THE PRESIDENTIAL IMAGE

THE PRESIDENTIAL IMAGE

A History from Theodore Roosevelt to Donald Trump

Edited by Iwan Morgan and Mark White

I.B.TAURIS
LONDON • NEW YORK • OXFORD • NEW DELHI • SYDNEY

I.B. Tauris
Bloomsbury Publishing Plc
50 Bedford Square, London, WC1B 3DP, UK
1385 Broadway, New York, NY 10018, USA

BLOOMSBURY, I.B. TAURIS and the I.B. Tauris logo
are trademarks of Bloomsbury Publishing Plc

First published in Great Britain 2020

Cover design by Alice Marwick

A catalogue record for this book is available from the British Library.

A catalog record for this book is available from the Library of Congress.

ISBN: HB: 978-1-7883-1359-9
         PB: 978-1-8386-0474-5
       ePDF: 978-0-7556-0208-7
      eBook: 978-0-7556-0207-0

Typeset by Integra Software Services Pvt. Ltd.
Printed and bound in Great Britain

To find out more about our authors and books visit www.bloomsbury.com
and sign up for our newsletters.

Iwan Morgan:
For my granddaughter, Juno
&
Mark White:
For my nephew and niece, Jonathan and Greta

CONTENTS

LIST OF FIGURES

Introduction

Chapter 1

Chapter 2

Chapter 3

Chapter 4

Chapter 5

Chapter 6

Chapter 7

Chapter 8

Chapter 9

Chapter 10

Chapter 11

Chapter 12

CO-EDITORS AND CONTRIBUTORS

Iwan Morgan is Professor of US Studies at the Institute of the Americas, University College London, and Commonwealth Fund Chair of American History in the UCL Department of History. He is a fellow of the Rothermere American Institute, University of Oxford, recipient of the British Association of American Studies Honorary Fellowship in 2014, and winner of the Neustadt Prize in 2010 for his book *The Age of Deficits: Presidents and Unbalanced Budgets from Jimmy Carter to George W. Bush* (University Press of Kansas, 2009). An authority on the modern American presidency, his various works include: *Reagan: American Icon* (I.B. Tauris, 2016), a *Times/Sunday Times* Politics Books of the Year for 2016; [as editor] *Presidents in the Movies: American History and Politics on Screen* (Palgrave, 2011), and *Nixon* (Arnold, 2002).

Mark White is Professor of History at Queen Mary, University of London. His scholarship has examined US foreign relations and the American presidency. He is the author of eight books, including *Missiles in Cuba* (Ivan Dee, 1997), *Against the President* (Ivan Dee, 2007, shortlisted for the Neustadt Prize), *The Presidency of Bill Clinton*, ed. (I.B. Tauris, 2012), and *Kennedy: A Cultural History of an American Icon* (Bloomsbury, 2013). He has also worked on film and theatre, and in 2005 wrote a biography, *Kenneth Branagh*, for Faber and Faber. He has written for the *Independent* and *BBC History Magazine*, appeared on BBC Radio 4, and contributed to a recent television documentary on JFK. He has received research awards from the John F. Kennedy Presidential Library, Franklin and Eleanor Roosevelt Institute, and the Harry S. Truman Library.

Michael Patrick Cullinane is Professor of US History at the University of Roehampton, London. He gained a PhD in History from University College Cork. He has taught at UC Cork, the University of Leicester, and Northumbria University. His research has explored US foreign policy, especially during the presidency of Theodore Roosevelt, as well as the role played by the media and the issue of memory in American history. He has authored twenty publications, including *Liberty and American Anti-Imperialism: 1898–1909* (Palgrave Macmillan, 2012), *The Open Door Era: United States Foreign Policy in the Twentieth* Century, co-authored (Edinburgh University Press, 2017), and *Theodore Roosevelt's Ghost: The History and Memory of an American Icon* (Louisiana State University Press, 2017).

John Dumbrell is Emeritus Professor of Government at Durham University and was previously Professor of Politics at the University of Leicester and the University of Keele. He is the author of numerous books on the modern American presidency in general and US foreign policy in particular, including: *The Carter Presidency: A Re-evaluation* (Manchester University Press, 1995); *American Foreign Policy: Carter to Clinton* (Palgrave, 1996); *A Special Relationship: Anglo-American Relations from the Cold War to Iraq* (Palgrave, 2006); *Clinton's Foreign Policy: Between the Bushes, 1992–2000* (Routledge, 2009); and *Rethinking the Vietnam War* (Palgrave, 2012).

Bob Green was awarded his PhD at Queen Mary University of London for his dissertation on the domestic policy of the Jimmy Carter presidency. He teaches at Queen Mary and is presently engaged on turning his doctoral study into a published monograph.

Clodagh Harrington is Senior Lecturer in American Politics at De Montfort University. She has also served as Chair of the American Politics Group. Her scholarship encompasses the American presidency, US foreign policy, and the nature of political scandal in America. She has published essays on the rhetoric of Condoleezza Rice, Barack Obama's leadership, and the Tea Party Movement. She edited and contributed to the international collection *Obama's Washington: Political Leadership in a Polarized Era* (ILAS, 2015) and is presently co-writing a book on the impact of the Trump presidency on Obama's legacy for publication by Edinburgh University Press.

Dean Kotlowski is Professor of History at Salisbury University, Maryland. His extensive publications include the books *Nixon's Civil Rights: Politics, Principle, and Policy* (Harvard University Press, 2002) and *Paul V. McNutt and the Age of FDR* (Indiana University Press, 2015). He has published over forty chapters and articles, including in such major journals as *Diplomatic History*, *Pacific Historical Review*, *Journal of Policy History*, and *Business History Review*. In addition to making numerous media appearances, he has been an historical advisor to the U.S. Mint, National Archives, and the Richard Nixon Library and Museum, which commended his work. He has been a Fulbright scholar three times, to the Philippines (2008), Austria (2016), and Australia (2002).

Tony McCulloch is Senior Fellow in North American Studies at the UCL Institute of the Americas. He has also taught at the universities of Middlesex, Hertfordshire, and Canterbury Christ Church where he was Head of History and American Studies and Director of Canadian Studies. He is a former chair of British Association of Canadian Studies and has played a very active role in the Transatlantic Studies Association. He has written extensively on US foreign policy, particularly during the presidency of Franklin Roosevelt. He is presently working on a two-volume history of Anglo-US relations in the age of FDR for publication by Edinburgh University Press.

Mara Oliva is Lecturer in Modern American History at the University of Reading. She received a PhD at the Institute for the Study of the Americas, University of

London, and has taught at various universities, including Queen Mary, University of London. A specialist in modern US diplomatic history and its domestic dimensions, she has published numerous articles and a book, *The Eisenhower Administration, American Public Opinion and the People's Republic of China* (Palgrave, 2018). She is the co-editor of *The Trump Presidency: From Campaign Trail to World Stage* (Palgrave, 2019) and is currently researching a monograph on Richard Nixon.

Sean J. Savage is Professor of Political Science at Saint Mary's College, Notre Dame, Indiana. A specialist on presidents and party politics, he has published, in addition to numerous articles, the following monographs: *Roosevelt: The Party Leader, 1932–1945* (University Press of Kentucky, 1991), *Truman and the Democratic Party* (University Press of Kentucky, 1997), and *JFK, LBJ, and The Democratic Party* (SUNY Press, 2004). He earned an Emerging Scholar Award from the American Political Science Association for the first of these and won a Choice Award for Outstanding Academic Title of 2005 for the third.

Tim Stanley is a historian, journalist, and broadcaster, specializing in US history and politics. He is a columnist and leader writer for the *Daily Telegraph*, writes for CNN, and appears regularly on BBC Question Time. He has a PhD in History from Trinity College, Cambridge; has taught at the universities of Oxford, London and Sussex; and covered the 2016 US presidential election for the *Telegraph*. He is the author of four books, including *Kennedy vs. Carter: The Battle for the Democratic Party's Soul* (University Press of Kansas, 2010), *Making Sense of American Liberalism*, co-editor (University of Illinois Press, 2012), and *Citizen Hollywood: How the Collaboration between LA and DC Revolutionized American Politics* (Thomas Dunne, 2014).

John Thompson is Emeritus Reader in American History at St. Catherine's College, Cambridge. An authority on US foreign policy and its domestic repercussions in the early decades of the twentieth century, his publications include: *Reformers and War: American Progressive Publicists and the First World War* (Cambridge University Press, 1987), *Woodrow Wilson* (Pearson Longman, *Profiles in Power* series, 2002), and *A Sense of Power: The Roots of America's Global Role* (Cornell University Press, 2015).

Introduction

THE IMAGE OF THE PRESIDENT: AN OVERVIEW

Iwan Morgan and Mark White

Image has been an important element of political leadership and statecraft from the days of the Roman emperors through medieval and pre-modern European monarchies to the heads of government, whether democratic or autocratic, of modern times. It has been a particularly significant instrument of presidential governance in the United States from the inception of the chief executive's office in the late eighteenth century through its various stages of development into the early twenty-first century. Effective image-making has helped presidential candidates to win election, to gain support for their leadership in office and to shape their reputation in history. On the other hand, image-making can be a double-edged sword if presidents do not live up to the leadership persona that helped to get them elected or if historical opinion turns against what a president represented. It is too much to claim that image is paramount to ensure presidential success. Other factors are clearly of comparable or greater importance, notably a president's clarity of vision; the political skills he possesses to turn this into reality; and the domestic, international and partisan contexts in which he must operate. Nevertheless, history shows that image, put simply what the president appears to be in terms of his personality, ability and values, is an important variable in shaping his (and one day, her) perceived effectiveness as America's leader.

Presidential image is never a simple phenomenon because its assessment ultimately lies in the eye of the beholder and is sensitive to historical change. The differing perceptions of Ronald Reagan at various stages of his political life and its aftermath help to illustrate this. When he swapped Hollywood stardom to run as the Republican challenger for governor of California against Edmund 'Pat' Brown in 1966, the Democratic incumbent looked to paint him as a right-wing extremist. This proved a miscalculation of the first order because Reagan's movie roles had marked him out as a 'good guy' – he had played a villain only in one of his fifty-four films. As a chastened Democratic fundraiser recalled, '[T]he first thing you've got to have in politics is recognition.... You take an actor who had the image of a good guy; man, you can't overcome it. You just can't make him a bad guy anymore.'[1] Nevertheless, Reagan's Hollywood background shaped adverse perceptions of him among America's allies after his election as president in 1980.

Some NATO heads of government worried that he would conduct international affairs in a manner akin to their celluloid image of him as a gun-slinging cowboy. When visiting the White House in May 1981, Helmut Schmidt was pleasantly surprised to learn that Reagan had started corresponding with Kremlin boss Leonid Brezhnev in the hope of reducing US-Soviet tensions. Sensing that he had misjudged the president, the West German chancellor urged him to visit West European capitals to dispel his image as 'a cowboy or one who only appears in cowboy films.'[2] Reagan was far too polite to point out that he had only made six Westerns in his 25-year movie career.

For many Americans, Reagan's optimism about America's future rather than his Hollywood past largely moulded their image of him as president. When he took office, the stagflation-hit economy was in the grip of its worst crisis since the Great Depression of the 1930s, the Soviet Union had seemingly gained the upper hand in the Cold War and the Watergate-affected presidency appeared to have lost the capacity for leadership. Reagan made it his mission to reassure the nation through word as much as deed that its greatest days lay ahead rather than behind it. When he left office, the economy was enjoying one of the longest booms in its history, America was on the brink of Cold War victory and the presidency had regained its position as the epicentre of power in American government. Having recorded unusually high levels of pessimism about the future on the part of the American public in the late 1970s, the Gallup poll found that opinion on this score had reverted to a strong sense of optimism by the early 1990s. Remembrance of the fortieth president's role in renewing national pride and optimism burnished his image in history, particularly after his death in 2004. While Reagan's average Gallup poll approval rating over the course of his presidency was just 52.8 per cent, twenty-first-century Gallup surveys asking respondents to identify the nation's greatest presidents of all time would find any one of three heading the list – Abraham Lincoln, John F. Kennedy and Reagan, who came top in 2001, 2005 and 2011.[3]

In his seminal book, *Presidential Power*, Richard Neustadt contended, 'An image of the office, not an image of the man, is the dynamic factor in a President's prestige. Impressions of the person will form early and last long, but the values men assign to what they see can alter rather quickly.' This dean of presidential scholars based that assertion on the changes he perceived in popular assessment of Harry S. Truman and Dwight D. Eisenhower. In his estimate, Truman's image evolved from being a little man not big enough to fill Franklin D. Roosevelt's shoes on his sudden accession to the presidency on the latter's death in April 1945 to the master politician who won a surprise re-election in 1948, but then receded into being that of a mere politician when his Korean War leadership seemed ineffective in 1951–2. In Eisenhower's case, the reassuring image of calm and experienced leadership that helped him win sweeping re-election in 1956 became a negative quality owing to the president's apparent inability to respond energetically to the new challenges posed by the Soviet launch of Sputnik and a sharp recession in 1957–8. In the case of both presidents, according to Neustadt, 'the sense of what he *was* does not seem to have changed' but 'the sense of what he *ought* to be' had changed.[4]

While acknowledging that expectations of the presidential office can affect popular perceptions of the strengths and weaknesses of a president, this volume places more emphasis on the intentional construction of presidential image as an instrument of leadership and historical reputation than did Neustadt's classic study of the presidency. Though image is commented on in the presidential literature, its formation and significance have not received much systematic study to date. There is a body of scholarship that explores the importance of image for successful presidential candidacies.[5] Some scholars have also started to examine the significance of image to the leadership of individual presidents and their historical reputation.[6] To date, however, there has been little systematic attempt to investigate image-making across a range of presidents. Several academic analysts have started to explore the specific methods through which presidents construct their image. Political scientist Bruce Miroff has examined the use of spectacle whereby presidents promote their identity through their performances at stage-managed public events that draw on 'a wellspring of archetypal cultural memories and deeply embedded national myths.'[7] Meanwhile historian David Greenberg has considered the use of spin to put the president's persona, politics and policy in best light before the court of public opinion.[8] Though it makes no claim to comprehensive coverage of this subject, this volume is intended as a contribution to enhance understanding of an understudied field of presidential history and politics through examination of various aspects of presidential image-making pertaining to twelve presidents who held office between 1901 and 2020.

Of course, presidents who held office before the dawn of the twentieth century were hardly unmindful of the benefits of image for their leadership. Having learned how portraits of him could aid the cause of American independence during the Revolutionary War against Britain (best exemplified by Charles Willson Peale's 1779 painting commemorating his victory at the Battle of Princeton), George Washington willingly sat for artistic depictions of him as president. Among the most famous is the so-called 'Lansdowne portrait,' a full-length painting done by Gilbert Stuart in 1796, the 64-year-old Washington's final year in office [see below]. This perfectly captures him as the embodiment of the harmony, industry and frugality that he considered necessary to make Americans a great people.

The portrait presents Washington as he appeared on public occasions dressed in a manner befitting a republican chief executive rather than a monarch or an aristocrat: a black velvet suit, white shirt with lace ruffles, black stockings and shoes, and dress sword. It references his past and present leadership through the titles of the tomes featured in the painting – the *General Orders* (his command of the Continental Army in the Revolutionary War) and the *Constitution and Laws of the United States* (his presidency of the Constitutional Convention of 1787) under the table and the *Federalist Papers* and the *Journal of Congress* atop it. The pose chosen for the portrait alludes to Washington's address to Congress, a body represented by the ornate chair, the columns and the curtain, on 8 December 1795. To symbolize the achievements of his leadership as general and president, the sky in the background has dark clouds to the left representing the trials through which the young republic has passed and a rainbow on the right signifying the peace and prosperity it now enjoys. It was an image of the president that became widely circulated through popular engravings of Stuart's portrait. Having been commissioned by Lord Lansdowne, the British statesman who negotiated the 1783 treaty that ended the American War of Independence (under his then title, Lord

Shelburne), the original was despatched to England. It was through Stuart's copies of the portrait that it became known to American audiences. One of these now hangs in the East Room of the White House as a permanent reminder to his successors of Washington's greatness.[9]

The development of photography offered presidents another avenue for image-making in the mid-nineteenth century. Abraham Lincoln was the first significant beneficiary of this new medium thanks to the camera artistry of Matthew Brady. The almost-full-length studio portrait that Brady took of Lincoln on 27 February 1860

Figure I.1 Gilbert Stuart's 'Lansdowne portrait' of George Washington Non-copyright, Source: Wikipedia Commons.

on his visit to New York City to speak at the Cooper Union, the occasion for the first exposition of his opposition to slavery expansion before an audience outside his home state of Illinois, is a masterpiece of the genre. It perfectly captures the national role which Lincoln sought as an aspirant candidate for the Republican presidential nomination in the forthcoming election. The setting is deliberately sparse: a column symbolizes democratic institutions and two books – possibly the Bible and the Constitution – signify the subject's dedication to time-honoured moral and national values. Against a neutral background that lacks any décor, Lincoln places his hand on the volumes to suggest mastery of their content. His features are distinct and his eyes gaze at the camera rather than away from it, the conventional pose of the time. He is dressed in a plain three-piece suit with white shirt, is clean-shaven and has a confident appearance, all of which invite those seeing his photographic image to trust his abilities as a leader [see below].

The portrait became a cover for *Harper's Weekly* and *Frank Leslie's Weekly*, both popular magazines with sizeable circulations, and featured in the popular Currier & Ives lithographs of the Cooper Union address. As well as being reproduced in many newspapers, it appeared on postcards, campaign buttons and headed notepaper. The substance of Lincoln's Cooper Union address helped to win him the Republican presidential nomination and ultimately the presidency, but the image of the Brady portrait contributed to this success by presenting him in perfect harmony with the character and style of the office he sought. Lincoln himself would acknowledge, 'Brady and the Cooper Union address made me president.' Facing the Civil War crisis soon after taking office, the now-bearded sixteenth president intuitively understood the need to sit as often as possible for Brady and other photographers because they were helping to give a face to the Union cause, one that could appear in many places at once – his own.[10]

Notwithstanding the significance of image for late eighteenth- and nineteenth-century presidents, this volume focuses on their twentieth- and early twenty-first-century successors to make good the relative paucity of study of the image of modern office-holders. It does so for the following reasons. Firstly, the presidency has been the driving force in American politics almost continuously in this period, whereas it played this role only intermittently in its first century of existence.[11] Secondly, the growth of presidential power since 1900 has been accompanied by the expansion of the presidency as an institution that includes, *inter alia*, public communication and public relations aides (speechwriters, press officers, pollsters and public liaison aides, to name but a few) who are charged with putting the incumbent president and his image in best light. Even in its infancy in the first third of the twentieth century, one historian observed, 'the modern presidency was as much about the appearance of being a leader as it was about the actual qualities that the executive displayed in office.'[12] Finally, the rise of the modern presidency coincided with the rapid expansion of new technology that facilitated the promotion and dissemination of presidential image. This process began with the emergence of cheap, mass-circulation newspapers that could reach an increasingly literate public; continued through the development of motion picture newsreels, radio, and television; and culminated in the internet-based media of the early twenty-first century.[13]

Figure I.2 Matthew Brady photograph of Abraham Lincoln on the day of his Cooper Union Speech in New York City, 27 February 1860. Non-copyright, Source: Wikipedia Commons.

This book offers a history of presidential image since 1900 that is broad in scope but not exhaustive. It does not contain chapters on all twenty presidents who have held office since the dawn of the twentieth century. It also focuses on specific aspects of image-making in the case of most of those chosen for analysis. The intention is to provide a representative selection of presidents who variously exemplified the importance of political context, racial change, new technology and cultural portrayals in image-making. This is not to suggest that the presidents omitted from this volume were insignificant in this regard. Doubtless they can offer rich subjects for analysis by other scholars engaged in exploration of image-making. Indeed, it is to be hoped that this volume can contribute through its case studies to broader interest in presidential image as a field of inquiry.

In some cases, the decision to select certain presidents over others was straightforward. Warren Harding, Calvin Coolidge and Herbert Hoover, the Republican presidents of the 1920s, each employed the new technology of radio as an instrument of public communication but never came close to matching Franklin D. Roosevelt's exploitation of the medium for image-building in the 1930s. Other cases made for more difficult calls. Harry S. Truman was selected for inclusion over Dwight D. Eisenhower because he offers such an interesting contrast of inattention to image-building as president and positive imagery in history (the availability of an excellent monograph on the latter's image was also a factor[14]). The most difficult decision was the omission of George W. Bush whose image-building strategy of portraying himself as the heroic War on Terror leader would come a cropper (as is briefly discussed at the end of this chapter). In large part, his omission reflected the fact that the historiography of his presidency is in its early stages, but this will surely produce an in-depth analysis of his image-making in time.[15] That said, both of Bush's successors make it into our volume before they have become the subject of historical study. Their inclusion reflects their unique status: Barack Obama as the first president of African descent and the first hip hop president; Donald Trump as the first president without previous experience of government office or military command and the first Twitter president.

Our volume, as conceived, explores aspects of presidential image in the case of twelve office-holders: Theodore Roosevelt (1901–9), Woodrow Wilson (1913–21), Franklin D. Roosevelt (1933–45), Harry S. Truman (1945–53), John F. Kennedy (1961–3), Lyndon B. Johnson (1963–9), Richard M. Nixon (1969–74), Ronald Reagan (1981–9), Bill Clinton (1993–2001), Barack Obama (2009–17) and Donald Trump (2017–). Each author's chapter in the book is complete in itself, but our common purpose has been to answer one or more of the following questions in our analysis of image-making: Is presidential image the creation of the president and his aides in pursuit of a carefully conceived public relations strategy – or is it more the work of the president's critics and opponents in their negative depiction of him? Does it have more to do with the way that the print and broadcasting media interpret what the president says and does? How do cultural outputs – books, plays, films, paintings and music – contribute to the construction of presidential image? What role can the new technology of the day play in promoting presidential image? Is a president's image static or does it change over time? To what extent does it become the instrument of those seeking to influence the politics and policies of their own times after he has left office? Finally, is presidential image important, and if so, why?

In 'Performing the Presidency: The Image of Theodore Roosevelt on Stage,' Michael Patrick Cullinane explores the influence of plays on the historical image of Theodore Roosevelt (TR). While other cultural forms are universally recognized as shaping influences on popular memory of presidents and other historical figures, theatre has attracted less attention in this regard, but the Broadway and London success of Lin-Manuel Miranda's *Hamilton* (about 'founding father' and first Treasury Secretary Alexander Hamilton) is a reminder of its importance.

Unlike other cultural outputs, theatre depicts the presidency through a live re-enactment that offers audiences changing insights into its subject in contrast to movies and paintings. This chapter examines several productions that feature quite different perceptions of Theodore Roosevelt from the negative imagery of Joseph Kesselring's *Arsenic and Old Lace*, first performed in 1939, to the more sympathetic interpretation in Jerome Alden's *Bully*, written in 1977, and ultimately to postmodern experimental productions – Daniel Ortberg's *Dirtbag Teddy Roosevelt* in 2014 and The TEAM's *RoosevElvis* in 2015. As Cullinane shows, each of these derived their depictions of TR both from the historical contexts in which they were originally written and the evolving historiography manifest in contemporary biographies of him. As such, they provide a unique insight into the reconstruction and continuing evolution of a long-dead president's image to reflect changing perspectives of the past.

In 'Woodrow Wilson: Professor and Idealist,' John Thompson explores the development of Wilson's image from his 1910 campaign to become New Jersey governor, through his tumultuous presidency, to the years after his death. Initial portrayals, such as those in political cartoons, emphasized Wilson's academic background as president of Princeton University, a professorial image that both helped and hurt him. To admirers, it suggested both intellectual authority and integrity; to detractors, however, it suggested a troubling naiveté about the power realities of political life. Once Wilson entered the White House, and especially after the outbreak of war in Europe posed new challenges for America, criticisms of his image intensified. Leading the assault, Theodore Roosevelt accused the professor-president of lacking the virile strength needed to conduct the nation's foreign policy. This exemplified a major theme of Thompson's chapter, namely that to a great extent Wilson's image was fashioned by the views and objectives of others, whether friend or foe. Hence in the debate over Wilson's cherished League of Nations and his attempts to shape the peace settlement in general, he was portrayed as the embodiment of high-minded principle on the one hand, as weak and ineffectual, on the other hand. Thompson makes two other important points. One is how Wilson's image became internationalized but meant different things to different peoples abroad. Secondly, as with other presidents, Wilson's image changed over time. The Second World War boosted his image in the eyes of many who believed that the breakdown of the peace showed that he had been right about the need for US participation in the League of Nations. The big-budget 1944 Hollywood film *Wilson* both reflected and added to this perception of Wilson as wise and prescient. To 'realist' scholars, however, the failure of the League of Nations to prevent war exposed the crucial flaw in Wilson as a man and leader oblivious to the overriding importance of power in international politics.

In 'The Roosevelt Image on Trial: FDR, the Radio and the Supreme Court Battle of 1937,' Tony McCulloch explores how Franklin D Roosevelt's unsuccessful effort to 'pack' the Supreme Court in 1937 challenged his image as a master politician. FDR is conventionally rated – alongside George Washington and Abraham Lincoln – as one of America's three greatest presidents. He won four terms as president, an unprecedented and unrepeatable feat, including the largest election victory hitherto in 1936, but he miscalculated in seeking to reorganize the Supreme Court to overcome its opposition to his New Deal reforms. In thereby threatening the constitutional separation of the powers, FDR enabled his conservative critics to saddle him with the negative image of a potential dictator. In these circumstances, the president could not rally his normal sources of popular support through use of radio. His defeat on the issue encouraged the rise of a bipartisan conservative coalition in Congress that stymied further advancement of his New Deal programme. Nevertheless, FDR's case also demonstrated the fluidity of presidential image. Had he served only two terms in office, he would likely have been remembered as a president who ultimately over-reached and would probably have been rated only among the 'near great' presidents. Despite his setback on court-packing, his image as a tried-and-tested leader helped him win a third term in office in 1940 against the backdrop of a new war in Europe. When the United States became involved in the Second World War, he developed a new image as the 'Soldier of Freedom', which guaranteed his place in the trio of 'great' presidents.

In '**Truman: The Everyman**,' Sean Savage examines how the image of Harry S. Truman has changed from a generally negative to a far more flattering depiction and considers how this reflected shifts in US history and the values of the American public. Truman is an unusual case, perhaps a modern president *sui generis*, in the scant attention he paid to his own image. He was intent on distinguishing his own personality from the office of the presidency. Failure to do so, he believed, would inevitably lead to abuse of the presidential office. Initially, Truman's image – apart from high ratings in 1945 due to the victories over Germany and Japan – suffered from the inevitably unfavourable comparison made with the political megastar who preceded him, Franklin D. Roosevelt; the perception that he had unsavoury ties to corrupt machine politics in his home state of Missouri and tolerated corrupt officials in his administration; and the sense that he was not up to the challenge of the complex issues facing postwar America. After his presidency, however, Truman's image and reputation improved considerably. Historians have consistently rated him a 'near great' president, particularly for his handling of foreign policy during the early Cold War – an approach that contained the growth of Soviet power and laid the foundations for America's ultimate success in the conflict. After his death in 1972, the American people came to share this enthusiasm for Truman. In the context of Watergate, stagflation and the other tribulations of the 1970s, the Truman years seemed like a halcyon period. Reflecting this, glowing portrayals of an admirably humble yet courageous Truman became commonplace in popular culture thanks to positive representations of him in films, music and theatrical plays.

In '**The Art of John F. Kennedy**,' Mark White considers how portraiture influenced the thirty-fifth president's image. To a considerable extent, JFK was successful in controlling his own image. Having a father who had worked as a Hollywood producer, he grew up with a more precocious understanding of how to manipulate image than any presidential predecessor. Even before reaching the White House, he succeeded in crafting a dazzling image as literary figure, war hero, sex symbol, family man and man of faith. On the issue of agency, then, he succeeded in defining how he appeared to the American people both in life and even in death. Artists played a significant part in this process of image-making.

White examines how Norman Rockwell, Pietro Annigoni, Elaine de Kooning and Robert Rauschenberg depicted him in portraits, several of which were undertaken with JFK's approval. Unsurprisingly, their work generally flattered him, burnishing his image yet further. Rockwell's painting, completed during the 1960 presidential campaign, served to counter criticisms about Kennedy's youth, inexperience and Catholic allegiance. De Kooning's body of work on JFK emphasized his dazzling image and referenced his sex appeal. Rauschenberg reflected on the tragedy of the assassination in Dallas and asserted JFK's greatness as president, not least for his far-sighted commitment to space exploration. It was only Italian artist Pietro Annigoni, in his cover for *Time* magazine, who provided a more sober portrait of Kennedy, one that revealed his inner turmoil as well as the pressures of the presidential office. This darker view of Kennedy anticipated a later, more critical wave of historical scholarship that debunked the 'Camelot' myth of his presidency.

In **'We *Shall* Overcome': Lyndon B. Johnson as the Civil Rights President,'** Dean Kotlowski considers the development of LBJ's image as the greatest civil rights president in history, mainly based on his role in promoting enactment of the Civil Rights Act of 1964, the Voting Rights Act of 1965 and the Civil Rights Act of 1968. His chapter explores LBJ's evolution from racial conservative as Texas Senator in the 1950s to racial liberal as president. It also examines Johnson's efforts to safeguard his image as the civil rights president despite his failure to support the African American freedom struggle on some occasions, notably over the seating of the Mississippi Freedom Democratic Party at the Democratic National Convention in 1964. It further considers how LBJ's image as the greatest ally of racial change survived the break with Martin Luther King over his criticism of the Vietnam War because others in the civil rights establishment, notably Roy Wilkins and A. Phillip Randolph, stayed loyal to the president. Finally, Kotlowski demonstrates that LBJ's reputation with historians in the fifty years since his presidency has improved to the point that his civil rights record is given more weight than Vietnam, permitting their reassessment of him as a 'near great' president. Conversely, LBJ's civil rights image in popular culture has moved in the opposite direction, with controversial movie depictions of him as a less than forthright supporter of black protest in Lee Daniels' *The Butler* (2014) and Ava DuVernay's *Selma* (2014). Whatever his limitation in this regard, supporters and critics find agreement in Johnson's image as a leader struggling to make and to shape history as a civil rights president in the face of the still-strong forces of white supremacy.

In **'*Nixon in China*: Presidential Image in Modern Opera,'** Mara Oliva considers how the John Adams opera, premiered in 1987, offered a more positive image of Richard Nixon than the Watergate-stained one. After reviewing Nixon's image problems during his political career and his campaign for rehabilitation that began soon after he resigned the presidency in 1974, she shows how the musical oeuvre complemented his hopes of being remembered as a great foreign-policy leader. Its insightful and credible portrayal of Nixon as a complex and very human leader engaged in what was the greatest venture of his presidency to forge detente with Communist China was far removed from his unsavoury 'Tricky Dick' image. Memories of Watergate were still too recent for early showings to foster a 'new Nixon' in the public mind. Nevertheless, as Oliva suggests, the growing capacity of opera as a musical form to reach younger, more diverse audiences in the twenty-first century could benefit the 37th president's posthumous image as those seeing new productions of Nixon in China are more likely to appreciate that there was more to him than the Watergate scandal that indelibly defined his image for his contemporaries.

In 'Jimmy Carter: The Unravelling of an Image,' Bob Green considers Jimmy Carter's efforts to develop an image that would resonate with the American public and align with the post-Watergate political climate. He used his life experience to present himself as a Washington outsider who could make government work efficiently and a leader who could be trusted. By highlighting his diverse roles as farmer, engineer, businessman, planner, scientist, governor and born-again Christian, he projected an intriguing, multi-faceted image on the campaign trail in 1976. His engineering and scientific credentials signified his capacity to bring rationality and efficiency to government, whilst his religiosity validated his promise of honesty. As president, he used symbolism to reinforce this image as a leader working for the common good, dispensing as far as possible with ceremony, getting out to meet the people and in public rhetoric admitting the lack of assured solutions for the nation's problems. Seeing himself as a trustee of the people, he refused to play politics, but thereby fell afoul of the deal-making culture in Congress and the rising tide of conservatism across America. Even worse, his inability to resolve complex economic and international problems undermined his image of competence. The public grew weary of his moralistic calls for self-sacrifice and the media increasingly portrayed him as indecisive and ineffectual. The unravelling of the image he established for himself in the 1976 election made Carter vulnerable to defeat at the hands of Ronald Reagan, a Republican opponent who radiated confidence in America's future and his own ability to ensure better days ahead.

In 'In Black and White: Ronald Reagan's Image on Race,' Iwan Morgan explores Reagan's positive image for white Americans as the president who restored national optimism following the 1970s malaise and his negative image for African Americans as a president utterly lacking in sympathy for their problems. This dichotomy suggests that presidential image is for the most part highly racialized in construction, reception and remembrance. Morgan examines Reagan's 'dog-whistle politics' in his gubernatorial and presidential campaigns as the source of his appeal to blue-collar whites who felt threatened by black advancement, his efforts to promote an ideal of colour-blind conservatism that excused government obligation to assist racial minorities, and his largely adversarial relationship with African American leaders who pressed him to do more to make the promise of America a reality for blacks. Finally, he reviews differing perceptions of the fortieth president's image on race from the vantage of the twenty-first century. During Barack Obama's tenure of office, conservatives lionized him as a leader whose free-market, anti-statist ideals had done more for black economic uplift than the supposedly socialist doctrines of the first black occupant of the Oval Office. Conversely, Reagan's image went from bad to worse in black popular culture, with his emergence as a villain in hip hop, now the world's most popular musical genre. Thanks mainly to white Americans, Reagan still rides high in national memory. As the United States becomes ever more racially and ethnically diverse, however, it could well be that negative images of him become the new orthodoxy.

In his chapter, '**Bill Clinton's Primary Colours: Making the Image of the forty-second President,**' John Dumbrell sheds light on the issue of agency in presidential image-making. He emphasizes the extent to which Clinton has sought to bolster his reputation and burnish his image. In his 2004 autobiography and the 2018 novel he wrote with James Patterson, *The President Is Missing*, he portrayed himself – either directly or by implication – as a leader with a powerful life story, a social conscience and political dexterity. The famous picture of a young Bill Clinton meeting President John F. Kennedy in the summer of 1963 (used in his 1992 presidential campaign) added some Camelot lustre to his image. In addition to these efforts at self-promotion, Clinton enjoyed high public approval ratings as president, particularly during his second term. Despite this, Clinton could not prevent the core of his image from being connected to ideas about his flawed character, sexual excesses and compromised ideals. The 1996 novel *Primary Colors*, written by journalist Joe Klein but published anonymously, played an important role in entrenching these negative notions about Clinton. The bestselling book told the story of a gifted politician Jack Stanton running for president. As a Southern governor with skeletons in his closet, and with a wife who resembled Hillary Clinton and various aides who seemed based on Bill Clinton's own advisors, the parallel between Jack Stanton and Bill Clinton was clear. Accordingly, the novel became widely regarded as both a history of the 1992 presidential campaign and a dissection of Clinton's character and political style. The impact of the book was enhanced two years later by a Hollywood film based on Klein's novel. Despite a generally successful presidency, Dumbrell concludes, it is this sense of a flawed Clinton that is now central to his image.

In '**Hip Hop and Hope: Managing the Outlier Status of Barack Obama,**' Clodagh Harrington analyses Barack Obama's image as 'America's first hip hop president,' whose embrace of his 'otherness' on the 2008 campaign trail encouraged belief among his younger supporters, especially non-white ones, that his promise of change was real. One early indication of his unusual appeal was graffiti artist Shephard Fairey's creation of the iconic 'Hope' image poster that became a cultural phenomenon as Obama's campaign poster. In office, the new president demonstrated awareness of the cultural significance of rap music by declaring that he saw a place for hip hop in the nation's dialogue. Nevertheless, he did not receive a free pass from performers of this music genre. Though lauded by some, others criticized him in two main regards. As a black president, or at least as a bi-racial one who chose to identify as black, he was inevitably held to a higher standard by many of those who viewed him as one of their own. He was also taken to task, at times with vitriol, by those who took exception to, for example, his drone usage abroad and immigration restrictions at home. Harrington identifies four genres of hip hop that presented differing images of Obama ranging from very supportive to very critical, namely effusive, instructive, adversarial and unconscious. For his own part, Obama looked to shore up his outlier image as his presidency entered a second term by close association with some rappers, notably in enlisting Kendrick Lamar's involvement in his post-presidential mentoring project for disadvantaged youth, *My Brother's Keeper*. Nevertheless, however tarnished his image for some hip hoppers, the fissures between Obama and this musical community looked increasingly irrelevant as the Trump presidency fostered a toxic racial environment and focused on the roll-back of its predecessor's legacy.

In **"'All Publicity Is Good Publicity:" Donald Trump, Twitter and the Selling of an Outsider in the 2016 Presidential Election,'** Tim Stanley explores Donald Trump's use of social media, particularly Twitter, to shape his own image. Twitter has been as important to his image as radio was to FDR and television was to JFK. Trump's tweeting, argues Stanley, needs to be understood in the context of the decades-long battle between conservatives and the liberal section of the American media. The Right had long believed that the mainstream media exhibited a liberal bias that delegitimized conservatism. Twitter offered a way to alter media discourse to its advantage, as Trump demonstrated in his 2016 presidential campaign. For Stanley, the style and content of Trump's tweeting had their roots in his earlier career. He had long believed in the importance of self-promotion and a robust approach in taking on adversaries. He had long discussed the need for America's allies to pay more for their own defence, and for the US government to protect domestic manufacturing from international competition. In both the Republican primaries of 2016 and then the fall campaign against Hillary Clinton, he used Twitter to develop his image as a plain-speaking, anti-establishment, outsider businessman, and also to tarnish his opponents – often through the use of pithy, pejorative nicknames such as 'Lyin' Ted' Cruz and 'Crooked Hillary'. Moreover, his tweeting was capable of changing the news cycle when it turned against him, as it did with the controversy that broke out when a tape from 2005 surfaced in which Trump boasted of sexual assault. The importance of Trump's use of Twitter, Stanley makes clear, relates not only to his domination of social media but also the way it compelled traditional media, namely television and newspapers, to report his tweets and hence increase their coverage of him and his message.

Finally, in this introductory review, it is worth reflecting on the image-making travails of George W. Bush, the forty-third president, who held office from 2001 to 2009. Though not the subject of a chapter in this book, his experience offers an object lesson of the dangers for presidents when their image-making falls foul of reality. The transformative consequences of the 9/11 al-Qaeda attacks on New York and Washington for American politics and foreign policy engendered a new imperial presidency that challenged the constitutional limits of presidential power even more than its Cold War predecessor.[16] In these circumstances, Bush seized the opportunity to build his image as a bold, competent and resolute commander-in-chief charged with waging the War on Terror.

The public relations campaign in support of this reached its high point with what the *New York Times* called 'one of the most audacious pieces of presidential theater in American history'. Given a free hand by Congress to make war on Iraq because of its government's supposed links with terrorists, Bush celebrated the rapid ouster of Iraqi leader Saddam Hussein in spectacular style. On 1 May 2003, he landed a fighter plane on the deck of the USS *Abraham Lincoln* (actually anchored close enough to the California coast to be reached by helicopter), posed for pictures in his flight jacket with cheering sailors, and – after changing into a blue suit – took the podium to announce the end of 'major combat operations'

Figure I.3 George W. Bush declares 'mission accomplished' on board the nuclear aircraft carrier USS *Abraham Lincoln* on 1 May 2003, STEPHEN JAFFE/AFP/Getty Images.

with a banner behind him announcing 'MISSION ACCOMPLISHED' [see above]. With television pictures capturing the warm glow of the late afternoon sun on Bush's visage, NBC commentator Chris Mathews effused about his 'amazing display of leadership,' adding, 'I think we like having a hero as our president.'[17]

The sense that Bush was the personification of presidential infallibility began to permeate the comments of aides close to him. Journalist Ron Suskind reported a breath-taking assertion by an anonymous official (likely to have been senior advisor Karl Rove):

> The aide said that guys like me were 'in what we call the reality-based community,' which he defined as people who 'believe that solutions emerge from your judicious study of discernible reality.' [...] 'That's not the way the world really works anymore,' he continued. 'We're an empire now, and when we act, we create our own reality. And while you're studying that reality – judiciously, as you will – we'll act again, creating other new realities, which you can study too, and that's how things will sort out. We're history's actors... and you, all of you, will be left to just study what we do.'[18]

Bush and his team would soon discover that nemesis follows hard on the heels of hubris. Far from ending the Iraq war, Saddam's overthrow turned out to be the beginning of a prolonged military occupation, expensive in both lives and treasure, to combat an insurgency that showed no signs of ending by the time Bush left office. The national euphoria generated by the president's strutting performance aboard the *Abraham Lincoln* soon gave way to disillusion. Five months after that event, *Time* magazine ran a cover featuring Bush in flight gear with the headline 'MISSION NOT ACCOMPLISHED.'[19]

As the Iraq War turned sour, Americans increasingly wondered whether Bush was, as one scholar put it, 'a heroic liberator or a callow poseur.'[20] The ineffectual response to the Hurricane Katrina disaster in New Orleans in August 2005 then raised doubts about his competence to manage domestic crisis, let alone a foreign one. The president's heroic image took a final battering when the worst economic downturn since the Great Depression of the 1930s blighted his final months in office. Bush departed the White House with his Gallup job approval rating at a lowly 34 per cent in January 2009, a far cry from the stratospheric 90 per cent approval he had enjoyed amid the post-9/11 rally-round-the-flag mood of national unity in late 2001.[21] Other than Richard Nixon, he had also become the modern president most pilloried in popular culture. Among the many examples of this trend, Stephen Colbert regularly lampooned Bush's proclivity for 'truthiness' (a preference for something to *feel* true rather than *be* true) on his Comedy Central cable channel show; Steve Zahn satirized his bumbling response to Hurricane Katrina in 'Shame, Shame, Shame' on the soundtrack of the HBO series *Treme*; and director Oliver Stone portrayed him in distinctly unheroic terms in the biopic *W*, released in 2008.

Of course, some presidents – Franklin D. Roosevelt and John F. Kennedy are among the standout examples – had far greater success in image-making than George W. Bush. Nevertheless, the latter's experience showed the danger of creating an image that could not be sustained. Bush was arguably the author of his own downfall on this score. Other presidents – Woodrow Wilson and Jimmy Carter are obvious examples – found themselves unable to live up to their preferred image because of circumstances beyond their control. And no matter how effective a president was in the politics of image, his appeal could not carry across the whole of society, as Ronald Reagan discovered. For the most part, presidential image is a highly contested entity both during a president's lifetime and when history becomes his judge. The contributions to this volume look to explore this complex, controversial and continuous element of modern presidential politics.

Notes

1   DeGroot, Gerard, *Selling Ronald Reagan: The Emergence of a President* (London: I.B. Tauris, 2015), p. 172.

2   'Memorandum of a Conversation with Chancellor Helmut Schmidt, May 21, 1981,' National Security Council-Executive Secretariat: Subject Files-48, Ronald Reagan Presidential Library.

3   Morgan, Iwan, *Reagan: American Icon* (London: I.B. Tauris, 2016), pp. 325–27.

4   Neustadt, Richard E., *Presidential Power and the Modern Presidents: The Politics of Leadership from Roosevelt to Reagan* (New York: Free Press, 1990), p. 80.

5   See, for example, Shannon, David A., 'The Presidential Image,' *Challenge*, 4 (1956): 42–6; Rosenberg, Shawn, Lisa Bohan, Patrick McCafferty and Kevin Harris,

'The Image and the Vote: The Effect of Candidate Presentation on Voter Preference,' *American Journal of Political Science*, 30 (February 1986): 108–27; Hacker, Kenneth L., ed., *Presidential Candidate Images* (Lanham, MD: Rowman and Littlefield, 2004).

6   These studies include: Blake, David Haven, *Liking Ike: Eisenhower, Advertising, and the Rise of Celebrity Politics* (New York: Oxford University Press, 2016); Cullinane, Michael, *Theodore Roosevelt's Ghost: The History and Memory of an American Icon* (Baton Rouge: Louisiana State University Press, 2017); Greenberg, David, *Nixon's Shadow: The History of an Image* (New York: Norton, 2003); and White, Mark, (i) *Kennedy: A Cultural History of an American Icon* (London: Bloomsbury, 2013), and (ii) 'Son of the Sixties: The Controversial Image of Bill Clinton,' *History*, 103 (January 2018): 100–23.

7   Miroff, Bruce, *Presidents on Political Ground: Leaders in Action and What They Face* (Lawrence: University Press of Kansas, 2016) [quotation p. 10].

8   Greenberg, David, *Republic of Spin: An Inside History of the American Presidency* (New York: Norton, 2016).

9   'Life Portraits of George Washington,' https://www.mountvernon.org/george-washington/artwork/life-portraits-of-george-washington/; Miles, Ellen, 'Gilbert Stuart Paints George Washington,' *facetoface: A Blog from the National Portrait Gallery*, no date, https://npg.si.edu/blog/gilbert-stuart-paints-george-washington.

10   Levy, Marie Cordie, 'Matthew Brady's Abraham Lincoln,' *American Studies Journal*, 60 (2016), http://www.asjournal.org/60-2016/matthew-bradys-abraham-lincoln/; Widmer, Ted, 'Lincoln Captured!' *New York Times Opinionator*, 15 May 2011, https://opinionator.blogs.nytimes.com/2011/05/15/lincoln-captured/. See too Meredith, Roy, *Mr Lincoln's Cameraman: Matthew B. Brady* (New York: Dover, 1974).

11   See, for example, Graubard, Stephen, *The Presidents: The Transformation of the American Presidency from Theodore Roosevelt to George W. Bush* (London: Penguin, 2004); Gould, Lewis L., *The Modern American Presidency*, 2nd ed. (Lawrence: University Press of Kansas, 2009); Leuchtenburg, William E., *The American President: From Teddy Roosevelt to Bill Clinton* (New York: Oxford University Press, 2015).

12   Gould, *Modern American Presidency*, p. 78.

13   Desilver, Drew, 'From Telegram to Instagram, a Look at Presidents and Technology,' *Pew Research Center Facttank*, 13 February 2015, http://www.pewresearch.org/fact-tank/2015/02/13/from-telegrams-to-instagram-a-look-at-presidents-and-technology/; Cunningham, Sean, 'A Short History of Presidential Communication: How Our Leaders Went from the Telegraph to Twitter,' *RealClearLife*, 14 July 2018, http://www.realclearlife.com/history/short-history-presidential-communication/.

14   Blake, *Liking Ike*.

15   For a recent historical biography, see Nichter, Luke, *George W. Bush: Life of Privilege, Leadership in Crisis* (Haupaugge, NY: Nova Science, 2012).

16   Rudalevige, Andrew, *The New Imperial Presidency: Renewing Presidential Power after Watergate* (Ann Arbor: University of Michigan Press, 2005).

17   Greenberg, *Republic of Spin*, pp. 435–6.

18   Suskind, Ron, 'Without a Doubt,' *NYT Magazine*, 17 October 2004, pp. 44–51, 64, 102, 106.

19   'So, What Went Wrong?' *Time*, 6 October 2003, pp. 30–7.

20   Greenberg, *Republic of Spin*, p. 436.

21   'Presidential Approval Ratings – George W. Bush,' *Gallup*, https://news.gallup.com/poll/116500/presidential-approval-ratings-george-bush.aspx.

Chapter 1

PERFORMING THE PRESIDENCY: THE IMAGE OF THEODORE ROOSEVELT ON STAGE

Michael Patrick Cullinane

Cultural representations of Theodore Roosevelt have flourished since his death in 1919. Over one hundred motion pictures portrayals exist, from cameos in short and silent films to TR in leading roles, and even TR in animated television sitcoms like *The Simpsons*. In pop culture, we find Roosevelt in literature, fine art, music and fashion, and his speeches are regularly invoked by politicians, sports stars, celebrities and corporate leaders. Although its impact is largely neglected by scholars and commentators, particularly in comparison to these other mediums, theatre has also played an important role in our perception of Roosevelt. If its capacity to shape historical imagery is generally underestimated, a recent controversy offers ample evidence of its power to do so.

In 2015, the social media campaign Women on 20s pressured the Obama administration to replace Andrew Jackson's profile on the $20 bill with that of a famous American woman. Shortly after the campaign began, the US Treasury Department announced that it would include more women on greenbacks, but instead of replacing Jackson it reported that Alexander Hamilton would vacate the front of the $10 note.[1] Hamilton's devotees reacted with fury. After all, he was the first person to lead the Treasury Department and founded the very mint that produced American currency. Hamilton biographer Ron Chernow said the decision effectively corrected 'one historic injustice by committing another.' In the same corner, former Secretary of State Hillary Clinton and former Federal Reserve Chairman Ben Bernanke urged the Treasury to reconsider.[2] Almost a year after he declared the redesign, Treasury Secretary Jack Lew changed his mind. Hamilton would stay put, and Lew decided that Andrew Jackson would make way for the abolitionist Harriet Tubman on the front of the $20 note. The turnaround owed less to the pressure of the Women on 20s campaign or the disapproval from political heavyweights like Clinton and Bernanke. Hamilton was spared because an eponymous theatre production had set his life to a hip-hop musical.[3] Written and produced by Lin-Manuel Miranda, *Hamilton: The Musical* has set box office records, won unequivocal critical acclaim and has brought the story of the Founding Fathers to a new generation by way of contemporary pop culture.

Perhaps more than any previous theatre production, *Hamilton* has demonstrated the power of performing arts for historical image.

Presidential images in film, television, music, art and architecture have an unmistakable effect on our impression of the past.[4] As sociologist George Lipsitz put it, culture is 'not a sideshow.'[5] It reflects human experience and communicates popular discourses; it defines shared truths and distinguishes social boundaries. Cultural outputs often demonstrate how the past undergoes dramatic re-conceptualization. In this way, the past never remains static, even if the appearance of a painted portrait or the architecture of a monument endures unchanged over hundreds of years. New audiences consume timeworn cultural outputs differently, and even if the creation of culture begins with the intentions of its author(s), throughout its existence a cultural product belongs to the audience(s) that derive meaning from it. As such, historical images tend to modify according to their context. It is why Hamilton remains on American currency, and why Jackson was scheduled to make way for Tubman. A century from now, that might change – Jackson might reappear and Hamilton might disappear. The past is contested ground, and the battle over historical image plays out in cultural mediums.

When it comes to the American presidency, the place of the chief executive as head of state, head of government and a nationally elected figure generates pervasive public attention. The office attracts countless memorialists who construct myriad images intended to portray the past in ways that have meaning for future generations. Consequently, the image of former presidents encourages periodization, metanarratives and myth. Presidential representations in culture often hasten meme-making. For example, the nineteenth century's 'Age of Jackson' persists in public memory, as does the apparent 'greatness' of the four presidents carved on Mount Rushmore.[6] Caricatures range from abstract portraits like Jim Shaw's 2006 'Untitled' tapestry to the ludicrous depictions of Abraham Lincoln as a zombie slayer or a vampire hunter in cinematic portrayals. Not all these images endure and resonate with successive generations, but many do, and each leaves an imprint, no matter how small. Think of the impression made by Lincoln's immense statue set in a memorial temple on the national mall, or the Lincolniana traded over eBay for thousands of dollars, or Daniel Day-Lewis's portrayal of the sixteenth president in Steven Spielberg's *Lincoln*. Cultural productions craft our perception of the past in enduring ways. Journalist Jackie Hogan argues that in learning about presidential representations 'we learn about ourselves, about who we are and who we wish we could be.'[7]

What distinguishes theatre productions from other cultural outputs is the portrayal of presidents or the presidency through live performance. Theatre literally stages the past, allowing audiences to experience a re-enactment. We might accept that a degree of fiction and dramatization is necessary to theatre, but like the re-enactment of military battles, live acting produces an experiential familiarity with the past, dispossessed of Hollywood special effects and the artistic licence that often accompanies motion pictures. As live spectators, the audience recognizes historical agency, and the performance of the past can 'leave us with a renewed sense of history as a lived experience of time, of history as *becoming*.'[8] Perhaps more than any other medium, the performing arts challenge our notions of time and historical action, be it the anachronistic hip-hop songs of *Hamilton*, the deeply researched re-enactments of the American Civil War that bring Confederates 'out of the attic,' in spoken word recitals or in abstract acts of expression through dance or display.[9] Audiences interact with live actors; performers grapple with how best to depict the past to achieve their impression of historical characters. These unique attributes of theatre have an impact on popular memory and make it a worthy cultural medium to study and to better help us understand presidential image and its representations. And yet, curiously, the performing arts have remained largely overlooked by scholars of the presidency.[10]

Of course, theatre productions have some significant drawbacks for analysing image. Unpopular or semi-popular productions tend to fade quickly from public consciousness – if they held it at all. In addition, because presidential images have such considerable cache among the public, audiences and critics instinctively consider an actor's likeness to the president and this can make the theatre 'more an impersonation than a real drama.'[11] Despite these obstacles, hundreds of theatrical representations of the presidency exist, and the theatre offers a rich tableau of our evolving perception.

To further appreciate the impact of theatrical productions on presidential image, this chapter examines four stage representations of the twenty-sixth president, Theodore Roosevelt, from two popular Broadway plays, namely Joseph Kesselring's *Arsenic and Old Lace* (1939) and Jerome Alden's *Bully* (1977), to an off-Broadway production from The TEAM's *RoosevElvis* (2015), and a spoken-word performance from Daniel Mallory Ortberg called 'Dirtbag Teddy Roosevelt' (2014). Theatrical performances of these four productions provide a diverse range of representations and show that TR's image remains deeply contested in this particular art form. This chapter also aims to demonstrate the role of stage writers, actors and producers in shaping different perspectives of Roosevelt's image and will illustrate how theatre derives inspiration from historical context. The stage, much like film or television, belongs to a moment in which history is performed, but unlike motion pictures, theatre is often re-staged in new venues, with new casts and at times when audiences hold different perspectives. Because of this, performance art provides a unique insight into the evolution of image.

The Most Adolescent of Men

As president, Theodore Roosevelt projected an image of activism on behalf of the national interest both at home and abroad. In his autobiography, he set out what became known as his 'stewardship theory' that America's chief executive had both the right and the duty to do anything the country's interests required provided he operated within the Constitution and the laws. 'I acted for the public welfare,' he declared. 'I acted for the common well-being of all our people.' In pursuit of this end, he displayed acute awareness of his symbolic role. Not only did he set the political agenda through speeches and close relations with the media, he also commanded public attention, historian David Greenberg noted, 'by mastering the tools and techniques of persuasion and image craft that would, decades later, come to be known as *spin*.'[12] Photographs of him were part of this strategy in conveying a sense of his gravitas, command and competence to do what was right for the country (see below). Though successful in promoting this self-image during his presidency, it did not long survive his early death at the age of sixty in January 1919. Theatre would play its part in the debunking of the image that the twenty-sixth president had so assiduously developed during his tenure in office.

Figure 1.1 Theodore Roosevelt projects confidence in America and himself in a 1908 photograph. Library of Congress, LC-DIG-ppmsca-36041, unrestricted use.

In 1931, journalist Henry Fowles Pringle published the first revisionist biography of Theodore Roosevelt. Pringle cut his teeth as an investigative reporter in New York before turning his hand to biography writing. He drew inspiration from a school of political critics known as debunkers who aimed to revise the portraits of political idols. Roosevelt was ripe for such revision. Biographies that had hitherto appeared since Roosevelt's death, mostly written by individuals who had known him, emphasized his greatness and his goodness. Pringle's book cast off the portrait of a saintly, high-minded character and transformed public perception by rendering the president a juvenile delinquent and reckless demagogue. In his telling, Roosevelt's trust-busting and government regulations became the product of an insufferable ego. Pringle presented Roosevelt's domestic policies as narcissistic, and his foreign policies as eager interventions designed to extend presidential power. The arbitration of the Russo-Japanese War, according to Pringle, was 'gratifying, but much less enjoyable' than the charge up San Juan Heights in the Spanish-American War.[13]

Until Pringle, no biographer had so obviously tipped the scales of Roosevelt's popular memory against him. In fact, the image of an adolescent Roosevelt was so convincing that few new biographies appeared in the 1930s or 1940s, and none challenged Pringle's revisionist narrative. What made Pringle's reversal of Roosevelt's saintly image so credible and compelling was the vast archival research on which he based his portrait. Consequently, historians for more than a generation hailed Pringle's biography as a 'first-rate contribution' of 'scholarly thoroughness, judgment, and detachment.'[14] Awarded the Pulitzer Prize in 1932, his 'crazy Teddy' portrait established itself as TR's standard image.[15]

A debunked Roosevelt did not escape self-parody. Pringle constructed an image by overemphasizing a single character trait: adolescence. On nearly every page, the biographer refers to Roosevelt's 'juvenile' personality, most zealously in the years surrounding the War of 1898. For Pringle, Roosevelt's service in the Rough Riders was defined by childish exuberance. His young adulthood and the pre-presidential years became a whirl of frenzied, impulsive and infantile moments defined as a psychological overcompensation for personal demons, such as his asthma and his father's failure to serve in the Civil War. When writing about Roosevelt's political career, Pringle portrays an immature adult affected by an 'overly enthusiastic' ardour and an unreasonably high 'estimate of his services.'[16] Whether assessing TR as governor of New York, vice-president, or president, Pringle's predominant image of TR emphasizes his subject's adolescent nature. Roosevelt's lifelong friend, journalist William Allen White, complained that the impression left the reader with 'every unpleasant side and angle' and the publisher Harcourt Brace advertised the book as an opportunity to discover the faults in TR's personality.[17]

On Broadway, Pringle's portrayal appeared most clearly in Joseph Kesselring's comedic play *Arsenic and Old Lace*. A German-American playwright from New York City with only minor credits to his name hitherto, Kesselring wrote the four-act *Arsenic and Old Lace* in 1939 and brought it to Broadway in 1941.[18] The play parodies the homicidal deeds of the fictional Brewster family. The protagonist, Mortimer Brewster, brings his fiancé to visit the home of his elderly aunts Martha and Abby. The women seem delicate septuagenarians, innocent and charitable, but they harbour a deadly secret. Martha and Abby offer room and board to lonely men before poisoning them with elderberry wine spiked with arsenic. The men, they insist, are depressed bachelors and the aunts murder them to relieve them of their loneliness. When Mortimer discovers a dead body at their house, the plot unravels, and the audience gradually uncovers the odious crime.

Although *Arsenic and Old Lace* initially appears to bear no connection to Theodore Roosevelt, in Act 1 the audience is introduced to Mortimer's brother, Teddy, who lives with his aunts and believes he is the twenty-sixth president. In a play with a farcical storyline, more than a few twists, and an overabundance of quirky characters, Teddy Brewster stands out for his antics and psychosis. Played by seasoned Shakespearean actor John Alexander, Teddy is meant to be the same age as his dapper brother Mortimer but looks and acts many years younger. He dresses in Rough Rider khakis and screams 'CHARGE' each time he climbs the stairs, imitating Roosevelt's pursuit of Spanish soldiers up San Juan Hill. When forced to explain his outfit, shovel and the long periods spent in the basement, he tells his brother, 'I'm off to Panama,' but he is actually burying his aunts' victims in the cellar. The play reaches its climax when a psychiatrist diagnoses Teddy as delusional before committing him to an asylum. At that point, Mortimer must convince Teddy to sign the commitment papers in his own name 'Brewster,' and Kesselring goes to great fictional length to connect the Teddys:

> Mortimer: The name Brewster is code for Roosevelt.
> Teddy: Code for Roosevelt?
> Mortimer: Yes. Don't you see? Take the name Brewster, take away the B, and what have you got?
> Teddy: Rooster!
> Mortimer: Uh-huh. And what does a rooster do?
> Teddy: Crows.
> Mortimer: It crows. And where do you hunt in Africa?
> Teddy: On the veldt!
> Mortimer: There you are: crows – veldt!
> Teddy: Ingenious! My compliments to the boys in the code department.

Kesselring's script and dialogue aim to show the gaping inconsistencies between myth and reality. The audience's first impression of Aunts Abby and Martha as charitable old ladies reverses when Mortimer uncovers their deadly secret. At the end of the play, he also discovers that he was adopted, and rather than react with surprise, the revelation brings relief. He can distance himself from the Brewsters and dismiss the fear of following in his family's footsteps. As with the rest of the characters, Teddy Brewster gradually changes. At first, he appears lovable and deluded, only to become dark and menacing.

In 1944, Frank Capra directed the film adaptation of *Arsenic and Old Lace*, starring Cary Grant as Mortimer and John Alexander reprising his stage role as Teddy. While Capra's movies often deliver a political moral, film critics treated his rendering of *Arsenic and Old Lace* 'as sheer entertainment without any real substance.'[19] That is a mistake. Capra adapted Kesselring's play because he could accentuate elements of it to make a political point. Like other Capra movies, such as *Mr. Smith Goes to Washington* (1939) or *It's a Wonderful Life* (1946), *Arsenic and Old Lace* demystifies, even debunks history in the same way Pringle revised the Roosevelt portrait. Kesselring and Capra crafted an image of TR that relied on Pringle's psychological profile. The play and film de-mythologize an American icon, and when theatre companies staged *Arsenic and Old Lace* across the country in smaller venues, they told actors playing Teddy Brewster to think of Roosevelt as Peter Pan, the boy who never grew up.[20] The emotionally adolescent Teddy Brewster demands the audience's attention by shouting, thundering around the stage, trumpeting a bugle and pretending to hold cabinet meetings. Traits like this initially seem innocent and perhaps nothing more than parody, but they represent the prevailing public image of Theodore Roosevelt in the 1930s and 1940s established by Henry Pringle. The daft acts of Teddy Brewster conceal the faults of a dangerous and unhinged collaborator and, in that depiction, Kesselring perpetuated the crazy Teddy image.

Recalibrating the Image

The infantile Depression-era image of Theodore Roosevelt went through considerable change during the Second World War. At the outset of the war, before American intervention, the Warner Bros. studio produced *The Monroe Doctrine* (1939), a short film that extolled the virtues of neutrality and deployed Theodore as the forerunner to Franklin D. Roosevelt. Although Warner Bros. produced the first overtly anti-Nazi film the same year (*Confessions of a Nazi Spy*), the studio faced pressure from government censors who wanted it to maintain a semblance of impartiality.[21] That lasted until the United States lined up with the Allies in 1941 and began supplying war material to Great Britain. Shortly before Pearl Harbor and the American declaration of war on the Axis Powers, Warner Bros. revisited Theodore's image and recalibrated it to that of an interventionist in another short film, *Teddy and the Rough Riders* (1941). Like the earlier depiction of TR as an advocate of neutrality, this revised historical image was designed to relate to Franklin D. Roosevelt and the changing nature of American foreign policy.

On the stage, however, crazy Teddy persisted. Theatrical treatments of Theodore Roosevelt took nearly forty years to adjust. There are two possible explanations for this. First, Franklin D. Roosevelt attracted so much attention from playwrights and producers that TR's recalibration went unexplored. Dore Schary's *Sunrise at Campobello* nearly swept the Tony Awards in 1958 and the production was adapted into a film in 1960. Second, the performance industry suffered catastrophic economic setbacks in the 1950s and 1960s. These decades may have witnessed a new era in performance styles, but the number of theatres dwindled throughout the country. Cinema had overtaken theatre as the favourite form of entertainment decades earlier, and the rise of television further eviscerated takings at the box office. Even worse for revenue were the changes taking place in the music industry. Sales in rock and roll diverted Americans' disposable income from once-popular show-tunes albums.[22]

It was not until the late 1970s that theatre recovered, and only then did performances reconsider Theodore Roosevelt. By the end of the 'Me Decade' as writer Tom Wolfe dubbed the 1970s, small off-off Broadway plays proved a sustainable model, albeit not a highly lucrative one, for playwrights and actors. Theatre proliferated outside traditional centres of performance and inspired a new generation of artists. Along with changes effecting production of plays and musicals, the political and social climate of the 1970s induced a sense of declining U.S. leadership, a sentiment that seemed to permeate all parts of American life. *Newsweek's* Pete Axthelm called the 1970s an era without heroes: 'Once, we routinely asked our kids who their heroes were. Today we fumble for answers when they ask us if there are any heroes left. Vietnam and Watergate played their part in all this, as we learned to beware our leaders and to scrutinize them warts and all.'[23] Public cynicism spread to the presidency; Richard Nixon, Gerald Ford and Jimmy Carter could hardly match the heroics of George Washington, Abraham Lincoln or Theodore Roosevelt.[24]

In the very same issue of *Newsweek*, contrarian editorialist George Will disagreed with Axthelm, but only in part. The problem as Will saw it was the ever-rising expectations on public figures and particularly for leaders to have heroic personalities. An honest appraisal of most historic figures would present 'a rounded portrait of the person's ambiguities, doubts, and defects,' but that 'does not mean that the person does not deserve to be thought of as heroic.'[25] It did imply, however, 'that those people who want to have heroes must outgrow the desire for cartoon characters, or monumental bronze statues.'[26] The blame for shifting expectations belonged to a mass media that brought public audiences ever closer to celebrities, politicians and each other in ways they never expected, Will contended, and by the late twentieth century that proximity ensured that 'warts-and-all' assessments of historical characters became the typical depiction, even if the public still craved fearlessness, boldness and nobility in their leaders.

Several biographers seized upon this 1970s malaise to write about Theodore Roosevelt as the quintessential American hero from a bygone era, although they did not do so as hagiographers had in the 1920s. Rather, this new Roosevelt brimmed with as many faults as he had virtues. Edmund Morris, a Kenyan-born writer who immigrated to the United States in 1968, became curious about TR after the disgraced Richard Nixon referenced his distant predecessor in his last days as president. Nixon not only quoted from TR's oft-cited 'Man in the Arena' speech for his official Farewell Address, but also referred to Roosevelt just minutes before he departed the White House the following day. In his last public remarks as president, Nixon likened his departure to that of Roosevelt restarting his life after his wife and mother died on the same day. The comparison confounded Morris. So did John Milius's 1975 movie, *The Wind and the Lion*, which Morris deplored as an 'erroneously ridiculous' film 'aimed at adolescents,' one that filled 'their heads with phony history.'[27] Both Nixon and Milius attempted to co-opt the heroics of

Roosevelt in moments of national disgrace, be it Watergate or the Vietnam War. As a result, Morris started writing a screenplay in 1975 about Roosevelt's youth and rise to high office, but the project floundered until he decided to develop it into a biography. Four years later, he released *The Rise of Theodore Roosevelt*, a nearly 900-page treatment of TR's pre-presidential years.

The literary community anointed Morris's book the new standard narrative, a biographical portrait that overtook Pringle's crazy Teddy. With access to the latest archival materials, Morris crafted a vivid image, submerging his subject in a multitude of human contradictions revealed in thick description. *The Rise of Theodore Roosevelt* depicted a man capable of being at once a New Yorker and a cowboy, a reformer and a conservative, a sickly asthmatic and an exuberant naturalist, a cool political operator and a fiery activist. Columnist Nicholas von Hoffman called it the homecoming of 'the Theodore Roosevelt of patriotic legend,' coupled with a priggish 'boy scoutism' that captured elements of Pringle's portrait.[28] Morris's book combined hagiography and bunk, producing an image of a hero with substantial defects.

In 1981, David McCullough published *Mornings on Horseback*, a Roosevelt biography that covered roughly the same period as Morris's book. 'I was interested in knowing what was involved in the metamorphosis of this most conspicuous animate wonder,' McCullough explained, and contended that Morris left gaps that a more experienced writer – namely, himself – could expand on.[29] *Mornings on Horseback* focused on Roosevelt's family, making them the protagonists in TR's life and recounting his rise through childhood experiences, demonstrating new approaches to biography that stemmed from academic scholarship in social history and culture studies. Psychological analysis, the agency of women and minorities, and understudied components of personality based on family, class, religion and geography helped to depict Theodore Roosevelt as a 'fixed core within an individual persona' that evolved from social mores, a man not easily reduced to a single dimension or affected by one 'primal event.' Whereas Henry Pringle emphasized Roosevelt's adolescent spirit as an all-encompassing attribute, such a singular measurement of the man appeared entirely out of place in the 1970s and 1980s.[30]

Playwrights and stage actors followed these trends in biographical reappraisal, much the way they did in the 1930s when Pringle shifted the perception of Roosevelt. The best example came from Jerome Alden who wrote *Bully: An Adventure with Teddy Roosevelt* (1977), a one-man show that opened at the Playhouse Theatre in Wilmington, Delaware, before its popularity prompted a move to the 46th Street Theatre in New York, where it ran for over a year.[31] One of Roosevelt's favourite cries, 'bully,' has two meanings. Roosevelt typically used it as a positive affirmation; a 'bully good time' would be a 'very good time.' But, as a noun, a bully is a person who intimidates others, and not coincidentally this dichotomy has also come to represent Roosevelt who has been criticized as a political bully. Echoing the era's biographies that cast Roosevelt as both a hero and hooligan, Jerome Alden seized on the word as the basis for his portrayal. Starring veteran stage and screen actor James Whitmore, who in 1975 had appeared in a similar one-man play about

President Harry S. Truman, *Give 'Em Hell Harry*, *Bully* included many of the hallmark characteristics of Kesselring's and Pringle's crazy Teddy. The show began with a 'loud roaring, good-natured laugh from the back of the theatre,' followed by a marauding Roosevelt who 'charges briskly down the aisle to the front of the orchestra wearing a khaki riding outfit [and] campaign hat.'[32] But, unlike the deranged Teddy Brewster, the audience meets a many-sided Roosevelt who makes references to bird calls in nature and obscure English literature, and lectures on scientific discoveries, ancient history and fine art. All the while, Whitmore bounds on point-to-point treks with unseen contemporaries many of whom challenge and contest Roosevelt.

Bully synthesizes previous caricatures. Alden's play, set during the 1912 presidential election, breaks away from the events of Roosevelt's Progressive campaign in flashbacks and flash-forwards to explore Roosevelt's youth and the presidential years. Whitmore even demonstrates Roosevelt's enduring energy in retirement. More than any previous performance, *Bully* aimed to reflect on Roosevelt's life from the perspective of old age (Roosevelt died in 1919 at sixty). The play illustrates a man whose greatest accomplishments are behind him, and as such *Bully* is a kind of presidential memoir that illustrates the contradictions in human personalities and behaviour over time. The most humorous parts of Whitmore's monologue come in the unseen exchanges with critic H. L. Mencken, to whom his Roosevelt jibes that 'you chaps [in the newspaper industry] never could "peg" me, could you? Liberal-radical-conservative-populist-progressive-monorchial-imperialist!'[33] Indeed, Whitmore's Roosevelt includes all these types, and the show's self-deprecating humour disarms any serious consideration about psychosis. Instead, *Bully* depicts TR's arrogance as a gallant conviction shaped by the times.

The Roosevelt in *Bully* reaches hero-status when an assassin's bullet fails to stop him delivering a speech in Milwaukee. No matter how ill-fated and doomed to fail, the Bull Moose campaign drives on to become instrumental in the recalibration of American politics. After the 1912 campaign, Whitmore hangs up his 'army greatcoat' and puts on an 'old sweater,' but the adventure continues almost unabated. 'I ran away again,' Whitmore tells the audience, 'This time to the jungles of the Amazon.'[34] The second act of *Bully* plods through the often uninteresting daily routine of a father and husband interspersed with the exceptional labours of a modern explorer and political powerhouse. Unlike Pringle's interpretation of a man overcome with ego, Alden's Roosevelt enjoys the banal elements of retirement, such as reading literature, rowing on Oyster Bay and watching his children grow up, all the while longing for renewed glory by leading a regiment into battle in the Great War. The death of Roosevelt's youngest son Quentin in aerial combat over France in July 1918 leaves him in mourning, mindful of the contradictory feelings of glory and sorrow inherent in battle. The play attempts to plumb the depths of human complexity and frailty in a figure best known until that point as routinely reckless or brazenly valiant.

Bully received as much criticism as it did acclaim. Admiring its examination of 'the vagaries of Roosevelt,' Clive Barnes of the *New York Times* called the play 'the best of its kind.'[35] His colleague Richard Eder, by contrast, criticized the lack of historical interest for modern audiences, but detected 'snatches of intimacy' that complicate our understanding of TR's life, and particularly the later years in which he 'putters, but putters with passion ... Mr. Whitmore is at his best as this creaky, futile, but moving figure.'[36] Loved, or mildly disliked, *Bully* reflected the changing interpretation of Roosevelt, depicting him as neither entirely heroic nor exclusively adolescent. Theatre-goers seemingly opted for Whitmore's version over Kesselring's in *Arsenic and Old Lace*. In 1977, a restaging of Kesselring's play ran in Queens with poor reviews, and the Broadway revival in 1986, staged at the very same theatre as *Bully* less than a decade after Whitmore's performance, flopped. Frank Rich criticized Michael John McGann's portrayal of Teddy Brewster as 'a tiresome loudmouth,' observing 'all that remains funny are the gags about critics and the theater.'[37] Conversely, *Bully* became the basis for Jerome Alden's 1987 musical *Teddy and Alice*. With the revival of the stage show in 1997–9, now starring John Davidson as Roosevelt, *Bully* went on to become the most popular theatre portrayal of Roosevelt.

Experimental Performances

Exploring gender and sexuality have been major themes in theatre productions since the 1960s. Literary critic Christopher Bigsby argues that such explorations came about when Broadway suffered an economic downturn in the mid-century and:

> regional theatres spread throughout the country, generating plays that then fed back to Broadway, reversing the flow of the prewar world. And if audiences diversified on a regional basis, so they did on that of race, gender, national origin, and sexual preference. In other words, as the ruling metaphor of American society changed, from melting pot to rainbow, the theatre acknowledged this. The presumed homogeneity of the audience no longer prevailed.[38]

What accompanied commercial theatre productions in the 1980s and 1990s was experimental theatre that pushed cross-gender and cross-racial casting, confessional-style autobiographical performances and anti-authoritative recital art that 'sought to exorcise what they saw as the rationalist, positivist, racist, imperialist, and capitalist' impulses in American society.[39] As a figure of authority and normative masculine privilege, Theodore Roosevelt was naturally excluded from the first wave of experimental performances. Instead, Jerome Alden's masculine, boisterous and daring Roosevelt became the typical treatment, and a number of family-friendly plays about Roosevelt-as-president or one-man shows akin to *Bully* embarked on successful national tours in the first decade of the twenty-first century.[40] But, as experimental theatre styles endured and have even become the mainstream in performance art, Theodore Roosevelt's image has gravitated away from Alden's complex, but essentially normative, American hero.

In 2015, The TEAM, a Brooklyn theatre collective committed to performance art that reconsiders the American experience, staged *RoosevElvis*, a comedy in which protagonist Ann grapples with her innermost thoughts about gender, socializing and love in Midwest America. Ann's debilitating introverted personality has held her back from dating, but by dressing up as Elvis at home she finds the courage to come out of her shell as well as the closet. Ann realizes she might be a lesbian and begins internet dating, choosing to go on a date with Brenda, an outgoing woman who likes taxidermy, the outdoors and Theodore Roosevelt. Their first date – a weekend camping trip in the Badlands where Roosevelt once ranched – goes disastrously awry, and in her disillusion with modern courtship, Ann decides that she will drive south to Graceland, the home of Elvis, to find inspiration. But this is no ordinary road trip: Ann's journey descends into a hallucinogenic fugue in which the spirits of Elvis Presley and Theodore Roosevelt 'battle for what type of man or woman Ann should become.'[41] Elvis (Libby King) and Roosevelt (Kristen Sieh) dominate the play as variations of American masculinity. Elvis is a softly spoken, sensitive stud and somewhat bashful in comparison to Roosevelt who is portrayed as a prude, eager-to-please Victorian. 'I have great admiration for him,' Sieh recounted in her performance notes. '[I] approached playing him with warmth and empathy, rather than any kind of ironic remove. That said, he is definitely a clown. He throws himself into everything with absolute commitment.'[42]

James Whitmore's performance in *Bully* established Roosevelt as a composite character, but Sieh adds all-new angles to the former president's persona. Her own hyper-femininity perceptibly contrasts with Roosevelt's reputation for hyper-masculinity (she said Katherine Hepburn was the inspiration for Roosevelt's voice and mannerisms), and the play's focus on identity, gender, androgyny, sex, race and class allows audiences to wonder about Roosevelt's likely opinions on LGBTQ issues, Black Lives Matter and even neo-liberal economics. 'Once we've had our reason overthrown and our logic drummed into submission' by the unconventional casting of women as quintessential American men, 'the play lets us in on the reality behind the dream state,' Helen Shaw commented in *Time Out*.[43] Exploring human multitudes in a way unimagined by Kesselring and Alden, *RoosevElvis* demonstrates that identity runs deeper than social designations, status and norms in its depiction of Theodore Roosevelt's historical image.[44]

One of the *RoosevElvis* playwrights, Jake Margolin, said the play's inspiration stemmed from The TEAM's regular conversations 'about how we see ourselves in constant relation to icons of "greatness," regardless of our own potential.' He wondered 'whether Teddy Roosevelt and Elvis Presley pictured themselves through the eye of the camera and whether they heard a score for their internal biopics.'[45] Roosevelt certainly considered his image during his lifetime. For example, he crafted a Western cowboy persona despite spending less than four months in the Badlands. Historians have pointed out that his upbringing in Manhattan exuded wealth and privilege antithetical to the mythical cowboy. As for masculinity, Roosevelt's hunting prowess or sportsman image jars with the reality that he never shot song birds and preferred tennis to football.[46] Those contradictions came out in Alden's *Bully*, but what *RoosevElvis* asks us to consider is how other historical characters may have occupied Roosevelt's inner monologue. Since TR wrote biographies on Oliver Cromwell, Thomas Hart Benton and Gouverneur Morris, we could make a guess at those three, or perhaps we might include the heroes of the *Nibelungenlied* or the gods of mythology he so adored. In any case, the thought raises the potential of a polygonal Roosevelt, with even more sides than Alden's character.

The postmodern turn in performance art that defied gender norms and twisted realistic narratives into fantasies like *RoosevElvis* also found adherents beyond Broadway. Scripted and unscripted performance art has become part of twenty-first-century public life, in flash mobs, street recitals, happening festivals like Burning Man or impromptu poetry slams. The character of Theodore Roosevelt has found his way into some of these performances. In 2014, Daniel Mallory Ortberg, a feminist writer and actor, performed 'Dirtbag Teddy Roosevelt,' an act in which a nonsensically loud and impetuous Roosevelt barks orders at his presidential successor William Howard Taft. An obviously exaggerated take on the crazy Teddy trope, the show purposely convolutes Roosevelt's traits in the same way *RoosevElvis* treats the former president:

TAFT!
GET IN HERE THIS INSTANT!
THE BOYS IN THE WAR DEPARTMENT ARE LETTING ME USE THEM
TO RECREATE THE BATTLE OF SAN JUAN HILL AND WE NEED YOU
TO PLAY SAN JUAN HILL.
TAFT!
TAFT!
WAKE UP YOU WALRUS!
what is it
THERE'S A WAR ON AND YOU DIDN'T TELL ME!
where's a war
we're not at war
NOT HERE, YOU BLOATED MUSTACHE-HOLDER, IN RUSSIA
I, yes
there is a war in Russia
WELL I'M GOING THERE TO PUT A STOP TO IT
their war is with the Japanese, Mr. President, it's not with us
IF I CAN'T HAVE A WAR YOU CAN BE DAMNED SURE THE RUSSIANS
AND THE JAPANESE AREN'T GOING TO HAVE ONE[47]

'Dirtbag Teddy Roosevelt' emerged from Ortberg's first book, *Texts from Jane Eyre*, an imagination of how literary characters might communicate in the twenty-first century with cellular phones.[48] It turns out that the likes of Scarlett O'Hara, Daisy Buchanan and Jane Eyre are 'a bunch of weirdos, losers, needy douchebags, obnoxious strivers.'[49] So is Dirtbag Teddy Roosevelt. The objective of Ortberg's performance is not to disparage Roosevelt for cheap laughs, but to show how out of place Victorian culture is in the contemporary world. 'There's a sense the canon should be entirely dismissed or completely revered because it's the canon and you can't touch it and you can't make fun of the things white men like, because it breaks their tiny, precious hearts,' Ortberg attempted to clarify in a recent interview. He acknowledged, however, 'It would be hard to write... if there wasn't love at the core of it.'[50]

Conclusion

Despite abundant scholarship that can help present a realistic characterization of Theodore Roosevelt in historical context, absurd theatrical performances persist. At the 2014 World Cup in Brazil, a man dressed in khakis, calling himself Teddy Goalsevelt became the *de facto* mascot for Team USA soccer. He even ran for FIFA president in 2015.[51] Dozens of impersonators perform Roosevelt at National Park sites, academic symposia and corporate leadership seminars.[52] Joseph Kesselring's Teddy Brewster in *Arsenic and Old Lace* and Jerome Alden's Roosevelt in *Bully* appear positively uncomplicated in comparison to these portrayals, or even when viewed alongside Ortberg's 'Dirtbag Teddy Roosevelt' and The TEAM's *RoosevElvis*. They do, however, share something in common. The performed image of Theodore Roosevelt matches the historiographical turns, especially in biography writing, as well as the general trend in cultural representations.[53] Theatre portrayals of Roosevelt have transitioned from monolithic impressions in Pringle and Kesselring's psychotic adolescent image into a complex character of high intellect and frequent enthusiasm in Morris and Alden's 'great man' portrayals. The latest style, certainly a different kind of caricature that is deliberately anachronistic, depicts a man with countless sides from a different era from whom we can learn.

The other common element among many portrayals on stage, and certainly in terms of the four performances considered here, is humour. The character of Theodore Roosevelt appears as light-hearted, amusing and fun-loving, even if that playful exuberance is consciously tongue-in-cheek, masquerading as dangerous machismo. Although far fewer stage performances of Roosevelt exist when compared to the dozens of film and television representations, playwrights and producers use Roosevelt to inject humour into uncomfortable topics, a shared theme that says something about the broad affection for a president with a fair share of admirers and detractors. In his own life, Roosevelt enjoyed those witty caricatures of him created by humorists. He invited satirist Finely Peter Dunne to the New York Governor's Mansion in 1899 after Dunne spoofed Roosevelt's autobiographical account of the Rough Riders' charge up San Juan Heights. Writing as one of his characters Mr. Dooley, Dunne said the book should be called 'Alone in Cuba.' Roosevelt responded, 'I regret to state that my family and intimate friends are delighted with your review of my book. Now I think you owe me one; and I shall exact that when you next come east you pay me a visit.'[54] Dunne and Roosevelt struck up a close relationship after that meeting, and so have the performers and writers who depict Roosevelt on stage. It appears that they cannot help but find something to love alongside something to loathe in their parodies.

Notes

1   Women on 20s, 'Campaign & Results' (http://www.womenon20s.org); Calmes, Jackie, 'Woman's Portrait Will Appear on the $10 Bill,' *New York Times* [*NYT*], 17 June 2015.

2   Chernow, Ron, 'Save Alexander Hamilton!' *POLITICO*, 18 June 2015, https://www. politico.com/magazine/story/2015/06/save-alexander-hamilton–119176; 'Why Is Alexander Hamilton, 1st US Treasury Chief, Leaving the $10 Bill?' *Chicago Tribune*, 18 September 2015.

3   Calmes, Jackie, 'Harriet Tubman Ousts Andrew Jackson in Change for a $20,' *NYT*, 20 April 2016; Phillips, Amber, 'How Politics and Hip-Hop Saved the Hamilton $10 Bill – and Put Harriet Tubman on the $20,' *Washington Post*, 20 April 2016. Andrew Jackson's legacy has experienced a revival of sorts with President Donald Trump invoking 'Old Hickory' and telling reporters that replacing Jackson with Tubman is 'pure political correctness.' Trump's Treasury Secretary Steve Mnuchin has said the redesigned $20 bill is not a priority for his Department. See Temple-West, Patrick, 'Mnuchin Dismisses Question about Putting Harriet Tubman on $20 Bill,' *POLITICO*, 31 August 2017, https://www.politico.com/story/2017/08/31/harriet-tubman-20-dollar-bill-steven-mnuchin–242217.

4   For an explanation of sites of memory and cultural outputs as mnemonic markers, as well as the anthropological practices of humans as acts of intergenerational cultural transmission, see Winter, Jay, 'Historians and Sites of Memory' and Boyer, Pascal, 'Cognitive Predispositions and Cultural Transmission,' in Pascal Boyer and James V. Wertsch, eds., *Memory in Mind and Culture* (Cambridge: Cambridge University Press, 2009), pp. 252–72, 288–319.

5   Lipsitz, George, *Time Passages: Collective Memory and American Popular Culture* (Minneapolis: University of Minnesota Press, 1990), pp. 3–4, 14–17.

6   Polsky, Andrew J., 'No Tool Is Perfect: Periodization in the Study of American Political Development,' *Polity*, 37 (October 2005): 523–30; Taliaferro, John, *Great White Fathers: The True Story of Gutzon Borglum and His Obsessive Quest to Create the Mt. Rushmore National Monument* (New York: Public Affairs, 2004), p. 2.

7   *Abraham Lincoln vs. Zombies* (director Richard Schenkman, 2012); *Abraham Lincoln: Vampire Hunter* (director Timur Bekmambetov, 2012); Sandage, Scott A., 'A Marble House Divided: The Lincoln Memorial, the Civil Rights Movement, and the Politics of Memory, 1939–1963,' *Journal of American History*, 80 (June 1993): 135–67; Ward, Geoffrey, *The Civil War*, PBS miniseries (director Ken Burns, 1990); *Lincoln* (director Steven Spielberg, 2012); Hogan, Jackie, *Lincoln, Inc.: Selling the Sixteenth President in Contemporary America* (New York: Rowman and Littlefield, 2011), p. 2.

8   Bechtel, Roger, *Past Performance: American Theatre and the Historical Imagination* (Lewisburg, PA: Bucknell University Press, 2007), pp. 19–24.

9   Horowitz, Tony, *Confederates in the Attic: Dispatches from the Unfinished Civil War* (New York: Vintage Books, 1999), pp. 3–17; Schneider, Rebecca, *Performing Remains: Art and War in Times of Theatrical Reenactment* (New York: Routledge, 2011), pp. 1–18, 87–98.

10 Several collections and monographs analyse presidential images in motion pictures, art, architecture and material culture, but even examinations of individual presidents on this score only fleetingly consider performance art. There is one notable exception: political science professor Bruce Altschuler has sought to 'begin filling the gap' by researching more than forty plays performed and written since 1900. See Altschuler, Bruce, *Acting Presidents: 100 Years of Plays about the Presidency* (New York: Palgrave Macmillan, 2010).

My own work on Theodore Roosevelt, notably *Theodore Roosevelt's Ghost: The History and Memory of an American Icon* (Baton Rouge: Louisiana State University Press, 2017), is somewhat guilty of overlooking theatre, and this chapter offers a correction.

11 Altschuler, *Acting Presidents*, p. xi.

12 Roosevelt, Theodore, *An Autobiography* (New York: Macmillan, 1913), p. 357; Greenberg, David, *Republic of Spin: An Inside History of the American Presidency* (New York: Norton, 2016), p. 23.

13 Pringle, Henry F., *Theodore Roosevelt: A Biography* (New York: Harcourt, Brace, 1931), p. 264.

14 'Review: Theodore Roosevelt: A Biography by Henry F. Pringle,' *International Affairs*, 12 (March 1933): 284.

15 Kathleen Dalton, an eminent Theodore Roosevelt biographer, believes that historian Richard Hofstadter's impression of TR derived from Pringle's and even 'magnified Pringle's view that TR had been rather mad. Together, Pringle and Hofstadter put forth the Crazy Teddy theory which became historical gospel.' See Dalton, Kathleen, 'Changing Interpretations of Theodore Roosevelt and the Progressive Era,' in Christopher M. Nichols and Nancy C. Unger, eds., *A Companion to the Gilded Age and Progressive Era* (Malden, MA: Wiley-Blackwell, 2017), p. 298.

16 Pringle, *Theodore Roosevelt*, pp. 13, 144, 149–50, 180.

17 Pringle, Henry F., 'Roosevelt's Vigorous Mind in Action,' *NYT*, 30 November 1930; White, William Allen, 'Review of *Theodore Roosevelt*,' and (Harcourt Brace) Advertisement in *Saturday Review of Literature*, 7 November 1931, p. 257, 265.

18 For the play's text, see Kesselring, Joseph, *Arsenic and Old Lace* (London: Weinberger, 2001). For discussion of contemporary reviews, see Krutch, Joseph Wood, 'Homicide as Fun,' *The Nation*, 25 (January 1941): 108–9.

19 Gunter, Matthew C., *The Capra Touch: A Study of the Director's Hollywood Classics and War Documentaries, 1939–1945* (Jefferson, NC: McFarland, 2011), p. 46.

20 Johnson, Eric, 'The Character of Teddy Brewster in Arsenic and Old Lace' (Master of Fine Arts Dissertation, Minnesota State University at Mankato, 1989), p. 32.

21 Warner Bros., the most anti-fascist of the Hollywood studios, initially clashed with FDR over his foreign policy of non-involvement with regard to the developing war crisis in Europe, in part because of its first-hand experience of Nazi violence and xenophobia. In 1936, Nazi Brownshirts allegedly murdered the studio's German-Jewish salesman in Berlin. Warner Bros. ceased distribution in Germany and produced *Confessions of a Nazi Spy* (1939), a film that met with FDR's disapproval. The film censor said it 'unfairly represented' Hitler and threatened to fracture transatlantic neutrality. FDR even asked Warner Bros. to shelve any explicitly anti-Nazi films. See Cullinane, *Theodore Roosevelt's Ghost*, pp. 133–5.

22 Aronson, Arnold, 'American Theatre in Context, 1945-present,' in Don B. Wilmeth and Christopher Bigsby, eds., *The Cambridge History of American Theatre: Post World War II to the 1990s* (Cambridge: Cambridge University Press, 2000), pp. 123–4.

23 Axthelm, Pete, 'Where Have All the Heroes Gone?' *Newsweek*, 6 August 1979.

24 When Reagan announced his candidacy for president in the 1980 election, he accused every White House occupant from Lyndon B. Johnson to Jimmy Carter of lacklustre leadership that corroded the political system. He promised a return to prosperity by adhering to old-fashioned values of individual liberty and American democracy. He promised to be the hero they were not, a leader capable of returning the United States to 'greatness' in an 'unbelieving world.' Reagan, Ronald, 'Announcement of Presidential Candidacy,' 13 November 1979, http://www.reagan.utexas.edu.

25 Will, George, 'Fashions in Heroes,' *Newsweek*, 6 August 1979.

26   Ibid.

27   'Q&A with Edmund Morris,' *C-SPAN*, 4 November 2010, http://www.c-span.org/
     video/?296436-1/qa-edmund-morris; Morris, Edmund, *This Living Hand: And
     Other Essays* (New York: Random House, 2013), pp. 128–9; Morris, Edmund,
     'The Distortion of History: "The Wind and the Lion,"' *TRA [Theodore Roosevelt
     Association] Journal*, 1 (Summer/Fall 1975): 9–10, 12.

28   von Hoffman, Nicholas, 'A Bully Portrait of the Legendary Teddy,' *Chicago
     Tribune*, 25 March 1979.

29   Ward, Geoffrey C., 'The Making of Theodore Roosevelt,' *NYT*, 26 July 1981.
     McCullough admitted that he aimed to resurrect Roosevelt from 1930s depictions
     that began with Henry Pringle and culminated in the Frank Capra adaptation of
     Joseph Kesselring's play *Arsenic and Old Lace*. See 'Book Notes,' *TRA Journal*, 7
     (Summer 1981): 22–3.

30   Banner, Lois W., 'Biography as History,' *American Historical Review*, 114
     (June 2009): 579–86. The cultural turn also gave rise to the postmodern turn, a
     theoretical approach denying that biography, or indeed histories, could locate
     meaning and truth from the resources available to researchers. Biographers were
     affected by this, but as Nigel Hamilton relates, with 'no credible alternative to the
     grand récit of life chronicling,' the writing of biography continued to churn over
     human existence. See Hamilton, Nigel, *Biography: A Brief History* (Cambridge, MA:
     Harvard University Press, 2007), pp. 206–12.

31   Other examples reflect the changing nature of Roosevelt's legacy and the theatre industry.
     Jon Phillip Palmer's *Teddy in That Splendid Little War* (1976) was commissioned by the
     Berkeley University Bicentennial Committee and sponsored by the Committee for Arts
     and Lectures. It depicted a heroic Roosevelt with plenty of shortcomings and made use
     of the patriotic fervour that accompanied the bicentennial celebrations.

32   Alden, Jerome, *Bully: An Adventure with Teddy Roosevelt* (New York: Crown
     Publishers, 1979), p. 1.

33   Ibid., p. 12.

34   Ibid., p. 52.

35   Clive Barnes quoted in 'Bully,' *Samuel French*, https://www.samuelfrench.com/p/1129/
     bully.

36   Eder, Richard, 'Drama "Bully" Talks Softly,' *NYT*, 2 November 1977.

37   Rich, Frank, 'The Stage: "Arsenic and Old Lace" Revival,' *NYT*, 27 June 1986. *Teddy
     and Alice*, which ran for seventy-seven shows at the Minskoff Theatre in midtown
     Manhattan, examined Roosevelt's psychological state of being at the time of his first
     wife's death in 1884 and his inability to recover from her passing. Alice Roosevelt,
     TR's daughter by his first wife, becomes the musical's antagonist through her
     outspokenness and ill-mannered conduct. Roosevelt can either manage the country,
     or Alice, but not both. Alden, Jerome, *Teddy and Alice: A Musical*, in the Theodore
     Roosevelt Collection, Subject Files: Plays, Houghton Library, Harvard University;
     Rich, Frank, 'Theater: A Musical, "Teddy and Alice",' *NYT*, 13 November 1987.

38   Bigsby, Christopher, 'Introduction' in Wilmeth and Bigsby, *Cambridge History of
     American Theatre*, p. 2.

39   Ibid., p. 14.

40   The Irish Arts Center reprised *Bully* in 2006 with William Walsh as Roosevelt.
     Kesselring's *Arsenic and Old Lace* is a mainstay of High School theatre as well as local
     and regional stage revivals. Children's shows in the late twentieth century include
     the musical *Teddy Roosevelt* by Theatreworks/USA and the Kennedy Center of
     Performing Arts staging of *Teddy Roosevelt and the Treasure of Ursa Major* (2006).

Other musicals included Power Productions' *Teddy: A Rough and Ready Musical* (1981). Heroic plays also crowded the field, notably *Teddykins: An American Hero* (2000), a biographical performance not unlike *Bully*, and *King of the Mountains* (2016), a story about John Muir and Roosevelt as early environmental champions. For re-runs of *Bully*, see advertisement for the 1998 version in the Theodore Roosevelt Collection, Subject Files: Plays, Houghton Library, Harvard University; and Gates, Anita, 'Bully: Even Caught in the Footlights, a Bull Moose Can Still Roar,' *NYT*, 19 July 2006. Scripts and marketing material for *Teddy Roosevelt* (Theodore Roosevelt Birthplace), *Teddy: A Rough and Ready Musical* can be found in the Theodore Roosevelt Collection cited above. See also Kidd, Ronald, *Teddy Roosevelt and the Treasure of Ursa Major* (New York: Simon & Schuster, 2008); Maley, Patrick, 'King of the Mountains at Luna Stage Is a History Lesson Best Left Forgotten,' *Star Ledger*, 18 October 2016.

41 The TEAM, 'RoosevElvis Press Kit,' http://theteamplays.org/wp-content/uploads/2012/01/RoosevElvis-press-kit.pdf.

42 'A Note on the Performances,' *RoosevElvis* (London: Oberon Books, 2015), p. 4.

43 Shaw, Helen, 'RoosevElvis,' *Time Out New York*, 18 October 2013.

44 In the prelude to the script, The TEAM cite Walt Whitman's famous adage: 'Do I contradict myself? Very well, then I contradict myself, I am large, I contain multitudes.'

45 Jake Margolin, 'A Note from One of the Writers,' *RoosevElvis*, pp. 1–2.

46 On the mythical cowboy image versus the New York dandy, see Kohn, Edward, *Heir to the Empire State: New York and the Making of Theodore Roosevelt* (New York: Basic Books, 2014), pp. ix–xv, 85–104. On football and tennis, see Watts, Sarah, *Rough Rider in the White House: Theodore Roosevelt and the Politics of Desire* (Chicago: University of Chicago Press, 2010), p. 8. On Roosevelt's disapproval of being depicted in tennis costume, and his advice to successor William Howard Taft to avoid playing golf, see Theodore Roosevelt to William Howard Taft, 14 September 1908, in Morison, Elting E. et al, eds., *The Letters of Theodore Roosevelt*, Vol. 6 (Cambridge: Harvard University Press, 1952), pp. 1234–5.

47 Ortberg, Mallory, 'Dirtbag Teddy Roosevelt' was originally published on *The Toast* (http://the-toast.net/2014/09/16/dirtbag-teddy-roosevelt) but was removed when this online blog closed in 2017. For Ortberg's live performance, see 'Dirtbag Teddy Roosevelt,' *YouTube*, https://www.youtube.com/watch?v=nfKSa0MCrg0.

48 Ortberg, Mallory, *Texts from Jane Eyre: And Other Conversations with Your Favorite Literary Characters* (New York: Henry Holt, 2014).

49 Lange, Maggie, 'Mallory Ortberg on the Great Jerks of Literature,' *The Cut*, 30 October, 2014, https://www.thecut.com/2014/10/mallory-ortberg-on-the-great-jerks-of-literature.html.

50 Ibid.

51 Channick, Robert, 'Teddy Goalsevelt Throws Hat in FIFA Presidential Ring,' *Chicago Tribune*, 5 June 2015.

52 Keith McGough, 'Front Page, Theodore Roosevelt … Today,' www.theodoreroosevelt.com, available on the Internet Archive's Way Back Machine (https://archive.org/web). The director of the Theodore Roosevelt Association, John Gable, barred TR impersonators from attending its meetings or sponsored events in character. For a commentary on 'imposters,' see Roosevelt, Tweed, 'Forgotten Fragments: Impostors!' *TRA Journal* 35 (Winter–Spring 2014): 27–31.

53 See Cullinane, *Theodore Roosevelt's Ghost*; Dalton, 'Changing Interpretations of Theodore Roosevelt and the Progressive Era.'

54 Theodore Roosevelt to Peter Finely Dunne, 28 November, 1899, in Finley Peter Dunne Papers, Folder: Correspondence, 1899–1905, Library of Congress, Washington, DC.

Chapter 2

WOODROW WILSON: PROFESSOR AND IDEALIST

John Thompson

The images of public figures derive from those features of their backgrounds and personalities that are seen by their supporters, their opponents or the public as distinctive and revealing. In the case of Woodrow Wilson, his earlier academic career and his Presbyterian background (as the son of a minister) have most often shaped perceptions of him. Wilson himself was among those who also regarded his Scots-Irish heritage as a significant element in his identity and image. Responses to this image have been sharply divided, for Wilson has been one of those political figures who arouse strong feelings – either of allegiance or of hostility. And this has not only been among Americans. By leading the United States into the Great War and calling for a new international order capped by a League of Nations, Wilson became a world figure. He was received almost as a Messiah by huge and enthusiastic crowds when he arrived in Europe to take part in the Paris peace conference. Yet many of those who initially cheered him at home and abroad became bitterly critical when the terms of the eventual settlement seemed a betrayal of their hopes. Wilson's public reputation suffered a further blow when his efforts to secure Senate approval of the League of Nations were unsuccessful but rose twenty years later when the predictions he had made of the consequences of American non-participation seemed vindicated by the coming of the Second World War. In 1944, a Technicolor Hollywood blockbuster portrayed him as a prophet and a martyr to the cause of world peace. In subsequent decades, Wilson has continued to be identified above all with his vision of a new world order and has been seen by both admirers and critics as the embodiment of an idealist approach to international relations.

It was not until he was fifty-three years old that Woodrow Wilson entered politics. Before that he had had an academic career during which he had written several notable books on American government and history. It was as President of Princeton University that he had achieved national prominence through widely publicized contests with the university's board of trustees. At a time when the progressive movement against 'plutocracy' and 'boss politics' was at its height, Wilson seemed a potentially strong candidate for electoral office to the leaders of the Democratic Party in New Jersey. They secured his nomination for the governorship, which he won with a handsome majority in 1910. Like his chief sponsors, Wilson himself always saw this as a step to the presidency.[1]

Unsurprisingly, Wilson's public image was shaped by his previous career; in political cartoons, he was commonly portrayed in academic cap and gown. He was generally referred to as 'Dr. Wilson,' while opponents spoke sarcastically of 'the schoolmaster in politics.' Joseph P. Tumulty, a young supporter who would soon become Wilson's secretary, was deeply involved with ward politics and recognized that being regarded as 'the "highbrow" candidate' was potentially damaging. It could easily be associated with both unworldliness and a condescending attitude to 'plain folks.' In his memoir, Tumulty emphasized that Wilson's style of campaigning countered such preconceptions:

> Those who had gathered the idea that the head of a great university would appear pedantic and stand stiff-necked upon an academic pedestal from which he would talk over the heads of the common people were forced, by the fighting, aggressive attitude of the Doctor, to revise their old estimates.... His homely illustrations evoked expressions of delight, until it seemed that this newcomer in the politics of our state had a better knowledge of the psychology of the ordinary crowd than the old stagers who had spent their lives in politics.

Nevertheless, Tumulty also recounts how he attempted to warm up Wilson's relations with old pros among the politicians who found the governor's reserved social manner off-putting: 'I very frankly told him one day at luncheon that many members of both legislative bodies felt that he was too stiff and academic and that they were anxious to find out for themselves if there was a more human side to him.' Tumulty then arranged a dinner, at the close of which one senator challenged Wilson to a Virginia Reel: 'the crowd of men were soon delighted to see ... the new Governor out on the floor and his long legs were soon moving in rhythm with the music.'[2]

The professorial image also had positive aspects that were naturally emphasized by those promoting Wilson's cause. Intellectual authority was obviously one of these. In Tumulty's account, Wilson's speeches in 1910 represented 'an application to practical politics of the fundamental principles of responsible government which he had analyzed in his earlier writings.... His trained habit of thinking through concrete facts to basic principles was serving him well in this campaign; this trained habit of clear exposition in the Princeton lecture hall was serving him well.'[3]

The professorial image also suggested an independence and integrity that would eschew vulgar political calculation and the dirty deals associated with professional politicians. Wilson himself always sought to project this image while at the same time demonstrating a strength of character that would belie the association of academic intellectualism with ineffectualness in the real world. He managed to do both at the very start of his governorship by breaking very publicly with Senator James 'Sugar Jim' Smith, the political boss who had been the leading sponsor of his nomination when the latter sought his backing for a second term in the US Senate. In this contest, Tumulty admiringly recalled:

> My chief, no longer an amateur, taught me, by precept and example, that effective fighting can be conducted without resort to the tricks and duplicities of those who place political advantage above principle. Woodrow Wilson made new rules for the game, and they were the rules which men of honor adopt when conducting their private business on principles of good faith and truth-telling.[4]

Cartoonists portrayed the new governor literally kicking the bosses out of his office.

As Wilson became a leading contender for the presidency in 1912, opponents like newspaper baron William Randolph Hearst delighted in always referring to him as 'Professor Wilson.' Far from seeing this image as a liability, his supporters highlighted it when placing Wilson's name in nomination for president at the Democratic National Convention in 1912. In the conclusion of his eulogistic speech, his friend Judge John W. Westcott hailed him as 'the seer and philosopher of Princeton, the Princeton schoolmaster, Woodrow Wilson.'[5] After a lengthy and tense contest, Wilson secured the necessary two-thirds majority for the nomination on the forty-sixth ballot. According to one observer, Wilson's speech of acceptance shortly afterwards was greeted by 'enthusiastic men and women who looked upon him as the Moses of progressivism – a great intellect applied to the confusion and chaos of politics.'[6]

In pitting Wilson against Theodore Roosevelt, the 1912 presidential campaign marked the beginning of a political rivalry that grew ever more intense and personal until Roosevelt's death in January 1919. In 1912, the charismatic TR was the largest figure on the American political scene. An unprecedentedly young ex-president, he projected a larger-than-life image of vigorous leadership. Generally referred to as 'Colonel Roosevelt' in recognition of his leadership of 'the Rough Riders' (a voluntary cavalry regiment) in the Spanish-American War, he kept the image of virile physicality alive through overseas expeditions of exploration and big-game hunting. And he continued to make the political weather. In a speech at Osawatomie, Kansas, where John Brown had led an antislavery raid in the run-up to the Civil War, he invoked the spirit of that 'heroic struggle' in calling for 'a new nationalism' of advanced progressivism.[7] Such radicalism was unacceptable to more conservative Republicans who obstructed Roosevelt's bid for their party's presidential nomination in 1912. Launching his own 'Bull Moose' Progressive party in response to this rebuff, he became the main threat to Wilson's election prospects as its presidential candidate.

Wilson was very conscious of TR's appeal and of his own comparative disadvantage in the personality contest. As he wrote in August to a friend,

> It depends upon what the people are thinking and purposing whose opinions do not get into the newspapers, – and I am by no means confident. He appeals to their imagination; I do not. He is a real, vivid person, whom they have seen

and shouted themselves hoarse over and voted for, millions strong; I am a vague, conjectural personality, more made up of opinions and academic prepossessions than of human traits and red corpuscles.[8]

Despite these differences of personality, Wilson and TR had much in common as college-educated men who stood both for high standards in public life and for progressive reform that sought to rein in the power of big business by expanding the authority of the federal government. As rival candidates, however, they found it expedient to present their differences, particularly on how 'the trusts' should be regulated, as fundamental and momentous. To this end, Roosevelt dismissed Wilson's approach as 'a bit of outworn academic doctrine that was kept in the schoolroom and the professorial study for a generation after it had been abandoned by all who had experience of actual life.' Nevertheless, most observers would have agreed with the journalist William Allen White's judgement that between them 'was that fantastic imaginary gulf that has always existed between tweedle-dum and tweedle-dee.'[9] When pressed on the similarity between Wilson's principles and his in a post-election interview with a New York editor, Roosevelt reportedly conceded, 'I suppose I am a little hard on Wilson. What I object to about him is his mildness of method. I suppose, as a matter of fact, (tapping himself on the chest), Wilson is merely a less virile *me!*'[10]

This supposed lack of virility became a major theme in Roosevelt's fierce criticism of the way Wilson conducted the nation's foreign relations after entering the White House in March 1913. The attacks initially focused on the disorderly situation in Mexico, where revolution had given rise to complex internal conflicts. TR and other Republicans called for forceful intervention to protect American citizens from assaults and US companies from expropriation. Criticism of his alleged failure to uphold American rights and interests in Mexico persisted throughout Wilson's presidency, but the European war took centre stage from the moment of its outbreak in August 1914. Again, Republicans accused Wilson of weakness in defending America's interests – in this case, of not firmly upholding the country's neutral rights against the actions of the belligerents. The most fraught issue was the German use of submarines against merchant vessels. When the Cunard liner, RMS *Lusitania*, was torpedoed by a German U-boat in May 1915 and sank with the loss of 1200 lives, including 128 Americans, Roosevelt declared that it was 'inconceivable that we can refrain from taking action in this matter, for we owe it not only to humanity but to our own national self-respect.' Wilson responded to the *Lusitania* sinking by sending a Note to Berlin demanding that the Germans abandon the use of submarines against merchant ships and pressed this demand in further Notes, especially after the sinking of another British liner, the *Arabic*, in August. Roosevelt described this method of proceeding as 'worthy of a Byzantine logothete' and he mocked one of the protests as 'No. 11,765, series B.' 'When the urgent need of the nation was for action', Wilson had 'met the need purely by elocution.' Attributing the president's failure to take more forceful action to physical cowardice, TR privately fulminated, 'Wilson has done more to emasculate American manhood and weaken its fiber than anyone else I can think of.' In the 1916 election campaign, he publicly evoked 'the shadows of men, women and children who have risen from the ooze of the ocean bottom and from graves in foreign lands; the shadows of the helpless whom Mr. Wilson did not dare protect lest he might have to face danger.'[11]

As Roosevelt recognized, however, the country was not in a 'heroic mood' and the great majority of Americans wanted to avoid war. After Wilson's diplomatic pressure elicited from Germany a pledge not to attack passenger liners and a tacit suspension of submarine warfare, the president was hailed for securing 'peace with honor.' 'Woodrow Wilson may well forgive in condescending pity the men who have ridiculed and stabbed him,' a Presbyterian journal wrote. 'His patience and self-control and calmness and reason and conscience have now put him far above their criticism and envy. He stands laurelled with victory.' This theme was developed in a way that highlighted the professorial image evoked by Senator Ollie M. James of Kentucky at the Democratic National Convention of 1916 that nominated Wilson for a second term.

> Four years ago they sneeringly called Woodrow Wilson the schoolteacher; then his classes were assembled within the narrow walls of Princeton College. They were the young men of America. Today he is the world teacher, his class is made up of kings, kaisers, czars, princes, and potentates. The confines of the schoolroom circle the world. His subject is the protection of American life and American rights under international law.... Without orphaning a single American child, without widowing a single American mother, without firing a single gun, without the shedding of a single drop of blood, he wrung from the most militant spirit that ever brooded above a battlefield an acknowledgement of American rights and an agreement to American demands.[12]

Wilson himself was very conscious that this extravagantly lauded triumph was a precarious one, dependent on the balance of arguments and forces in Berlin where there were powerful voices, particularly in the Navy, calling for a resumption and intensification of the submarine campaign. If this point of view prevailed, it would be impossible for him to uphold 'peace with honor.' This knowledge led Wilson to change his position on the need for greater military 'preparedness,' something for which Roosevelt had long been calling. The president's proposals for substantial increases in both the Army and the Navy met strong resistance in Congress, particularly within the Democratic Party where there were many supporters of the anti-interventionist position advocated by William Jennings Bryan, who had resigned as secretary of state in June 1915 in protest at Wilson's demands that Germany suspend submarine attacks on passenger ships. But adoption of this issue helped Wilson to counter Roosevelt's gibes that this professor lacked the robust Americanism needed to stand up for the nation's interests. At Tumulty's suggestion, the president personally headed a large 'preparedness parade' in the nation's capital on 4 July 1916, and one in New York City shortly afterwards. Carrying a large American flag but wearing casual civilian clothes and a boater hat, Wilson projected an image at once patriotic and un-militaristic. 'As soon as the moving pictures throughout the country began to feature the President leading the demonstration, these parades became less frequent and finally obsolete,' Tumulty recorded with satisfaction. 'By getting into the "front line" the President had cleverly outwitted his enemies.'[13]

Wilson's awareness that the German government might at any time force him to choose between war and a humiliating climb-down from the position he had taken on the submarine issue had another, even more consequential, effect on his policy. It gave greater urgency and force to his efforts to bring an end to the European war. It was to encourage the Allies, particularly the British, to accept an early, negotiated peace that in May 1916 he implicitly committed the United States to upholding the consequent settlement by pledging that it would participate in a postwar league of nations 'to prevent any war begun either contrary to treaty covenants or without warning and full submission of the causes to the opinion of the world – a virtual guarantee of territorial integrity and political independence.' To justify domestically this break with the hallowed tradition of non-involvement in European politics, he insisted that settlement should accord with basic American principles, notably that 'every people has a right to choose the sovereignty under which they shall live.'[14]

Making the establishment of a reformed international order the goal of his policy also provided a rationale for preparedness that could gain support from those progressives who found the assertion of America's national interests and neutral rights too narrow and selfish an objective. The journalist Ray Stannard Baker, who had gained a national reputation as a 'muckraker,' gave voice to this outlook in an article for *Collier's* magazine in 1916:

> The idea of duty, the duty of the President, the duty of Congress, the duty of the Democratic Party, the duty of the nation, loom large in everything that Mr. Wilson says or does. He talks indeed about rights also, as he has talked about the rights of the Mexicans to control their own affairs, but when he thinks of America he seems to think first of our duties, afterward of our rights. Mr. Wilson is Scotch Presbyterian in his origin and I fancy that this point of view, more or less unconscious, is deeply ingrained in his very nature.[15]

Baker was to become the president's press secretary during the Paris peace conference and later his admiring biographer. Himself of puritanical bent, he did much to implant this image of Wilson's character formation in the minds of those sympathetic to the twenty-eighth president, both at the time and in subsequent years.

Wilson's commitment to American participation in a future League of Nations and enunciation of principles that should shape the postwar settlement raised his profile internationally. His approach was very similar to that of the radical liberals in Britain who had founded the Union of Democratic Control (UDC) shortly after the outbreak of war. Not surprisingly, this section of British opinion warmly welcomed the president's May 1916 speech, which A.G. Gardiner of the London *Daily News* claimed had opened 'a new chapter in the history of civilization.' This was not, however, the preponderant response in the Allied countries where people were deeply offended by Wilson's detached and studiously neutral attitude to the conflict in which they were currently engaged so passionately. In European political circles, this resentment fed into an incipient image of the president as both self-righteous and naïve. 'If the Creator needed seven days to organize a couple of creatures of which the first born instinctively tore each other apart, Mr. Wilson, in one sovereign word, is going to create men such as have never been seen, whose first need will be love and universal harmony,' sardonically observed Georges Clemenceau, not yet in government.[16]

This divided European response to Wilson gained in intensity when the president made a more direct and public effort to bring the war to an end in the winter of 1916–17. In a Note to all the belligerent powers calling on them to specify the terms on which they would be willing to stop fighting, he observed that 'the objects' which both sides sought were 'virtually the same, as stated in general terms to their own peoples and to the world.' When neither side replied helpfully to this Note, Wilson sought to increase the pressure on the belligerent governments by an address to the Senate which was transmitted in code to US embassies in Europe so that they could ensure its full publication locally. In this speech, the president expressed the hope that he was 'speaking for the silent mass of mankind everywhere who have as yet had no place or opportunity to speak their real hearts out concerning the death and ruin they see to have come already upon the persons and the homes they hold most dear.' Declaring that 'no covenant of co-operative peace that does not include the peoples of the New World can suffice to keep the future safe against war,' he warned that 'there is only one sort of peace that the peoples of America could join in guaranteeing.' A stable settlement would have to embody the liberal principles he had set out earlier, including the establishment of a league of nations. Above all, it would have to be 'a peace without victory' because 'victory would mean a victor's peace imposed upon the vanquished ... and would leave a sting, a resentment, a bitter memory upon which terms of peace would rest, not permanently, but only as upon quicksand.'[17]

Reaction in the Allied countries to these attempts to bring about an early end to the war was for the most part very hostile, with strong exception being taken to the apparent implication that there was a moral equivalence between the two sets of belligerents. In Britain, Conservative leader Andrew Bonar Law gave perfect voice to this animus: 'what Mr. Wilson is longing for, we are fighting for.' To the more sympathetic commentators, Wilson was, in the words of the *Pall Mall Gazette*, 'as unlucky as he is highminded. His zeal for humanity has evoked a step that will create the bitterest resentment among all who are fighting, working, and dying for the very principles he has at heart.' Others were less charitable. Sir George Otto Trevelyan, father of a UDC leader, saw the president as 'the quintessence of a prig.' 'This professor, with his dogmatism and inspired airs,' the French diplomat Paul Cambon observed, 'is acting like a knave.' Prime Minister David Lloyd George, newly ensconced in 10 Downing Street, shared this opinion and, according to one of his biographers, 'found little high purpose in Wilson and much political calculation, ... [and] a dread of belligerency.'[18] This view of Wilson accorded with that of Roosevelt and his friend, Senator Henry Cabot Lodge of Massachusetts, both passionate supporters of the Allies' cause.

Few Americans, however, felt this degree of partisanship in the European war and the president's moves for peace won wide approval at home. His address to the Senate, in particular, was met by what one historian has called 'a cacophony of approving voices.' 'This,' the *New York Times* declared, 'is not merely a guarantee of peace, it is a moral transformation.' Progressives and Socialists were particularly enthusiastic. The address 'will reverberate throughout history,' the editor of the *New Republic* wrote. In Europe, too, it was on the left that Wilson found his greatest support. The French Socialist party registered 'with joy the admirable message of President Wilson,' while delegates to the British Labour party conference cheered for five minutes after the address had been read to them. Wilson had become, in Arthur Link's words, 'the hero, leader, and spokesman of the various liberal, labor, and socialistic groups throughout the western world who had themselves long since worked out the programme that the President now proposed.'[19]

Less than a week after Wilson had delivered his address to the Senate, Germany announced that it was embarking on a new submarine campaign, one that would for the first time target the merchant vessels of neutral nations as well as those of its enemies. Wilson remained reluctant to go to war but after the Germans started sinking American ships he agreed with the unanimous view of his cabinet that there was 'no alternative.' He made it clear that the chief reason for his hesitation was his knowledge that the country was divided, with the indignant demands for war from pro-Allied partisans on the East Coast balanced by continuing opposition to intervention among progressive legislators from the Middle West and South where sentiment remained more neutralist. It was to these latter regions that Wilson owed his recent re-election and when he came to make the case for war to Congress he sought to do this in a way that appealed to his own supporters.[20]

The president emphasized that the fundamental aim of his policy had not changed since his address to the Senate: 'our object now, as then, is to vindicate the principles of peace and justice in the life of the world.' The road to this goal now included the defeat of 'selfish and autocratic power' but the United States would be fighting 'for the ultimate peace of the world and for the liberation of its peoples, the German peoples included: for the rights of nations great and small and the privilege of men everywhere to choose their way of life and obedience.' In his stirring peroration, he held out a vision of the world to come: 'a universal dominion of right by such a concert of free peoples as shall bring peace and safety to all nations and make the world itself at last free.'[21]

In this way, Wilson succeeded in persuading most of the more progressive and pacifistic wing of American opinion to support the war effort. However, the shift from neutrality to belligerency on the side of the Allies led to a great change in the view he presented of the origins and significance of the European conflict – a change that brought him much closer to the position long held by Roosevelt and other Republicans. This re-positioning within the spectrum of domestic debate complicated and aggravated the political difficulties Wilson faced as he became the leader of a nation at war rather than the advocate of peace. These political difficulties, and the manner of his response to them, had effects on the president's image – reinforcing some established impressions but also highlighting aspects of his personality that had previously been largely unknown or overlooked.

Critics and opponents who had come to see Wilson as an unprincipled political opportunist found confirmation of this view in the abrupt change in the president's appraisal of the nature of the European conflict. In reply to a friendly journalist who had praised Wilson's war address, Theodore Roosevelt wrote:

> what is perfectly impossible, what represents really nauseous hypocrisy, is to say that we have gone to war to make the world safe for democracy in April when sixty days previously we had been announcing that we wished a "Peace without victory," and had no concern with the "causes or objects" of the war. I do not regard any speech as a great speech when it is obviously hypocritical and in bad faith; nor do I regard the making of such a speech of service to the world. I regard it as a damage to the cause of morality and decency.[22]

After the declaration of war, Wilson's principal objective was to mobilize the country for the conflict. Some of the ways in which he sought to do this brought his previous image as a liberal and man of peace into question. The administration's actions to suppress dissent, including the exclusion from the mail of radical publications that opposed the war, provoked protests from even devoted followers.[23] The president's rejection of calls for an early peace along lines very similar to those he had set out in his January speech was also troubling to liberals. In rebuffing such appeals from external sources as different as the Petrograd Soviet and Pope Benedict XV, Wilson argued that a 'stable and enduring peace' could not be achieved by negotiations in the current situation because 'we cannot take the words of the present rulers of Germany as a guarantee of anything that is to endure.' This change of stance together with the uncompromising bellicosity of the president's speeches in the summer and fall of 1917 led some to fear that the great power of the United States was being used to serve the imperialistic purposes of the Allies. This argument gained credibility when the Bolsheviks, following their seizure of power in November, published the secret treaties in which the states fighting the Central Empires had promised each other territorial gains. In propaganda directed at the workers in all nations, the Bolsheviks called for an immediate 'peace without annexations or indemnities, on the basis of the self-determination of peoples.'[24]

'What I am opposed to is not the feeling of the pacifists, but their stupidity,' Wilson declared, as he responded to 'the dreamers in Russia.' 'My heart is with them, but my mind has a contempt for them. I want peace, but I know how to get it, and they do not.'[25] To unsympathetic observers, such a remark was a manifestation of the arrogance and egotism that they saw becoming a more prominent facet of Wilson's image during the war years, and particularly during the peace-making and the fight over the League of Nations. Like other war presidents, Wilson was accused of stretching the powers of the office beyond its constitutional limits – and not only by Republicans in Congress. The charge that he was an autocrat gained strength not only from his obvious domination of the policymaking process but also from aspects of his personality that became more widely commented on in his second term than they had been in his first.

In 1918, however, Wilson not only largely revived his standing with American liberals as the enlightened advocate of a new world order but projected this image to Europe and beyond. His Fourteen Points address and subsequent speeches, delivered as the United States was for the first time mobilizing its immense economic resources and ample manpower to exercise its potential weight in international politics, made Wilson a world figure. His words were disseminated by not only the international news agencies but also the activities of the Committee on Public Information (CPI), a wartime agency run by the journalist George Creel. By various methods including wireless, the CPI circulated the speeches to countries across the globe, though its main efforts were centred on Europe where it had offices in several capitals. Hundreds of thousands of posters were produced and distributed with the text of the Fourteen Points and later addresses, both in the original and translated into numerous languages. Nationalists in every continent came to see the American president as a saviour or liberator. Among the disaffected subjects of the Austro-Hungarian empire, the historian Victor Mamatey writes, there grew

> a veritable Wilsonian myth which portrayed the President as a new Messiah who would cure the world of all its ills and tender succour even to the most humble. His personality and habits naturally contributed to the growth of this myth: aloof and reticent, he would break his Olympian silence only occasionally with speeches couched in a Miltonesque English ... To Europeans generally, his speeches, circulated in hasty and execrable newspaper translations, in enemy countries moreover censored, were impressive but largely incomprehensible – a fact which stimulated rather than weakened the growth of the Wilsonian myth. The exalted and inscrutable are natural ingredients of myth.

As historian Erez Manela has recently shown, nationalists in Egypt, India, China and Korea were similarly enthused. If Wilson had come to Asian capitals at the end of the war, the Indian intellectual V.S. Srinivasa Sastri wrote, 'it would have been as though one of the great teachers of humanity, Christ or Buddha, had come back to his home.'[26]

It was only in the Fourteen Points that Wilson addressed specific territorial issues and doing so brought out the difficulty of reconciling some of the general principles he had earlier proclaimed – most notably, the call for 'a peace without victory' and the principle 'that every people has a right to choose the sovereignty under which they shall live.' It was with regard to the Austro-Hungarian empire that this tension was most sharp and the promise of no more than 'the freest opportunity of autonomous development' to its 'peoples' in Point X was seen as betrayal by Czech and Yugoslav nationalists. Later, however, after efforts to induce Vienna to make a separate peace were recognized to have failed, the United States backed ever more strongly the claims to independence of the Czechoslovaks and

Yugoslavs, explicitly repudiating in October the terms of Point X. In other ways, too, Wilson's speeches acquired a more radical tone as the months passed. 'On the one hand stand the peoples of the world,' he declared in July, 'people of many races and in every part of the world.... Opposed to them, masters of many armies, stand an isolated, friendless group of governments who speak no common purpose but only selfish ambitions of their own by which none can profit but themselves.' 'The counsels of plain men have become on all hands more simple and straightforward and more unified than the counsels of sophisticated men of affairs,' he insisted in September. 'Statesmen must follow the clarified common thought or be broken.'[27]

A consistent theme in Wilson's speeches continued to be that the United States was fighting the German government, not the German people, and that there should be a moderate peace. 'We have no jealousy of German greatness,' he said in the Fourteen Points address, 'and there is nothing in this program that impairs it.' 'Punitive damages, the dismemberment of empires, the establishment of selfish and exclusive economic leagues, we deem ... no proper basis for a peace of any kind, least of all for an enduring peace,' he assured the Pope. As the end of the war came in sight with American troops now heavily engaged in the fighting, he insisted that the terms of peace should 'mete out' an 'impartial justice' that 'must involve no discrimination between those to whom we wish to be just and those to whom we do not wish to be just.'[28]

Given such statements, it is not surprising that when the rapid advance of the Allied armies led the German government to request an armistice, it was to Wilson that they turned, declaring their willingness to accept the programme set out in his Fourteen Points and subsequent pronouncements as the basis of the peace negotiations. By responding to this approach Wilson defied calls for the American army to march to Berlin and demand 'unconditional surrender'. 'Let us dictate peace by the hammering of guns and not chat about peace to the accompaniment of the clicking of typewriters,' declared Roosevelt, who claimed that an agreement based on the 'thoroughly mischievous' Fourteen Points would represent 'the conditional surrender of the United States.' In pre-Armistice negotiations with the Allies, Wilson's emissary, 'Colonel' Edward M. House, secured agreement that the Fourteen Points (with two reservations by Britain and France) should be the basis of the peace but accepted military terms for the armistice that rendered Germany impotent to resist any further demands. This led Max Weber to observe that,

> It is the peculiar destiny of the world that the first man to be its true ruler should be a professor. How much he is a professor we see in the great act of stupidity he has committed in the armistice terms. If he doesn't prevent Germany from entering into peace negotiations in a disarmed state, then his own rule will be at an end.[29]

Nevertheless, the Fourteen Points had been accepted as the basis of the peace, which confirmed a general impression that Wilson would be in a position to shape the settlement. 'When President Wilson left Washington he enjoyed a prestige and a moral influence throughout the world unequalled in history,' John

Maynard Keynes wrote a year later. 'In addition to this moral influence the realities of power were in his hands.... Europe was in complete dependence on the food supplies of the United States; and financially she was even more absolutely at their mercy.... Never had a philosopher held such weapons wherewith to bind the princes of this world.' This perception led millions of people to invest their hopes for the postwar period in the American president. On his arrival in Europe to take part in the peace conference, he was greeted by huge, cheering crowds wherever he went. Banners and newspaper headlines hailed 'Wilson, the Just', 'the Saviour of Humanity', 'the Moses from Across the Atlantic.' 'In that brief interval,' H.G. Wells recalled, 'all humanity leapt to accept and glorify Wilson.... He was transfigured in the eyes of men. He ceased to be a common statesman; he became a Messiah.'[30]

In the nature of things, such millennial expectations were bound to be disappointed. In the first place, some of the hopes conflicted with each other. In Italy, where Wilson had been so ecstatically greeted in January, his determined resistance to Italian claims to Fiume and parts of Dalmatia largely inhabited by Yugoslavs led to such anger that Americans were officially advised to keep their distance from the demonstrating crowds. The peace sought by the French who had thronged to acclaim Wilson as the man who had sent millions of American troops across the ocean to help liberate their country was quite different from that expected by the Germans who looked to him to deliver the 'impartial justice' he had promised. In the event, it was the latter who felt more deceived; the publication of the draft treaty in May 1919, an American observer in Berlin reported, led to denunciations of Wilson as 'the greatest hypocrite in all history.' A similar sense of betrayal was expressed by some of the liberals at home and abroad who had been the president's most fervent supporters. The *New Republic*, a weekly whose editors had been close to the administration, blasted the treaty in an issue emblazoned with the headline, 'THIS IS NOT PEACE.'[31]

Like others whose hopes had been dashed, the *New Republic* laid the blame squarely on Wilson, whose 'lack of courage and knowledge and administrative capacity has yielded a settlement which means a Europe of wars and revolution and agony.' In this, the editors were following the lead of William C. Bullitt, who had resigned as a junior member of the American delegation in a bitter public letter to the president. As 'one of the millions who trusted confidently and implicitly in your leadership and believed that you would take nothing less than "a permanent peace" based upon "unselfish and unbiased justice", Bullitt wrote, 'I am sorry that you did not fight our fight to the finish.' It was, however, not an American, but an English liberal who expressed this point of view in a way that had the most widespread and lasting effect on Wilson's image. In *The Economic Consequences of the Peace*, published in December 1919, the 36-year-old John Maynard Keynes portrayed the president as so 'incompetent in the agilities of the council chamber' as to be 'a blind and deaf Don Quixote' who could be 'bamboozled' by 'men much sharper than himself.' Notwithstanding his university background, 'his temperament was not primarily that of the student or the scholar' but 'essentially theological not intellectual, with all the strength and the weakness of that manner of thought, feeling, and expression.' Keynes concluded that 'the President was like a nonconformist minister, perhaps a Presbyterian.'[32] This theme was carried to an extreme in a book that Bullitt later co-wrote with Sigmund Freud, which stressed Wilson's alleged ignorance of European languages, culture and geography, and his immersion in 'the ideas and ideals of the middle-class Bible-reading British.' On the basis of biographical data supplied by Bullitt, Freud diagnosed Wilson as suffering from an unresolved Oedipus complex that caused him to identify his Presbyterian minister father with God and himself with Jesus Christ.[33] Yet while critics linked what they perceived as the president's failings to his Presbyterian background, some of his admirers remained impressed by the qualities they associated with it. As Wilson's press secretary in Paris, Ray Stannard Baker saw 'a character dominated by stern inner principles.... what was imputed to him as stubbornness seemed to me to be courage of conviction.'[34]

Whereas liberal critics blamed Wilson for failing to realize his peace programme, the target of Freud's attack was the programme itself – which 'gave the impression of the method of Christian Science applied to politics.' The view that Wilson's vision of a new world order ignored human nature was a common one in European conservative circles, voiced during the Paris negotiations by Clemenceau and the Italian foreign minister, Sidney Sonnino. In a more moderate way, it also figured in the critique of the League of Nations Covenant by Republican leaders such as Lodge and Elihu Root. The attack focused particularly on the undertaking by Member states in Article 10 'to respect and preserve as against external aggression the territorial integrity and existing political independence' of all other Member states. The most significant of the 'reservations' that Lodge led the Republican majority in the Senate to attach to the treaty was a repudiation of any obligation under Article 10 'unless in any particular case' Congress chose to act.[35]

Wilson described this as a nullification of a commitment that was 'the very backbone of the whole covenant' and refused to accept any of Lodge's reservations. It was in an attempt to put public pressure on the Senate to approve the treaty without such reservations that the president embarked on a cross-country speaking tour in September 1919 – 'going to talk to the boss,' as a cartoon showing Wilson heading for the door from a meeting with Congress was captioned. In twenty-two days, Wilson travelled eight thousand miles and delivered thirty-two major addresses, all but one of them without benefit of amplification. This tremendous physical effort by a man already in poor health had to be cut short when he collapsed shortly after speaking in Pueblo, Colorado; a few days after his return to Washington, he suffered an ischemic stroke that left him partly paralysed. However, he never contemplated resignation and the extent of his disability was concealed by his White House circle. As part of this effort, a photograph was commissioned showing the president at his desk signing a document. But the document was held in place by his wife, and the picture was taken from the right side, concealing the fact that his face sagged on the left and his left arm dangled.[36]

His intransigence probably strengthened by the effects of the stroke, Wilson continued to reject the Lodge reservations, and in the final vote on the treaty in March 1920, it was a combination of 'irreconcilable' isolationists and Democratic Senators still loyal to the president who prevented the treaty with the reservations

Figure 2.1 Hiding Woodrow Wilson's disability: The image of the president at work, 1920. Non-restricted use, Public Domain. Source: Wikipedia Commons.

attached from achieving the necessary two-thirds majority. At the time and since, Wilson's behaviour has seemed perverse to those who have seen the value of America's participation in the League as outweighing any limitations on its commitment.[37] It seemed to many to be further evidence of the president's arrogance – with some even suggesting it was motivated by a vain pride in his authorship of the Covenant. Certainly, Wilson's obsession with the League, together with his seclusion in the White House, contributed to his growing unpopularity as postwar America experienced inflation, strikes, race riots and a Red Scare. In the 1920 election, the Republicans triumphed in one of the greatest landslides in American history after a campaign that targeted 'Mr. Wilson' personally for his alleged despotism and 'disregard of the lives of American boys or of American interests.'[38]

Yet by no means everyone turned against Wilson. The first day of the Democratic Convention witnessed a great demonstration in his favour and his name would have been put in nomination for a third term (as he himself wished) had those acquainted with his real physical condition not killed the idea. 'The grim old schoolmaster there in Washington still has power in the land,' Ray Stannard Baker wrote with satisfaction.'[39] Franklin D. Roosevelt played a prominent part in the Wilson demonstration at the Convention and it helped him secure the vice-presidential nomination. Roosevelt later spearheaded the fund-raising effort that led to the establishment in 1922 of the Woodrow Wilson Foundation, which established an annual prize and made grants to promote the cause of internationalism. Wilson was a joint recipient of the 1920 Nobel Peace Prize, and in Europe, particularly in the new national states created from the Austro-Hungarian empire, the president was widely memorialized. Someone arriving in interwar Prague, Mamatey writes, 'would detrain at the Wilson Station. Coming out of the station, he would face the Wilson Square and the Wilson Park, with a statue of President Woodrow Wilson in its center.' In the United States, Wilson remained a hero to members of the League of Nations Association and others who attempted to keep the issue of American membership alive.[40]

The international crises of the 1930s and the outbreak of the Second World War revived and intensified both negative and positive appraisals of Wilson. To 'Realist' critics, the failure of the League of Nations and the crumbling of the Versailles order reflected the illusions underlying Wilson's approach to international politics. Like Weber earlier, the British scholar E.H. Carr saw the fault as lying with a class to which he himself belonged: Wilson was 'the most perfect modern example of the intellectual in politics.' 'Utopianism, with its insistence on general principles may be said to represent the characteristic intellectual approach to politics,' with 'some supposedly general principle, such as "national self-determination," "free trade" or "collective security"' being 'taken as an absolute standard.' Carr contrasted this with the 'fundamentally empirical' character of 'the bureaucratic approach to politics,' which eschewed the formulation of principles and sought to handle each particular problem 'on its merits.' Wilson and his followers had been blind both to the fact that the interests of different nations inevitably conflicted and to the determining role of power in international politics, while over-estimating the potency and wisdom of public opinion: 'The whole conception of the League of Nations was from the first closely bound up with this twin belief that public opinion was bound to prevail and that public opinion was the voice of reason.' The core features of Carr's critique, originally published in 1939, were developed in the next twenty years by American writers, notably Walter Lippmann, Hans J. Morgenthau and George F. Kennan, who all saw Wilson as the arch exponent of a naïve, national self-righteousness that had been fostered by a century of secure isolation from world politics.[41]

To loyal Wilsonians, on the other hand, the coming of the Second World War was the result of America's failure to join the League of Nations and a confirmation of their hero's vision. In a speech at Wilson's tomb in the basement of Washington Cathedral on Armistice Day 1941, Under-Secretary of State Sumner Welles asked, 'who saw straight and who thought straight twenty years ago?' It was 'that great seer, statesman, patriot, and lover of his fellow men – Woodrow Wilson.' The rehabilitation of Wilson gathered impetus after the Pearl Harbor attack brought the United States itself into the war. 'Had we but followed the brilliant statesmanship of Woodrow Wilson, who in my judgment is one of the great world figures of the ages,' Senator James C. Eastland declared in 1943, 'we would not be in this war, and this world would live in peace.' The Wilson revival gathered pace in 1944 as it became central to the campaign against 'isolationism' in the build-up to the Dumbarton Oaks conference that laid the basis for the postwar United Nations. A number of books, of varying scholarly quality, were published on Wilson's role in the peacemaking and his fight with Lodge over the League of Nations; a pictorial biography was published in *Look* magazine with the subtitle 'the Unforgettable Figure Who Has Returned to Haunt Us.'[42]

The highpoint of the Wilson revival, and by far its most remarkable product, was the major motion picture produced by Twentieth-Century Fox that opened at the Roxy Theatre in New York in August 1944. The film *Wilson* was very much the project of the studio head, Darryl F. Zanuck, a passionate internationalist who as a young man had served in France during the First World War. Inspired by the desire to develop popular support for the United Nations, Zanuck did not want the movie to be 'for highbrows only.' The result was a Technicolor production complete with eighty-seven songs of the period, many sung by groups of Princeton undergraduates. Running for more than two and a half hours, it cost more to make than any previous motion picture, topping even *Gone with the Wind* in this respect. (If it was a flop, Zanuck told a reporter, 'I'll never make another film without Betty Grable.') The sets that were built included reproductions of the House of Representatives Chamber, the Hall of Mirrors at Versailles and various rooms in the White House. Most spectacular was the re-creation of the 1912 Democratic Convention at which Wilson had been nominated. Staged in the Los Angeles Shrine Auditorium, with over 1500 conventioneers in period seersuckers shouting and marching with banners and placards in support of the various candidates as bands played, this took six days to film.

Wilson was played by little-known Scots-Canadian actor Alexander Knox, who won praise (and an Academy Award nomination for best actor) for a sympathetic and accurate characterization that drew on his own Presbyterian upbringing. Although Knox delivered passages from some of Wilson's speeches and newsreel footage of the peace conference featured in the film, several scenes were fictional and clearly designed to show Wilson as a regular guy, knowledgeably supporting the Princeton football team and singing with his family round the piano. In the most extreme piece of invention, he and Mrs. Wilson were shown serving food in a canteen to doughboys about to set off for France. The film attracted large audiences in New York and eastern cities, where it was effective propaganda for the United Nations, but did poorly in middle America, and by the end of its national run had registered a net loss of 2 million dollars. Nor, to Zanuck's lasting resentment, did it win the Oscar for best picture of the year.[43]

In the post-1945 period, Wilson continued to be seen above all as an idealist. A major study of American responses to the First World War, Robert E. Osgood's *Ideals and Self-Interest in America's Foreign Relations* was structured around the contrast between Wilson's approach to international politics and that of nationalists and realists. Osgood portrayed Wilson's idealism as a naïve position which experience had taught Americans to transcend, but other scholars were more sympathetic to it. Arthur S. Link, who devoted a whole lifetime of scholarship to the study of the twenty-eighth president, argued that what he saw as Wilson's consistent stand for a postwar settlement that would command the durable support of all the major powers represented 'a higher realism' than that of 'the European leaders who thought that ... they could impose their nation's will upon other great peoples'. Link described the president himself as '*primarily a Christian idealist* ... a man who almost always tended to judge policies on whether they were right by Christian standards, not whether they brought immediate material or strategic advantage.' The conviction that 'Wilson in the twentieth century represents idealism in action' led an eminent British judge to research and write a major study of the president's policymaking during the period of neutrality in which he concluded that Wilson was 'under the control of an ideal' that 'sought to introduce into international affairs the Christian ideal of peace upon earth for men of goodwill to be brought about through the Christian ethic of service to others.'[44]

In addition to being a distinguished jurist, Patrick Devlin had a strong religious commitment himself. His view of Wilson can be seen as a notable example of the extent to which Wilson's image was projected upon him by the desires and needs of others. The extravagant hopes invested in him in 1918 were the product not only of the euphoria usual after victorious wars but also of a more general and recurrent yearning for a philosopher-king whose wise and righteous leadership would produce good government and justice for all. Likewise, the intense hostility directed at Wilson reflected an often-felt aversion to politicians who are perceived to be claiming an unjustified moral superiority and to be peddling illusions in order to enhance their own popularity and power. In this clash of archetypes, the historical figure whose utterances and actions reflected a pragmatic adjustment to changing circumstances to a much greater degree than either his admirers or his detractors recognized was rather lost to view.

Notes

1   Cooper Jr., John Milton, *Woodrow Wilson: A Biography* (New York: Knopf, 2009), pp. 120–6. Cooper's is now by far the best biography of Wilson.

2   Tumulty, Joseph P., *Woodrow Wilson as I Know Him* (London: William Heinemann, 1922), pp. 31, 75; Lawrence, David, *The True Story of Woodrow Wilson* (London: Hurst and Blackett, 1924), p. 39.

3   Tumulty, *Woodrow Wilson*, pp. 35–6.

4   Ibid., p. 71.

5   Link, Arthur S., *Wilson: The Road to the White House* (Princeton, NJ: Princeton University Press, 1947), pp. 382, 447.

6   Lawrence, *The True Story*, p. 184.

7   Cooper, John Milton, *The Warrior and the Priest: Woodrow Wilson and Theodore Roosevelt* (Cambridge, MA: Harvard, 1983), pp. 144–7.

8   Wilson to M.A. Hulbert, 25 August 1912, in Link, Arthur S. et al., eds., *The Papers of Woodrow Wilson* [henceforth *PWW*] (Princeton, NJ: Princeton University Press, 1966–94), Vol. 25, pp. 55–6.

9   Cooper, *The Warrior and the Priest*, pp. 187–209.

10 Lawrence, *The True Story*, pp. 83–4.

11 Roosevelt, Theodore, *Fear God and Take Your Own* Part (New York: George H. Doran, 1916), p. 32; Harbaugh, William H., *The Life and Times of Theodore Roosevelt* (New York: Oxford University Press, 1975), pp. 447–50; Osgood, Robert Endicott, *Ideals and Self-Interest in America's Foreign Relations: The Great Transformation of the Twentieth Century* (Chicago: University of Chicago Press, 1953), pp. 140, 144, 150–1.

12 Harbaugh, *Theodore Roosevelt*, p. 456; *The Presbyterian Banner*, 9 September 1915, quoted in Link, Arthur S., *Wilson: The Struggle for Neutrality 1914–1915* (Princeton, NJ: Princeton University Press, 1960), p. 586; Tumulty, *Woodrow Wilson*, p. 185.

13 Tumulty, *Woodrow Wilson*, p. 247.

14 'Address in Washington to the League to Enforce Peace,' 27 May 1916, *PWW*, 37, pp. 113–16.

15 'Wilson,' *Collier's*, 7 October 1916, p. 6.

16 Knock, Thomas J., *To End All Wars: Woodrow Wilson and the Quest for a New World Order* (Princeton, NJ: Princeton University Press, 1992), pp. 36–8, 78–80; Martin, Laurence W., *Peace without Victory: Woodrow Wilson and the British Liberals* (New Haven, CT: Yale University Press, 1958), pp. 68–9; Link, Arthur S., *Wilson: Campaigns for Progressivism and Peace 1916–1917* (Princeton, NJ: Princeton University Press, 1965), pp. 27–8.

17 Link, *Wilson: Campaigns for Progressivism and Peace*, pp. 217–19, 253–5, 265–8; 'Address to the Senate,' 22 January 1917, *PWW*, 40, pp. 533–9.

18 Link, *Wilson: Campaigns for Progressivism and Peace*, pp. 230–1, 271–4; Fry, Michael G., *And Fortune Fled: David Lloyd George, the First Democratic Statesman, 1916–1922* (New York: Peter Lang, 2011), pp. 91–5.

19 Link, *Wilson: Campaigns for Progressivism and Peace*, pp. 269–72; Knock, *To End All Wars*, pp. 113–15; Link, Arthur S., *The Higher Realism of Woodrow Wilson* (Nashville, TN: Vanderbilt University Press, 1971), p. 106.

20 Link, *Wilson: Campaigns for Progressivism and Peace*, pp. 396–426; Seymour, Charles, ed., *The Intimate Papers of Colonel House* (London: Houghton Mifflin, 1925), II, p. 467.

21 'Address to Congress,' 2 April 1917, *PWW*, 41, pp. 519–27.

22 Theodore Roosevelt to William Allen White, 3 August 1917, quoted in Osgood, *Ideals and Self-Interest in America's Foreign Relations*, pp. 271–2.

23 Knock, *To End All Wars*, pp. 133–7.

24 Robert Lansing to W.H. Page, 27 August 1917, *PWW*, 44, pp. 57–9; 'To the Provisional Government of Russia,' 22 May 1917, *PWW*, 42, p. 366; Mayer, Arno J., *Political Origins of the New Diplomacy, 1917–1918* (New Haven, CT: Yale University Press, 1959), pp. 194–5.

25 'Address to the American Federation of Labor,' 12 November 1918, *PWW*, 45, p. 14.

26 Manela, Erez, *The Wilsonian Moment: Self-Determination and the International Origins of Anticolonial Nationalism* (New York: Oxford University Press, 2007), especially pp. 45–52, 55; Mamatey, Victor S., *The United States and East Central Europe 1914–1918: A Study in Wilsonian Diplomacy and Propaganda* (Princeton, NJ: Princeton University Press, 1957), pp. 107–8.

27 'Address to Congress,' 8 January 1918, *PWW*, 45, pp. 534–9; Mamatey, *The United States and East Central Europe*, pp. 209–15; 'Address at Mount Vernon,' 4 July 1918, *PWW*, 48, pp. 515–16; 'Address in the Metropolitan Opera House, New York,' 27 September 1918, *PWW*, 51, pp. 132–3.

28 'Address to Congress,' 8 January 1918, *PWW*, 45, p. 538; Robert Lansing to W.H. Page, 27 August 1917, *PWW*, 44, p. 59; 'Address in the Metropolitan Opera House, New York,' 27 September 1918, *PWW*, 51, p. 130.

29 Knock, *To End All Wars*, pp. 165–6, 169–75, 181–4; for Max Weber, see Nordholt, Jan Willem Schulte, *Woodrow Wilson: A Life for World Peace* (Berkeley and Los Angeles: University of California Press, 1991), pp. 277, 280.

30 Keynes, John Maynard, *The Economic Consequences of the Peace* (New York: Harcourt, Brace and Howe, 1920), p. 3; Knock, *To End All Wars*, pp. 194–5; Wells, H.G., *The Shape of Things to Come: The Ultimate Revolution* (London: Hutchinson, 1933), p. 96.

31 Ambassador T.N. Page to American Mission in Paris, 24 April 1919, *PWW*, 58, pp. 91–3; 'Address in the Metropolitan Opera House, New York,' 27 September 1918, *PWW*, 51, p. 130; Schwabe, Klaus, *Woodrow Wilson, Revolutionary Germany, and Peacemaking, 1918–1919: Missionary Diplomacy and the Realities of Power* (Chapel Hill, NC: University of North Carolina Press, 1985), pp. 333–4; Cooper Jr., John Milton, *Breaking the Heart of the World: Woodrow Wilson and the Fight for the League of Nations* (Cambridge: Cambridge University Press, 2001), pp. 97–8.

32 *New Republic*, 7 June 1919, quoted in Cooper, *Breaking the Heart of the World*, p. 97; William C. Bullitt to the President, 17 May 1919, *PWW*, 59, pp. 222–3; Keynes, *Economic Consequences*, pp. 41–4.

33 Freud, Sigmund, and William C. Bullitt, *Thomas Woodrow Wilson: A Psychological Study* (Boston: Houghton Mifflin, 1967). The limited and dubious factual basis of this book is stressed in Link, *The Higher Realism of Woodrow Wilson*, pp. 143–53.

34 Baker, Ray Stannard, *American Chronicle* (New York: Charles Scribner's Sons, 1945), p. 459.

35 Freud and Bullitt, *Thomas Woodrow Wilson*, pp. xii–xiii; Cooper, *Breaking the Heart of the World*, pp. 75, 78–9, 166.

36 Cooper, *Breaking the Heart of the World*, pp. 142, 262; cartoon from *Chicago Daily News* in Knock, *To End All Wars*, p. 174ff; photograph in Nordholt, *Woodrow Wilson*, p. 240ff. On the nature and effects of Wilson's stroke, see Cooper, *Woodrow Wilson*, pp. 532–40, 544–9.

37 To Thomas A. Bailey, it was 'a supreme act of infanticide. With his own sickly hands Wilson slew his own brain child – or the one to which he had contributed so much.' Bailey, Thomas A., *Woodrow Wilson and the Great Betrayal* (Chicago: Quadrangle Books, 1963), p. 277.

38 'Republican platform,' *PWW*, 65, p. 415n.

39 Baker to Brand Whitlock, 11 August 1920, quoted in Baker, *American Chronicle*, p. 479.

40 Cooper, *Woodrow Wilson*, pp. 565–9; Mamatey, *The United States and East Central Europe*, p. vii; Divine, Robert A., *Second Chance: The Triumph of Internationalism in America during World War II* (New York: Atheneum, 1967), pp. 10–19.

41 Carr, E.H., *The Twenty Years' Crisis, 1919–1939: An Introduction to the Study of International Relations* (New York: Harper and Row, 1964), pp. 13–19, 32–6; Lippmann, Walter, *U.S. Foreign Policy: Shield of the Republic* (Boston: Little, Brown and Company, 1943), and *U.S. War Aims* (Boston: Little, Brown and Company, 1944); Morgenthau Jr., Hans, *In Defense of the National Interest* (New York: Knopf, 1951); Kennan, George F., *American Diplomacy 1900–1950* (Chicago: University of Chicago Press, 1951).
42 Divine, *Second Chance*, pp. 45, 152, 168–9.
43 Ibid., pp. 169–71; Knock, Thomas J., "'History with Lightning': The Forgotten Film *Wilson*," *American Quarterly*, 28:5 (Winter 1976): 523–43. *Wilson* cost $5,200,000 to produce; *Gone with the Wind* $4,250,000.
44 Osgood, *Ideals and Self-Interest in America's Foreign Relations*; Link, *The Higher Realism of Woodrow Wilson*, pp. 136, 129; Devlin, Patrick, *Too Proud to Fight: Woodrow Wilson's Neutrality* (London: Oxford University Press, 1974), pp. 464, 678.

Chapter 3

THE ROOSEVELT IMAGE ON TRIAL: FDR, THE RADIO AND THE SUPREME COURT BATTLE OF 1937

Tony McCulloch

Introduction

On 10 April 1937, the Gridiron Club, the exclusive association of Washington DC press bureau chiefs, held its annual spring dinner at the Willard Hotel. There could be only one issue to provide the central theme for the evening's topical entertainment – the controversy surrounding President Franklin D. Roosevelt's proposal to reorganize the Supreme Court by adding a new justice for every sitting judge over the age of seventy. The so-called 'court-packing' plan would have increased the membership of this august body from its current complement of nine to fifteen. Attending the prestigious Gridiron dinner as guests were FDR, his son James, Vice President John Nance Garner, other Cabinet officials, members of Congress and prominent leaders of business and labour. Three Supreme Court judges were also present – Associate Justices James Clark McReynolds and Harlan Stone and Chief Justice Charles Evans Hughes, who was seventy-five the next day and received a rendition of 'Happy Birthday to You' from Gridiron members.

FDR attended the Gridiron dinners throughout his presidency without ever really enjoying them. On this occasion, he made an uncontroversial speech that contained only one indirect reference to the age of retirement and a mild joke at the expense of his vice president – a critic of the Court proposal.[1] In contrast, the issue dominated the various satirical sketches performed by Gridiron members that evening. One skit, located in 'old Castile,' portrayed FDR as 'Don Quixote' interacting with his henchman, 'Sancho Panza Garner'. 'Seest thou not yon castle of finance?' Don Quixote remarks to his sidekick. 'There lies some poor forgotten wight under dire oppression to whose relief I am brought hither.' 'Them's windmills, Boss,' answers Panza. 'They grind the corn. They're useful.'

In another skit, located in what was described as the 'modest suburban home of a prince of privilege,' a group of 'economic royalists' gathered by a fireside to hear FDR on the radio. A female listener was immediately won over. 'From now on I'm a New Dealer,' she declared. 'You couldn't understand a word he said,' protested one of the others. 'Of course not,' she replied. 'But what difference does it make?

Oh, that lovely voice!' This exchange was accompanied by a song that extolled the virtues of the president's radio performances.

> We hear a voice which softly rings
> The Voice on the Radio.
> It promises so many things
> The Voice on the Radio.
> In dreams we drift thru a twilight haze
> Under the spell of a magic phrase
> And visions fair of Happy Days
> The Voice on the Radio.

The final act of the evening saw the fifteen members of the new Supreme Court walk on to the stage to the 'March of the Toys,' played by the Marine Band Orchestra. 'This court is far too crowded,' said one justice. 'What do you expect in a packed court – a private room and bath?' replied another. When the chief justice asked for nominees to join the Supreme Court, anyone contributing more than $1,000 to the 1936 Democratic campaign could put his own name forward, while smaller donors had to settle for the Circuit Courts of Appeal. A messenger from the president then arrived with the instruction to hurry up declaring the new laws constitutional as it had already taken two hours to get them through Congress. When the chief justice pointed out that he did not know what was in them, he was told not to worry as nor did Congress. To which he replied, implicitly drawing a contrast between the obedience FDR expected of today's judiciary and the judicial giants who had established the independence of the third branch of national government in the early republic: 'Gentlemen of the court, get out your rubber stamps! And, above all, keep your minds off John Marshall!'[2]

The fact that the 1937 Gridiron dinner was so dominated by the Supreme Court battle underlined its significance at the start of FDR's second term and the integral role of the media in the controversy. The image its satirical sketches conveyed of Roosevelt was that of a patrician reformer concerned to stand up for the needs of the 'forgotten man' and his family against the opposition of the 'economic royalists,' namely the anti-New Deal business elite. They additionally portrayed him as a leader with almost mystical powers of persuasion, especially via the medium of radio. This was the common image of FDR in the wake of his landslide re-election as president in November 1936. It also accords with the scholarly perception of him as a consummate politician and leader. Historian William Leuchtenburg referred to Roosevelt as 'the Great Campaigner,' while political scientist Richard Neustadt considered him the greatest exponent of the 'power to persuade,' the essential instrument in a president's political armoury.[3]

As the Gridiron skits demonstrated, the Supreme Court controversy raised concerns about FDR's methods and motives in advocating such a far-reaching change in the judicial branch of government without seeking a constitutional amendment. It also called into question his ability to persuade the American public, notably through his mastery of radio broadcasting, that he was pursuing the right course for the nation rather than just for himself. Thus, in a very real sense, the Roosevelt image as a great reformer and a 'Great Campaigner' was on trial during the Supreme Court battle of 1937. In exploring this aspect of the controversy, this essay begins by considering the nature and origins of FDR's image as a New Dealer and political communicator in his first term. It then examines the Supreme Court battle and the media's role in it, before assessing whether the outcome dented perceptions of FDR as the embodiment of the great reformer and great communicator. Finally, by way of conclusion, the essay discusses the resilience of the 'Roosevelt image' that continues to undergird his twenty-first-century reputation as a great president.[4]

The Roosevelt Image

Presidential image is, of course, a multi-faceted concept and, like beauty, it lies largely in the eye of the beholder. It is a construct of, among other things, public opinion, the political elite, the academic community and the cultural media. There is also a distinction to be made between presidential image as perceived by domestic and foreign audiences. In addition, it is important to note that although FDR's electoral success was second to none, he was both a unifier and a divider during the Great Depression years. He was a hero to the common people who made up the bulk of his voter support; he was a traitor to his class insofar as many in the upper stratum of society were concerned; and he was the propagator of alien doctrines to his conservative political opponents, both Republican and Democrat, as the architect of big-government liberalism that supplanted the traditional ascendancy of individualism and states' rights in American political culture.

Until the New Deal transformed it, the Democratic party had supported Jeffersonian ideals of small government and predominantly represented the interests of the white South in national politics. By 1936, FDR's socio-economic programmes had mobilized the support of a new urban voter coalition outside Dixie that would give his party a lock on the presidency until the end of the 1960s. Its constituent elements included Northern city dwellers, ethnics, labour union members, African Americans, women and the unemployed, all of whom benefitted from his expansion of federal authority and responsibility. By contrast, more conservative Democrats, mainly but not exclusively based in the South, regarded the New Deal as a threat to constitutional principles of limited national government and the sovereignty of the states.[5]

Historians generally have a positive image of FDR and rank him alongside George Washington and Abraham Lincoln as one of America's three greatest presidents. For James MacGregor Burns, his first major biographer and arguably the best, 'Roosevelt was one of the master politicians of his time, certainly the most successful vote getter. His political artistry grew out of long experience with the stuff of American politics: men's ambitions, fears, and loyalties operating through conventions, primaries, elections, offices, constitutions, opinion agencies.'

Referencing Machiavelli's view that a leader needs to show boldness and cunning at different times, he entitled the first volume of his FDR biography, *The Lion and the Fox*. More recently, Robert Dallek has written: 'Roosevelt, like his cousin Theodore, was an instinctively brilliant politician,' who 'principally relied on his feel for the public mood to guide him in leading the country'. Nor is this view of FDR confined to US historians – a poll of British academics in 2011 rated him America's greatest president, ahead of both Washington and Lincoln.[6]

When examining the nature of FDR's political image, and especially the role of the media in its construction, it is important to note that it originated at a time when radio and newsreels were in their infancy. Key elements of FDR's image, regarding his personal qualities, his words and his actions, had already been formed before he became president, but it was only after he entered the White House that they reached full maturity with the help of new media. A significant early influence was the family name that benefitted from association with the dynamism and progressivism of Theodore Roosevelt, FDR's distant cousin. Woodrow Wilson was not oblivious to the advantages of including a Democratic Roosevelt in his administration when appointing the young FDR Assistant Secretary of the Navy – a post occupied by his illustrious relative in the Spanish-American War of 1898. Franklin Roosevelt served in this capacity during the Great War and, like 'Uncle Teddy,' he emerged from his wartime experience with his reputation enhanced, if not quite to the same extent.[7]

Like his eminent forbear, FDR climbed another rung on the political ladder with his nomination as vice president in 1920, an elevation reflecting Democratic hopes that his illustrious name would attract support from progressive Republican voters. The main medium for the formation of political image at this time remained the press but newsreels were gaining in importance – and FDR became a star in both during the 1920 campaign. Following his vice-presidential nomination, the *New York Times* gave Roosevelt a big spread on its front page and newsreel footage showed him as a tall, handsome figure, with a winning smile and an adoring family – Eleanor and their five children, plus doting mother Sara. Notwithstanding the landslide Republican victory, the 38-year-old FDR's energetic campaigning provided a beacon of hope for Democratic revival and marked him out as a future presidential contender.[8]

Roosevelt's protracted convalescence after contracting polio in 1921 was a great personal setback but did not kill his political ambition. With the assistance of Eleanor Roosevelt and Louis Howe, his faithful advisor, he was able to enhance his public image at a time when the Democratic party was badly divided over Prohibition, the Ku Klux Klan and immigration. His 'Happy Warrior' speech on behalf of Al Smith's bid for the Democratic presidential nomination at the 1924 national convention in New York City won widespread praise from pundits and politicos both for the quality of its delivery and the bravery he showed in making his way to the podium on crutches for his return to the political spotlight. Though failing to gain the nomination in 1924, Smith won it four years later with the help of another nominating address by FDR at the national convention in Houston. On this occasion, Roosevelt got to the podium not on crutches but supported by the strong right arm of his son James, who performed a similar role on many subsequent occasions when FDR was governor of New York and later president.[9]

Smith in turn persuaded a reluctant Roosevelt to run for governor of New York to boost his own chances of winning the Empire State in his presidential race against Herbert Hoover. Sensing that the Republican tide was too strong, FDR preferred to bide his time to run for president in 1936, but he was fearful of becoming a pariah in his own party if he ignored its presidential candidate's call to arms. Smith predictably went down to defeat, even losing his home state of New York, but Roosevelt won the gubernatorial race with a vigorous campaign that bucked the nationwide GOP trend. Like Theodore Roosevelt before him, FDR used the New York governorship to establish a national reputation, proving himself a creative and dynamic state leader in facing the growing challenge of the Great Depression in the early 1930s. This record was instrumental in propelling him to the Democratic nomination for president in July 1932. Signifying his determination not to be bound by orthodoxy if he won office, he broke precedent by flying to Chicago, where the Democratic National Convention was in session, to accept the nomination in person. Addressing the delegates, he said: 'Let it be symbolic that in so doing I broke traditions. Let it be from now on the task of our Party to break foolish traditions.' Pledging 'a new deal for the American people,' he mounted an energetic campaign that promised strong action against the economic crisis if elected president without being specific about what he intended to do. The unpopular incumbent Herbert Hoover proved no match for the dynamic challenger – lacking a record to defend, his efforts to portray his opponent as an untried second-rater got nowhere, as did his later attempts to depict him as a dangerous radical.[10]

The unobtrusive physical support from sons James and Elliot and others (notably military aide Edwin 'Pa' Watson) during Roosevelt's public appearances as presidential candidate and then president was an important aspect of what one historian has called 'FDR's splendid deception.' With the collusion of the media (reinforced by Press Secretary Stephen Early's strict rules about how FDR was to be photographed and filmed), he succeeded in hiding the true extent of his disability from the American public and, indeed, the world. In the 1932 campaign, too, Roosevelt and his aides misleadingly framed his condition as temporary and likely to continue improving, a narrative that paralleled the promise of economic recovery he offered the nation. In fact, FDR remained wheelchair-bound for the rest of his life and needed assistance to undertake almost any activity that would have involved use of his legs. Had the full scale of his paralysis been known to the public, he would likely never have made it to the White House. Even if he had won election as president, it is almost inconceivable that he could have developed and sustained the image of being a strong leader if he was widely perceived as incapable of unassisted mobility in the wake of his polio attack.[11]

The 'Great Campaigner'

From the moment he took office with the nation's financial system on the verge of meltdown, Roosevelt exuded an image of confidence in his ability to put things right. His Inaugural Address on 4 March 1933, in which he famously declared that

Americans had 'nothing to fear but fear itself,' set the tone for bold and optimistic leadership that contrasted markedly with Hoover's hesitation and pessimism in the face of the crisis. On 6 March, he declared a 'bank holiday' that temporarily closed financial institutions to prevent further runs; on 9 March, he secured and signed legislation from Congress giving his administration authority to take steps to restore confidence in the banks; and on 12 March, he gave his first Fireside Chat explaining his intentions and asking people to keep their money in the reopened banks, a request that elicited an overwhelmingly positive response.[12]

Roosevelt's Republican predecessors, Calvin Coolidge and Hoover, had used radio as a medium of communication, but neither came close to matching him as a speaker over the airwaves. The first Fireside Chat was broadcast on a Sunday evening, a day and time when he would be heard by the largest audience of the week. FDR's calm and measured explanation of the banking crisis and the steps he would take to resolve it did much to restore popular confidence in the nation's financial system. Of equal significance, the radio address established his presidential image as a friend or neighbour who joined ordinary people in their homes to talk about the problems of the times. [See image below of FDR's first Fireside Chat.] In the days that followed, the White House received a huge volume of mail in response to the talk, setting a pattern for subsequent Fireside Chats and establishing a unique dialogue between president and people. Thanks to FDR's 'conspicuous courage, cheerfulness, energy, and resource,' Sir Ronald Lindsay, the British Ambassador reported, 'the starved loyalties and repressed hero-worship of the country have found in him an outlet and a symbol.'[13]

However, some of the measures adopted by Congress during the early months of the New Deal met with more criticism, especially the National Industrial

Figure 3.1 FDR delivers his first Fireside Chat, 12 March 1933 (Photo by © CORBIS/ Corbis via Getty Images)

Recovery Act, the Agricultural Adjustment Act and the devaluation of the dollar. FDR delivered two more Fireside Chats – on 7 May and 24 July – to explain and defend his policies directly to the American people, referring in the latter to 'the hundred days which had been devoted to the starting of the wheels of the New Deal.' The 'Bombshell message' that Roosevelt sent to the World Economic Conference in London on 3 July rounded off this intense period of activism. Rebuking the delegates for their continued adherence to the 'old fetishes of so-called international bankers,' FDR told them not to focus on currency stabilization but to discuss trade policy and other economic issues. Now increasingly concerned at the direction of the New Deal, Sir Ronald Lindsay commented of the president whom he had so greatly praised just a short time ago: 'Mr Roosevelt is, in these complex matters, an almost complete amateur and an opportunist, in a country where both types tend to predominate.'[14]

While Roosevelt's image abroad was now dented, at home public opinion and the press remained largely favourable to him. The 'Bombshell message' was regarded in the United States as a financial declaration of independence from Europe. Frank Knox, a leading Republican and the owner of the influential *Chicago Daily News*, who had served under TR in the 'Rough Riders' during the Spanish-American War, welcomed what he called its dose of 'Rooseveltian realism, which does not hesitate to call a spade a spade.' Henry Stimson, another Republican admirer of Theodore Roosevelt, arriving in Britain on 12 July on vacation, also approved of Roosevelt's message although not the language that had been employed. He felt that FDR's character was impulsive and similar in this respect to that of Theodore Roosevelt – whose anti-trust policies he had supported as a US attorney for New York from 1906 to 1910.[15]

The 'Hundred Days' and the 'Bombshell message' consolidated FDR's initial image as a strong leader in the TR mould who was putting the United States first. In fact, he had gone beyond TR in his advocacy on behalf of 'the forgotten man,' a stance that Al Smith condemned as a call to 'class warfare.' Smith subsequently joined the Liberty League, an organization of conservative businessmen and politicians formed to defend 'American values' against the perceived radicalism of the New Deal. In response to their accusations that he was acting like a dictator, Roosevelt insisted that he was defending American democracy by safeguarding ordinary people from the economic ravages of the Great Depression. The increased congressional majorities won by the Democrats in the 1934 midterm elections suggested that FDR was winning the argument against his conservative critics, but he now faced grassroots anger that the New Deal had not gone far enough to help the common people. Senator Huey Long of Louisiana; Father Charles Coughlin, the so-called 'radio priest'; and Francis Townsend, the California physician who advocated old-age pensions became the champions of this populist protest. Long posed the greatest danger to FDR's re-election because he could draw many votes away from the president by running as a third-party candidate, but his assassination in September 1935 eliminated that threat. Even so, Roosevelt was aware that Coughlin and Townsend could still mobilize popular opposition if the New Deal failed to deliver reforms that benefitted the mass of people.[16]

FDR's relationship with the media was obviously an important ingredient in his electoral success. He felt that most newspaper owners, exemplified by *Chicago Tribune* publisher Robert 'Colonel' McCormick, were largely pro-business GOP supporters. By contrast, with the help of a very efficient press office headed by Steve Early, Roosevelt developed a good relationship with most journalists. Reporters valued FDR's bi-weekly press conferences as a constant source of news, appreciated not having to submit written questions in advance as required by his Republican predecessors and enjoyed interacting with a president so willing to give them copy. By and large newspaper correspondents wrote favourable articles about FDR throughout his first term, but editorial opinion grew more critical as the New Deal became more interventionist on socio-economic issues in 1935. The Revenue Act established a 'wealth tax,' the Social Security Act introduced federal old age pensions and unemployment insurance, and the National Labor Relations Act greatly strengthened trade union rights. Breaking with Roosevelt, whom he had initially supported, media mogul William Randolph Hearst made his newspaper chain a powerful voice of opposition to the New Deal.[17]

Faced with the hostility of newspaper owners, FDR valued the radio and newsreels as ways of communicating his message to the public. With some 60 per cent of households owning a radio in 1932, the market continued to grow in defiance of economic conditions – there were estimated sales of 8 million new sets in 1936 and 9 million in 1937. In 1934, the licensing of radio stations became the responsibility of the newly established Federal Communications Commission. This independent regulatory agency consisted of five commissioners, nominated by the president and confirmed by Senate to serve for five years, and a chair designated by the president. Although no more than three commissioners could be chosen from the same political party, authority to appoint them became an important presidential power, one that FDR was not shy of using. Through Steve Early, the Roosevelt White House paid close attention to radio station audience sizes and their reporting of the president when broadcasters sought licence renewal.[18]

Newsreels became a significant medium of political communication that featured in virtually every movie-house programme as the silent-film era gave way to the 'talkies.' Their popularity led to the opening of all-newsreel theatres, beginning with the Embassy Theater in New York in November 1929. Seeing a market for pictorial depiction of current affairs, a handful of newsreel chains opened houses in other cities as the 1930s progressed. According to W. French Githens, managing editor of Pathé News and founder of Newsreel Theaters Inc, 'We soon discovered that in Franklin Delano Roosevelt we had the greatest single attraction. Announcement of his Fireside Chats, which were always filmed, brought hundreds of patrons to the theater. Anti-New Dealers came to hiss. The vigorous years of the New Deal under FDR and the rise of Mussolini, Hitler, Stalin, and Chiang Kai-shek aroused great interest in newsreels.'[19]

The 'vigorous years of the New Deal' saw an unprecedented amount of legislation that empowered federal involvement in new areas of economic regulation, social welfare provision and protection of labour rights. In Roosevelt's first term, the principal opposition to these innovations came not from the Republican Party or conservative Democrats but from the Supreme Court. Four of the nine justices on the Court – Pierce Butler, James Clark McReynolds, George Sutherland and Willis Van Devanter – became known to the press as the 'four horsemen' for their steadfast opposition to key features of the early New Deal as an unconstitutional expansion of federal authority. When joined by Associate Justice Owen Roberts and, on occasions, Chief Justice Charles Evans Hughes in the 1935 term, this conservative bloc invalidated some key Roosveltian measures, notably the National Industrial Recovery Act, the Agricultural Adjustment Act, the Railroad Act and the Coal Mining Act. FDR feared that subsequent New Deal reforms such as the Social Security Act and the National Labour Relations Act would be invalidated sooner or later by the conservatives on the Court unless they could be curbed during his second term.[20]

In the meantime, the 1936 presidential election turned into a referendum on Roosevelt's leadership and his reforms. The Republican platform began with the words: 'America is in peril.' Charging that 'the New Deal Administration has dishonoured American traditions,' it urged 'all Americans, irrespective of party, to join us in defense of American institutions.' FDR responded with a stirring speech accepting his party's presidential nomination at its national convention in Philadelphia. In the city where the Continental Congress had adopted the Declaration of Independence in 1776, the president reminded his audience that the Founding Fathers had ended political tyranny, but he went on to warn that the rise of modern industry had brought with it a new tyranny of 'economic royalists,' whose 'new dynasties' threatened democracy by creating huge inequalities of wealth. 'Here in America,' he declared, 'we are waging a great and successful war. It is not alone a war against want and destitution and economic demoralization. It is more than that; it is a war for the survival of democracy. We are fighting to save a great and precious form of government for ourselves and for the world.'[21]

The Supreme Court Battle of 1937

FDR believed that there was only one issue in the 1936 presidential election – himself. To the extent that it was a contest between two contrasting images of Roosevelt, the outcome was a clear victory for FDR as reformer and 'Great Campaigner' over FDR as threat to constitutional democracy. He won a huge personal victory, gaining forty-six out of forty-eight states (all except Maine and Vermont), 523 electoral votes against 8 for his Republican opponent, Governor Alf Landon of Kansas, and almost 61 percent of the popular vote. Thanks to his coattails, the Democrats increased their already large majorities in both houses of Congress. To some pundits, the result put the continued existence of the Republican Party in doubt. The Union party that Father Coughlin and Francis Townsend had organized to promote William Lemke's independent presidential candidacy had proved a damp squib. After its rout, the 'radio priest,' whose anti-Roosevelt tirades had reached a wide audience, announced that he was going off the air.[22]

FDR barely mentioned the Supreme Court during the campaign, but his smashing electoral victory emboldened him to propose a radical plan for its reorganization. In his inaugural address on 20 January 1937, he acknowledged that the state of the nation was much improved in comparison to its condition four years earlier, but much remained to be done to fulfil 'our progressive purpose.' Encapsulating the New Deal's unfinished business in a short, simple, but striking sentence, Roosevelt declared, 'I see one-third of a nation ill-housed, ill-clad, ill-nourished.' Anxious that the Supreme Court might invalidate his initiatives to help those in most need, he was in a great hurry to reform it without going through the drawn-out process of constitutional amendment. Based on the advice of Attorney-General Homer Cummings, the president intended to enlarge the Court by appointing up to six new justices. The patently devious rationale for such a dramatic change entailed dressing it up as part of a broader Judiciary Bill based on the need for 'new blood' in view of the advanced age of some current justices. FDR kept the plan a closely guarded secret that he did not share with Democratic National Committee chair James Farley and party leaders in Congress until the eve of making it public at his press conference on 5 February 1937.[23]

Republicans predictably opposed what soon became known as FDR's 'court-packing' plan, seeing it as vindication of their 1936 campaign warnings about the New Deal's threat to American institutions. Frank Knox, the GOP's vice-presidential candidate who had compared FDR to TR in 1933, now saw nothing in common between them apart from their family name. Henry Stimson, whom TR had appointed a US attorney, was also critical of his cousin's disrespect for the Constitution in the pages of his diary. Republican traditionalists like Herbert Hoover were also up in arms at the threat to the separation of the powers.[24] For the most part, however, Republicans left it to the Democrats to criticize the plan, which many of them proceeded to do – in the press and on the radio.

Opposition in the Senate from conservative Democrats like Harry Byrd of Virginia and Josiah Bailey of North Carolina was to be expected, but some prominent liberals joined in the attack. Burton Wheeler of Montana, hitherto a strong New Dealer, played a leading role in masterminding the defeat of the Judiciary Bill. In addition to putting forward an alternative proposal for popular review of Supreme Court decisions, first suggested by Theodore Roosevelt in 1912, he obtained a private letter from Chief Justice Hughes containing reassurances that the nine justices were up to date with their docket and did not require additional appointments to keep on top of their work.[25]

In also coming out against the court-packing plan, several eminent journalists portrayed FDR as posing a threat to America's constitutional democracy. Most damningly, Walter Lippmann noted the similarities between his proposed judicial reform and the actions of dictators in Europe. In his view, FDR was to all intents and purposes acting on the assumption that democracy could not function in America unless power was centralized in his hands, but that development would only destroy what it was intended to save.[26] Even normally supportive newspapers like the *New York Times* accused Roosevelt of engaging in 'political sharp practice' by hiding a major constitutional change 'under the name of judicial reform.' This was a mild rebuke in comparison with editorials elsewhere that depicted Roosevelt as a tyrant in the making. 'Nothing can disguise the naked sword that has been drawn,' opined the *Brooklyn Eagle*. 'Already possessing far more power than any peace-time President has ever held, with an unprecedented control over both Houses of Congress, he has asked for power over the judiciary. This is too much power for any man to hold in a country that still calls itself a democracy.' Disdaining FDR's failure to mention his plans during the recent election campaign, the *Baltimore Sun* accused him of being 'disingenuous with the people.'[27]

Losing the Battle

This widespread attack on the Court plan put FDR on the defensive. He initially hoped that speeches and interviews from loyalists like Secretary of the Interior Harold Ickes and pressure on Democratic members of Congress from New Deal groups with an interest in Court reform, notably labour unions, would suffice. Before long, however, it was clear that he would have to make an open appeal for support. With the fox giving way to the lion, FDR launched a double-pronged attack in early March – addressed first to his party and then to the public in a Fireside Chat. At a Victory Dinner at the Mayflower Hotel, Washington DC, on 4 March, he called on Democrats to be bold. Mindful of the rise of dictators in Europe and of home-grown demagogues in the mould of Huey Long, he warned: 'If we do not have the courage to lead the American people where they want to go, someone else will.' Harold Ickes adjudged this address 'the greatest he has ever made … it will go down in history as one of the outstanding speeches delivered by an American statesman.'[28]

A few days later FDR confided to Ickes that he was struggling with how to frame his Fireside Chat. In the event, he emulated his second Inaugural Address in contending that America now faced a crisis greater than the one in March 1933 – 'the need to meet the unanswered challenge of one-third of a Nation ill-nourished, ill-clad, ill-housed.' Over the past half-century, he warned, the balance of power between the three branches of national government had been undermined by the judiciary 'in direct contradiction of the high purposes of the framers of the Constitution.' Ending on a high note, he refuted charges of acting like a dictator: 'It is my purpose to restore that balance. You who know me will accept my solemn assurance that in a world in which democracy is under attack, I seek to make American democracy succeed.'[29]

Voicing the scepticism of the *New York Times*, Washington bureau chief Arthur Krock anticipated that FDR would appoint 'party men' rather than accomplished jurists to the Supreme Court. Public reaction to the fireside address was more favourable but did not elicit the same level of support as FDR's earliest efforts. The White House received many letters from Democratic voters and self-declared independents expressing admiration for the president but declaring him wrong on this issue. Others were very critical of the Court proposal as undemocratic and dangerous, with some expressing concern that FDR was aiming to become a dictator. Most correspondents put their trust in FDR to do the right thing because of the 'fearless courage' he had shown in taking on the bankers and corporations. 'We workers are with you to the end of this bitter fight,' wrote one listener, while an African-American living in Louisiana called Roosevelt 'a shepherd for your flock' and suggested he nominate a black justice among the new appointments to the Supreme Court.[30]

The Gallup poll findings indicated that FDR's campaign met with some success. Following his Victory Dinner speech and Fireside Chat, respondent approval for the Court plan increased from 41 per cent to 46 per cent and opposition fell from 50 per cent to 44 per cent, with 'don't knows' at 9 to 10 per cent. Popular support for the plan remained marginally stronger than opposition to it until the Court upheld the National Labor Relations Act of 1935 in a landmark ruling on 4 April. With the urgency of Court reform appearing to decrease, opposition thereafter rose to 46 per cent while support fell to 44 per cent. Associate Justice Willis Van Devanter's announcement on 18 May that he would retire at the end of the current judicial term then opened the way for FDR to replace one of the 'Four Horsemen' with a liberal nominee. Public support for reform consequently dropped to its lowest point at 31 per cent while opposition rose to 45 per cent and climbed thereafter to 50 per cent.[31] Gallup polls suggested that public opposition never ran higher than 50 per cent and popular approval ranged from 31 per cent to 46 per cent. Though FDR's support was far from anaemic, it was not sufficiently robust to persuade doubtful members of Congress to vote for the scheme. The sudden death on 14 July of Senate Majority Leader Joseph Robinson of Arkansas, who was leading the fight for judicial reform in the upper chamber and had been promised the first vacancy on the Supreme Court, proved the final blow for presidential hopes. On 22 July, the Senate voted by 70 to 20 to send the Judiciary Bill back to committee without the Supreme Court clauses and the resulting Judiciary Act was signed by FDR on 24 August. Explaining this outcome, William Leuchtenburg suggested that the 'greater the insecurity of the times, the more people cling to the few institutions that seem unchangeable.' In any event, the Supreme Court plan was dead, and no American president has thereafter attempted to reorganize the judiciary.[32]

Winning the War

FDR would later claim that he had 'lost the battle but won the war' over judicial change. According to historian James MacGregor Burns, however, the impact of the controversy on Congress and the Democratic party meant that the president had 'lost the battle, won the campaign, but lost the war.' Certainly, FDR had failed to achieve a radical reorganization of the Supreme Court and the issue had widened the divide between liberal and conservative Democrats, but the event that helped to deliver the *coup de grace* to the court-packing plan – the resignation of Associate Justice Willis Van Devanter – also brought judicial conservatism closer to its Appomattox. This was the first of five judicial vacancies created by retirement or death within a three-year period. By the end of FDR's second term, the Supreme Court had to all intents and purposes become the Roosevelt Court. Four further nominations in his third term confirmed this reality. Only George Washington in the early years of the Supreme Court had nominated more justices. A decade later, five of his nominees joined with three of Harry S. Truman's appointees to render the epochal school-desegregation decision, *Brown v. Topeka*, under the leadership of liberal Republican Earl Warren, Dwight D. Eisenhower's first judicial nominee.[33]

Following the Judiciary Bill defeat, FDR went by train on a tour of the Pacific Northwest to inspect various New Deal public-works projects. In a rear platform address at Boisie, Idaho, the president likened himself to 'an old mythological character by the name of Antaeus,' whose strength redoubled every time his foot touched the ground. 'I feel that I regain strength by just meeting the American people.'[34] The subtext was clear: he may have stumbled with Congress, but the people were still with him. A reinvigorated Roosevelt used another Fireside Chat on 12 October to draw a line under the Supreme Court imbroglio. This radio address gave perfect form to Roosevelt's image as a great campaigner through its confident expression in the wellbeing of American democracy.

'Five years of fierce discussion and debate,' the president asserted, 'five years of information through the radio and the moving picture, have taken the whole nation to school in the nation's business. Even those who have most attacked our objectives have, by their very criticism, encouraged the mass of our citizens to think about and understand the issues involved, and understanding, to approve.' FDR had pointedly not referred to the role of the press in his paean to the country's democratic spirit, but he was confident that hostile newspaper owners could not destroy the bond between people and president based on their agreement that activist government was necessary to resolve the nation's problems. Americans, he avowed, 'are less concerned that every detail be immediately right than they are that the direction be right. They know that just so long as we are traveling on the right road, it does not make much difference if occasionally we hit a "Thank you ma'am".'[35]

Lauding this optimistic address, *New York Times* radio editor Orrin Dunlap conjured up an arresting image of FDR's peerless skills of political communication through the medium by referring to him as 'a Blondin of the wavelengths,' whose 'all-American voice ... [had] lifted the art of broadcast speaking to lofty heights'. For the political parties planning their 1940 campaign, he continued, 'part of the problem may be to find a voice as well as a man' because politicians and broadcasters were now of one mind that 'no matter how strong a candidate's prestige and character, if he has a weak voice personality on the radio, he has one if not two strikes on him when he steps up to the "mike."' The 'magnetic technique' that made FDR the master of the medium was not a complicated one: 'Naturalness is the keynote. He talks smoothly and in a conversational tone, seldom faltering on a single word; rarely does he cough or clear his throat during a half-hour "chat."' In Dunlap's estimate, FDR was 'born with a radio personality,' making it 'a difficult assignment' for any other candidate to measure up to him. The question was already being asked: 'Who have the Democrats to offer with a voice like Roosevelt's; who have the Republicans?'[36]

Two weeks later, Arthur Krock reflected in the *New York Times* on FDR's position following the Supreme Court controversy. In his assessment, whatever their divisions over court-packing, conservative Democrats, especially in the South, still had a tribal loyalty to the party, and liberals remained strongly supportive of the president's New Deal. Meanwhile, the GOP's 'strategy of silence' during the Court controversy may have appeared to be clever politics at the time, but it had won them few new adherents. A realignment of political forces would therefore be very difficult to achieve without 'a great leader with a powerful personality and record appealing to the country' and at present FDR was 'the only national leader on the scene or in sight.'[37]

FDR's image as a strong leader would arguably suffer more damage from the outcome of the 1938 mid-term elections than it had from the Supreme Court controversy. His largely unsuccessful efforts to purge anti–New Deal Democrats by supporting liberal challengers in the primaries raised doubts about his control over his own party. The so-called Roosevelt recession of 1937–8 also did much to precipitate the Republican comeback in the mid-terms. In the new Congress that met in 1939, the Democrats held majorities in both chambers, but an informal coalition of Republicans and conservative Democrats had the votes to block further significant expansion of the New Deal. Sensing that FDR was at the nadir of his prestige, columnist Raymond Clapper commented, '[C]learly … President Roosevelt could not run for a third term even if he so desired.'[38] A half-century before Bill Clinton would forge his 'Comeback Kid' image, FDR would mount an even greater political recovery to win four more years as president.

The international situation and the threat of war in Europe had significant impact on the environment of American politics. As Roosevelt biographer Roger Daniels observed, his annual message in January 1939 and the congressional response to it prefigured his relations with the legislature for the remainder of his presidency: 'As long as his chief concern was national defense and eventually the prosecution of the war, he could usually count on majority support drawn from both sides of the aisle for most of his proposals. But when he endeavoured to expand the New Deal, he would often encounter serious difficulties.' In this address, his avowal to build up America's military strength to keep it safe from attack was broadly well received, but his insistence that the nation's programme of social and economic reform was 'a part of defense as basic as armaments themselves' drew far less support.[39]

The outbreak of war in Europe led to another Fireside Chat on 3 September confirming American neutrality but – unlike Woodrow Wilson in August 1914 – not asking for neutrality in thought as well as action. However, the president did make 'the simple plea that partisanship and selfishness be adjourned; and that national unity be the thought that underlies all others.'[40] Clearly Roosevelt was shifting his image from the rather divisive reformer of the 1930s to the unifying leader of the wartime era. Indeed, from this point in time, all his Fireside Chats would have a war-related theme. In combination with his formal presidential speeches, best exemplified by his 1941 State of the Union address,[41] they would do much to educate Americans about their nation's democratic purpose in eventually joining the conflict. With the dramatic success of the German blitzkrieg in the summer of 1940, FDR effectively created an administration of national unity by appointing eminent Republicans Frank Knox as Navy Secretary and Henry Stimson as Secretary of War. Both had been trenchant critics of his court-packing plan but were strong supporters of his efforts to move American public opinion away from isolationism.

The apparent imminence of Adolf Hitler's total victory in the European conflict also formed the backdrop to FDR's nomination for an unprecedented third-term as president by the Democratic National Convention in Chicago. His image as a strong and experienced leader was to prove essential in his defeat of his relatively untested Republican challenger, Wendell Willkie, in the November presidential election. This was no landslide victory on the scale of 1936, but it was still a comfortable one by 54.7 to 44.8 percent of the popular vote and by 449 to 82 votes in the Electoral College. In one way, the outcome confirmed the continued importance of the New Deal voter coalition that had formed in support of the Democrats in FDR's first term. In another way, it was also a triumph for the Rooseveltian image. As Republican House minority leader Joseph Martin of Massachusetts later observed, 'There are times, and 1940 was one when the party that seems best able to prosecute a war is invincible. In the last analysis, the people trusted Roosevelt's experience in coping with the situation that confronted the country.' For that reason, it is reasonable to conclude that no other Democratic candidate could have won the presidency in 1940.[42] FDR was genuinely reluctant to run again but he was determined to uphold both national security and the New Deal. During his third term, 'Dr New Deal' became subordinate to 'Dr Win-the-War.' However, the spirit of New Deal reformism never entirely disappeared and would find expression in his 1944 State of the Union address with its vision of promoting an Economic Bill of Rights once the war was won.[43]

Conclusion

If FDR's image and, indeed, his presidency were on trial during the Supreme Court episode, the outcome of the 1940 presidential election suggests that he was acquitted by the jury that matters most in American politics – public opinion. The defeat of his Judiciary Bill did not mean that his powers of persuasion were in decline. The Gallup poll findings suggest that he was able to carry a significant proportion of the population with him, and in the month following his Fireside Chat on the Court, a plurality. But in a political system defined by checks and balances, there is a limit to the constitutional change that any president can achieve without securing a formal amendment to the Constitution – even one as popular as Roosevelt. However, FDR's radio presence remained a potent weapon in exercising the 'power to persuade' as was demonstrated by his leadership during the Second World War, when he delivered over half of his total of thirty Fireside

Chats to far larger audiences than in peacetime. In December 1940, his 'garden hose' analogy for Lend Lease and the 'arsenal of democracy' metaphor in his Fireside Chat showed that FDR retained his rhetorical powers and his mastery as 'the Voice on the Radio' – a mastery that won the admiration of Winston Churchill in beleaguered Britain as well as the president's supporters at home. The 'Great Campaigner' had not lost his touch.[44]

How then do we explain the resilience of the Roosevelt image? Essentially the image of FDR as a charismatic and reforming president had already been established by the start of his second term. As the Gridiron skits suggested, the main issue raised during the Supreme Court controversy centred upon his judgement in adopting the 'Court packing' plan. While some doubted his motives, what concerned many critics were his methods, which would be dangerous in the hands of a dictatorial successor. Had he stood down in 1940, FDR would probably have been regarded by history as a 'near great' president – somewhat akin to Theodore Roosevelt, Woodrow Wilson and Harry S. Truman. From 1940, however, as the threat from Nazism grew and was reinforced by Japan after the attack on Pearl Harbor, Roosevelt the progressive reformer became Roosevelt the defender of democracy. As James MacGregor Burns put it, 'the Lion and the Fox' gave way to the 'Soldier of Freedom' and FDR's image – at home and abroad – as one of America's greatest presidents was assured.[45]

Notes

1 'Remarks of the President at the Gridiron Club Dinner, Washington DC,' 10 April 1937, http://www.fdrlibrary.marist.edu/_resources/images/msf/ msf01473. For FDR's views on the Gridiron dinners, see Winfield, Betty Houchin, *FDR and the News Media* (New York: Columbia University Press, 1994), p. 60.
2 '15 Rubber Stamps in Gridiron "Court",' *New York Times* [*NYT*], 11 April 1937.
3 Leuchtenburg, William E., *In the Shadow of FDR: From Harry Truman to Ronald Reagan* (Ithaca, NY: Cornell University Press, 1983), p. x; Neustadt, Richard, *Presidential Power and the Modern Presidents* (New York: Macmillan, 1990), pp. 11, 135–7.
4 Leuchtenburg, *Shadow of FDR*, pp. vii–xi.
5 For the classic study of Depression-era politics, see Leuchtenburg, William, E., *Franklin D. Roosevelt and the New Deal, 1932–1940* (New York: Harper & Row, 1963). Excellent political biographies of FDR include: Maney, Patrick, *The Roosevelt Presence: The Life and Legacy of FDR* (Oakland: University of California, 1998); Hamby, Alonzo, *Man of Destiny: FDR and the Making of the American Century* (New York: Basic Books, 2015); and Daniels, Roger, *Franklin D. Roosevelt: Road to the New Deal, 1882–1939* and *Franklin D. Roosevelt: The War Years, 1939–1945* (Urbana: University of Illinois Press, 2015 and 2016).
6 Burns, James MacGregor, *Roosevelt: The Lion and the Fox* (New York: Harcourt, Brace, 1956), p. ix; Dallek, Robert, *Franklin D Roosevelt: A Political Life* (London: Allen Lane, 2017), p. x; Morgan, Iwan, 'The Top US Presidents: First Poll of UK Experts,' https://www.bbc.co.uk/news/world-us-canada-12195111. Regarding

Roosevelt's top spot in the latter, see McCulloch, Tony, 'Simply the Best: FDR as America's Number One President,' in Michael Patrick Cullinane and Clare Frances Elliott, eds., *Perspectives on Presidential Leadership: An International View of the White House* (New York: Routledge, 2014), pp. 113–31.

7   Burns, *Lion and Fox*, pp. 47–66; Maney, *Roosevelt Presence*, pp. 12–29; Dallek, *Roosevelt*, pp. 40–69.

8   Burns, *Lion and Fox*, pp. 67–80; Dallek, *Roosevelt*, pp. 70–3; 'Unanimous for Roosevelt,' *NYT*, 7 July 1920; FDR newsreel, 1920–32, https://www.youtube.com/watch?v=Fl6WBhavFgU.

9   Burns, *Lion and Fox*, pp. 83–122; Dallek, *Roosevelt*, pp. 74–100; 'Roosevelt Offers Name of Governor Smith,' *NYT*, 27 June 1924; 'Roosevelt Names New York Governor,' *NYT*, 28 June 1928.

10 'Address Accepting the Democratic Presidential Nomination in Chicago,' 2 July 1932, Gerhard Peters and John T. Woolley, The American Presidency Project [hereafter APP], https://www.presidency.ucsb.edu/node/275484; Ritchie, Donald A., *Electing FDR: The New Deal Campaign of 1932* (Lawrence: University Press of Kansas, 2007).

11 Gallagher, Hugh Gregory, *FDR's Splendid Deception: The Moving Story of FDR's Massive Disability - And the Intense Efforts to Keep It from the Public* (St. Petersburg, FL: Vandamere, 1999); Tobin, James, *The Man He Became: How FDR Defied Polio to Win the Presidency* (New York: Simon & Schuster, 2013).

12 Alter, Jonathan, *The Defining Moment: FDR's Hundred Days and the Triumph of Hope* (New York: Simon & Schuster, 2006), pp. 245–52; 'Fireside Chat on Banking,' 12 March 1933, APP, https://www.presidency.ucsb.edu/node/207762; Greenberg, David, *Republic of Spin: An Inside History of the American Presidency* (New York: Norton, 2016), pp. 189–98.

13 Levine, Lawrence, and Cornelia Levine, *The People and the President: America's Conversation with FDR* (Boston: Beacon Press, 2002), pp. 29–59; Leuchtenburg, William E., *The FDR Years: On Roosevelt and His Legacy* (New York: Columbia University Press, 1995), p. 7.

14 Burns, *Lion and Fox*, pp. 176–9; Dallek, *Roosevelt*, pp. 133–66; FDR, 'Wireless to the London Conference,' 3 July 1933, APP, https://www.presidency.ucsb.edu/node/208290; Lindsay, 27 July 1933, Foreign Office 371, 16600, A5782/17/45, UK National Archives, Kew.

15 Knox, Frank, 'Boldness of President Clears Away Fog,' *Chicago Daily News*, 3 July 1933; Henry Stimson Diary, Vol. 26, 14 and 16 July 1933, Stirling Library, Yale University, New Haven.

16 Burns, *Lion and Fox*, pp. 161–226; Brinkley, Alan, *Voices of Protest: Huey Long, Father Coughlin, and the Great Depression* (New York: Knopf, 1982), pp. 169–93.

17 White, Graham, *FDR and the Press* (Chicago: Chicago University Press, 1979), pp. 5–24, 49–52; Winfield, *FDR and the News Media*, pp. 27–51, 127–32.

18 Winfield, *FDR and News Media*, pp. 103–25; Ryan, Halford R., *Franklin D Roosevelt's Rhetorical Presidency* (Westport, CT: Praeger, 1988), pp. 109–30; Craig, Douglas B., *Fireside Politics: Radio and Political Culture in the United States, 1920–1940* (Baltimore, MD: Johns Hopkins University Press, 2000).

19 Fielding, Raymond, *The American Newsreel: A Complete History, 1911–1967*, 2nd ed. (Jefferson, NC: McFarland, 2006), p. 124.

20 Burns, *Lion and Fox*, pp. 227–46; Daniels, *FDR: Road to New Deal*, pp. 230–3, 253–5.

21 'Republican Party Platform of 1936,' 9 June 1936, APP, https://www.presidency.ucsb.edu/node/273386; FDR, 'Acceptance Speech for the Renomination for the Presidency, Philadelphia, PA,' 27 June 1936, APP, https://www.presidency.ucsb.edu/node/208917.

22 Leuchtenburg, William E., 'The Election of 1936,' in William E. Leuchtenburg, ed., *The FDR Years* (New York: Columbia University Press, 1995), pp. 101–58.

23 For the Supreme Court battle, see Leuchtenburg, William E., *The Supreme Court Reborn: The Constitutional Revolution in the Age of Roosevelt* (New York: Oxford University Press, 1995); and Shesol, Jeff, *Supreme Power: Franklin Roosevelt vs the Supreme Court* (New York: Norton, 2010). For historiographical analysis, see Shaw, Stephen 'The Supreme Court,' in William Pederson, ed., *A Companion to Franklin D. Roosevelt* (Hoboken, NJ: Blackwell Publishing, 2011), 427–41.

24 Krock, Arthur, 'In the Nation – Two Results of Supreme Court Argument,' *NYT*, 10 February 1937. For Republican responses, see Knox, editorial, *Chicago Daily News*, 6 February 1937; and Stimson Diary, Vol. 28, 27 March 1937.

25 McKenna, Marian C., 'Prelude to Tyranny: Wheeler, FDR, and the 1937 Court Fight,' *Pacific Historical Review*, 62 (November 1993): 405–31; Wheeler, Burton K., *Yankee from the West* (New York: Doubleday, 1962), pp. 320–3.

26 Krome, Frederick, 'From Liberal Philosophy to Conservative Ideology? Walter Lippmann's Opposition to the New Deal,' *Journal of American Culture*, 10 (Spring 1987): 57–64; Ronald Steel, *Walter Lippmann and the American Century* (Livingston, NJ: Transaction Publishers, 1999), pp. 319–26.

27 White, *FDR and the Press*, pp. 69–79; 'Opinions of the Nation's Press on Court Plan,' *NYT*, 6 February 1937.

28 'Address to Democratic Victory Dinner, Washington, DC,' 4 March 1937, APP, https://www.presidency.ucsb.edu/node/209418; Ickes, Harold, *The Secret Diary of Harold Ickes*, Vol. II: *The Inside Struggle, 1936–1939* (New York: Simon and Schuster, 1954) [27 February 1937], p. 88.

29 'Fireside Chat,' 9 March 1937, APP, https://www.presidency.ucsb.edu/node/209434; Ryan, *Rhetorical Presidency*, pp. 121–4; Ickes, *Secret Diary*, II, 15 March 1937, p. 95.

30 Editorial, *NYT*, 11 March 1937; Krock, 'In Washington – a Formula for Choosing Supreme Court Judges,' *NYT*, 11 March 1937; Levine and Levine, *The People and the President*, pp. 163–200.

31 Caldeira, Gregory A., 'Public Opinion and the US Supreme Court: FDR's Court-Packing Plan,' *American Political Science Review*, 81 (December 1987): 1139–53.

32 Leuchtenburg, *FDR and New Deal*, pp. 232–6; McKenna, 'Prelude to Tyranny,' pp. 430–1; Caldeira, 'Public Opinion,' pp. 1139–40.

33 Burns, *Lion and Fox*, p. 315; Urofsky, Melvyn, 'The Roosevelt Court,' in William Chafe, ed., *The Achievements of American Liberalism: The New Deal and Its Legacies* (New York: Columbia University Press, 2003), pp. 63–98.

34 'Remarks at Boise, Idaho,' 27 September 1937, APP, https://www.presidency.ucsb.edu/node/208784.

35 'Fireside Chat,' 12 October 1937, APP, https://www.presidency.ucsb.edu/node/208891.

36 Dunlap, Orrin, 'Speaking of Voices,' *NYT*, 7 November 1937. See too Ryfe, David Michael, 'Franklin Roosevelt and the Fireside Chats,' *Journal of Communication*, 49 (December 1999): 80–103.

37 Krock, Arthur, 'Roosevelt Shapes the Line Up for 1940,' *NYT*, 24 October 1937.

38 Clapper, Raymond, 'Return of the Two-Party System,' *Current History*, 49 (December 1938), 14. For the politics of 1938, see Dunn, Susan, *Roosevelt's Purge:*

How FDR Fought to Change the Democratic Party (Cambridge, MA: Belknap Press, 2010).

39   Daniels, *FDR: War Years*, p. 1; 'Annual Message to Congress,' 4 January 1939, APP, http://www.presidency.ucsb.edu/ws/?pid=15684.

40   'Fireside Chat,' 3 September 1939, APP, https://www.presidency.ucsb.edu/node/209990.

41   See Engel, Jeffrey A., ed., *The Four Freedoms: Franklin D. Roosevelt and the Evolution of an American Idea* (New York: Oxford University Press, 2016).

42   Martin, Joseph, *My First Fifty Years in Politics* (New York: McGraw-Hill, 1960), 120. For the 1940 election, see Dunn, Susan, *1940: FDR, Willkie, Lindbergh, Hitler – the Election Amid the Storm* (New Haven, CT: Yale University Press, 2013); and Jeffries, John, *A Third Term for FDR: The Election of 1940* (Lawrence: University Press of Kansas, 2017).

43   'State of the Union Address,' 11 January 1944, http://www.fdrlibrary.marist.edu/archives/stateoftheunion.html.

44   'Press Conference,' 17 December 1940, APP, https://www.presidency.ucsb.edu/node/209409; 'Fireside Chat,' 29 December 1940, APP, https://www.presidency.ucsb.edu/node/209416.

45   Burns, James MacGregor, *Roosevelt: The Soldier of Freedom, 1940–1945* (New York: Harcourt Brace and Company, 1970), pp. ix–xiv.

Chapter 4

TRUMAN: THE EVERYMAN

Sean J. Savage

During his nearly eight-year presidency, Harry S. Truman seemed to be indifferent about his presidential image and status in public opinion polls.[1] He wrote in his memoirs that he ignored polls because 'they did not represent a true cross section of American opinion' and 'did not represent facts but mere speculation.'[2] He also noted that his public approval rating was 36 per cent in the spring of 1948 when he began his presidential campaign.[3] Truman, moreover, insisted that he made policy decisions without any concern or calculation about how they would affect his presidential image, public approval ratings, ability to win the presidential election of 1948 or the electoral performance of Democratic congressional candidates. Truman knew beforehand that his decisions to submit civil rights legislation to Congress and begin the racial integration of the military would be unpopular, especially with southern Democrats who dominated the major committees of Congress.[4] Likewise, when Truman made decisions that were initially controversial, such as the Berlin airlift[5] and the diplomatic recognition of Israel,[6] there is no conclusive evidence that he cared about how these policies would affect his image, poll ratings or the outcome of the 1948 presidential election.

Despite Truman's inattention to it, his image has undergone significant change since he became president in 1945 in accordance with shifts in American and world history and the evolving perceptions of both the public and scholars regarding what constitutes a desirable presidential image. In their biographies of Truman, historians Alonzo L. Hamby and Robert Dallek adjudged that his presidential image has changed more than those of other presidents because of how much American society has changed. Hamby concluded that Truman became 'an American icon' not because of what he did as president but because of 'who Americans believe him to be.'[7] According to Dallek, Truman's personal character of 'ultimate good sense and honesty' and propriety in his conduct demonstrated 'how circumstances and human decency can ultimately produce a successful life – and a presidency that resonates as a model of how someone can acquit himself in the highest office.'[8] The thirty-fourth president's image as an American everyman, well captured in an early official photograph of him [see below], endured throughout his tenure – even though he would grow in stature as a consequence of his momentous decision-making.

Figure 4.1 Harry S. Truman: The Common Man as president, Harry S. Truman Library, public domain. Frank Gatteri, United States Army, Harry S. Truman Library & Museum.

With the rise of the so-called 'modern presidency' under Franklin D. Roosevelt (FDR), Americans and people of other nations began to expect more from American presidents in providing effective leadership to solve or alleviate both domestic and international policy problems.[9] Richard E. Neustadt, a political scientist who served in the Truman administration, has explained how presidential power is influenced by a president's image to various audiences. These images are influenced by public expectations of a president. Likewise, these images and expectations of a president as an individual are affected by the image and expectations of the presidency as an office at that time. In *Presidential Power and the Modern Presidents*, Neustadt wrote, 'An image of the office, not an image of the man, is the dynamic factor in a President's prestige. Impressions of the person will form early and last long, but the values men assign to what they see can alter rather quickly.'[10]

Two factors largely influenced Truman's initially unfavourable presidential image. First, his immediate predecessor was the political colossus, FDR. Second,

America's president, regardless of who he was as an individual, had to make crucial decisions from 1945 to 1952 that greatly affected the future both of the United States and the world. In his book about the first four months of Truman's presidency, A.J. Baime wrote, 'Never had fate shoehorned so much history into such a short period.'[11]

Ever since 1948 when historians began to rank presidents, FDR has been bracketed with Abraham Lincoln and George Washington as one of the three great presidents in US history.[12] Regardless of whether FDR was loved or hated or whether his policies have been evaluated as successful or disastrous, he is widely regarded as the founder of the modern presidency.[13] Since he remade the office, Americans and leaders of other nations have expected much more from its holder than they did prior to his tenure. Roosevelt's response to the consecutive crises of the Great Depression and the Second World War greatly increased the powers, responsibilities and expectations of the American presidency.[14]

More so than any of his predecessors in the White House, FDR personalized the presidency to the extent that there seemed to be little or no difference between the office of president and the man himself. In his study of Roosevelt's Great Depression leadership, historian William E. Leuchtenburg concluded, 'Franklin Roosevelt personified the state as protector. It became commonplace to say that people felt towards the President the kind of trust they would normally express for a warm and understanding father who comforted them in their grief or safeguarded them from harm.'[15] Likewise, Edgar E. Robinson argued that FDR's style of leadership, communication and rapport with millions of Americans helped to strengthen the democratic legitimacy of American government in general and the presidency in particular at a time when they were severely strained and challenged by the economic chaos and suffering of the 1930s. According to Robinson, FDR 'represented fairly well the level of conception, understanding, and purpose that characterized the mass of the American people of his time.'[16]

Roosevelt's adroit use of radio addresses to Americans, notably his 'Fireside Chats,' developed an intimate relationship with the American people that increased his ability to use public opinion to influence Congress in policymaking and circumvent the mostly Republican-owned news media.[17] Political scientist Theodore J. Lowi contended that FDR's political skills, notably his communicative ability and projection of confidence in his leadership, and his image as the protector of the common people enabled him to establish the first plebiscitary presidency. In such a presidency, the incumbent derives much of his power and effectiveness from his ability to communicate directly with and influence the public through modern mass media, such as radio and television. In Lowi's estimate, '[FDR's] legacy can be summed up in a single concept, the plebiscitary presidency. He set its foundations and determined its initial directions.'[18] In his study of leadership, political scientist James MacGregor Burns similarly concluded, 'Roosevelt was a consummate manager of public opinion – probably, if one could measure these things, the most skillful and effective in American history.'[19]

In his analysis of how every post-1945 president has been compared to FDR, William E. Leuchtenburg elaborated on how and why the 'shadow of FDR' weighed so heavily on Truman. As Roosevelt's last vice president and successor in the White House, Truman was the most rigorously evaluated and compared to FDR, often to the detriment of his own presidential image. For example, FDR's communication style and skills were simultaneously aristocratic and folksy, engaging and inspiring, reassuring and rousing. By contrast, Truman's speeches, especially prepared speeches on public policy that were broadcast first on radio and later via television, were often dry and bland and spoken in his flat, droning Missouri accent. Even the legitimacy of Truman's status and authority as president was difficult for the shocked, grieving members of Roosevelt's administration and family to accept. Leuchtenburg noted, 'So much did Roosevelt dominate the Truman years that one of FDR's former advisors put forth the novel claim that Roosevelt continued to be president of the United States beyond the grave.'[20]

The way by which Truman became FDR's last vice president weakened his presidential image and legitimacy. Historian Robert H. Ferrell has examined how and why FDR chose Truman as his running mate in the 1944 presidential election.[21] With his health rapidly deteriorating and his focus on winning the war and establishing a stable peace, FDR apparently gave little thought to who would replace Henry A. Wallace, his vice president and a political liability, as his running mate at the Democratic National Convention.

In 1942, Truman, then Missouri senator, had recommended Robert E. Hannegan to the position of collector of internal revenue for the eastern district of Missouri. This was a pay-off for his success in delivering enough votes from St. Louis for Truman's razor-thin victory over Governor Lloyd Stark by 40.9 to 39.6 per cent of ballots cast in the fiercely contested 1940 Democratic senatorial primary in Missouri. Hannegan then became commissioner of internal revenue in 1943 and chairman of the Democratic National Committee (DNC) the following year.[22] In the latter post, he became aware of FDR's receptivity to having a new vice-presidential running mate in 1944. He was also confident of being able to persuade the president of Truman's attractiveness as a compromise candidate for the number 2 position on the Democratic ticket. Hannegan reminded FDR of the national fame and bipartisan respect for his integrity that Truman had earned through his chairmanship of the Senate Special Committee to Investigate the National Defense Program, which exposed waste, fraud and incompetence in the award of defence contracts. Through his influence with the White House staff, Hannegan also arranged for influential, pro-Truman Democrats to meet with FDR. As DNC chair, he was also in a position to give Truman maximum exposure through scheduling him as a speaker at Democratic state conventions and fundraising dinners.[23]

By the time of the 1944 Democratic National Convention in Chicago, FDR was willing to accept either Truman or William O. Douglas, a Supreme Court justice, as his running mate. At Hannegan's request, he sent a public letter explaining this to convention delegates. With Truman receiving broad, diverse support from Catholic machine bosses, unions and southerners, he was easily nominated for vice president.[24] Truman's route to the vice presidency through the murky corridors of machine politics tarnished his image among pro-Wallace progressives, anti-boss liberals and anti-Cold War Democrats in the early stages of his accidental presidency. In *Truman: The Rise to Power*, Richard L. Miller portrays Truman as a calculating career politician who was ethically comfortable with and adept at the amoral, transactional, *quid pro quo* relationships of machine politics. In his telling, the future president Truman made his way in the politics and government of Jackson County, Missouri, as a member of the notorious, corrupt Kansas City machine headed by Tom Pendergast. He also furnished evidence that the financial and electoral support of machine politicians in Missouri was essential to Truman's rise from election as County Court judge in 1922 to election as US senator in 1934.[25]

The American public was dramatically reminded of Truman's machine antecedents when Tom Pendergast died on 26 January 1945. Having served a term in federal prison for tax evasion, the former boss had become something of a pariah to the national Democratic Party. Nevertheless, Truman insisted on attending the funeral of his former ally just a few days after being sworn in as vice president. The only elected official of note to do so, he always acknowledged that Pendergast was his friend and never asked him to do a dishonest deed.[26] The gesture revived memories of Truman's one-time reputation as 'the senator from Pendergast.' In Alonzo Hamby's words, the vice president's critics 'saw his pilgrimage as an outrage that reaffirmed his loyalty to a crooked machine and underscored his status as a political hack.' Not everyone shared their disdain, however. Many people, Truman biographer David McCullough argued, 'saw something admirable and courageous in a man risen so high who still knew who he was and refused to forget a friend.'[27]

By the end of Truman's presidency, there were examples of alleged and proven corruption in his administration, especially within the Bureau of Internal Revenue (BIR) and the Reconstruction Finance Corporation (RFC). Although the influence-peddling scandals of the BIR and RFC had their origins in the Roosevelt administration, Truman received most of the blame, partially because of his image as a machine politician. In *The Truman Scandals*, Jules Abels, a conservative economist who served in the Eisenhower administration, wrote that Truman's tolerance of corruption in his administration and his belated, inadequate response to it were rooted in his association with the Pendergast machine.[28] In a more balanced study, *The Truman Scandals and the Politics of Morality*, historian Andrew J. Dunar concluded that the public's association of Truman's presidential image with corruption was exacerbated by his poor judgement in appointing White House staff members, such as Harry Vaughan and Matthew Connelly, who accepted gifts from lobbyists, and then remaining stubbornly loyal to them.[29] I. F. Stone, a leftist columnist and critic of Truman, referred to the ethical climate of Truman's presidency as 'the era of the moocher. The place was full of Wimpys who could be had for a hamburger.'[30]

Other journalists contributed to the image of Truman as a president who knew about and tolerated widespread corruption and mediocre public service in his administration. In *The Truman Merry-Go-Round*, columnists Robert S. Allen and William V. Shannon wrote that he tended to appoint 'many mediocre associates and ill-chosen friends' who used their public offices for personal gain.[31] In a collection of his diary entries edited by Tyler Abell, columnist Drew Pearson noted that corruption in Truman's administration was worsened by the president's reluctance and even refusal to fire any of his appointees credibly suspected of corruption.[32] Based on their scandal-mongering, investigative articles, the book *Washington Confidential* (1951) by Jack Lait and Lee Mortimer depicted the ethical atmosphere of Washington DC during the Truman presidency as infused with corruption of all kinds.[33] In *The Presidents' Men*, a study of White House staffs from FDR to LBJ, journalist Patrick Anderson contended that it was Truman's 'manner to trust his aides too far, to assume their honesty, to give them a job and not look over their shoulders.'[34]

In contrast to these critics' portrayal of Truman's fidelity to subordinates as a serious character flaw, those who served in his administration recalled this quality as one of his greatest virtues. In their memoirs and oral history interviews, Truman's appointees, especially White House aides, fondly recalled Truman's loyalty to them and the generally high morale among his staff. In his published diary, Assistant Press Secretary Eben A. Ayers wrote admiringly about Truman's defiance towards columnists who wanted him to fire military aide Harry Vaughan for alleged influence peddling.[35] White House Counsel Clark M. Clifford similarly observed that Truman's 'compassion for his friends usually took precedence over the needs of government unless or until he felt he had been deceived or misled.'[36]

In an interview for the Truman presidential library, Dean Acheson, who served as secretary of state under Truman, recalled how much he valued the president's unyielding support of him, especially when accused of incompetence and 'softness' on communism. Acheson stated, 'I don't think there is any example of a president who so stood by his secretary as Truman had me.'[37] Paul G. Hoffman, a Republican industrialist whom Truman appointed as the administrator of the Marshall Plan to rebuild Europe's war-ravaged economy, told an interviewer that he admired Truman for not tolerating any political interference in the Marshall Plan and for his 'courage and never-failing common sense.'[38]

Truman's status as an affiliate to the political regime initiated by FDR has also shaped assessments of his presidential image. According to political scientist Stephen Skowronek, a handful of presidents – Thomas Jefferson, Andrew Jackson, Abraham Lincoln, FDR and Ronald Reagan – transformed American politics for anywhere between a quarter-century and a half-century through their success in overthrowing the existing political order and establishing a new one. These reconstructive leaders drew authority from their electoral repudiation of the old regime to build a new regime with different ideals, interests and commitments from the previously dominant orthodoxies.[39] Their political legatees were the 'orthodox-innovator' presidents who promised 'to continue the good work of the past and demonstrate the vitality of the regime in different times.' If regime-building presidents were succeeded by their former vice presidents, however, what Skowronek termed the 'politics of articulation' became a formidable challenge for the so-called 'heir apparent,' a category that included Martin Van Buren (1837–41), Harry S. Truman and George H. Bush (1989–93).[40]

The burden of expectation regarding the conservation and continuation of the reconstructive president's electoral, policy and institutional commitments falls heaviest on their shoulders. In their status as 'heir apparent,' they tend to be found wanting by the most devoted followers of their regime-building predecessors. In Truman's case, he succeeded in protecting and preserving the major policies of FDR's New Deal but failed to build anew on its liberal foundations. The core measures of his own Fair Deal programme, notably civil rights, national health insurance and federal aid to elementary and secondary education, failed to secure enactment by a Congress dominated by a conservative coalition of Republicans and Southern Democrats in his second term.[41]

During the first year of Truman's presidency, it was not unusual for some members of the former Roosevelt administration, like David Lilienthal, director of the Tennessee Valley Authority, to compare Truman to Alexander Throttlebottom.[42] A character in two Broadway musical satires written by George and Ira Gershwin, 'Of Thee I Sing' (first performed in 1931) and 'Let 'Em Eat Cake' (first performed in 1933), Throttlebottom is comically and absurdly incompetent and unqualified for high office. Like Truman, however, he is chosen as a compromise candidate for vice president in the smoke-filled hotel rooms of a national party convention in the first of these productions and becomes president in the second.

Truman's presidential image of mediocrity was reinforced by the sharp differences in the backgrounds of FDR and Truman. FDR was a patrician who grew up on a large estate in the Hudson River Valley of upstate New York. He had inherited wealth and was a graduate of the Groton School and Harvard University. He was a distant cousin of Theodore Roosevelt who, as president, gave away the bride, his favourite niece, at FDR's wedding. With his aristocratic bearing and aura of noblesse oblige, FDR personified the office of president to such an extent that even his bitterest enemies in the news media would not publish photographs of the paralysed president in his wheelchair or being carried by Secret Service agents.[43]

Truman, by contrast, was a plebian to FDR's patrician. Truman grew up on small farms in Missouri.[44] He was the only twentieth-century president who was not a college graduate. His parents could not afford to send him to college, and West Point rejected him because of poor eyesight. He never owned his own house. After service in the Great War, he went into business by opening a haberdashery shop in downtown Kansas City, but the failure of the venture in 1921 compelled him to declare bankruptcy and left him with debts that he did not pay off fully until 1935. He subsequently entered and initially succeeded in politics as a member of one of the most corrupt political machines in the nation.[45]

For some analysts of Truman's presidency, his background as an 'everyman' foretold a mediocre presidency. British journalist Alistair Cooke accepted the conventional wisdom that he would lose the 1948 presidential election. In his *Manchester Guardian* column, published on the day before the election, Cooke referred to Truman as a 'study of failure.'[46] He wrote that 'mediocre Presidents must depend on careful advice,' but Truman consulted 'political hacks' and military officers to whom he excessively deferred.[47] In 2016, historian Kenneth Weisbrode echoed Cooke's assessment of Truman and criticized David McCullough's biography as hagiographic revisionism.[48] Adjudging the thirty-third president as 'overrated,' he found similarities between Truman and George W. Bush in their personal traits and mediocrity. Weisbrode concluded, 'If we ask today who was Harry Truman, our answer would not be too different from what most Americans would have said in 1946.'[49] In his study of early postwar America, Joseph C. Goulden wrote that many Americans had an image of Truman when he succeeded to the presidency as 'a not especially bright fellow who could be anyone's next door neighbor; nice enough, in his own way, but did one really trust him with the country?'[50]

By contrast, those who worked closely with Truman, especially on foreign and defence policies, found that his supposedly ordinary 'everyman' image made his leadership and decision-making skills as president especially impressive. In his memoirs, former Secretary of State Dean Acheson wrote, 'As suggested in the Apologia, the President's task was reminiscent of that in the first chapter of Genesis – to help the free world emerge from chaos without blowing the whole world apart in the process. To this task, Mr. Truman brought unusual qualities.'[51] Other top Truman administration officials, such as General George C. Marshall and W. Averell Harriman, had similar impressions.[52] They perceived Truman as a deceptively ordinary 'everyman' with uncommon virtues and skills who rose to the challenges of the presidency during a dangerous period in American and world history.

Major events, problems and crises during Truman's first year as president included his meeting with Churchill and Stalin at Potsdam, his decision to drop atomic bombs on Japan, high inflation, shortages of housing and consumer goods, the rapid demobilization of the US military, major labour strikes, the signing of the charter of the United Nations (UN), the trials of German and Japanese war criminals, and Winston Churchill's 'Iron Curtain' speech referring to the beginning of the Cold War. Journalist Robert J. Donovan wrote, 'For President Truman, the postwar period did not simply arrive – it broke about his head with thunder, lightning, hail, rain, sleet, dead cats, howls, tantrums, and palpitations of panic.'[53] During this period, most of the criticism of Truman's policy decisions and public statements focused on his efforts to convert the US economy to a peace-time footing. Indeed, this issue more than any other contributed to a decline in Truman's public approval ratings and a Republican victory in the 1946 congressional elections.[54] Based on his experience during this hectic, complex period of presidential decision-making, Truman popularized his two favourite aphorisms, 'The Buck Stops Here!' and 'If you can't stand the heat, get out of the kitchen.'[55] Meanwhile, Truman's detractors quipped, 'To err is Truman.'

In his own memoirs, Truman wrote 'that being a President is like riding a tiger. A man has to keep on riding or be swallowed.'[56] He elaborated that this metaphor taught him how to make decisions as president. He would learn all the necessary facts and information, seek good advice, make clear, firm decisions, and then not worry about whether he had done the right thing. In his study of how Truman organized and managed his administration, Francis H. Heller noted these qualities of Truman's leadership and decision-making.[57] Richard E. Neustadt wrote, 'The source of Truman's confidence was his ability, in his own mind, to live up to that image of the President as man in charge. His confidence was highest when he saw himself deciding and initiating.'[58] Later, President George W. Bush drew inspiration from Truman's decision-making style.[59] Neustadt also wrote that Truman's belief in his moral and constitutional obligations to protect the image and power of his office for future presidents influenced his decisions.[60] Neustadt concluded that 'Truman's image of the office made him sensitive to anything that challenged his position as decider and proposer.'[61]

Polls of historians since 1962 have consistently ranked Truman as a 'near great' president along with the likes of Thomas Jefferson Andrew Jackson, Theodore Roosevelt and Woodrow Wilson.[62] A 2017 CBS News poll of historians ranked Truman at number six, above John F. Kennedy and Jefferson. This poll specified that Truman earned his high ranking because of his effective 'crisis leadership'.[63] What are the criteria for ranking presidents and distinguishing 'near great' presidents like Truman from 'great' presidents, such as FDR? Scholars Robert K. Murray and Tim H. Blessing found that historians who rate presidents consider such qualities as decisiveness, intelligence, potential for growth and change, and integrity. A 'great president' also provides moral, inspirational leadership with a distinct vision of the future.[64] According to Marc Landy and Sidney Milkis, 'great' presidents like Abraham Lincoln and Franklin Roosevelt led 'conservative revolutions' because they preserved the constitutional order by reforming it.[65] Thus, a 'near great' like Truman who immediately succeeds a 'great' president of the same party is primarily responsible for consolidating and continuing the 'conservative revolution' of that 'great' president.[66]

While historians have ranked Truman as a 'near great' president since 1962, the American public's perception of Truman and his image varied considerably during his presidency and did not become consistently favourable until after his death in 1972. During Truman's tenure, Americans tended to evaluate him according to current developments and whether his responses to them seemed effective. For example, Truman's public approval rating stood unusually high at 87 per cent in May 1945, shortly after the Second World War ended in Europe. It was almost as high at 82 per cent after Japan surrendered.[67] In the Gallup polls, Truman's lowest job approval rating was 23 per cent in an opinion survey undertaken in November 1951, when Americans were frustrated by the military and diplomatic stalemate in the Korean War and high inflation.[68] As a point of comparison, Richard M. Nixon's approval rating was 23 per cent when he resigned from the presidency in August 1974.[69] When Truman prepared to leave the White House in December 1952, his public approval rating was just 31 per cent.[70]

The generally high regard for Truman among presidential scholars is mostly based on his decision-making in international crises, such as the Berlin airlift of 1948–49 and his dismissal of General Douglas MacArthur because of their differences over Korean War policy in 1951, the long-term consequences of the containment policy, namely the peaceful end of the Cold War and the dissolution of the Soviet Union, and the economic rebuilding of Europe through the Marshall Plan.[71] As one scholar observed, by the middle of 1949 Truman's foreign policy 'had pulled Europe back from the brink of economic collapse, established an alliance structure for Western collective defence, and moved steadily toward rehabilitating West Germany as a core ally.'[72] Likewise, historian John Lewis Gaddis concluded that these and other policies of the Truman administration, such as the creation of the North Atlantic Treaty Organization (NATO) and the Truman Doctrine, prevented the Soviet Union from expanding its political domination into Western and Southern Europe.[73]

These lofty appraisals of Truman's policies in Europe have served to burnish his image in the years since he left the White House. The peaceful end of the Cold War and dissolution of the Soviet Union in the early 1990s seemed to further enhance Truman's image as a patient, resolute, farsighted strategist in establishing and implementing the containment policy against communism. Studies of the Korean War evaluate Truman's leadership somewhat more ambivalently. Truman's assertion of the Constitution's civilian supremacy over the military and application of the limited war concept by dismissing General Douglas MacArthur have generally been commended.[74] Historian H.W. Brands, for instance, concluded, 'Truman hadn't yielded to communist aggression in Korea, but neither had he panicked and let himself be stampeded into World War III, by Douglas MacArthur or others.'[75] In contrast, Richard Whelan offered a more pessimistic assessment of what Truman's policies achieved: 'The Korean War resolved nothing. It had arisen in the first place out of the extreme tension and frustrations of the Cold War, and it served mainly to intensify them.'[76] Likewise, Alex R. Hybel criticized Truman's decision to intervene militarily in the Korean War as being 'void of a systematic analysis.'[77]

The fact that the Korean War ended in a ceasefire in which the United States and its UN allies prevented the communist conquest of South Korea contributed to the improvement of Truman's presidential image with the American public during the 1970s. The accelerated US military withdrawal from the Vietnam War in the early 1970s made it clear that North Vietnam's communist government would soon rule all of Vietnam. The results of Truman's policies in the Korean War seemed like victory by comparison.[78]

The 1970s marked a significant improvement in Truman's presidential image with the American people and a greater familiarity with his life, presidency and policies for several reasons other than the different outcomes of the wars in Korea and Vietnam. Truman died in 1972, less than two years before Richard M. Nixon's resignation from the presidency in 1974 to avoid almost-certain impeachment over his obstruction of justice pertaining to Watergate. For the remainder of the 1970s, Americans experienced stagflation; rising rates of violent crime, divorce and illegal drug use; energy crises; and the brief, uninspiring presidencies of Gerald Ford and Jimmy Carter. All this made it the most miserable decade for the nation since the 1930s. By comparison, the postwar era looked like the long-lost high summer of American power, prosperity and presidential leadership.

Under these circumstances, many Americans became nostalgic for a past that was supposedly better, simpler, more honest and more optimistic. The celebration of the nation's bicentennial in 1976 lifted the national mood, but not for long. The sense that yesterday was somehow better than today found expression in popular culture, as was evident in such long-running television programmes as *The Waltons*, a drama about a southern, rural family during the Great Depression and the Second World War, and *Happy Days*, a situation comedy about a middle-class family during the 1950s. As the 1970s ended, polls found that Americans' habitual optimism about the future was giving way to a pessimism about what it might hold.

The image of Harry S. Truman benefitted from the nostalgia boom for a better past. Many Americans were shocked and repulsed by Nixon's cynical ruminations and vindictive orders to his subordinates revealed by the Watergate tapes. As Nixon prepared to leave the White House, a book based on interviews with Harry Truman conducted in the early 1960s was published and quickly became a national bestseller. Entitled *Plain Speaking: An Oral Biography of Harry S. Truman* and written by Merle Miller, it became the basis for a television movie broadcast in 1976 and starring Ed Flanders as Truman.[79] The same actor portrayed Truman in a television movie about his meeting with Churchill and Stalin at Potsdam, and in a 1977 Hollywood movie, *MacArthur*, which showed the thirty-third president as a doughty defender of civilian superiority over the disrespectful general, played by Gregory Peck.

In *Plain Speaking*, Truman conveys the image of an earthy, folksy, bluntly honest, commonsensical 'everyman' who rose to the challenges of the presidency without being overwhelmed by its responsibilities or corrupted by its powers and prestige. In his interviews with Miller, he made clear that he had rejected all financial offers that would exploit his status as a former president.[80] Truman was content to live on his modest government pension in his home town of Independence, Missouri. Throughout *Plain Speaking* and in published collections of his letters, lectures and speeches, Truman emphasized that every president needs to separate himself as a private individual from the office of president to guard against personalizing the presidency, becoming corrupt and violating the Constitution.[81]

Truman's status with the public and with presidential scholars was further improved by the publication in the early 1970s of the first edition of *The Presidential Character: Predicting Performance in the White House*. Its author, political scientist James D. Barber, evaluated presidents psychologically and behaviourally according to criteria which then categorized them into four types. The two most recent presidents, Lyndon B. Johnson and Richard M. Nixon, were active-negative, a type Barber depicted as having the worst mental health and a tendency to abuse power and rigidly pursue courses of action that damage the nation, such as Johnson's expansion of the Vietnam War and Nixon's efforts to cover up the Watergate scandals. By contrast, Barber categorized Truman as active-positive, someone mentally suited to the post and having self-confidence and wholesome values from which 'he drew the strength to grow in office, to develop through learning without anxiety, as a person and as a President.'[82] Meanwhile, the popularity of

Plain Speaking and the sharp contrast between Truman and Nixon stimulated a plethora of books about Truman that were intended for general audiences. Margaret Truman, the former president's daughter and only child, wrote a best-selling biography of him in the early 1970s. In it, she concluded that her father 'did his duty. I am confident that history will do him justice.'[83]

Fortunately for researchers of his life and presidency, Harry Truman was a prolific letter writer and occasionally wrote diary entries. Historian Robert Ferrell edited two of the most valuable published collections of these: *Dear Bess: The Letters from Harry to Bess Truman, 1910–1959* and *Off the Record: The Private Papers of Harry S. Truman*. *Dear Bess* includes details about Truman's long courtship of his future wife and how much he missed her when she spent much of his presidency in Independence rather than the White House. On occasions he confided in her his doubts about his ability to serve as president. In a letter dated 28 December 1945, Truman wrote, 'There ought to have been more brain and a larger bump of ego or something to give me an idea that there can be a No. 1 man in the world. I didn't want to be.'[84]

All of this created a sympathetic image of Truman as a man of uncommon modesty and humility. *Off the Record* contains selected letters and diary entries from 1945 to 1971. One of the purposes of Truman's diary entries and unsent letters was to vent his frustrations about the presidency. In a 1949 diary entry, he complained, 'I have very few people fighting my battles in Congress as I fought F.D.R.'s.'[85] This kind of evidence enlarged the sense of Truman as feisty.

The publication of these and other works contributed to more television movies and miniseries about or including Truman. Besides Ed Flanders's film appearances as Harry Truman, the actor James Whitmore played him in a one-man stage show, *Give 'Em Hell, Harry!*, later televised as a live performance. Whitmore's Truman was witty, feisty and scrupulously honest. One year before the appearance of *MacArthur*, the president's confrontation with his general was the subject of a television movie, *Collision Course: Truman vs. MacArthur*. E.G. Marshall played the feisty president taking on Henry Fonda's military man. Whitmore, Marshall and Flanders all portrayed him as unassuming but courageous in his determination to protect his constitutional authority as commander-in-chief of the armed forces and willing to suffer controversy with Congress and unpopularity with the American public for his dismissal of MacArthur.

Two rock songs in the 1970s musically promoted Truman's image as an honest, straightforward 'everyman' and the idea that Americans needed a president like Truman to restore their faith in their nation and the presidency in the post-Watergate era. In its song *Harry Truman*, the rock band Chicago commended Truman for his blunt honesty and staunch patriotism as Americans had become disillusioned by politicians' lies and expressed confidence that the deceased president would know what to do about this. In his song *So Long, Harry Truman*, Danny O'Keefe praised Truman for scrupulously following such virtues as never cheating a friend, doing what he thought was right and assuming responsibility for difficult decisions in both his presidency and personal life. O'Keefe's song was sung to the refrain that it was now hard to find an honest man.

David McCullough's best-selling 1992 biography of Truman became the basis of an *American Experience* documentary broadcast by the Public Broadcasting Service (PBS) and a dramatized Home Box Office (HBO) miniseries in 1995. In the HBO miniseries, the actor Gary Sinise portrayed Truman as a more complex, nuanced and conflicted historical figure compared to the aforementioned actors. Sinise's Truman is honest and committed to public service but is occasionally plagued by self-doubt and moral ambivalence from his days as a county judge immersed in machine politics to his agonized decision to drop atomic bombs on Japan. The television audience also sees Truman as a devoted husband and father who wanted his wife to be more supportive and wrote a threatening letter to a music critic who harshly reviewed his daughter's singing.

Both the PBS documentary and the HBO miniseries highlighted Truman's 1948 presidential campaign and upset victory. In common with a number of Truman biographies and campaign histories, they highlight the Democratic electoral success in retaining control of the presidency and in regaining control of Congress and as a personal victory for him.[86] In particular, they highlight voter attraction to Truman's feisty 'give 'em hell' rhetoric in his 'whistle stop' campaign by train.[87] Some studies of the 1948 presidential election, however, claim that other factors were more significant in contributing to Truman's victory.[88] Irwin Ross contended that the minor party presidential candidacies of Henry Wallace as an anti–Cold War leftist and Strom Thurmond as an anti–civil rights southerner helped to increase electoral support for Truman from Catholics and African Americans.[89] In his history of the 1948 campaign, David Pietrusza concluded, 'A multitude of reasons brought a single result.'[90] Historian Gary A. Donaldson emphasized Truman's success in developing a broad, diverse electoral coalition in 1947 and 1948.[91] In my book on Truman's relationship with the Democratic Party, I emphasized the importance of his party leadership in maintaining the New Deal voter realignment that had taken place in the 1930s.[92] All of this coverage of Truman's remarkable, against-the-odds victory in 1948 highlighted his resilience and indefatigability, thus bolstering his historical reputation and image.

Throughout his nearly twenty-year retirement from the presidency, Truman reaffirmed his 'everyman' image by living quietly in his hometown of Independence, Missouri. He continued his morning walks and worked in his office at his presidential library.[93] Unlike later former presidents, he refused to serve on corporate boards or charge enormous speaking fees. His admirable humility was once again apparent. In his 2009 book *Harry Truman's Excellent Adventure: The True Story of a Great American Road Trip*, Matthew Algeo detailed a 1953 private automobile trip of Harry and Bess Truman from Independence to New York City to visit their daughter and celebrate their wedding anniversary. Contemporary readers might be startled to learn that Truman drove his own car and did not have Secret Service protection or media coverage. As Algeo remarked, 'Harry and Bess Truman's road trip also marked the end of an era: never again would a former president and first lady mingle so casually with their fellow citizens.'[94] Truman's down-to-earth qualities, his lack of hubris – in short, his admirable common-man character, were highlighted once more.

From the 1990s to the twenty-first century, detrimental facts about Truman that tarnished his popular 'everyman' image became more widely known to the American public. Most notably, Truman made blunt, controversial statements that were increasingly perceived as racist, sexist and inappropriate. While the status of women and African Africans changed after Truman's presidency, his beliefs did not. During his long retirement, he continued to think that women should not be active and powerful in politics and to use racial epithets to refer to African Americans.[95] He supported laws and court decisions to advance and protect the civil rights of African Americans, but he criticized civil rights demonstrations and opposed interracial marriages.[96]

While Harry Truman seems to have done little during his presidency and long retirement to mould his image, he was always careful to distinguish himself as a person from the office of president. He always sought to protect the public's image of and respect for the presidency by safeguarding its constitutional powers, status and ethics. In his personal life, Truman wore garish tropical shirts while vacationing, played poker, enjoyed a glass of bourbon, threatened a music critic who disliked his daughter's vocal performance and did not change his prejudices about African Americans and women in politics. As president, Truman believed that he had a constitutional and moral obligation to his office to advance the civil rights of African Americans through executive orders and the submission of civil rights bills to Congress, preserve the civilian supremacy over the military by removing General Douglas MacArthur from command, intervene in the Korean War in order to fulfil the UN's obligation to deter aggression, recognize Israel and conduct the Berlin airlift to assert Western access to Berlin. Truman was content to let history and future generations evaluate his presidential record and image. In the future, as in the past and present, interpretations of the 'everyman' image, life and presidency of Harry S. Truman will be influenced by changes in the values, perspectives and experiences of Americans. In his biography of his old boss, journalist Jonathan Daniels, who served as FDR's last and Truman's first press secretary, concluded that his 'everyman' presidency taught Americans that 'their greatness lies in themselves.'[97]

Notes

1   Kernell, Samuel, *Going Public: New Strategies of Presidential Leadership* (Washington, DC: CQ Press, 1996), p. 23.
2   Truman, Harry S., *Memoirs: 1946–1952, Years of Trial and Hope* (New York: New American Library, 1956), p. 208.
3   Ibid.
4   Gardner, Michael R., *Harry Truman and Civil Rights: Moral Courage and Political Risks* (Carbondale: Southern Illinois University Press, 2002), p. 202.
5   Haydock, Michael D., *City under Siege: The Berlin Blockade and Airlift, 1948–1949* (Washington, DC: Brassey's, Inc., 1999), p. 153.
6   Cohen, Michael J., *Truman and Israel* (Berkeley: University of California Press, 1990), pp. 218–20.

7   Hamby, Alonzo L., *Man of the People: A Life of Harry S. Truman* (New York: Oxford University Press, 1995), p. 641.

8   Dallek, Robert, *Harry S. Truman* (New York: Thorndike Press, 2008), pp. 152–3.

9   Savage, Sean J., *Roosevelt: The Party Leader, 1932–1945* (Lexington: University Press of Kentucky, 1991), p. 1.

10 Neustadt, Richard E., *Presidential Power and the Modern Presidents* (New York: Free Press, 1990), p. 80.

11 Baime, A.J., *The Accidental President: Harry S. Truman and the Four Months That Changed the World* (New York: Houghton Mifflin Harcourt, 2017), p. x.

12 Ragsdale, Lyn, ed., *Vital Statistics on the Presidency: Washington to Clinton* (Washington, DC: CQ Press, 1996), pp. 27–8.

13 Rozell, Mark J., and William D. Pederson, eds., *FDR and the Modern Presidency: Leadership and Legacy* (Westport, CT: Praeger, 1997).

14 Savage, *Roosevelt: The Party Leader, 1932–1945*, p. 183.

15 Leuchtenburg, William E., *Franklin D. Roosevelt and the New Deal, 1932–1940* (New York: Harper & Row, 1963), p. 331.

16 Robinson, Edgar E., *The Roosevelt Leadership, 1933–1945* (Philadelphia, PA: Lippincott, 1955), p. 17.

17 Burns, James MacGregor, *Roosevelt: The Lion and the Fox* (New York: Harcourt, Brace and Company, 1956), p. 205.

18 Lowi, Theodore J., *The Personal President: Power Invested, Promise Unfulfilled* (Ithaca, NY: Cornell University Press, 1985), p. 65.

19 Burns, James MacGregor, *Leadership* (New York: Harper Torchbooks, 1978), p. 281.

20 Leuchtenburg, William E., *In the Shadow of FDR: From Harry Truman to Ronald Reagan* (Ithaca, NY: Cornell University Press, 1983), p. 3.

21 Ferrell, Robert H., *Choosing Truman: The Democratic Convention of 1944* (Columbia: University of Missouri Press, 1994).

22 Jordan, David M., *FDR, Dewey, and the Election of 1944* (Bloomington: Indiana University Press, 2011), p. 52.

23 Savage, Sean J., *Truman and the Democratic Party* (Lexington: University Press of Kentucky, 1997), pp. 17–21.

24 Ferrell, *Choosing Truman*, p. 88.

25 Miller, Richard L., *Truman: The Rise to Power* (New York: McGraw Hill, 1986), pp. 217–61.

26 Miller, Merle, *Plain Speaking: An Oral Biography of Harry S. Truman* (New York: Berkley Medallion, 1974), pp. 413–14.

27 Hamby, *Man of the People*, 287; McCullough, David, *Truman* (New York: Simon & Schuster, 1992), p. 336.

28 Abels, Jules, *The Truman Scandals* (Chicago: Regnery, 1952), p. 29.

29 Dunar, Andrew J., *The Truman Scandals and the Politics of Morality* (Columbia: University of Missouri Press, 1984), pp. 58–65.

30 Stone, I.F., *The Truman Era, 1945–1952* (New York: Random House, 1972), p. xxi.

31 Allen, Robert S., and William V. Shannon, *The Truman Merry-Go-Round* (New York: Vanguard Press, 1950), p. 229.

32 Abell, Tyler, ed., *Drew Pearson Diaries: 1949–1959* (New York: Holt, Rinehart and Winston, 1974), p. 186.

33 Lait, Jack, and Lee Mortimer, *Washington Confidential* (New York: Crown Publishers, 1951).

34 Anderson, Patrick, *The President's Men* (New York: Doubleday, 1968), p. 134.

35 Ferrell, Robert H., ed., *Truman in the White House: The Diary of Eben A. Ayers* (Columbia: University of Missouri Press, 1991), p. 296.
36 Clifford, Clark M., *Counsel to the President: A Memoir* (New York: Random House, 1991), p. 282.
37 Neal, Steve, ed., *HST: Memories of the Truman Years* (Carbondale: Southern Illinois University Press, 2003), p. 6.
38 Ibid., p. 162.
39 Skowronek, Stephen, *The Politics Presidents Make: Leadership from John Adams to Bill Clinton* (Cambridge, MA: Belknap Press, 1997).
40 Ibid., pp. 41–3; Zinman, Donald A., *The Heir Apparent Presidency* (Lawrence: University Press of Kansas, 2016), pp. 8–32.
41 Savage, *Truman and the Democratic Party*, p. 164.
42 Leuchtenburg, *In the Shadow of FDR*, pp. 19–20.
43 Graber, Doris A., *Mass Media and American Politics* (Washington, DC: CQ Press, 2002), p. 242.
44 McCullough, *Truman*, pp. 39–88.
45 Dorsett, Lyle W., *The Pendergast Machine* (New York: Oxford University Press, 1968), p. 71.
46 Cooke, Alistair, *America Observed: From the 1940s to the 1980s* (New York: Collier Books, 1988), p. 27.
47 Ibid., pp. 29–30.
48 Weisbrode, Kenneth, *Year of Indecision, 1946: A Tour through the Crucible of Harry Truman's America* (New York: Viking Press, 2016), p. 25.
49 Ibid., pp. 39–40.
50 Goulden, Joseph C., *The Best Years, 1945–1950* (New York: Atheneum, 1976), p. 211.
51 Acheson, Dean, *Present at the Creation: My Years in the State Department* (New York: Norton, 1987), p. 730.
52 Isaacson, Walter and Evan Thomas, *The Wise Men* (New York: Simon & Schuster, 1986), pp. 253–87.
53 Donovan, Robert J., *Conflict and Crisis: The Presidency of Harry S. Truman, 1945–1948* (New York: Norton, 1977), p. 107.
54 Savage, *Truman and the Democratic Party*, p. 97.
55 McCullough, *Truman*, p. 481.
56 Truman, Harry S., *Memoirs: 1946–1952, Years of Trial and Hope* (New York: New American Library, 1956).
57 Heller, Francis H., ed., *The Truman White House: The Administration of the Presidency, 1945–1953* (Lawrence: University Press of Kansas, 1980).
58 Neustadt, *Presidential Power and the Modern Presidents*, p. 147.
59 Draper, Robert, *Dead Certain: The Presidency of George W. Bush* (New York: Free Press, 2007), p. 402.
60 Neustadt, *Presidential Power and the Modern Presidents*, pp. 148–9.
61 Ibid., pp. 149–50.
62 Ragsdale, *Vital Statistics*, pp. 27–8.
63 Associated Press, 'Presidents Ranked from Worst to Best,' *CBS News*, 2018, https://www.cbsnews.com/pictures/presidents-ranked-from-worst-to-best-presidential-historians-survey-2017/39.
64 Murray, Robert K., and Tim H. Blessing, *Greatness in the White House: Rating the Presidents, George Washington through Ronald Reagan* (University Park: Pennsylvania State University Press, 1994), pp. 41–63.

65 Landy, Marc, and Sidney M. Milkis, *Presidential Greatness* (Lawrence: University Press of Kansas, 2000), p. 6.

66 Ibid., p. 200.

67 Ragsdale, *Vital Statistics*, p. 194.

68 Ibid., p. 194.

69 Ibid., p. 201.

70 Ibid., p. 194.

71 Spanier, John, *American Foreign Policy since World War II* (Washington, DC: CQ Press, 1992), pp. 47–53.

72 Sestanovich, Stephen, *Maximalist: America in the World from Truman to Obama* (New York: Knopf, 2014), p. 37.

73 Gaddis, John Lewis, *The Cold War: A New History* (New York: Penguin Press, 2005), p. 34.

74 Alexander, Bevin, *MacArthur's War: The Flawed Genius Who Challenged the American Political System* (New York: Berkley Publishing Group, 2013); and Pearlman, Michael D., *Truman and MacArthur: Policy, Politics, and the Hunger for Honor and Renown* (Bloomington: Indiana University Press, 2008).

75 Brands, H.W., *The General vs. the President: MacArthur and Truman at the Brink of Nuclear War* (New York: Doubleday, 2016), p. 398.

76 Whelan, Richard, *Drawing the Line: The Korean War, 1950–1953* (Boston, MA: Little, Brown and Company, 1990), p. 373.

77 Hybel, Alex R., *U.S. Foreign Policy Decision-Making from Truman to Kennedy* (New York: Palgrave, 2014), p. 85.

78 Brands, *The General vs. the President*, p. 398.

79 Miller, *Plain Speaking*, pp. 20–1.

80 Ibid., p. 460.

81 Gallen, David, *The Quotable Truman* (New York: Carroll and Graf, 1994), p. 42.

82 Barber, James D., *The Presidential Character: Predicting Performance in the White House* (Englewood Cliffs, NJ: Prentice Hall, 1992), p. 339.

83 Truman, Margaret, *Harry S. Truman* (New York: Pocket Books, 1974), p. 634.

84 Ferrell, Robert H., ed., *Dear Bess: The Letters from Harry to Bess Truman, 1910–1959* (New York: Norton, 1983), p. 524.

85 Ferrell, Robert H., ed., *Off the Record: The Private Papers of Harry S. Truman* (New York: Penguin Books, 1980), p. 168.

86 Daniels, Jonathan, *The Man of Independence* (New York: J.B. Lippincott, 1950); and Phillips, Cabell, *The Truman Presidency: The History of a Triumphant Succession* (New York: Macmillan, 1966).

87 Golway, Terry, *Give 'Em Hell: The Tumultuous Years of Harry Truman's Presidency, in His Own Words and Voice* (Naperville, IL: Sourcebooks, 2011); White, Philip, *Whistle Stop: How 31,000 Miles of Train Travel, 352 Speeches, and a Little Midwest Gumption Saved the Presidency of Harry Truman* (Lebanon, NH: Fore Edge Books, 2014); Karabell, Zachary, *The Last Campaign: How Harry Truman Won the 1948 Election* (New York: Vintage Books, 2000).

88 Busch, Andrew E., *Truman's Triumphs: The 1948 Election and the Making of Postwar America* (Lawrence: University Press of Kansas, 2012).

89 Ross, Irwin, *The Loneliest Campaign: The Truman Victory of 1948* (New York: New American Library, 1968), pp. 270–1.

90 Pietrusza, David, *1948: Harry Truman's Improbable Victory and the Year That Transformed America's Role in the World* (New York: Union Square Press, 2011), p. 407.

91 Donaldson, Gary A., *Truman Defeats Dewey* (Lexington: University Press of Kentucky, 1999), p. 219.

92 Savage, *Truman and the Democratic Party*, p. 139.

93 Clark, Anthony, *How Presidents Rewrite History, Run for Posterity, and Enshrine Their Legacies* (Charleston, SC: Createspace Independent Publishing Platform, 2015), p. 4.

94 Algeo, Matthew, *Harry Truman's Excellent Adventure: The True Story of a Great American Road Trip* (Chicago: Chicago Review Press, 2009), p. 3.

95 Ferrell, *Truman in the White House*, p. 78; Miller, *Plain Speaking*, p. 195.

96 Leuchtenburg, William E., *The White House Looks South: Franklin D. Roosevelt, Harry S. Truman, and Lyndon B. Johnson* (Baton Rouge: Louisiana State University Press, 2005), pp. 151–225; Algeo, *Harry Truman's Excellent Adventure*, p. 223.

97 Daniels, *The Man of Independence*, p. 19.

Chapter 5

THE ART OF JOHN F. KENNEDY

Mark White

On the last night of his life, Thursday, 21 November 1963, President John F. Kennedy fell asleep surrounded by art. Arriving at the Hotel Texas in Fort Worth late that evening, after two days campaigning in the Lone Star state in preparation for his re-election bid a year hence, Jack and Jacqueline Kennedy were taken to room 850. They discovered that their suite had been hung, to mark the occasion of this presidential visit, with major works of art, a dozen in total. There were a Van Gogh, a Monet, a Picasso, and a Henry Moore sculpture. The Kennedys assumed these were all cheap reproductions. They were not, for local collectors had loaned them, apparently to make up for the way the hotel had slighted the First Couple by giving its best room to Texan Vice President Lyndon B. Johnson and his wife Lady Bird. In retrospect, this conversion of the Kennedys' hotel suite into an art gallery on the final night of JFK's life was appropriate, for as Charles Darwent put it in the *Guardian*, 'More than any previous first couple, the Kennedys had set out to make themselves icons, creatures of the eye, works of art.'[1]

It was also the case that artists had played a role in John Kennedy's personal and professional life. He was good friends with the New England painter William Walton. He had an affair during his presidency with bohemian artist Mary Meyer, sister-in-law of one of JFK's closest friends in the media, Benjamin C. Bradlee. Luminaries of the contemporary art scene, including abstract expressionist Mark Rothko, were invited to some of those legendary White House soirées which the Kennedys used to present themselves as patrons of the arts in America. This added to the sense that John and Jackie Kennedy exhibited a cultural sophistication that contrasted sharply with the apparent philistinism of Dwight and Mamie Eisenhower.[2]

The most important connection between JFK and the world of art was the way in which portraits of him shaped his iconic image. Image was exceedingly important to Kennedy, and more than any other president he succeeded in crafting an image that the American people found seductive. That image was of course influenced by depictions of him – for instance, in the newspapers and on television – that were sometimes beyond his control. But to a great extent, he was able himself to fashion the precise image he wished to convey to the American public.

With his father Joseph P. Kennedy's experience as a film producer in Hollywood in the 1920s and his extensive knowledge of public relations, JFK grew up with a precocious understanding of the importance of image. 'It's not what you are that counts, but what people think you are,' Joe Kennedy told his children. 'We're going to sell Jack like soapflakes,' he declared on another occasion. Not surprisingly, therefore, JFK soon developed a strong interest in the art of self-presentation. During the Second World War, he journeyed to California to see his close friend Charles Spalding, who was working in Hollywood for actor Gary Cooper. Spalding recalled:

> Jack was beginning to notice the parallels between people out there, like personalities drawing crowds. Why did [Gary] Cooper draw a crowd? And the other people out there: Spencer Tracy and Clark Gable and others who were floating through that world. So even though he was terribly self-conscious about it, he was always interested in seeing whether he had it – the magnetism – or didn't have it. We'd spend hours talking about it.[3]

Even before running for president, Kennedy succeeded in crafting a potent, multi-faceted image. In 1940 his first book, *Why England Slept*, a reworking of his Harvard undergraduate dissertation on the British appeasement of Nazi Germany, was published with help from his father and the business tycoon's friends. It was praised in reviews and sold well. It established the first component of JFK's image, namely that he was a man of letters. Three years later, his naval service in the Pacific aboard *PT-109*, for which he was decorated with a Navy and Marine Corps Medal and the Purple Heart, added another: he was a war hero. His subsequent political campaigns always stressed his military valour. He was also regarded as a sex symbol, from the time of his first (and successful) campaign for the House of Representatives in 1946. Years before he became president, he was described as the most handsome man in Washington and the most eligible bachelor in the country.[4]

Paradoxically, given his libertine lifestyle (even after his 1953 marriage to Jacqueline Bouvier), JFK was viewed as a symbol of family life. His father was one of the most prominent businessmen in the country and had been Franklin D. Roosevelt's Ambassador at the Court of St. James. His mother's father had been Mayor of Boston. His siblings were very active and visible in support of his political campaigns. By 1961, Robert F. Kennedy was attorney general and the second most powerful man in America, and by 1963 Edward M. Kennedy was senator for Massachusetts. Consequently, JFK was regarded not so much as a lone political figure but as a representative of a dynasty. Gorgeous photospreads in magazines such as *Life* and *Time* of Jack, Jackie and (after her birth in 1957) their daughter Caroline enlarged the sense of JFK as a familial symbol.[5]

The key issue in the 1960 presidential campaign, at least during the Democratic primaries, was Kennedy's religion: would a Catholic president owe his allegiance to the American Constitution or Rome? This was a vexing political problem for

Kennedy, one he handled by emphasizing his strong support for the traditional US separation of church and state. The one advantage of this aspect of the 1960 campaign was that it added another element to his evolving image – as a man of faith – for the premise of the discussion of his Catholicism was that his religious convictions were sincere.[6]

By the time Kennedy was elected president on 8 November 1960, Americans saw him as a war hero, man of letters, man of faith, sex symbol and family symbol. He seemed perfect. Although he had White House aides to advise him on relations with the press, he was essentially his own image guru. With his assassination on 22 November 1963, another strand was added to the tapestry of his image: a poignant sense of tragedy. When Jackie Kennedy a week later, in an interview for *Life* magazine, revealed that she and the late president had enjoyed listening to a record of the hit Broadway musical *Camelot*, by Frederick Loewe and Alan Jay Lerner, she succeeded in creating a name for the Kennedy legend by forever associating him with the Arthurian legend. Tragedy and myth, combined with JFK's assiduous self-promotion during his own lifetime, made for one of the most powerful images in American history.[7]

A key part of Kennedy's appeal was his visual impact. In pictures taken by leading photographers such as Richard Avedon and Mark Shaw, he beguiled many Americans. Such was the impression he made in 1960 in the first-ever televised presidential debate with Richard M. Nixon – as assured, attractive and a very plausible president – he moved ahead of the Republican nominee in the polls for the first time and stayed ahead until Election Day. Testimony to the importance of his more appealing appearance was the fact that the overwhelming majority of television viewers thought JFK had won that first debate, whereas radio listeners called it a tie or even a narrow victory for Nixon. The way in which artists portrayed Kennedy, both before and after Dallas, was also an important part of the process by which a visual sense of JFK was conveyed to the American people. To some degree, Kennedy could control this process as works by Norman Rockwell, Pietro Annigoni and Elaine de Kooning were commissioned by the *Saturday Evening Post*, *Time* magazine and the Harry S. Truman Presidential Library respectively, and only took place with JFK's approval and cooperation. Even then, he could not always anticipate the final work. In fact, Annigoni's portrait would appal him. The assassination served as a dark source of inspiration for artists such as Robert Rauschenberg. Martyrdom had been a major theme in early devotional art; it was salient in artistic depictions of Kennedy too. This essay, then, will examine these works in exploring how art has influenced the image of one of the most iconic presidents of recent times.[8]

The first notable artistic depiction of Kennedy was by Norman Rockwell for the cover of *Saturday Evening Post* on 29 October 1960. The context to Rockwell's portrait was the febrile 1960 presidential campaign in which JFK was battling the Republican nominee, Vice President Richard Nixon. A Rockwell portrait of Nixon appeared in the same publication a week later. Rockwell's work for the *Saturday Evening Post* was long-standing and legendary. He had produced his first cover for the *Post* in 1916. By the time his collaboration with the *Saturday Evening Post* ended forty-seven years later he had illustrated more than 300 covers.[9]

Rockwell would later furnish an account of his encounter with Kennedy in preparation for the oil on canvas he would produce:

> It was a cold, misty morning in Hyannis Port. Mr. Kennedy leaned out of an upstairs window in his pyjamas and said to go right on into the house, he would be down in a minute. While Mr. Kennedy ate his breakfast, I selected a room in which to take photographs. As I posed him, I remarked that I thought a rather dignified, serious pose would be best; his youthful appearance should not be emphasized. He agreed. Afterward we walked onto the breakwater near the house to see his sailboat. As we were returning to the house, Mr. Kennedy suggested that we try the pose again. He felt that he had been a little stiff the first time. We did, and his expression was just what I had wanted – serious, with a certain dignity, but relaxed and pleasant, not hard.[10]

Superficially, Rockwell's painting can be viewed as a benign portrait of a handsome man, one devoid of any weightier significance. In reality, the painting was highly political, and Rockwell intended it to be so. As his comments to Kennedy indicate, his main objective was to render JFK in a way that obscured his apparent youthfulness. Kennedy was forty-three but his Cary Grant-suntan (which he deliberately maintained) and his luxurious hair (which received constant pampering) made him seem younger. This issue of his youth and alleged inexperience had become a major one in the campaign. It was the case that a Kennedy victory would make him the youngest elected president in American history. And from that fact alone it could be inferred that Kennedy would be a callow leader of the nation. To JFK's chagrin, that was precisely the claim that Republicans made in 1960. The Democratic candidate sought to refute it at campaign rallies, such as one in Alexandria, Virginia, on 24 August 1960, where he argued that although Nixon had served for eight years as vice president, he was 'experienced [only] in policies of retreat, defeat and weakness.' Kennedy's statements on this issue represented an eloquent rhetorical rebuttal of the claim that he was too green to be president.[11]

Rockwell's *Saturday Evening Post* cover was the pictorial coda to those statements. As he and Kennedy had agreed, JFK's youthful looks were obscured. Lines around his eyes and on his neck are prominent, suggesting a worldly experience on Kennedy's part. Kennedy stares directly at the viewer in a way that implies the self-confidence of experience rather than the diffidence of youth. The sense of a distinguished, venerable Kennedy is highlighted in a relative sense by Rockwell's *Saturday Evening Post* cover of Richard Nixon a week later: the intense, brooding Republican nominee looks younger than his forty-seven years and uncharacteristically carefree.[12]

Figure 5.1 Portrait of John F. Kennedy by Norman Rockwell, Printed by permission of the Norman Rockwell Family Agency. Copyright ©1960 the Norman Rockwell Family Entities. Reproduced with the generous assistance of a grant from the Isobel Thornley Bequest.

In addition to the way it suggested Kennedy had sufficient gravitas and experience to be president, Rockwell's portrait implicitly spoke to another key issue in the 1960 campaign: religion. No Catholic had ever been elected president, and the one time a major party did nominate a Catholic as their candidate – Democrat Alfred E. Smith in 1928 – he had been trounced. After Kennedy declared that he was a candidate for president, his Catholicism became the major issue in the Democratic primaries. Would he owe his allegiance to Rome or the American Constitution, asked his detractors? Kennedy was compelled to defend himself publicly, insisting he was committed to maintaining the traditional American separation of church and state, and observing that no one had suggested he was unfit to serve his country in the Second World War by virtue of his religion. Even after he had secured the Democratic nomination, he had to confront the religious issue, most famously in Houston on 12 September 1960 before a gathering of Protestant ministers.[13]

Fundamentally, this issue was one of bigotry. Prejudice against Catholics earlier in the twentieth century had been pronounced, and despite his background of wealth and privilege JFK grew up with a keen sense of it; his father had been barred from the most prestigious clubs at Harvard because he was Catholic and not from the WASP establishment. The religious issue in 1960 was akin to the Birther Movement in which some critics claimed that Barack Obama had not been born in the United States and was thus ineligible to be president. Both sought to propagate the idea that a presidential aspirant or president was un-American.[14]

In refuting that idea, Kennedy could not have been painted by a more suitable artist than Rockwell, for he was widely regarded as the foremost patriotic painter of Americana. His iconic covers for the *Saturday Evening Post* included his 1943 interpretation of President Franklin D. Roosevelt's Four Freedoms. His Four Freedoms paintings toured America, raising more than $130 million for the war effort. Often his work had a distinctly wholesome flavour. For instance, he painted a lot for the Boy Scouts of America. In 1939, he left his native New York for Vermont, and fourteen years later he moved to Massachusetts. Small-town New England life became a major theme of his work, and enlarged the sense that Rockwell was a recorder of traditional American virtues.[15]

This approach was evident in Rockwell's painting of Kennedy who comes across as warm, robust, dependable and humorous. But it is also apparent from his depiction of Kennedy's hair, which is short, close-cropped, befitting a soldier or naval officer, which is what JFK had been in the Second World War. Presumably Rockwell's depiction of his hair was reasonably accurate but in fact it was often bouffant, which gave him a boyish appeal, and in photographs from this period in the presidential campaign Kennedy's hair looks somewhat fuller than it does in Rockwell's portrait. This way, then, Rockwell referenced Kennedy's service in the US Navy, the most undeniably patriotic thing he had done.

Kennedy, then, was the beneficiary of Rockwell's patriotic credentials. The widely held view that he painted what was best and most unsullied about America meant that his portrait of JFK infused the Democratic candidate with a sense of quintessential Americanness, and usefully, in terms of the religious issue in the 1960 campaign, that served to discredit the idea that he was un-American.

Rockwell's portrait also proved to be of long-lasting significance. After Kennedy's assassination, which moved the painter greatly, the *Saturday Evening Post* decided to republish this painting on 14 December 1963, bordered in black to denote mourning for the slain leader. Hence Rockwell's portrayal of JFK marked both his election as president and his tragic demise. Three years later, Rockwell celebrated Kennedy's legacy by painting *The Peace Corps (J.F.K.'s Bold Legacy)*, which showed JFK alongside Peace Corps volunteers. It is easy to dismiss Rockwell, as many critics did, as a lightweight painter of cliché and syrupy nostalgia. There was more to Rockwell than that, however, as his paintings for *Look* magazine later in the sixties on civil rights and poverty made clear. And his portrait of Kennedy for the *Saturday Evening Post* succeeded in conveying to the American people, on the eve of his election, that JFK would be a president of substance.[16]

A very different sense of Kennedy as man and leader was provided by Pietro Annigoni's controversial portrait a year later for the 5 January 1962 cover of *Time* magazine, which had chosen the young president as their 'Man of the Year'. The painting was controversial because although commissioned as a celebration of Kennedy as leader, it was unflattering to say the least. Annigoni's watercolour depicted a dishevelled Kennedy, with his collar and tie skew-whiff, his hair unruly and his 'lazy' right eye exaggerated so that it appeared hooded, squint-eyed. Moreover, a sombre, joyless mood permeates the portrait. It is difficult to gauge precisely how Americans responded to artistic portrayals of JFK, but in the case of Annigoni's painting we know how Kennedy himself reacted: he loathed it. Fuming, he called Hugh Sidey of *Time* to complain: 'I hear you sons of bitches have done it again.' 'You've ruined me,' he added. Kennedy got to the nub of the matter: 'He's made me look cross-eyed.' 'Well,' retorted Annigoni on hearing that criticism, 'he *is* cross-eyed.' Many readers of *Time* magazine most likely shared Kennedy's distaste for this troubling presidential portrait.[17]

This could not have been what Kennedy had anticipated from Annigoni. On the contrary, the Italian appeared the ideal choice for this undertaking. Influenced by Renaissance masters such as Leonardo da Vinci and Titian, Annigoni was unrepentantly traditional in his approach and technique. Accordingly, it would have seemed unlikely that he would produce anything too radical or disturbing when he sat down in the White House to paint the president.[18]

An Annigoni portrait of Kennedy seemed appropriate for two other reasons. First, royal portraiture had made him an international star. In 1955, his romantic, idealized portrait of Queen Elizabeth II was widely admired. Similar commissions followed, including the Shah of Iran, other British royals and Pope John XXIII. Working in this genre, Annigoni was part of a venerable artistic tradition. Hans Holbein and Diego Velázquez were but two of the Old Masters whose royal portraits were a feature of their work.[19]

Annigoni's association with royal portraiture made him a fitting choice to paint JFK. The Kennedys today are often referred to as America's royal family. That description dates back to John Kennedy's inauguration as president on 20 January 1961. The pageantry of the occasion, Jackie's princess-like appearance, JFK's decision to have the great poet Robert Frost recite his verse in a way that was reminiscent of the British royal tradition of the Poet Laureate caused commentators to discuss the monarchical aspects of the occasion. Being royal became a part of Kennedy's image. To be painted by the man who had famously portrayed Elizabeth II was entirely apropos.[20]

Annigoni also seemed suitable because of the other type of painting for which he was renowned: devotional art. A man of faith, much of his work was religious. He painted church frescoes in the area of his adopted town, Florence, and in the

Figure 5.2 John F. Kennedy, Pietro Annigoni, 1961, Watercolor on paper, National Portrait Gallery, Smithsonian Institution; gift of *Time* magazine © Estate of Benedetto Annigoni

monastery at Monte Cassino, south of Rome. Kennedy's affiliation as a Catholic to Rome had been a major part of the 1960 presidential campaign, but most importantly there was a symmetry to Annigoni's painting of religious icons and his portrayal of America's great secular icon.[21]

As a facility for portraiture and devotional art made Annigoni a perfect choice for *Time*'s Man of the Year commission, it could not have been anticipated that he would produce a painting that was unflattering rather than reverential. What helps account for Annigoni's approach is his experience when he visited the White House to paint JFK. Annigoni was struck by the relentless pressure of Kennedy's presidential responsibilities. Frustratingly for the painter, Kennedy never sat still as he read papers and greeted a constant stream of visitors. It was the strain of office that struck Annigoni as he observed Kennedy, and it was this sense of the onerous, energy-sapping responsibilities of leadership that permeates the portrait.[22]

Kennedy may have regarded the painting as irritatingly unflattering and hence the work of an artist who had lost form during the completion of this commission. It is sounder to see Annigoni's portrait as brave, psychologically astute and prescient in his portrayal of JFK. There had been at least an implicit pressure on the Italian, as with any royal portrait painter, to produce an idealized depiction, with any physical or psychological imperfections concealed. Holbein's 1537 portrait of Henry VIII is a good example of how official portraits often became exercises in flattery. To eschew that approach, therefore, necessitated a certain amount of courage on Annigoni's part.[23]

Annigoni succeeded in not only avoiding the sycophantic but in fashioning a warts-and-all analysis of Kennedy's character, now a key theme in the historiography on JFK. Just as Shakespeare in *Richard III* used the 'Crookback's' physical deformity as a metaphor for the deformity of his mind, so Annigoni exaggerated Kennedy's physical imperfections to suggest a dark undertow to his superficial charm and good manners. Less pronounced than is implied in *Richard III*, Annigoni's Kennedy nonetheless has hunched shoulders. In that, the Italian's portrait was accurate. Kennedy had always suffered from back problems, having been born with one leg slightly shorter than the other. Spinal surgery in 1954 had gone so badly that he was read the last rites. In the White House he sat on a specially designed rocking chair, often wore a back brace under his shirt, and sometimes used crutches (as Antony Sher would later do in his landmark performance as Richard III for the Royal Shakespeare Company).[24]

More conspicuous than the hunched shoulders is Kennedy's 'lazy' right eye, which the painter exaggerated. It was this which had so vexed JFK. Not only was it aesthetically unpleasing, the pronounced 'lazy' eye made Kennedy look devious and hence utterly different from the inspiring combination of Hollywood glamour, selfless naval heroism and academic integrity that had hitherto defined his image.

What Annigoni was suggesting was that there was a greater complexity to Kennedy than was implied by his fulgent image – that behind the sheen lay his true character with its darker features as well as its nobler impulses. In this way, Annigoni anticipated the future direction of historical scholarship. Following a decade of idolatrous 'Camelot' biographies after Dallas, many historians provided a harsher interpretation of the Kennedy years. By the 1980s and 1990s, writers such as Garry Wills, Thomas Reeves and Seymour Hersh portrayed Kennedy as a belligerent Cold Warrior and a slow and reluctant supporter of civil rights whose flawed character was evident in a private life of Caligula-like debauchery.[25]

Annigoni's portrait was prescient in another sense. There is something funereal both in its sombre, joyless mood and in the suit and dark tie worn by Kennedy. Like Cary Grant in Alfred Hitchcock's *North by Northwest*, Kennedy wore suits that were immaculate, crisply cut and glamorous. That was no accident, for Kennedy was interested in fashion. At a May 1961 White House luncheon for Grace Kelly and her husband Prince Rainier of Monaco, the former Hollywood star was surprised when Kennedy asked whether she was wearing Givenchy; she was. He was fastidious in his own apparel, so much so that magazines such as *Esquire* devoted entire articles to his wardrobe, including his preference in lapels and the number of suit buttons – he plumped for two, not three. But the suit in Annigoni's portrait does not express Kennedy's usual sartorial elegance. The fabric seems heavy and burdensome, and the cut neither reveals nor flatters his athletic physique. The skew-whiff tie is of a man whose professional preoccupations have diverted him from any concern with his appearance. This sad, funereal sense evoked by Annigoni's portrait reveals a president with a painful sense of his own mortality. In this way, his painting anticipates Kennedy's demise in Dallas.[26]

What was even more impressive about Annigoni's portrait was the way he captured an authentic sense of the inner man. His charming manners and elegant style masked inveterate pain and sadness. Hidden from public view was the child so hurt by the cold detachment of his mother that he would later describe her as a 'nothing'; the boy whose unending sequence of illnesses – including scarlet fever, bronchitis, German measles, whooping cough and acute abdominal pains – often left him hospitalized and alone; the young man whose Addison's disease and chronic spinal problems took him to death's door; the brother who by his early thirties had lost his eldest sibling Joseph, Sr., when his aircraft exploded in the Second World War, his beloved sister Kathleen in a plane accident in 1948, and his sister Rosemary whose mental problems were exacerbated by a paternally arranged lobotomy, which resulted in her being confined for the rest of her life to a nursing home in the Midwest. Rembrandt's ability to paint eyes that movingly depict an interior world in all those self-portraits (less so in his other portraits) was acute. Annigoni, too, succeeded in conjuring up feelings of loss and melancholy in the eyes of John Kennedy.[27]

Charming, charismatic, witty, the child of a distant Irish-Catholic mother, one-half of a famous and glamorous couple and a sexual adventurer – there was much about Elaine de Kooning that must have been familiar to JFK. He met her in December 1962 at the family's winter home in Palm Beach, Florida, where she made preparatory sketches for a portrait of Kennedy for the Harry S. Truman Library in Independence, Missouri. Kennedy's artist friend William Walton had recommended de Kooning because she was not only a gifted and skilled painter but had a reputation as 'The Fastest Brush in the East.' She could complete a portrait in just one session. That would be helpful, reasoned Walton, given that a restless Kennedy would never consent to a long formal sitting.[28]

De Kooning was an unexpected choice for this assignment as she had received few formal commissions in her career, painting mainly her friends in New York. Moreover, she had been a major figure in the Abstract Expressionist art movement, and so a curious choice for a presumably sober presidential portrait. But, in retrospect, it was an inspired selection. She had been a precocious talent and student of art. With her mother, she began to visit New York's Metropolitan Museum of Art from the age of five, decorating her bedroom with reproductions by Raphael, Rembrandt and other Old Masters. By the age of eight, she was selling portraits of her classmates. That talent would be honed by a substantial training. She attended the Leonardo da Vinci Art School and the American Artists' School, but by her own account the most rigorous instruction she received was from her husband Willem de Kooning, whom she met in 1938, marrying five years later. Along with Jackson Pollock and others, this Dutch painter forged an Abstract Expressionist movement that would shift the centre of the art world from Paris to New York. Willem gave Elaine strict and traditional lessons on how to draw. He would ask her to draw a still life, analyse it, rip it up and tell her to start again. In addition to her talent and technique, Elaine de Kooning brought to bear a formidable intellect, which would manifest itself in her success as an art critic and teacher at Yale and elsewhere. 'She had this lightning-quick brain,' recalled the painter Jane Wilson. 'Wit would ricochet around the room.' A key issue with Elaine de Kooning's body of work, one she mulled over herself, is the extent to which it has been obscured by the greater prominence of her husband's career. But two major retrospectives of her work since her death in 1989, one at the Heckscher Museum in Huntingdon, the other at the Smithsonian's National Portrait Gallery, have helped create a consensus that she was an important artist in her own right.[29]

When she arrived at the Kennedy estate in Palm Beach on New Year's Eve 1962, JFK was surrounded by reporters. The impression he made on her was profound. 'He was incandescent, golden,' she recalled. 'And bigger than life. Not that he was taller than the men standing around; he just seemed to be in a different dimension. Also not revealed by the newspaper image were his incredible eyes with large violet irises half veiled by the jutting bone beneath the eyebrows.'[30]

Like Annigoni, de Kooning encountered a president who never remained still. Reading papers, chatting on the phone, writing notes, crossing and uncrossing his legs, talking to his advisors, he was, said de Kooning, 'always in action at rest.' But whereas Annigoni was frustrated by Kennedy's unwillingness to sit still for his portrait, de Kooning appears to have viewed it as part of the president's energy and dynamism. Moreover, she adapted her approach accordingly. Rather than one complete portrait, she produced many. Each time he shifted his pose, she began another sketch in charcoal, casein, pen-and-pencil or watercolour. She often changed her own perspective, sometimes sitting opposite him, sometimes standing at an easel – even climbing up a ladder. After four days, de Kooning had produced dozens of sketches and rough portraits. Attempting to record the variety of Kennedy's poses meant that de Kooning ended up producing a veritable body of work on him, and that is one reason why she is the most significant artist to have portrayed JFK. By the time Walton visited her New York studio in November 1963, she had been working away feverishly for eleven months since her time in Palm Beach on thirty-eight large oil paintings.[31]

During those Palm Beach sessions, she continued to be as dazzled by Kennedy as she had been at their initial encounter:

I was struck by the curious faceted structure of light over his face and hair – a quality of transparent ruddiness. This play of light contributed to the extraordinary variety of expressions. His smile and frown both seemed to be built-in to the bone. Everyone is familiar with the quick sense of humor revealed in the corner of his mouth and the laugh lines around the eyes, but what impressed me most was a sense of compassion.

For his part, Kennedy enjoyed this 'sitting' more than those he had with other artists. 'I just remember talking and laughing and having a lot of fun,' the painter Alex Katz said of his sitting with her; and in Kennedy's case, although she was more quietly deferential than she would ordinarily have been as her subject was busy running the country, there was the sort of playful banter between the two that Kennedy relished.[32]

There were two ways in which de Kooning succeeded in capturing Kennedy more perceptively than did any other artist: one was the extravagant libido of the private man, and the other was the brilliance of his image. Sex had been a salient feature of JFK's private life and his public image. His physical attractiveness elicited much comment from the press, beginning with his 1946 campaign for Congress. Accounts of Kennedy on the campaign trail during his quest for the presidency in 1960 reveal an intensity akin to an Elvis Presley concert. Women were seen swaying, jumping, screaming, swooning. One woman was overheard murmuring: 'Oh, Jack I love yuh, Jack, I love yuh, Jack – Jack, Jack, I love yuh.' The erotic was a key part of his appeal. What furnished a sense of authenticity to his sex-symbol status was the private reality of a philanderer of spectacular proportions. His father had encouraged JFK and his brothers to lead hedonistic sexual lives. Joe Kennedy, Sr., led by example, embarking on a tempestuous affair with Hollywood siren Gloria Swanson and even taking her on family holidays. He also tried to date his sons' girlfriends as well as his sons' friends' girlfriends. As a young man, JFK developed a promiscuous sex life that would be unaffected by his marriage in 1953 to Jacqueline Bouvier. His wide range of partners included prostitutes, Hollywood actresses, Mafia molls, and – as president – numerous White House staff, including a teenage intern.[33]

A commissioned portrait of Kennedy for a presidential library could not be expected to reveal his priapic proclivities. Rather it would necessarily be respectful, formal and most likely complimentary. De Kooning, however, did explore Kennedy's sexuality. In part that approach derived from the fact that during her time in Palm Beach she developed a crush on him. She acknowledged that she had been 'a teeny little bit in love with [Kennedy]. In love with his mind, in love with the whole idea of such a gallant, intelligent, handsome man leading the country and the world.' Two leading authorities have written that she was 'smitten by Camelot. She adored the president and may have hoped to entice him into an affair.' After the assassination in Dallas, she felt that she had 'lost a brother or a lover. It was a personal loss.'[34]

The emphasis on the sexual reflected not only de Kooning's feelings for Kennedy but also her bold approach to portraiture that inverted the usual relationship in the history of art between the man as artist and the woman as model. Whereas her husband Willem usually painted women, Elaine de Kooning preferred painting men. 'I wanted to paint men as sex objects,' she said, and indeed it was the case that in a number of her sitting portraits the men's legs are spread apart suggestively. In addition to what could be viewed as her progressive artistic agenda, de Kooning's approach was probably influenced by her own voracious sexual appetite, in which regard she could have given JFK a run for his money. She had affairs throughout her marriage and even – it is reputed – furthered her husband's career by sleeping with, as well as painting, art critic Harold Rosenberg, gallery owner Charles Egan and the *Art News* editor Thomas B. Hess.[35]

In her portrait of Kennedy, de Kooning placed the emphasis on JFK the man rather than JFK the leader by stripping away the political context of presidential authority. What remains is a handsome, youthful-looking man in the Floridian sunshine. As writer Amy Pastan said of de Kooning's Kennedy portraits in the 2015 retrospective at Washington's National Portrait Gallery, they scream 'youth, movement, and intensity. There are no symbols of power or democracy.'[36]

De Kooning was able to focus on Kennedy's sexuality directly because he compelled her to do so. One morning during their Palm Beach sessions, he suddenly threw his leg over the arm of his chair so that his crotch was conspicuous. 'Is this pose all right?' asked JFK. 'Well,' replied de Kooning, 'it's supposed to be an official portrait,' implying that it would be more appropriate for her own private collection. Kennedy smiled and held the pose. 'I thought,' recalled de Kooning, 'Ok, I'll take what I get.' She smiled, nodded at him and proceeded to produce a casein sketch. She ended up doing two drawings of Kennedy in this unorthodox position, enjoying the informality of his pose. She was struck too by the sexually candid nature of the pose. As she observed, 'there was the presidential crotch, right at the center of the drawings.' That was appropriate for a man for whom sexual indulgence was central to his life.[37]

The intriguing postscript to these 'presidential crotch' drawings came after the assassination when Jackie Kennedy visited de Kooning's studio. Having already acquired some of de Kooning's portraits of JFK from a gallery, she indicated a desire to see more of them; hence the visit to her studio. But the meeting went badly. De Kooning found the former First Lady haughty and her attitude appeared to be, according to the artist, 'Well, here I am and I can have what I want.' As it turned out, what she wanted was the 'presidential crotch' drawings. The strong-willed de Kooning refused, saying she had decided to keep those for herself. In other words, they belonged to her *personal* collection on JFK. Unused to such a lack of deference, a furious Jackie Kennedy remarked, 'Well, they make him look like a fag on the Riviera.' 'They look good to me,' retorted the artist, and given the way JFK had exposed himself in his pose for those drawings, Jackie must have known what it was about them that appealed to de Kooning. After this tense exchange, she decided against ever letting Jackie Kennedy acquire any more of her JFK portraits.[38]

Decoding this encounter requires an understanding of Jackie Kennedy's priorities after Dallas. Foremost amongst them was an intense desire to bolster

Figure 5.3 John F. Kennedy, Elaine de Kooning, Oil on canvas, 1963, National Portrait Gallery, Smithsonian Institution. © 1963 Elaine de Kooning Trust.

her late husband's reputation. She was very concerned that historians might remember him uncharitably. Her use of the Camelot metaphor to compare her husband to King Arthur in the interview she gave to *Life* magazine a week after the assassination, her successful request to Lyndon Johnson that he rename the NASA Space Center the Kennedy Space Center, her insistence on having an Eternal Flame at his burial site in Arlington Cemetery, and her editing of the key early biographies of JFK by Theodore C. Sorensen and Arthur M. Schlesinger, Jr., were all part of her drive to use myth to counter history.[39]

Jackie Kennedy understood that post-Dallas reverence for JFK throughout the country was dependent on an admiration for him as a man as well as a political leader. She had been well aware of her husband's infidelities. Once whilst giving a White House tour to a *Paris Match* reporter, she passed by Secretary Priscilla Wear's desk and said in French, 'This is the girl who supposedly is sleeping with my husband.' Her suspicion was well-founded, and at one point there were at least three other women working in the White House doing the same thing. JFK had relied on a discreet Fourth Estate that would not search for sexual scandal and not report it if it did find any. During his lifetime, his image as a symbol of family life, transmitted to the American people by irresistible pictures of him with Jackie and their children, was not compromised by media coverage of his libidinous escapades. She was determined after Dallas that his reputation be glorified, not sullied.[40]

That constitutes the most cogent explanation as to why Jackie Kennedy sought to obtain de Kooning's 'presidential crotch' pictures. Unlike her husband, Jackie was a connoisseur of art history. Her hero was the French art historian André Malraux. Hence, she was not a naïve, ill-informed interpreter of artwork. She knew what those pictures were all about. She knew they were the most candid representation of her husband's exuberant sexuality ever committed to canvas. They were hardly the most dazzling pictures in de Kooning's Kennedy oeuvre. It seems unlikely therefore that Jackie Kennedy would have chosen these two works on aesthetic grounds. Rather she wanted to get the 'presidential crotch' sketches out of de Kooning's hands and to eradicate any possibility they would end up in the public domain.

One other related factor may well explain Jackie Kennedy's determination to obtain these pictures. They had resulted from a moment of genuine intimacy between her husband and the artist. There was a sense of JFK revealing his true self to de Kooning. He loved gossip and no doubt William Walton or another friend would have told him about her bohemian past and numerous affairs, in which case he would have been confident that she would be amused rather than offended when he showed his crotch. Vexation at what was a type of erotic encounter between JFK and de Kooning is another plausible reason as to why Jackie wanted to get those sketches out of the artist's hands. But for de Kooning, the Kennedy pictures continued to have erotic meaning. When Walton visited her studio in autumn 1963, he saw that she had put her Kennedy pictures and other images of him on all the walls, including her kitchen, bathroom – and bedroom. As writer Thurston Clarke puts it, when Elaine de Kooning 'made love, she saw him.'[41]

De Kooning captured Kennedy's potent image as well as his sexual potency. In the account she gave in December 1964 of her work on the Kennedy pictures, she explained how after the Palm Beach sessions she felt compelled to factor into her portraits a sense of his image:

Everyone has his own private idea of President Kennedy. The men who worked with him had one impression, his family another, the crowds who saw him campaigning another, the rest of the world, which saw him only in two dimensions, smiling or frowning on a flat sheet of paper or a TV screen, still another – and this last, by far the most universal. Beside my own intense, multiple impressions of him, I also had to contend with his "world image" created by the endless newspaper photographs, TV appearances, caricatures. Realizing this, I began to collect hundreds of photographs torn from newspapers and magazines and never missed an opportunity to draw him when he appeared on TV. These snapshots covered every angle, from above, below, profile, back, standing, sitting, walking, close-up, off in the distance. I particularly liked tiny shots where the features were indistinct yet unmistakable. Covering my walls with my own sketches and these photographs, I worked from canvas to canvas…always striving for a composite image.[42]

De Kooning understood that his image was important to how he was viewed. She wanted her portraits to capture the allure of that image. The way she achieved that was through her use of colour. De Kooning had fused her immersion in Abstract Expressionism with a penchant for figuration as revealed in her portraiture. Her technique was to sketch rapidly her subject's most conspicuous features, and then to overlay – as one pundit put it – 'slashes of vivid, colourful paint in all directions, in and outside the lines, and the image emerges with a jazzy energy'. A pivotal experience for de Kooning in her use of colour was her appointment in 1957 as a visiting professor at the University of New Mexico in Albuquerque. She had never before visited the American Southwest. Dazzled by the New Mexico landscape, she began to paint in more vibrant hues.[43]

In the case of de Kooning's Kennedy portraits, her sumptuous use of green, light blue and gold captures the sunny Floridian setting but also the allure of JFK's image: dazzling, intoxicating, seductive, with a strong suggestion of indulgent pleasure. De Kooning's portraits were not simplistically idolatrous. His posture and facial expression do not transmit a sense of heroic fearlessness. He often looks wistful. There is sometimes a slight frown and a sadness in the eyes. A man with a complex psychology is suggested. But still de Kooning's luxurious colours and the remarkable 'presidential crotch' sketches capture the brilliance of his image and his irrepressible sexuality more strikingly than did any other painter.

With the assassination in Dallas on 22 November 1963, John Kennedy's presidency was over, his life abruptly terminated, but he lived on in the collective memory of the American people. His eventful presidency, enduring image and tragic slaying ensured that this would be the case anyway. But his memorialization – schools and streets named in his honour; stamps and coins adorned with his image; biographies written as panegyrics – vivified Americans' memory of him. Artists played an important role in this memorialization of JFK, including Robert Rauschenberg.[44]

Rauschenberg was a protean talent. After training in Paris, North Carolina and New York, he displayed a Leonardo-like curiosity, constantly pursuing new lines of intellectual enquiry. He moved from abstract expressionism to Combines (paintings embedded with actual objects such as radios and fans) and on to transfer-drawings. Later on, he would choreograph live-performance shows, utilize technology in his art and produce sculptural works out of cardboard. Throughout, his approach was characterized by his use of whatever materials were close at hand, including old tyres or stones; the relishing of collaboration with other artists, such as the composer John Cage and the choreographer Merce

Cunningham; travel as a bridge to other cultures and to a broader personal understanding of different artistic traditions; and, most fundamentally, his opposition to the idea that painting was pre-eminent. Small wonder that artist Jasper Johns claimed Rauschenberg had 'invented more than any artist since Picasso.'[45]

A key chapter in Rauschenberg's story was his visit in 1962 to Andy Warhol's studio in New York. It resulted in his decision to focus on the making of silkscreens. With his transfer-drawings, Rauschenberg had applied lighter fluid to a magazine image, then used an empty ballpoint pen to transfer that image onto another piece of paper. The transferred image, which was the same size as the original, would often be strikingly ghost- or dream-like. With silkscreens, a technique used in commercial printing, Rauschenberg could both enlarge the transferred image and reproduce it numerous times. Beginning in 1962 and ending in 1964, he produced many silkscreens.[46]

In autumn 1963, Rauschenberg was working on a silkscreen with a prominent image of JFK, but the president was slain before its completion. The impact on the artist was profound, in part because the tragedy took place in the state where he was born and raised. Stunned by the assassination, he also felt that the enormity of the event was somehow appropriate given what he perceived to be the magnitude of Kennedy's presidential achievements. 'One of the things that was so shocking about his death,' said Rauschenberg, 'was that it was so believable; it wasn't out of scale with the strength and abruptness of all the things he'd done in office.' Uncertain at first as to whether it would be in good taste to continue to use this image of Kennedy, he decided to do so, and by 1964 had completed the silkscreen, *Retroactive II* [shown below].[47]

The image of Kennedy which Rauschenberg used was juxtaposed with other images, including a parachuting American astronaut, a military vehicle and an Old Master painting in which a woman gazes at her reflection in a mirror. *Retroactive II* was a pictorial representation of the Camelot school's lavish praise for Kennedy's life and leadership, and herein lies the key significance of the work. Rauschenberg had long been a fan of Kennedy. During the 1960 campaign, he had been impressed by Kennedy's progressive attitude to social issues such as civil rights. So inspired was he that as the election results came in on 8 November 1960 he began work on a solvent transfer drawing called *Election* with images of John and Jackie Kennedy, George Washington, an American eagle and a Greek sculpture. He sent the work to the Kennedys as a present to mark JFK's election victory. After Kennedy's death, Jackie and historians such as Sorensen and Schlesinger promoted a Camelot interpretation of his record as one of presidential greatness. In his boundless admiration for the late president, Rauschenberg was singing from the same hymn sheet. *Retroactive II* ensured that the effort to remember JFK by idealizing him was made in the world of modern art as well as historical writing.[48]

In *Retroactive II* the image of Kennedy selected by Rauschenberg was apt for a celebration of his life. He looks confident, and the way his finger jabs to emphasize

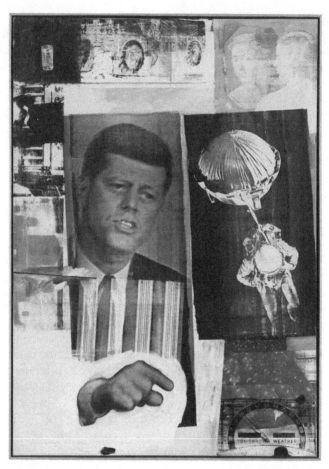

Figure 5.4 Robert Rauschenberg, *Retroactive II*, 1963. Oil and silkscreen ink on canvas, 84 × 60 inches (213.4 × 152.4 cm). Collection, Museum of Contemporary Art Chicago, Partial gift of Stefan T. Edlis and H. Gael Neeson. ©Robert Rauschenberg Foundation.

the point he is making adds to this sense of self-assurance. He is also Hollywood immaculate and debonair: the crisply-cut suit, perfectly coiffed hair and gleaming teeth. But it is not only the image of Kennedy that glorifies him. By including an American astronaut Rauschenberg drew attention to what many would regard as one of the most visionary aspects of his presidency: his determination to press ahead with space exploration and, as he vowed in May 1961, to send a man to the moon by the end of the decade. 'Rauschenberg would later come to associate the progress of the Space Race,' one art historian has observed, 'with the youthful promise of the Kennedy presidency.' It is striking that Rauschenberg's method for portraying JFK as an inspiring visionary was the same as Jackie Kennedy's. In the days after the assassination she made it a priority to persuade Lyndon Johnson to rename the NASA Space Center as the Kennedy Space Center, and even to change the name of Cape Canaveral to Cape Kennedy. She understood, as did Rauschenberg, that exploring the stars was a more eye-catching part of Kennedy's legacy than say his policy on housing or tax.[49]

In addition to Kennedy's space policies, Rauschenberg also referenced the way he had met the challenges of the Cold War by including an image of a military vehicle. JFK's handling of the Berlin Crisis of 1961 and of the Cuban Missile Crisis the following year were indeed examples of Kennedy's cool and adroit leadership in the international arena. It is instructive to note that Rauschenberg began to make silkscreens in autumn 1962, around the time when Kennedy defused the Missile Crisis, his greatest presidential achievement.[50]

As well as praising Kennedy as president, *Retroactive II* reflected on the tragedy of his assassination. In the image of Kennedy, the way his hand is disconnected from the rest of his body references his bodily disintegration on 22 November. Also included is an image of fruit that appears cannonball-like, which alludes to the gun violence that had killed Kennedy. There is also a thermometer with the approximate temperature in Dallas, 20 degrees, on the day of the assassination. The tragedy of the assassination, as well as Kennedy's bravura leadership, was a theme of *Retroactive II*.

Beyond these themes, there was another way Rauschenberg's silkscreen suggested the brilliance of Kennedy's leadership and the tragedy of his loss. Unlike Norman Rockwell, Rauschenberg was a cutting-edge artist. Accordingly, he seemed the right artist for the depiction of a president who had been path-breaking in a number of ways. The youngest elected president, Kennedy had launched new initiatives such as the Peace Corps and the Alliance for Progress. And his dazzling telegenic image was unprecedented too. The very fact that the avant-garde Rauschenberg regarded JFK as an appropriate subject for his art in itself conveyed the idea that Kennedy had been innovative, even cool.

The work of Rockwell, Annigoni, de Kooning and Rauschenberg played a significant role in shaping the image of John F. Kennedy. For the most part, these works glorified JFK. Rockwell's portrait served to refute the allegations made during the 1960 presidential campaign about Kennedy's youth, inexperience and Catholicism. De Kooning's vast body of work on Kennedy highlighted his dazzling image and sex-symbol status. Rauschenberg's silkscreen emphasized both the tragedy of his assassination and the extent of his presidential achievements, including his visionary leadership on space exploration. It was Pietro Annigoni who presented a more complex view of Kennedy. He conveyed a sense of the pressures of the presidential office and the inner pain and sadness of the man. In this way, it was Annigoni who succeeded in anticipating the future direction of historical scholarship with its warts-and-all interpretation of Kennedy rather than the image of perfection as man and leader propagated by the Camelot school.

Agency is a key issue in presidential image. For his part, JFK was the antithesis of Harry Truman who paid little attention to the cosmetic side of the presidency.

Kennedy was meticulous, indeed brilliant in his understanding of image and how to fashion it so as to impress. No one in the White House has ever been his superior in this regard. And it is to his credit. In a televisual era, image has really mattered to presidential credibility. How Jimmy Carter ended his presidency made that clear. So, Kennedy was justified in attaching importance to image. It would only be troubling if there were occasions when he placed his own appearance ahead of the national interest when it came to policy-making. But there are no instances of that. Such was the power of Kennedy's image that when others did influence it – individuals beyond his control – their depiction of him was usually flattering. This was the case with many journalists but also those major artists who portrayed him. This added sheen to his already dazzling image.

Notes

1   Darwent, Charles, 'JFK in Art: All the President's Pictures,' *Guardian*,
    20 November 2013, https://www.theguardian.com/artanddesign/2013/nov/20/jfk-art-
    president-pictures.
2   Oral history of William Walton, # 1, John F. Kennedy Library [JFKL], Boston, MA,
    https://www.jfklibrary.org/asset-viewer/archives/JFKOH/Walton%2C%20William/
    JFKOH-WW-01/JFKOH-WW-01; Janney, Peter, *Mary's Mosaic: The CIA Conspiracy
    to Murder John F. Kennedy, Mary Pinchot Meyer, and Their Vision for the World* (New
    York: Skyhorse, 2012); memorandum, dinner at the White House, 13 April 1962,
    Papers of Arthur M. Schlesinger, Jr., box WH-15, JFKL.
3   Documentary, *The Kennedys* (PBS, 1992); Hamilton, Nigel, *JFK: Reckless Youth*
    (London: Arrow paperback ed., 1993), p. 753; Blair, Joan and Clay Blair, *The Search
    for JFK* (New York: Berkley, 1976), pp. 482–3.
4   See White, Mark, 'Apparent Perfection: The Image of John F. Kennedy,' *History: The
    Journal of the Historical Association*, 330 (April 2013): 226–46.
5   Ibid.
6   The classic work on the 1960 presidential campaign is White, Theodore H., *The
    Making of the President 1960* (New York: Atheneum, 1961 paperback ed.).
7   White, Theodore H., 'An Epilogue: For President Kennedy,' *Life*, 55
    (6 December 1963), pp. 158–9; Theodore White typed notes of conversation with
    Jackie Kennedy on 29 November 1963, Personal Papers of Theodore H. White,
    box 59, JFKL.
8   White, *Making of the President, 1960*, pp. 325, 329.
9   Norman Rockwell, Portrait of John F. Kennedy, *Saturday Evening Post* cover, 29 October
    1960, Norman Rockwell Museum, https://www.nrm.org/2013/11/remembering-
    john-f-kennedy/, and Rockwell, Portrait of Richard M. Nixon, 5 November 1960,
    in 'Cover Gallery: Presidents,' *Saturday Evening Post*, 18 January 2017, https://www.
    saturdayeveningpost.com/2017/01/cover-gallery-presidents/; 'Norman Rockwell's 323
    Saturday Evening Post Covers,' Norman Rockwell Museum, https://www.nrm.
    org/2009/10/norman-rockwells-323-saturday-evening-post-covers/.
10 Quoted in Hart, Joan, 'Arts Everyday Living: Norman Rockwell's Presidential
    Portraits – Kennedy vs. Nixon,' http://artseverydayliving.com/blog/2012/10/
    presidential-elections/.

11 John Kennedy, speech at a Democratic rally, Alexandria, Virginia, 24 August 1960, JFKL, https://www.jfklibrary.org/asset-viewer/archives/JFKSEN/0910/ JFKSEN-0910-021.

12 Rockwell, Portrait of Kennedy, 29 October 1960, and Portrait of Nixon, 5 November 1960.

13 Goodwin, Richard M., *Remembering America: A Voice from the Sixties* (New York: Harper & Row, 1989 paperback ed.), pp. 83–5, 87–8; transcript of John Kennedy's statement at the Greater Houston Ministerial Association, 12 September 1960, in www.npr.org/templates/story/story.php?storyId=16920600.

14 Reeves, Thomas C., *A Question of Character: A Life of John F. Kennedy* (Rocklin, CA: Prima Publishing, 1992 paperback ed.), p. 21.

15 'Norman Rockwell: A Brief Biography,' Norman Rockwell Museum, https://www. nrm.org/about/about-2/about-norman-rockwell/. For a lucid overview of Rockwell's career, see Marling, Karal Ann, *Rockwell* (London: Taschen, 2010).

16 Rockwell, Norman, *My Adventures as an Illustrator* (New York: Harry N. Abrams, 1988), p. 412; 'Remembering John F. Kennedy,' Norman Rockwell Museum, https://www.nrm.org/2013/11/remembering-john-f-kennedy/; Halpern, Richard, *Norman Rockwell: The Underside of Innocence* (Chicago and London: University of Chicago Press, 2006), p. 128; 'The Peace Corps (J.F.K.'s Bold Legacy),' Norman Rockwell Museum, www.nrm.org/MT/text/PeaceCorps.html; 'Norman Rockwell: A Brief Biography.'

17 Pietro Annigoni, Portrait of John Kennedy, 1961, National Portrait Gallery, https:// npg.si.edu/object/npg_NPG.78.TC501; Halberstam, David, *The Powers That Be* (Urbana and Chicago: University of Illinois Press, 2000 reprint).

18 Obituary, 'Pietro Annigoni, 78, Dies in Italy; Noted for Portrait of Elizabeth II,' *New York Times* [*NYT*], 30 October 1988, http://www.nytimes.com/1988/10/30/obituaries/ pietro-annigoni-78-dies-in-italy-noted-for-portrait-of-elizabeth-ii.html; Pietro Annigoni, National Portrait Gallery, https://www.npg.org.uk/collections/search/ person/mp06620/pietro-annigoni.

19 Obituary, 'Pietro Annigoni,' *NYT*.

20 Lasky, Victor, *J.F.K.: The Man and the Myth* (New York: Macmillan, 1963), pp. 12, 14.

21 Obituary, 'Pietro Annigoni,' *NYT*.

22 Annigoni, Pietro, 'My Painting Meetings with Jacqueline, Kennedy, Queen Elizabeth and Pope John,' *Stile Arte*, 3 November 2014, https://www.stilearte.it/pietro-annigoni- i-miei-incontri-di-pittura-con-jacqueline-kennedy-la-regina-elisabetta-e-papa- giovanni/.

23 See portrait of Henry VIII, Walker Art Gallery, http://www.liverpoolmuseums.org.uk/ walker/collections/paintings/13c-16c/item-236761.aspx.

24 Dallek, Robert, 'The Medical Ordeals of JFK,' *Atlantic Monthly*, December 2002: 49–61, https://www.theatlantic.com/magazine/archive/2002/12/the-medical-ordeals-of- jfk/305572/; Sher, Antony, *Year of the King* (London: Nick Hern Books, 2004 reprint).

25 Wills, Garry, *The Kennedy Imprisonment: A Meditation on Power* (Boston: Little, Brown, 1982); Reeves, *A Question of Character*; Hersh, Seymour M., *The Dark Side of Camelot* (Boston: Little, Brown, and Company, 1997).

26 Oral history of Princess Grace of Monaco, pp. 1–4, JFKL; 'The Monogram on This Man's Shirt Is J.F.K.,' *Esquire* (January 1962), copy in JFKL.

27 For JFK's early years, including his medical problems and crises, see Hamilton, *JFK: Reckless Youth*; Dallek, Robert, *John F. Kennedy: An Unfinished Life* (London: Penguin, 2004 paperback ed.); Parmet, Herbert S., *Jack: The Struggles of John F. Kennedy* (New York: Dial, 1980).

28 Clarke, Thurston, *JFK's Last Hundred Days: An Intimate Portrait of a Great President* (London: Penguin, 2014), p. vii.

29 Moonan, Wendy, 'Why Elaine de Kooning Sacrificed Her Own Amazing Career for Her More-Famous Husband's,' *Smithsonian Magazine* (8 May 2015), http://www.smithsonianmag.com/smithsonian-institution/why-elaine-de-kooning-sacrificed-her-own-career-for-her-more-famous-husbands-180955182/; Stevens, Mark and Annalyn Swan, *de Kooning: An American Master* (New York: Knopf, 2016), pp. 159–61, 193, 211, 275–6, 567, 576, 579–80, 581–2; Strickland, Carol, 'Shining a Light on the Other de Kooning,' *NYT*, 21 November 1993.

30 de Kooning, Elaine, 'Painting a Portrait of the President,' in 'A President, Seen from Every Angle: Elaine de Kooning on Painting JFK, in 1964,' *ARTnews*, 10 April 2015, http://www.artnews.com/2015/04/10/a-president-seen-from-every-angle-elaine-de-kooning-on-painting-jfk-in-1964/.

31 Ibid.; Clarke, *JFK's Last Hundred Days*, pp. viii–xi; Cupic, Simona, 'The First Political Superstar: JFK as the New Image of History (1960–1963),' in Simona Cupic, ed., *The JFK Culture: Art, Film, Literature and Media* (Belgrade: American Corner, 2013), pp. 28–9.

32 De Kooning, 'Painting a Portrait of the President'; Strickland, 'Shining a Light on the other de Kooning.'

33 White, *Making of the President 1960*, p. 371. For detailed accounts of the sexual ethos and behaviour of the Kennedys, particularly JFK, see Reeves, *A Question of Character*; Hersh, *Dark Side of Camelot*; Wills, *The Kennedy Imprisonment*.

34 Cupic, 'The First Political Superstar,' pp. 30–1; Stevens and Swan, *de Kooning*, p. 433.

35 Cupic, 'The First Political Superstar,' p. 30; Moonan, 'Why Elaine de Kooning Sacrificed Her Own Amazing Career'; Stevens and Swan, *de Kooning*, pp. 240, 271–4, 346.

36 'Elaine de Kooning's JFK,' National Portrait Gallery, http://npg.si.edu/blog/elaine-de-koonings-jfk.

37 Quoted in Cupic, 'The First Political Superstar,' p. 30.

38 Clarke, *JFK's Last Hundred Days*, p. 362.

39 White, Mark, *Kennedy: A Cultural History of an American Icon* (London: Bloomsbury, 2013), pp. 85–97.

40 Oral history of Barbara Gamarekian, #1, p. 31, JFKL, https://www.jfklibrary.org/asset-viewer/archives/JFKOH/Gamarekian%2C%20Barbara/JFKOH-BG-01/JFKOH-BG-01.

41 Clarke, *JFK's Last Hundred Days*, p. ix.

42 De Kooning, 'Painting a Portrait of the President.'

43 Moonan, 'Why Elaine de Kooning Sacrificed Her Own Amazing Career'; Strickland, 'Shining a Light on the Other de Kooning.'

44 White, *Kennedy*, pp. 83–139.

45 Krcma, Ed., *Rauschenberg* (London: Tate, 2016), passim (including p. 5).

46 Entries for 18 September 1962 and 19 June 1964, Chronology, Robert Rauschenberg Foundation, https://www.rauschenbergfoundation.org/artist/chronology-new.

47 Retroactive I, Robert Rauschenberg Foundation, https://www.rauschenbergfoundation.org/art/art-in-context.

48 Krcma, Ed., *Rauschenberg/Dante: Drawing a Modern Inferno* (New Haven and London: Yale University Press, 2017), pp. 86, 88–9.

49 Rauschenberg, Robert, *Retroactive II* (1963), Museum of Contemporary Art Chicago, https://mcachicago.org/Collection/Items/1963/Robert-Rauschenberg-Retroactive-II-1963; Krcma, *Rauschenberg/Dante*, p. 62.

50 'Silkscreen Paintings (1962–64)', Robert Rauschenberg Foundation, https://www.rauschenbergfoundation.org/art/galleries/series/silkscreen-paintings-1962-64.

Chapter 6

'WE *SHALL* OVERCOME': LYNDON B. JOHNSON AS THE CIVIL RIGHTS PRESIDENT

Dean J. Kotlowski

'It is all of us, who must overcome the crippling legacy of bigotry and injustice,' President Lyndon B. Johnson told a joint session of Congress in March 1965, as he appealed for legislation to assure African American voting rights. 'And we shall overcome.'[1] By uttering the signature phrase of the civil rights movement, Johnson linked arms with African Americans as no previous president had. Arnold Arnoson, secretary of the Leadership Conference on Civil Rights, an umbrella organization of liberal groups, applauded this 'deeply-felt' address, noting that never had 'a civil rights bill come before Congress accompanied by so much zeal for its enactment.'[2] Johnson's words – along with the Voting Rights Act itself, signed by the president five months later [see below] – impressed many people. Charles Evers, a field secretary for the National Association for the Advancement of Colored People (NAACP), numbered Johnson among the 'few white folks who cared' about civil rights.[3] LBJ understood the resonance of his voting-rights efforts and success in winning passage of the Civil Rights Acts of 1964 and 1968. Near the end of his life, Johnson hosted at his ranch African American leader Leon Sullivan, to whom he delivered a forthright message: 'tell the people that we shall overcome.'[4] LBJ repeated those words a month before he died, in remarks at the Lyndon B. Johnson Library. Weeks afterward, the *Boston Globe* eulogized Johnson in an editorial titled 'L.B.J. – We Shall Overcome.'[5] The columnist Mary McGrory remembered the voting rights speech as Johnson's 'finest hour.'[6]

Johnson's rhetoric and record established his image as the civil rights president, the chief executive who did the most to achieve justice and equality for African Americans. Metamorphosing from conservative Texan senator to liberal US president, he appointed the first African Americans to sit in the Cabinet and on the Supreme Court, he promoted enactment of laws to outlaw discrimination and he instituted anti-poverty programmes that expanded opportunity for African Americans. Although Johnson did not overtly claim the title of Civil Rights President in the same way he assumed the moniker of the 'Education President,' he spoke movingly on behalf of racial equality.[7] Mainstream civil rights leaders

Figure 6.1 Lyndon B. Johnson signs the Voting Rights Act, 6 August 1965, with congressional leaders and civil rights leaders (including Martin Luther King) in attendance. LBJ Library photo by Yoichi Okamoto.

welcomed his gestures, appreciated his policies and affirmed his greatness. 'Johnson has done more to advance the cause of civil rights,' the 1963 March on Washington organizer, A. Philip Randolph, later asserted, 'than any president in the history of the country.'[8] Members of the black press agreed. During an exchange with Martin Luther King, Jr., on NBC's *Meet the Press* programme in 1967, Simeon Booker of *Ebony* observed that 'many people regard LBJ as a leader of the civil rights movement.'[9] Such perceptions shaped the historical literature. Kent Germany discerned a 'hero narrative' in studies of Johnson and civil rights, and Hugh Davis Graham identified LBJ as the movement's 'unanticipated hero.'[10] 'The black freedom struggle,' historian Steven Lawson explained, 'converted him from a routine defender of African Americans into the most vigorous advocate of racial equality ever to occupy the Oval Office.'[11] And Sylvia Ellis, in her monograph on Johnson's approach to the black struggle for freedom and equality, noted his desire 'to portray himself as a civil rights president.'[12] With a few exceptions, films and plays have accepted that interpretation.

Whatever its merits, talk of Johnson as the civil rights president remains problematic. LBJ's record on racial equality is largely, though not entirely, positive. He was not a civil rights leader, as King reminded Booker, but a politician responsive to the 'just aspirations of the Negro community.'[13] As a politician, he promoted his civil rights achievements selectively, when it advanced his interests. Moreover, Johnson the War President existed alongside, and even overshadowed,

Johnson the Civil Rights President. Richard Goodwin, who wrote the speech on voting rights, remembered that he 'loved' LBJ the moment he proclaimed, 'We shall overcome.' Yet within two years, Goodwin lamented, 'I would – like many others who listened that night – go into the streets against him.'[14]

The image that emerges is of a president striving to change history and to shape his legacy – and falling short. Johnson's civil rights and anti-poverty legislation, however commendable, failed to end racism and white privilege. Accordingly, LBJ's effort to cast himself as the civil rights president gained broad, although not universal, assent. In memory as in history, triumph, controversy and frustration defined the Johnson presidency on this score.

Johnson's Civil Rights Record

Johnson had to 'overcome' his own pre-presidential record in order to be seen as a civil rights president. Representing Texas in the US House of Representatives (1937–49) and the US Senate (1949–61), he seesawed on racial equality. On the one hand, he backed projects to benefit blacks economically and modest measures to protect voting rights. These endorsements reflected his empathy with the underprivileged, originating in his youthful instruction of impoverished Mexican-American schoolchildren in Texas in the late 1920s and his early embrace of the New Deal in the 1930s, with its optimism about government-inspired reform.[15] On the other hand, he bowed to the will of his overwhelmingly conservative white constituents and the bloc of powerful southern senators who promoted him to leadership posts in the upper house in the 1950s. During much of his congressional career, Johnson defended states' rights and voted against bills to discourage lynching and repeal the poll tax. As he looked to transcend his southern identity in order to win the White House in 1960, he steered the Civil Rights Act of 1957 through the Senate, while weakening its enforcement provisions.[16] Such manoeuvring reinforced another image of LBJ as a politician working both sides of the street.[17] Accordingly, he became 'poison' to many liberals, who protested his nomination as John F. Kennedy's vice-presidential running mate in 1960.[18] The labour lawyer, Joseph L. Rauh, Jr., mischievously organized liberal friends into a club, 'Johnsons Anonymous,' whose members took a drink 'every time they feel like attacking Johnson.'[19] A. Philip Randolph, LBJ's later champion when president, opposed his nomination for vice president, as did Bayard Rustin of the Southern Christian Leadership Conference (SCLC).[20]

Johnson began to emerge as a racial liberal while vice president. He chaired a committee to end bias in federal agencies and in companies with federal contracts. Although the panel posted modest breakthroughs, LBJ advocated civil rights publicly. Speaking in Gettysburg, Pennsylvania, on Memorial Day in 1963, he declared that a century after the Emancipation Proclamation 'the Negro remains in bondage to the color of his skin.' He rejected pleas for African Americans to exercise 'patience' and instead called on Americans to work to fulfil 'our hopes for universal freedom.'[21] The *Philadelphia Inquirer* praised Johnson for putting the civil rights crisis in 'proper perspective,' and the *Washington Post* applauded his 'eloquence,' 'courage' and 'vision,' as he 'summoned a bemused and lethargic Nation to face the challenge of its own high principles.'[22] According to columnist Drew Pearson, the speech had 'the groundswells of Lincoln's Gettysburg Address,' to the point that Kennedy aides were 'irked that it was the Vice President, not the President, who made it.'[23] Favourable coverage enhanced LBJ's civil rights credentials, as did praise from prominent African Americans. The psychologist Kenneth B. Clark later remarked that the Gettysburg speech 'opened up a new era of forthright civil rights leadership' from the White House.[24] Of course, grassroots protest in Birmingham, Alabama, had greater impact in forcing President John F. Kennedy to cast civil rights as a moral issue and push legislation outlawing discrimination in public accommodations, employment and federally funded programmes.

Courtship of civil rights leaders, along with a strong endorsement of JFK's bill, furthered Johnson's liberal reputation. On becoming president after Kennedy's assassination, he spoke with King, Randolph, Whitney Young of the National Urban League and NAACP Executive Secretary Roy Wilkins to affirm his support for the civil rights measure, which he championed in his first address to Congress: 'We have talked long enough in this country about equal rights ... It is time now to write the next chapter, and to write it in the books of law.'[25] The speech prompted the civil rights activist Stephen Spingarn to predict that LBJ would make 'a good President.'[26] Although African American leaders, grassroots protestors, congressional liberals and nationally minded conservatives played key roles in passing the Civil Rights Act in 1964, 'strategy and day-by-day tactics,' biographer Robert Caro averred, 'were laid out and directed by [Johnson].'[27] White House threats helped pry the bill from the House Rules Committee, while flattery encouraged Senate Minority Leader Everett McKinley Dirksen of Illinois to supply enough Republican votes to end a southern filibuster and ease its passage. On 2 July 1964, one hundred invited dignitaries assembled in the East Room of the White House to watch the president sign the measure into law on national television – and 'with 72 pens,' gushed the secretary of the Leadership Conference on Civil Rights.[28]

During Johnson's first two years as president, a combination of impulses, words and deeds revealed his support for civil rights. First, Johnson angled to be associated with racial equality. 'I'm going to be the best friend the Negro ever had,' the president informed Richard Goodwin. 'I've lived in the South a long time, and I know what hatred does to a man.'[29] In that vein, he pressed Whitney Young to assure blacks 'that I'm not a hater and a bigot.'[30] Second, LBJ built strong relationships with mainstream civil rights leaders – Randolph, Wilkins, Young and King – who, as Steven Lawson put it, 'joined him in playing by the rules of the legislative game.'[31] In particular Johnson corresponded frequently and fulsomely with Wilkins who, according to one presidential aide, was 'all the way with LBJ.'[32] Except for King, who used civil disobedience to achieve his ends and later criticized the Vietnam War, these leaders stuck by the president. Third, LBJ amassed an enviable record. According to historian William H. Chafe, the 1964

Civil Rights Act 'toppled' Jim Crow and the Voting Rights Act of 1965 'led to the massive increase in the franchise' for African Americans in the South.[33] Fourth, LBJ exhibited deep understanding of the challenges facing African Americans by insisting that economic progress must accompany the end to discrimination. He launched the War on Poverty in 1964, and a year later told the graduating class of Howard University that 'Negro poverty is not white poverty' and exclusion based on race or colour 'is matched by no other prejudice in our society.'[34] Finally, he took risks with white voters. During the election of 1964, the president denounced race-baiting. In New Orleans, he spoke of an unnamed southern senator who regretted that people in his state 'haven't heard a Democratic speech in 30 years. All they ever hear at election time is Negro, Negro, Negro.' A long silence, then 'scattered applause,' greeted Johnson's anecdote.[35]

Between 1963 and 1966, Johnson seized the civil rights mantle. He approved legislation passed in 1964 and 1965 in highly symbolic ceremonies. Surrounded by members of Congress and civil rights leaders, Johnson signed the Voting Rights Act in the Capitol, then gave a nationally televised address from a podium flanked by a bust and a statue of Abraham Lincoln.[36] LBJ's speeches tethered intense staff work with presidential ego. Goodwin and Assistant Secretary of Labor Daniel P. Moynihan composed the address at Howard, which they read to King and Young the night before Johnson delivered it.[37] Yet Johnson did not wish to share the adulation generated by the speech. Word of Moynihan's co-authorship leaked to the press, which upset LBJ and encouraged Moynihan to leave the administration.[38] Earlier, when reporters enquired about the origins of the 'We Shall Overcome' speech, LBJ aide Jack Valenti insisted that the president had written it.[39] To further highlight his leadership, Johnson sanctioned a film about his rights record, and the White House published his addresses in booklet form.[40] Fact sheets trumpeted the president's achievements – and ignored his pre-presidential votes against civil rights.[41] A copy of an anti-civil rights speech, made by LBJ in 1948, carried a warning to White House staffers: 'This is not EVER TO BE RELEASED.'[42] Conversely, criticism of Johnson drew sharp responses. When Franklin D. Roosevelt, Jr., chair of the Equal Employment Opportunity Commission, questioned the president's resolve to fight job discrimination, Johnson asked where Roosevelt had been 'the past several years.'[43]

Among his many breakthroughs, LBJ named the first African Americans to serve on the board of governors of the Federal Reserve (Andrew Brimmer), in the Cabinet (Secretary of Housing and Urban Development Robert Weaver) and on the U.S. Supreme Court (Thurgood Marshall). Between 1966 and 1968, he pressed for legislation to end discrimination in the selection of juries and the sale of housing, and the Leadership Conference on Civil Rights applauded his advocacy.[44] In the aftermath of King's assassination, the measure passed both houses and Johnson signed it, in what he called one of his 'proudest moments' as president.[45] Kudos from the Leadership Conference, with its close ties to the NAACP, underscored the White House's alliance with mainstream black leaders, including Randolph, to whom LBJ wrote: 'We will continue to work together for the other triumphs of justice.'[46] He courted prominent African Americans such as the novelist Ralph Ellison, whom he named to the National Council on the Arts, and the former Brooklyn Dodger Jackie Robinson, a Republican who managed to praise him: 'No American in public office has grown, as you have. No President could have affected the progress in our drive for human dignity as you have done.'[47] Johnson reinforced his civil rights credentials by aligning himself with Lincoln, whom he extolled for leading the country towards 'the establishment of a multi-racial community.'[48] According to African American journalist and Democratic Party hand Louis Martin, LBJ could proclaim '"We Shall Overcome" and no Black could question his sincerity.'[49]

In some respects, however, Johnson's embrace of civil rights proved less than firm. He failed to placate the Mississippi Freedom Democratic Party, an African American contingent seeking to displace that state's lily-white delegation at the Democratic National Convention in 1964. To avoid disruption of LBJ's convention – or coronation, some said – the White House vainly offered the Freedom Democrats token concessions, including the seating of two of their members as at-large delegates. The attempted compromise showed that Johnson the Dealmaker existed alongside – and at times in opposition to – Johnson the Civil Rights President. It also highlighted the realism of LBJ, who wished to avoid alienating white voters and southern lawmakers.[50] With respect to school desegregation, anathema to most white southerners, he achieved progress, but remained attuned to the 'political sensitivity' of enforcement – and left the task of implementing the Supreme Court's decision in *Brown v. Board of Education* (1954) to his successor, Richard Nixon.[51] More worrisome, LBJ's Great Society programmes raised expectations that proved difficult to meet.

Johnson's rhetoric, legislation and anti-poverty exertions did little to improve the lives of African Americans in cities, which exploded in rioting between 1965 and 1968. 'By and large the average black man in the ghetto has not profited within the past ten years,' averred Floyd B. McKissick, director of the National Congress of Racial Equality. Race relations shifted, as young African American leaders like McKissick rejected political norms, non-violent protest and racial integration in favour of community organizing and assertions of racial pride, black separatism and black power. According to Stokely Carmichael, chair of the Student Nonviolent Coordinating Committee, 'Black people across the country are becoming politically aware of their position, of their strength.'[52] Urban unrest fuelled white backlash demands to re-establish law and order, to which even liberals succumbed. 'There is no room in this country,' Vice President Hubert H. Humphrey declared in 1967, 'for violence, lawlessness, disorder, riot, arson, hooliganism.'[53] To remain out front of the law-and-order issue, Johnson signed the Omnibus Crime Control and Safe Streets Act of 1968 over the objections of the Leadership Conference on Civil Rights, which denounced the measure for stripping citizens of 'constitutional protections' and sanctioning 'broad invasions of privacy.'[54]

Rioting, Black Power and challenges to his vision of a multi-racial society whipsawed LBJ. On the one hand, Johnson's Department of Justice established 'a secret intelligence unit' to monitor urban unrest and 'Black Nationalist groups.'[55] On the other hand, White House officials considered, and ultimately rejected, outreach to Black Power advocates. Although these activists 'represent a lot of genuine frustration and anger,' Louis Martin advised, 'they aren't looking for conversation.'[56] LBJ instead remained close to established civil rights leaders, despite concerns about such a posture. As Ulric Haynes, Jr., an African American member of Johnson's National Security Council, explained: 'The Roy Wilkinses, Whitney Youngs, Dorothy Heights, Senator Brooke and others of the "Old Guard" are more reflective of the attitudes and approaches of whites than they are of those of Blacks.'[57]

After leaving office, Johnson endeavoured to prove his empathy for urban blacks, admitting to Doris Kearns Goodwin: 'I've moved the Negro from D+ to C-. He's still nowhere. He knows it. And that's why he's out in the streets. Hell, I'd be there too.'[58] While president, however, he bristled at criticism that he had failed to better the lives of African Americans. The 1968 report of the National Advisory Commission on Civil Disorders, which blamed white racism for black-white division and recommended increased investment in federal anti-poverty programmes, 'incensed him.'[59] As his presidency came to a close, LBJ found himself in a predicament partially of his own making. 'You are the principal civil rights leader in the country,' aide Harry McPherson told him in 1966, following a summer of urban rioting. 'This was of powerful assistance to you in 1964. It is something of a liability now. In my judgment, you cannot shake off that leadership. You are stuck with it, in sickness as in health.'[60] In this setting, Johnson began to pass up opportunities to address civil rights issues.[61]

Johnson's decision to dispatch US combat troops to Vietnam shattered his presidency, overshadowed his domestic accomplishments and, in varying degrees, strained his ties with civil rights leaders. The war had scant impact on his rather distant relationship with Jackie Robinson, who had backed LBJ in 1964 chiefly because Republican standard-bearer Barry Goldwater proved too conservative on civil rights.[62] In contrast, Vietnam halted LBJ's cordial association with Martin Luther King, Jr. In 1965, King had wept when the president proclaimed, 'We shall overcome.' Two years later, he attacked Johnson's Vietnam policy for exemplifying 'white colonialism,' inflicting 'atrocities' on the Vietnamese people and draining resources needed to fight poverty and injustice in America.[63] Vietnam also unsettled LBJ's staunchest allies. In 1968, A. Philip Randolph praised Johnson's 'war on white racism,' but also counselled disengagement from Vietnam.[64] Meanwhile, civil rights organizer Bayard Rustin had to deny newspaper reports that he favoured Johnson's re-election in the face of anti-war criticism by black activists.[65] Nevertheless, on LBJ's death in 1973, Rustin acknowledged: 'With the exception of Lincoln, no president contributed as much to the struggle for racial equality as did Lyndon Johnson.'[66]

The Making of the Civil Rights President

Robert Caro has asserted that Johnson 'wanted his presidency to be remembered in history for its great civil rights legislation.'[67] LBJ told Doris Kearns Goodwin: 'If I am ever to be remembered, it will be for civil rights.'[68] To that end, he wrote several reflective, and self-serving, letters on race during his last days in office. 'Time was catching up to the United States in the area of civil rights,' he informed one member of his administration, 'and I felt compelled to move the freedom process along as fast and as far as I could.'[69] To Clarence Mitchell, director of the NAACP's Washington bureau, Johnson expressed gratitude 'for all you have done for our common cause.'[70]

After LBJ exited the White House, his record acquired a unique lustre, partially because his successor, Richard Nixon, advanced the cause of civil rights via administrative action rather than landmark legislation or stirring speeches.[71] Johnson kept the focus on his record in his memoirs, published in 1971, in which he stressed his lack of prejudice, empathy for African American subordinates denied access to public accommodations and resolve to expend 'every ounce of strength I possessed to gain justice for black Americans.'[72] A year later, Johnson burnished his civil rights credentials before a gathering of African American professionals. He conceded that much work lay ahead, reiterated the breakthroughs made on his watch and invoked a familiar refrain: 'As I said on another occasion before a Joint Session of Congress one late evening seven years ago, "We shall overcome."'[73] Finally, Johnson maintained his ties with friendly black leaders, notwithstanding his sometimes boorish methods. For example, the Lyndon B. Johnson Library offered Ralph Ellison autographed copies of LBJ's memoirs – at the discounted price of $15 each. Ellison purchased three books.[74]

Partially to underscore LBJ's leadership, the Johnson Library organized a seminar on civil rights in December 1972. The occasion marked the opening of papers related to civil rights and an opportunity to ponder new ways to further 'equal opportunity.'[75] The programme, and the topic, proved as much personal as academic. According to historian Robert Dallek, 'Johnson looked forward to the symposium with pleasure; it was a chance to remember the greatest moments of his presidency.'[76] Among the guests were friends such as Ellison, and speakers included Lady Bird Johnson, Hubert Humphrey and mainstream civil rights leaders, such as Roy Wilkins, whose 'eloquent recapitulation' of Johnson's role in 'the Civil Rights movement' heartened the former president.[77] In his opening remarks, LBJ advocated action, especially in registering African American voters; emphasized the progress made over the past decade; and repeated the catchphrase 'we shall overcome.'[78]

Yet conversations about race, including this one, oftentimes unfold in unforeseen ways. At the end of the symposium, Kendall Smith of the Task Force on Racism and Roy Innis of the Congress on Racial Equality insisted that they, too, be permitted to speak.[79] Johnson agreed, and afterwards returned to the podium, where he advised the attendees to avoid verbal salvos and posturing, to draft specific proposals and to submit them to President Nixon.[80] In closing, he noted that 'to be black in a white society is not to stand on level and equal ground,' and for that reason, 'we must overcome unequal history before we overcome unequal opportunity.'[81] The crowd responded with a standing ovation, and Georgia state representative Julian Bond, a past critic of Johnson, hailed the former president as a 'human-hearted man.'[82] LBJ's summary comments, on the subject for which he most wanted to be remembered, represented his last public remarks. He died six weeks later.

Obituaries and retrospectives in the press lauded Johnson's support for civil rights. To be sure, newspapers struggled to assess LBJ's legacy amidst the Vietnam War, from which the US government was extricating itself when the former president died. Some editorial writers handled Johnson's death circumspectly by citing his attributes: patriotism, diligence, ambition, activism, political savvy, authenticity, compassion and 'larger than life' persona.[83] Many deemed him a tragic figure – a president of ability and arrogance who posted historic achievements at home while overreaching abroad.[84] Titled 'The Cruel Shadow', a cartoon in Little Rock's *Arkansas Gazette* showed a statue of Johnson, with his barely visible domestic enactments inscribed on the pedestal, shaded by a gigantic rock emblazoned with the words 'Escalation of Vietnam War 1965–1968'.[85] Nevertheless, many newspapers praised his record on race. 'His outstanding contribution,' the *Buffalo Evening News* averred, 'came in civil rights.'[86] The *Des Moines Register* agreed: 'His greatest achievement was in civil rights.'[87] Similar commentary was to be found in the South, where conservatives had resisted LBJ's policies. 'No president since Lincoln had created such a stir in Alabama,' a columnist for the *Birmingham News* observed.[88] The *St. Louis Post-Dispatch* noted 'that veteran civil rights spokesmen regard him as the greatest leader for their cause since Abraham Lincoln.'[89]

African American leaders celebrated Johnson's life and work. Unlike the mainstream press, African American newspapers eschewed chatter about a tragic presidency, refrained from emphasizing the war and focused on LBJ's domestic record. 'So great were his contributions on behalf of equal rights,' the *Baltimore Afro-American* editorialized, 'that his regretted role in the Vietnam disaster did not and cannot undo them.'[90] The *Atlanta World* hailed a legacy in civil rights 'unmatched by any other president.'[91] Both the *Norfolk Journal and Guide* and the *New York Amsterdam News* dubbed him the 'greatest civil rights president.'[92] Of course, scattered hisses resounded among the cheers. One letter-writer reminded the editor of the *Afro-American* that Johnson 'steadily lost minority support during the latter part of his term.'[93] Yet even black leaders not closely associated with Johnson extolled him. According to Ralph Abernathy of the Southern Christian Leadership Conference, 'black people and poor people in particular lost one of the greatest friends of democracy.'[94] The warmest words came from the president's long-standing allies in the movement. 'From the standpoint of poor white Americans and of non-white minorities,' Roy Wilkins wrote in his newspaper column, LBJ was 'the best' president.[95] Ralph Ellison similarly called Johnson 'the greatest American president for the poor and for the Negroes.' In 2006, historian Randall Woods ended his nearly 900-page biography of LBJ by quoting the novelist's words.[96]

Woods's citation of Ellison's tribute reflected a scholarly consensus that exalted LBJ's civil rights record. 'The effusive praise from key African-American leaders,' explained Kent Germany, author of a historiographical overview of Johnson and civil rights, 'punctuates a hero narrative in which civil rights victories and the ending of Jim Crow counter the dismal perceptions of his handling of Vietnam.' As he observed, such biographies and memoirs as Doris Kearns Goodwin's *Lyndon Johnson and the American Dream* (1976), Paul Conkin's *Big Daddy from the Pedernales* (1986), Joseph A. Califano's *The Triumph and Tragedy of Lyndon*

Johnson (1991), Robert Dallek's *Flawed Giant* (1998) and Woods's *LBJ* paint 'sympathetic portraits' of Johnson and civil rights.[97] To be sure, most of these works acknowledged his shortcomings, as did specialized studies that critiqued his surveillance of the Mississippi Freedom Democrats, King and others; his blaming of urban rioting on black radicals; and his spotty enforcement of school desegregation.[98] And Robert Caro disputed talk that Johnson lacked prejudice by recounting tales of young Lyndon playing cruel pranks on black people.[99] Nonetheless, most historians compared his record favourably with that of other presidents. In *Nixon's Piano: Presidents and the Politics of Race from Washington to Clinton* (1995), Kenneth O'Reilly credited only Lincoln and LBJ with tackling 'head-on' the subjugation of African Americans. Reviewing O'Reilly's book, Mary McGrory lamented that so many presidents had been so 'timid' on race.[100] Johnson's record also impressed other presidents. 'He did civil rights,' Nixon acknowledged, 'which was his one big achievement.'[101]

Films and plays generally have portrayed Johnson's presidency as complicated, matching exposé of the misadventure in Vietnam with favourable depictions of his civil rights initiatives. The conventions of historical scholarship of course do not apply to filmmakers and playwrights who stream existing stories through their 'own sensibility, interests, and talents.'[102] At the same time, historical adapters must balance dramatic licence against the need to remain faithful to factual accuracy, lest their work come under fire. Many biographical motion pictures (biopics) and plays about LBJ thus embody a 'warts-and-all' perspective.[103] Johnson's decisions with respect to Vietnam served to highlight the underside of his administration, while his 'we-shall-overcome' handling of African American rights provided a necessary counterpoint. Yet such an even-handed approach to the Johnson presidency left little room for calculating the pluses and minuses of LBJ's racial policies and thus furthered his image as the civil rights president.

David Grubin's documentary *LBJ*, which aired on public television in 1991, highlighted Johnson's complex overall record *and* his strong leadership on civil rights. 'Few presidents would ever know more triumph,' the narrator David McCullough began. 'Few suffered such a swift and tragic fall.' Civil rights, he continued, represented Johnson's 'first test,' and he passed it. Aided by motion pictures, photographs, testimonies and measured narration, the documentary acknowledged LBJ's southern roots and political compromises, then spotlighted his racial liberalism. 'He said over and over and over again,' recalled Roger Wilkins, nephew of Roy Wilkins and a Johnson appointee, 'I am going to be the president who finishes what Lincoln began.' White House assistant Jack Valenti and civil rights leader James Farmer stressed Johnson's push for the Civil Rights Act of 1964 over warnings that its enactment would cost him the South in the next election. Undaunted, he won passage of that law and of the Voting Rights Act. Indeed, footage of Johnson standing before Congress and declaring 'We shall overcome' segued into sights and sounds of African Americans singing 'We Shall Overcome' as they prepared to march across Alabama in support of voting rights. The film rendered the War on Poverty uncritically and sidestepped such shortcomings as the surveillance of black radicals, the Mississippi Freedom Democratic Party imbroglio and the glacial pace of school desegregation. Moreover, the urban riots emerged as 'a brutal fact of American life,' the by-product of white racism and a tragedy parallel to LBJ's Vietnam policy, which the documentary covered thoroughly. The film encouraged viewers to reconsider this presidency.[104] 'This is not a one-dimensional LBJ portrait, all monster, no saving grace,' journalist Haynes Johnson exclaimed.[105] 'However one finally assesses Johnson's accomplishments against his disasters,' observed *New York Times* television critic Walter Goodman, 'he seems more appealing here than he did a quarter century ago.'[106]

Path to War (2002), broadcast on Home Box Office (HBO), varied little in perspective from *LBJ*. Beginning with the inauguration of Johnson (Michael Gambon) in 1965, director John Frankenheimer examined how LBJ and his advisors led the United States into Vietnam. Frankenheimer depicted Johnson empathetically as a president caught between his predecessors' promises to defend South Vietnam and his overwhelmingly hawkish team.[107] Such empathy extended to LBJ's handling of voting rights, a lesser subject in this war-themed movie. Frankenheimer showed Johnson briefly venting about street protestors, and then conferring with Martin Luther King (Curtis McClarin), proclaiming 'We shall overcome' before Congress, and persuading Alabama Governor George C. Wallace (Gary Sinise) to request federal troops to protect civil rights workers marching from Selma to Montgomery. The Oval Office exchange between Johnson and Wallace proved captivating. It originated in memoirs, such as those of Goodwin, who depicted Johnson steering the diminutive governor to a sunken sofa, buttonholing him and appealing to his sense of legacy: 'Do you want a Great ... Big ... Marble monument that reads, "George Wallace – He Built"? ... Or do you want a little piece of scrawny pine board lying across that harsh, caliche soil, that reads, "George Wallace – He Hated"?'[108] *LBJ* also recreated the Wallace-Johnson encounter, employing on-camera testimony from two officials present – a vignette that, according to Goodman, exemplified Grubin's 'mastery of the television documentary.'[109] Such storytelling reinforced LBJ's image as a strong advocate of civil rights.

Johnson revisionism benefitted from the passage of time and a willingness by liberals in America's culture industries to look anew at the president's entire record. Frankenheimer stated that his perspective had evolved from condemnation of LBJ for taking America into Vietnam to adjudging him a 'great man brought down by this tragic event.'[110] Director Rob Reiner, who had once hated Johnson because of the war, commented, 'Nobody had a greater domestic legislative achievement than him, except for FDR. But you can't take Vietnam away.'[111] Reiner's film *LBJ* (2017) underlined Johnson's savvy, vulgarity, duplicity, deal-making – and emergence as a civil rights liberal between his years as Senate majority leader and his endorsement of the 1964 Act. At one point, LBJ (Woody Harrelson) informs his longtime mentor, Georgia Senator Richard B. Russell (Richard Jenkins), that he is wrong to oppose racial equality. In another scene, Johnson pushes aside the political risks in pressing for enactment of the strongest possible rights bill. He asks his staff: 'What the hell's the presidency for?'[112] During an era when President Donald J. Trump routinely engages in race-baiting, and when gridlock reigns in Washington, Reiner wanted to focus on civil rights and a chief executive able to 'get legislative accomplishments.'[113] Accordingly, *LBJ* mentioned the Vietnam War only in passing before the end credits.

Further revisionism altered the laudatory interpretation of LBJ and civil rights. Two plays by Robert Schenkkan applied a warts-and-all perspective to Johnson's record on race. In *All the Way* (2012), Schenkkan concentrated on the first eleven months of LBJ's presidency, particularly his efforts to win passage of the Civil Rights Act and end the Mississippi Freedom Democratic Party dispute. Actor Bryan Cranston, who portrayed Johnson on Broadway and in the 2016 adaptation for HBO, saw *All the Way* as 'dramatizing LBJ's political acumen in getting things done by any means necessary.'[114] Audiences watched Johnson cajole – and mislead – black leaders and southern members of Congress, order FBI director J. Edgar Hoover to place the Mississippi Freedom Democrats 'under constant surveillance' and listen 'with delight' to FBI audiotapes of King's amorous liaisons.[115] But they also heard Johnson assert that white southerners had to stop 'eating them nigras for breakfast every morning' and tell King that 'John F. Kennedy was a little *too* conservative for my taste.'[116] In the end, LBJ secures enactment of the civil rights bill, holds onto most of the southern delegations at the Democratic Convention and gives a master class in politics. 'I had to drag [my Party] into the light kickin' and screamin' every inch of the way. Did it make you feel a little squeamish?' he asks the audience. 'Cause this is how new things are born.'[117] Critics applauded the realism of this drama, which earned the Antoinette Perry ('Tony') Award for best play (Schenkkan) and best actor (Cranston) in 2014. The sequel, *The Great Society* (2014), carried the story of Johnson's manoeuvring on race to the end of his presidency, using vignettes that upheld his hero image (the 'We Shall Overcome' speech) and questioned it (the shadowing of black radicals). The play culminates in frustration, as the war saps LBJ's anti-poverty programmes and offends his allies in the civil rights movement. 'Who the hell does King think he is telling me how to handle Vietnam?' Johnson (Jack Willis) fumes.[118]

Schenkkan's plays underscored that Johnson's civil rights legacy has been contested. In 1972, a reporter described the former president's exchange with Smith and Innis at the Johnson Library as 'a demonstration reminiscent of the turbulent 1960s.'[119] Thirty-six years later, LBJ resurfaced in the race between Democratic presidential frontrunners Hillary Clinton and Barack Obama. As the young, inspirational Obama claimed the oratorical mantle of King, the less eloquent but more experienced Clinton insisted that progress stemmed from mastery of policymaking. 'Dr. King's dream began to be realized when President Johnson passed the Civil Rights Act,' she told Fox News. 'It took a president to get it done.' Controversy ensued. 'The interview caused a flap on cable TV and the blogs, where it was cast by some as a slight against King,' journalists John Heilemann and Mark Halperin observed.[120] It also underlined racial division, as an African American candidate embraced a black icon while his white opponent defended a white president. Although Clinton later praised King, the dispute raised the question of who merits credit for civil rights advances, movement activists or elite actors.

Minority and female filmmakers interested in the grassroots dimensions of the rights struggle have shown less reverence for Johnson's record. *Lee Daniels' The Butler* (2013) narrated the life of Cecil Gaines (Forrest Whittaker), a servant who works at the White House between the 1950s and 1980s. Inspired by the experience of longtime, real-life butler Eugene Allen, Daniels uses Gaines to explore the opportunities and constraints of domestic service, the movement for civil rights and, to a lesser extent, the exploits of a succession of presidents on race. In the film, LBJ (Liev Schreiber) comes across as loud and crass, ordering aides to halt the protests at Selma while he sits on a toilet. His speech assuring 'Negroes' the right to vote provokes scorn from one of Gaines's coworkers (Cuba Gooding, Jr.): 'Since when did he start calling us Negroes? That nigger uses the word nigger more than I use it.' Daniels also addresses Vietnam, which Martin Luther King, Jr., (Nelsan Ellis) chides as LBJ's 'tragic error.'[121] The underside of the Johnson years received further attention in director Kathryn Bigelow's *Detroit* (2017), which examined the Detroit riot of 1967 and the atrocities perpetrated by white law enforcement officials against African Americans in the Algiers Hotel. Although Bigelow neither features Johnson on screen nor blames him directly for these acts of violence, she includes audio from an LBJ speech justifying the use of force to quell unrest as context for the government's armed occupation of the Motor City.[122]

More critical of Johnson – and controversial – was the director Ava DuVernay's *Selma* (2014). Craggy and cranky, its Johnson (Tom Wilkinson) emerged as more antagonist than ally to King (David Oyelowo). During their first on-screen encounter, LBJ insists that 'this voting thing is just going to have to wait.' At their next meeting, Johnson seethes over the projected Selma-to-Montgomery march, declines to push voting rights legislation and castigates King: 'I am sick and tired of you demanding and telling me what I can and what I can't do.' LBJ afterward requests to see J. Edgar Hoover, presumably to order FBI investigation of King. Ultimately, the president reluctantly backtracks and addresses Congress on voting rights because of grassroots pressure and concern about his historical reputation. The harsh portrait of Johnson provoked condemnation from an array of journalists, scholars and LBJ intimates, who accused DuVernay of misrepresenting the historical record. Leading the charge was Mark Updegrove, director of the Johnson Library, which devoted a page of its website to documenting both the debate over *Selma* and Johnson's close collaborations with King.[123] The brouhaha echoed the Democratic primaries in 2008 in its exchanges over who propels history and America's fault lines on race.[124] The critics of *Selma*, directed by an African American, were largely white figures at leading print, cultural and academic institutions. But when *Selma* showed Johnson patting King on the shoulder, a group of African American teenagers watching the movie 'bristled at the power dynamic between the men.' DuVernay, for her part, claimed artistic licence. She conceded that the original screenplay had been 'much more slanted to Johnson' and that she ultimately decided against 'making another white-savior movie.'[125]

Reflections

The story of Johnson's image as the civil rights president is one of a leader struggling to make and to shape history. The legislation he helped pass and his rhetoric about racial equality constituted the most impressive aspects of LBJ's record. With respect to moulding his legacy, perhaps his wisest decision was to court mainstream civil rights leaders. They testified to Johnson's successes, avoided dwelling on his lapses and surfaced in various cultural representations. In Grubin's documentary, former aide Roger Wilkins recalled feeling 'bonded' to Johnson following the voting rights speech when, as he explained, LBJ became 'the civil rights president that we wanted and needed.'[126] In *All the Way*, Roy Wilkins acclaims Johnson as 'the best President the Negro has had since Abraham Lincoln' during a conversation with King, Abernathy, Bob Moses and Stokely Carmichael. Interestingly, none of these grassroots-oriented leaders echo Wilkins's approbation, and all express varying degrees of criticism of American politics and government.[127] Johnson's initiatives with respect to race proved too mixed to win universal praise. However historically misleading, *Selma* reminded audiences that LBJ had to be coaxed into action by movement activists and that no president, no matter how strong his record, can single-handedly and entirely dismantle the structures of racism and white supremacy.

Johnson could take heart from one reality: his rising reputation among scholars. At the time of his death, the *Washington Evening Star* predicted that LBJ 'will be counted among this country's near-great presidents.'[128] Forty-five years later, in 2018 this prediction appeared to come true. Johnson placed tenth out of forty-four presidents in a poll conducted by the American Political Science Association.[129] This ranking suggests that LBJ's image as the civil rights president is finally overshadowing his image as the Vietnam president in historical memory. 'His leadership in civil rights and his domestic vision in the Great Society,' Doris Kearns Goodwin asserted in 2018, 'will stand the test of time.'[130]

Notes

1   'Special Message to the Congress: The American Promise,' 15 March 1965. Online by Gerhard Peters and John T. Woolley, The American Presidency Project [henceforth APP], https://www.presidency.ucsb.edu/node/242211.

2   Arnold Aronson to Cooperating Organizations, 24 March 1965, folder 3, box I-37, Leadership Conference on Civil Rights (LCCR) Papers, Manuscript Division, Library of Congress (LC), Washington, DC.

3   Charles Evers Oral History, 3 April 1974, p. I-25, Lyndon B. Johnson Library (LBJL), Austin, Texas.

4   'LBJ on Civil Rights: "We Shall Overcome",' *Philadelphia Inquirer*, 23 January 1973, p. A-6.

5   *Boston Globe*, 24 January 1973, p. 22.

6   Mary McGrory column, 'The Overpowering Man Was Overpowered,' 23 January 1973, folder 5, box 132, Mary McGrory Papers, LC.

7   Joanna Ruth Jackson Goldman Diary, 30 July 1964, folder 16, box 6, Eric F. Goldman Papers, LC.

8   A. Philip Randolph address, 2 September 1968, folder: Speeches 1968, box 42, A. Philip Randolph Papers, LC.

9   *Meet the Press* transcript, 13 August 1967, p. 4, box 231, Lawrence E. Spivak Papers, LC.

10   Germany, Kent B., 'African-American Civil Rights,' in Mitchell B. Lerner, ed., *A Companion to Lyndon B. Johnson* (Oxford: Wiley-Blackwell, 2012), p. 114; Graham, Hugh Davis, *The Civil Rights Era: Origins and Development of National Policy, 1960–1972* (New York: Oxford University Press, 1990), p. 475.

11   Lawson, Steven F., 'Mixing Moderation with Militancy: Lyndon Johnson and African-American Leadership,' in Robert A. Divine, ed., *The Johnson Years*, Vol. 3: *LBJ at Home and Abroad* (Lawrence: University Press of Kansas, 1994), p. 105.

12   Ellis, Sylvia, *Freedom's Pragmatist: Lyndon Johnson and Civil Rights* (Gainesville: University Press of Florida, 2014), p. 55.

13   *Meet the Press* transcript, 13 August 1967, p. 4, box 231, Spivak Papers, LC.

14   Goodwin, Richard N., *Remembering America: A Voice from the Sixties* (Boston, MA: Little, Brown, and Company, 1988), p. 334.

15   Caro, Robert A., *The Years of Lyndon Johnson*, Vol. III, *Master of the Senate* (New York: Knopf, 2002), p. 719.

16   Ellis, *Freedom's Pragmatist*, pp. 16–100.

17   Frank H. Thurmond to Lawrence E. Spivak, 3 October 1960, folder: Program Response to Lyndon Johnson 10/9/60, box 44, Spivak Papers, LC.

18   Morse Henry to Editor, *Louisville Courier-Journal*, undated (*c.* 10 July 1960), folder: Program Response – Candidates Special 7/10/60, box 43, Spivak Papers, LC.

19   Joseph L. Rauh, Jr., to Myer Feldman, 16 September 1960, folder 7, box 36, Rauh Papers, LC.

20   A. Philip Randolph Oral History, 29 October 1968, p. 10 and Bayard Rustin Oral History, 17 June 1969, tape I, p. 2, both in LBJL.

21   'Johnson Hits Racial Bias,' *Baltimore Sun*, 31 May 1963, p. 4.

22   'Moment of Challenge,' *Philadelphia Inquirer*, 3 June 1963, p. A-18; 'A Voice from the South,' *Washington Post* [*WP*], 1 June 1963, p. A-10.

23   *WP*, 9 June 1963, p. E-7.

24   Kenneth B. Clark to Harry C. McPherson, Jr., 3 January 1969, in *Civil Rights during the Johnson Administration, 1963–1969*, ed. Steven F. Lawson (Frederick, MD: University Publications of America, 1984), reel 5, frame 349 (hereafter '*CRDJA*').

25   Lawson, 'Mixing Moderation with Militancy,' 84; Caro, Robert A., *The Years of Lyndon Johnson*, Vol. IV, *The Passage of Power* (New York: Knopf, 2012), p. 430.

26   Stephen J. Spingarn to Roy Wilkins, 30 November 1963, folder: 1963 N-Z, box 7, Roy Wilkins Papers, LC.

27   Caro, *Passage of Power*, p. xv.

28   Aronson to Cooperating Organizations, 6 July 1964, folder 2, box I-37, LCCR Papers, LC.

29   Goodwin, *Remembering America*, p. 317.

30   Beschloss, Michael, ed., *Taking Charge: The Johnson White House Tapes, 1963–1964* (New York: Simon and Schuster, 1997), p. 147.

31   Lawson, 'Mixing Moderation with Militancy,' p. 83.

32   Lyndon B. Johnson (LBJ) to Wilkins, 30 January 1967, folder 1967; LBJ to Wilkins, 17 January 1969 and 23 January 1969, folder 1969 – all in box 8, Wilkins

Papers, LC. Louis Martin to Joseph Califano, 28 February 1968, *CRDJA*, reel 4, frame 809.

33 Quoted in Graham, *The Civil Rights Era*, p. 452.

34 Pamphlet, *The Road to Justice: Three Major Statements on Civil Rights by President Lyndon B. Johnson*, undated (ca. 1965), *CRDJA*, reel 11, frame 466.

35 Typescript report via Western Union, undated (Fall 1964), folder 5, box 107, David S. Broder Papers, LC.

36 Evers Oral History, p. I-18, LBJL; 'Johnson Signs Voting Rights Bill,' *New York Times* [*NYT*], 7 August 1965, p. 1, 8.

37 Daniel P. Moynihan to Wilkins, 3 January 1966, folder 1966, box 7, Wilkins Papers, LC.

38 Moynihan to LBJ, 8 March 1971, folder 3, box I-176, Daniel P. Moynihan Papers, LC.

39 Jack Valenti to LBJ, 16 March 1965, *CRDJA*, reel 9, frame 791.

40 Valenti to LBJ, 24 February 1966, *CRDJA*, reel 3, frame 837; *The Road to Justice*, undated, *CRDJA*, reel 11, frames 448–474; Lee C. White to Wilkins, 9 April 1965 (plus attached statements and booklet), folder 1965, box 7, Wilkins Papers, LC.

41 'Voting Record and Excerpts from Speeches of Lyndon B. Johnson on Civil Rights,' undated [*c.* December 1963], *CRDJA*, Reel 12, frames 308–315.

42 Caro, *Master of the Senate*, p. 739.

43 LBJ to Franklin D. Roosevelt, Jr., 27 November 1965, *CRDJA*, Reel 5, frame 641.

44 Aronson to Cooperating Organizations, 17 February 1967, folder 5, box I-37, LCCR Papers, LC.

45 'Remarks Upon Signing the Civil Rights Act,' APP, 11 April 1968, https://www.presidency.ucsb.edu/node/237920.

46 LBJ to A. Philip Randolph, 23 April 1968, *CRDJA*, reel 5, frame 70.

47 White House Social Secretary to Mr and Mrs Ralph Ellison, 20 December 1965, and Juanita D. Roberts to Ralph Ellison, 11 March 1967, folder 8, box 53, Part 1, Ralph Ellison Papers, LC; Jackie Robinson to LBJ, 4 February 1965, folder 17, box 5, Jackie Robinson Papers, LC.

48 'Remarks at a Ceremony at the Lincoln Memorial,' APP, 12 February 1967, https://www.presidency.ucsb.edu/node/238274.

49 Louis Martin memoir, undated, p. 198, folder 8, box 9, Louis Martin Papers, LC.

50 Anderson, Terry H., *The Movement and the Sixties* (New York: Oxford University Press, 1995), pp. 79–81.

51 Kotlowski, Dean J., 'With All Deliberate Delay: Kennedy, Johnson, and School Desegregation,' *Journal of Policy History*, 17:2 (2005): 177 (quotation), 179.

52 *Meet the Press* transcript, 21 August 1966, p. 3, box 225, Spivak Papers, LC.

53 *Meet the Press* transcript, 26 November 1967, p. 3, box 233, Spivak Papers, LC.

54 Aronson to Cooperating Organizations, 14 June 1968, folder 6, box I-37, LCCR Papers, LC.

55 Califano to LBJ, 18 January 1968, *CRDJA*, reel 4, frame 744.

56 Harry C. McPherson, Jr. to George Christian, 1 August 1967, *CRDJA*, reel 3, frame 717.

57 Ulric Haynes, Jr. to LBJ, 8 April 1968, *CRDJA*, reel 5, frame 3.

58 Goodwin, Doris Kearns, *Lyndon Johnson and the American Dream* (New York: St. Martin's Press, 1976), p. 305.

59 Dallek, Robert, *Flawed Giant: Lyndon Johnson and His Times, 1961–1973* (New York: Oxford University Press, 1998), p. 516.

60 McPherson to LBJ, 12 September 1966, *CRDJA*, reel 11, frame 650.

61 Dallek, *Flawed Giant*, pp. 221–6, 322–9; Johnson handwritten comment on Douglass Cater to LBJ, 19 May 1966, folder: Handwriting – President Johnson May 1966 [3 of 4], box 14 Handwriting Files, LBJL; Johnson handwritten comment on Ben Wattenberg to LBJ, 26 April 1968, *CRDJA*, reel 5, frame 87.

62 Robinson to LBJ, 18 April 1967, folder 17, box 5, Robinson Papers, LC.

63 Garrow, David J., *Bearing the Cross: Martin Luther King, Jr., and the Southern Christian Leadership Conference* (New York: Vintage, 1986), p. 545.

64 Randolph Address, 2 September 1968, folder: Speeches 1968, box 42, Randolph Papers, LC.

65 'Speaker Says Negro's Future Lies with Lyndon Johnson,' *Jackson Daily News*, 15 December 1967; Eleanor Holmes Norton to Bayard Rustin, 4 January 1968; and Rustin to the Editors of the *NYT* (29 December 1967) and *WP* (2 January 1968) folder 5, box 25, Bayard Rustin Papers, LC.

66 Bayard Rustin statement for *The Crisis*, undated [February 1973], folder 5, box 5, Rustin Papers, LC.

67 Caro, *Master of the Senate*, p. 711.

68 Goodwin, Doris Kearns, *Leadership in Turbulent Times* (New York: Simon and Schuster, 2018), p. 351.

69 LBJ to Frank E. Smith, 16 January 1969, *CRDJA*, reel 5, frame 329.

70 LBJ to Clarence Mitchell, 2 January 1969, *CRDJA*, reel 5, frame 321.

71 Kotlowski, Dean J., *Nixon's Civil Rights: Politics, Principle, and Policy* (Cambridge, MA: Harvard University Press, 2001), pp. 266–8.

72 Johnson, Lyndon Baines, *The Vantage Point: Perspectives of the Presidency, 1963–1969* (New York: Popular Library, 1971), p. 157.

73 LBJ address, 5 April 1972, folder 1972, box 9, Wilkins Papers, LC.

74 Harry Middleton to Mr and Mrs Ellison, 29 October 1971 and Ellison to Middleton, 21 November 1971, folder 8, box 53, Part 1, Ellison Papers, LC.

75 Middleton to Ellison, 27 October 1972, folder 8, box 53, Part 1, Ellison Papers, LC.

76 Dallek, *Flawed Giant*, p. 621.

77 Civil Rights Symposium Program, 11–12 December 1972, folder 8, box 53, Part 1, Ellison Papers, LC; LBJ to Wilkins, 12 December 1972, folder 1972, box 9, Wilkins Papers, LC.

78 'Rights Seminar,' *Austin American*, 13 December 1972, p. 6.

79 'LBJ's Remarks Avert Symposium Disorder,' *Austin American*, 13 December 1972, p. 1.

80 Typescript of the Austin remarks, undated, folder 6, box 58, McGrory Papers, LC.

81 Woods, Randall B., *LBJ: Architect of American Ambition* (New York: Free Press, 2006), p. 884.

82 'Johnson Looked Tired, Sick at Last Public Appearance,' *Washington Evening Star*, 23 January 1973, p. A-5.

83 See editorials in *Montgomery Advertiser*, 24 January 1973, p. 4; *Scranton Times*, 24 January 1973, p. 6; *Pittsburgh Press*, 23 January 1973, p. 28; *Hartford Courant*, 23 January 1973, p. 26; *Chicago Tribune*, 24 January 1973, pp. 1–16; *Birmingham News*, 23 January 1973, p. 18; *Cleveland Plain Dealer*, 23 January 1973, p. A-10; *Indianapolis Star*, 23 January 1973, p. 14; Max Frankel column, *Dallas Morning News*, 24 January 1973, p. A-29 (quotation).

84 See editorials in *Arkansas Gazette* (Little Rock), 24 January 1973, p. A-6; *Boston Globe*, 24 January 1973, p. 22; *Buffalo Evening News*, 23 January 1973, p. 36; *Louisville Courier-Journal*, 24 January 1973, p. 18; *Milwaukee Journal*, 23 January 1973, p. 12;

Newark Star-Ledger, 24 January 1973, p. 20; *Philadelphia Inquirer*, 23 January 1973, p. A-8; *Atlanta Constitution*, 23 January 1973, p. A-4.

85   *Arkansas Democrat* (Little Rock), 24 January 1973, p. A-6.

86   'Lyndon B. Johnson,' *Buffalo Evening News*, 23 January 1973, p. 36.

87   'Lyndon Johnson,' *Des Moines Register*, 24 January 1973, p. 6.

88   'Late President Shook the State to Its Core,' *Birmingham News*, 23 January 1973, p. 17.

89   'The Ultimate New Dealer,' *St. Louis Post-Dispatch*, 25 January 1973, p. C-2.

90   'LBJ Touched Us All,' *Baltimore Afro-American*, 3 February 1973, p. 4.

91   'Lyndon Baines Johnson,' *Atlanta World*, 25 January 1973, p. 4.

92   See editorials in the *Norfolk Journal and Guide*, 3 February 1973, p. 6, and *New York Amsterdam News*, 27 January 1973, p. A-4.

93   'Our Readers Say: President Johnson Assessed,' *Baltimore Afro-American*, 3 February 1973, p. 4.

94   'Southern President Dedicated Full Energies to Equal Rights,' *Buffalo Evening News*, 23 January 1973, p. II-18.

95   Roy Wilkins column, 3–4 February 1973, folder R&T Syndicate Newspaper Column MSS, January–March 1973, box 47, Wilkins Papers, LC.

96   Woods, *LBJ*, p. 884.

97   Germany, 'African-American Civil Rights,' pp. 113–14.

98   Lee, Chana Kai, *For Freedom's Sake: The Life of Fannie Lou Hamer* (Urbana: University of Illinois Press, 1999), pp. 86–9; Garrow, David J., *FBI and Martin Luther King, Jr: From 'Solo' to Memphis* (New York: Norton, 1981); O'Reilly, Kenneth, *Racial Matters: The FBI's Secret File on Black America, 1960–1972* (New York: Free Press, 1991); Levy, Peter B., *The Great Uprising: Race Riots in Urban America during the 1960s* (New York: Cambridge University Press, 2018), pp. 82–6; Kotlowski, 'With All Deliberate Delay,' pp. 166–79.

99   Caro, *Master of the Senate*, p. 715.

100   Mary McGrory column, 'Presidents and Prejudice' (reviewing O'Reilly's book), 14 December 1995, folder 7, box 58, McGrory Papers, LC.

101   Crowley, Monica, *Nixon Off the Record* (New York: Random House, 1996), p. 18.

102   Hutcheon, Linda with Siobhan O'Flynn, *A Theory of Adaptation*, 2nd ed. (New York: Routledge, 2013), p. 18.

103   Bingham, Dennis, *Whose Lives Are They Anyway? The Biopic as Contemporary Film Genre* (New Brunswick, NJ: Rutgers University Press, 2010), p. 17.

104   *LBJ* (1991) (Hollywood: Paramount Entertainment, 2008). DVD.

105   'The Many Sides of "LBJ",' *WP*, 30 September 1991, p. C-6.

106   'Behind the Scenes in L.B.J.,' *NYT*, 30 September 1991, p. C-13.

107   Director Interview, *Path to War* (2002) (Home Box Office, 2003), DVD.

108   Goodwin, *Remembering America*, p. 323.

109   'Behind the Scenes in L.B.J.'

110   Director Interview, *Path to War.*

111   'Rob Reiner's "LBJ" Pays Tribute to a President the Filmmaker Once "Hated",' *Here and Now*, 30 October 2017, http://www.wbur.org/hereandnow/2017/10/30/rob-reiner-lbj.

112   *LBJ* (2017) (Culver City, CA: SONY, 2018) DVD.

113   'Rob Reiner's "LBJ".'

114   Cranston, Bryan, Introduction to *All the Way*, by Robert Schenkkan (New York: Grove Press, 2014), p. viii.

115 Schenkkan, *All the Way*, p. 93 (first quotation) and p. 44 (second quotation).

116 Ibid., p. 107 (first quotation), and p. 36 (second quotation).

117 Ibid., p. 123.

118 Schenkkan, Robert, *The Great Society* (New York: Grove Press, 2017), p. 107.

119 'LBJ's Remarks Avert Symposium Disorder.'

120 Heilemann, John, and Mark Halperin, *Game Change: Obama and the Clintons, McCain and Palin, and the Race of a Lifetime* (New York: Harper, 2010), p. 185.

121 *Lee Daniels' The Butler* (2013) (Beverly Hills: Anchor Bay Entertainment, 2014). DVD.

122 *Detroit* (2017) (Beverly Hills: Twentieth Century Fox Home Entertainment, 2017). DVD.

123 '*Selma* Movie,' http://www.lbjlibrary.org/press/selma-movie.

124 'Film Casts Johnson as Villain, Restarting Civil Rights Debate,' *NYT*, 1 January 2015, pp. A-1, 14.

125 Dowd, Maureen, 'Not Just a Movie,' *NYT*, 18 January 2015, p. SR11.

126 *LBJ* DVD.

127 Schenkkan, *All the Way*, pp. 76, 77, 78 (quotation).

128 'LBJ,' *Washington Evening Star*, 23 January 1973, p. A-8.

129 Rottinghaus, Brandon, and Justin S. Vaughn, 'How Does Trump Stack Up against, the Best – and Worst – Presidents?' *NYT*, 19 February 2018, https://www.nytimes.com/interactive/2018/02/19/opinion/how-does-trump-stack-up-against-the-best-and-worst-presidents.html.

130 Goodwin, *Leadership in Turbulent Times*, p. xv.

Chapter 7

NIXON IN CHINA: PRESIDENTIAL IMAGE IN MODERN OPERA

Mara Oliva

On Monday, 21 February 1972, President Richard M. Nixon arrived in Beijing for a one-week visit that 'would change the world.' The image of Richard Nixon and the first lady, Pat Nixon, in a vivid red coat, waving while disembarking the 'Spirit of '76' airplane made headlines around the world. Chinese Premier Zhou Enlai (Chou En-lai) led the reception committee at the airport. He offered the president his hand, which Nixon shook for a long time hoping to make up for Secretary of State John Foster Dulles's deeply offensive refusal to greet Zhou at the Geneva conference in 1954. 'When our hands met, one era ended and another began,' Nixon later recorded in his memoirs. It was, indeed, a historic moment. For the first time since 1949, when China had been 'lost' to communism, an American president had officially acknowledged the People's Republic of China (PRC).[1]

The meticulously organized visit was the high point of Nixon's time in office. The photograph of the president shaking hands with Zhou endowed him with a new image as a man of peace [see below]. In a report headlined 'Historic Handshake,' Max Frankel of the *New York Times*, winner of a Pulitzer Prize for his coverage of the visit, declared that Nixon's trip marked 'the end of a generation of hostility between the US and China.' Journalist Leonard Silk hailed Nixon as the new Marco Polo. James Reston, the dean of Washington political correspondents and one of Nixon's arch-critics, declared this to be the president's finest hour. For much of 1971, troubled economic conditions at home had depressed Nixon's poll ratings. On his return from Beijing, however, a Gallup survey recorded his approval rating at 56 per cent, marking the commencement of an upward movement in his popularity that would culminate in his re-election later that year. The same poll also found that over two-thirds of respondents thought the China visit would be effective in 'improving world peace.'[2]

The image of the talented statesman became, in the words of historian David Greenberg, 'a life raft' for Nixon to rebuild his reputation following his Watergate disgrace. On 9 August 1974, after months of painful legal battles and impeachment hearings over his involvement in the cover-up of an array of clandestine and illegal activities undertaken by members of his administration, Nixon left the White

Figure 7.1 Richard Nixon's historic handshake with Chinese Premier Zhou En-lai, Beijing, 21 February 1972. Source: Wikipedia public domain usage.

House with his reputation in tatters and one of the lowest approval ratings in the history of the US presidency. Only 24 per cent of Americans polled by Gallup believed he should have stayed in office. His successful trip to China and other foreign policy achievements became the foundations on which he tried to rebuild his credentials. Throughout the late 1970s and the 1980s, with the help of the influential foreign policy establishment, he worked tirelessly to shift the public focus from the shameful Watergate episode to his more significant contributions to international affairs and world peace.

This chapter contends that John Adams's opera, *Nixon in China*, was a product of this relentless rehabilitation campaign. Conceived in 1983, the work is one of the few pre- and post-Watergate art forms that present a fairly positive image of the thirty-seventh president of the United States. Though it did not change the public's negative perception of Nixon, it explored the president's personal thoughts and emotions through one of his major diplomatic achievements, thereby contributing to a new conversation in which the image of a corrupted leader could co-exist with that of a gifted diplomat.[3]

Nixon's Image: A Review

A man of many masks, Richard Nixon underwent several changes of image over the course of a political career that stretched from his starring role as a freshman congressman in the Alger Hiss case in 1948 to his search for post-Watergate redemption in the final twenty years of his life. The complexity of his image is one reason why cultural representations of him far outnumber those of any presidential predecessors or successors. Nixon's numerous portrayals in films, television series, novels, plays and an opera, alongside his own vast production of autobiographical writings, have combined to make him a major figure in the nation's cultural life.[4]

While often portrayed initially as a populist, self-made man who fought for ordinary Americans, Nixon's willingness in his early political career to use anti-communist smear tactics against electoral opponents prompted comparisons with Senator Joseph McCarthy (R-WI). The two images were on display in the 1952 presidential election campaign. Press charges that he benefitted from a slush-fund of contributions from business supporters nearly got Nixon dumped as Dwight D. Eisenhower's running mate on the Republican ticket. Salvation came through a half-hour address on national television presenting himself as a common man of modest means, an image that struck a chord with the public. Back on the campaign trail, he engaged in virulent red-baiting by accusing the outgoing Democratic administration of Harry S. Truman of appeasing communism's global expansion and tolerating traitors in government. As vice president, a 'new Nixon' came on display, a responsible statesman given to respectable rhetoric as he built up to running for president in his own right, but the old one was sometimes unleashed to denigrate his political opponents. Commenting on this inconsistency, his Democratic opponent in the 1960 presidential campaign, John F. Kennedy, quipped, 'I feel sorry for Nixon because he does not know who he is, and at each stop he has to decide which Nixon he is at the moment, which must be exhausting.'[5]

For his part, Nixon considered himself the victim of a liberal Eastern establishment that was determined to destroy him. His representation as fundamentally untrustworthy in numerous cultural outputs, most notably Herblock's cartoons in the *Washington Post*, Gore Vidal's 1959 Broadway play *The Best Man* (made into a film in 1964) and Philip Roth's 1971 novel *Our Gang*, fed his fears on this score.[6] In reaction, he became increasingly obsessed with micromanaging his public image as a safeguard against the manifold enemies that he saw lining up against him. This, in turn, gave rise to a new field of enquiry into his psychological fitness for office that became a flourishing genre of Nixon studies in the 1970s and beyond.[7]

After two major setbacks, defeat by Kennedy in the 1960 presidential election and by Edmund 'Pat' Brown in the 1962 California gubernatorial election, Nixon had the image of a loser. He then staged the most successful political comeback in US history by winning the race for the White House in 1968. In office, he devoted more time, energy and resources to image-making than any other president excepting John F. Kennedy. 'I don't worry about images . . . . I never have,' Nixon lied on NBC's *Today Show* in March 1971. More truthfully, he wrote in his memoirs, 'In the modern presidency, concern for image must rank with concern for substance.' According to his closest aide, H. R. 'Bob' Haldeman, Nixon was 'a man obsessed with maintaining what he perceived to be the correct public image.'[8]

Convinced that the Northeastern metropolitan press, notably the influential *New York Times* and *Washington Post*, was biased against him, Nixon reached out to the American public through television. His favourite form of communication via this medium was the set-piece presidential peroration to the nation, which he delivered on thirty-two occasions during his five and a half years in office (his predecessor, Lyndon Johnson, had given only fifteen). Obsessed with projecting his 'true image', he surrounded himself with aides who had worked in advertising or television; he developed the White House's first full-fledged public relations unit (staffed by recruits from the J. Walter Thompson advertising agency); and in early 1971, he inaugurated the White House Television Office, which had the services of a full-time producer. Even before Watergate stained his presidency and its reputation in history, however, Nixon's intensive public relations efforts only served to make him appear devious, manipulative and insincere in the eyes of his critics (or 'enemies' as he dubbed them).[9]

Although Nixon's career in public office ended when he resigned the presidency, he would soon launch another comeback campaign to restore his reputation. True to form, even after his resignation, he refused to let others define him, his image or his legacy. As historian Iwan Morgan noted, Nixon 'became his own historian'.[10] In December 1974, a few months after President Gerard Ford had pardoned him, he wrote in his diary, 'So be it. We will see it through. We have had tough times before and we can take the tough ones that we will have to go through now.' With expenses and lawyer fees eating into his assets, he began working on his memoirs, published in 1978 and the first of ten books he was to author after Watergate. In the summer of 1975, British journalist David Frost paid him $600,000 for a long interview. This was eventually broken down into four 90-minute episodes, broadcast in May 1977. Forty-five million viewers watched the first episode on Watergate, the largest audience for a political interview on record.[11]

Frost/Nixon was followed by numerous television appearances, speaking engagements, writing opportunities for prestigious print media publications and frequent travels to meet foreign leaders. In re-telling the story of his life and political career, Nixon used two familiar themes: first, the Horatio Alger myth that had supposedly characterized his rags-to-riches rise in his early years; second, his foreign policy know-how that had contributed to major breakthroughs in the Cold War and could still provide valuable expertise for the improvement of international relations.[12] Hoping to reignite some of the support generated by his first visit to China, Nixon met again with Mao Zedong and other Chinese leaders in Beijing in February 1976. Five years after leaving the presidency, Nixon decided to end his 'exile' in his San Clemente, California, home and move back East to better conduct his rehabilitation. In October 1979, he bought a town house on East 65th Street in Manhattan and moved again into a modern house in Saddle River, New Jersey, in 1982. In both places the former president hosted dinners and parties for prominent journalists and the foreign policy establishment.

The investment paid off. While his guests appreciated the gravity of Watergate, they considered foreign affairs a more important aspect of his presidency and thus helped Nixon build his new image as an elder statesman. Those who had been part of his foreign policy team, in particular Secretary of State Henry Kissinger, became ever more vocal in praising Nixon's performance as historic. Even distinguished diplomatic historian John Lewis Gaddis acknowledged in his publications that Nixon's Cold War record was highly successful. At a time when the disastrous US intervention in Vietnam had weakened American power and prestige, Nixon had regained the initiative against the Soviet Union through his strategy of détente. The apex of this process came in May 1986 when Katharine Graham, the owner and publisher of the *Washington Post* newspaper that had broken the story of the Watergate conspiracy, authorized one of her publications, *Newsweek*, to print a feature article entitled: 'He's Back: The Rehabilitation of Richard Nixon.' This was followed a few months later by a private meeting between Nixon and Soviet leader Mikhail Gorbachev that gained the former president an invitation to the Reagan White House. Though Nixon's efforts never succeeded in erasing Watergate from the public's memory, he did manage to make his foreign policy achievements part of his permanent legacy. It is in this context that *Nixon in China* needs to be explored in order to appreciate the contribution it made in shaping the former president's image.[13]

Opera and Politics

In the history of opera, politics has often been a source of inspiration for composers who, in turn, through music, drama and poetry, have influenced their audiences' views of political events and politicians. But while most operas tend to be based on a distant past, *Nixon in China* centred on recent history. Fifteen years before enjoying the operatic dramatization of the president's meeting with Zhou and Mao, or the first lady's visit to a Beijing school, the audience had experienced these actual events through live television coverage of the Nixons' historic visit to China. Moreover, most of the characters were still alive when the opera premiered in Houston, Texas, in 1987. For this reason, *Nixon in China* has often been unfairly labelled a CNN opera, or, in the words of *New York Times'* Max Frankel, 'a media event about a media event.' Its director, Peter Sellars, vehemently rejected the criticism:

> I really want to emphasise that it is exactly the opposite. CNN is fast-breaking with instant reactions, and of course, the rush to judgment. Opera is about a long view. What opera offers is poetry, is music. *Nixon in China* shows what opera can do to history, which is to deepen it and move it into its more subtle, nuanced and mysterious corners.[14]

Sellars was right. *Nixon in China* offers the audience the opportunity to detach from the fast pace of contemporary affairs and, instead, to reflect on recent history and appreciate its significance and consequences. In this sense, it sits firmly in the postmodern tradition. By combining musical minimalism with still current political issues that had been instrumental in shaping the late twentieth century, American opera had succeeded in overcoming what political scientist John Bokina has called a 'repertory crisis.' Up to that point, the standard repertory had largely consisted of operas by the classical greats of the late eighteenth and nineteenth centuries, notably Mozart, Verdi, Rossini and Wagner. This had not only made it difficult for new operas to gain popularity, but it had also created a gap between composers and a new generation of audiences. By focusing on nuclear weapons, racism, the Cold War and terrorism, works such as Philip Glass's *Einstein on the Beach* (1976) and John Adams's *Nixon in China* and the *Death of Klinghoffer* (1991) managed to overcome the dominance of conservative operas in the repertory and generate new interest in this art form. Stage directors had been the driving force behind the shift.[15]

Indeed, it had been theatre director Peter Sellars who in 1983 approached John Adams about writing together an opera on Nixon's 1972 visit to China. Sellars had been reading Henry Kissinger's and Mao's memoirs in an effort to better understand the Vietnam War for his production of Joseph Haydn's *Armida*. His research led him to the idea for the opera. Adams had been busy studying Richard Wagner's operas and, in particular, the concept of mythmaking. Although initially sceptical, as he saw Nixon as a subject more suitable for late-night comedies, he realized that this offered a valuable opportunity to 'find our [US] mythology in our own contemporary history.' As he noted during an interview for *Playbill*, 'As Americans, we are obsessed with our president because that person embodies our national psyche, both the dark side – our paranoia and our tendency to abuse power – but also our idealism and our curiously American optimism.'[16]

To be sure, Nixon's trip was a sort of mythological moment in US history. For almost twenty-five years, China had been a mysterious and unpredictable threat. Its attempts at recapturing the island of Taiwan in the 1950s and its involvement in Korea and Vietnam had increased the possibility of a nuclear Armageddon in Asia and had sent waves of panic among the American people. Nixon's almost overnight announcement that he was going to China was the most significant breakthrough of the Cold War hitherto. From a geostrategic point of view, it made détente possible, and from a US public opinion point of view, it suddenly turned an unknown enemy into a potential ally.[17]

Sellars invited his Harvard friend and poet, Alice Goodman, to write the libretto. Meeting at the Kennedy Center in Washington DC, where Sellars was artistic director for the American repertory theatre, the three principals agreed that *Nixon in China* would be a political opera, in that it concerned political figures, but it would not be a political satire. Instead, it would be an exploration of a heroic event, and as such, it would be written in verse, specifically an eight-syllable couplet. Supported by assistants who researched in the Library of Congress and the Department of State archives for available source materials, the trio embarked in 1985–6 on an in-depth study of the historical events and characters involved.[18]

As the work progressed, their initial assumptions about the main characters radically changed. In particular, after reading Nixon's and Kissinger's memoirs and the vast literature emphasizing the former president's diplomatic achievements, their intense dislike for the president turned into an interest in understanding a very complicated human being. From the outset of his political career, and reaching a crescendo during the Watergate scandal investigations, newspapers and news reports had dissected his public and private life. According to Sellars, this long and intense media coverage had created the false impression of familiarity with Nixon in the minds of many Americans. As he remarked in an interview for *Playbill*, '[W]e think we know everything about these people, of course, we really hardly know them at all.' The aim of the work, therefore, evolved into an in-depth study of characters beyond their public masks.[19]

The result was a three-act opera that captured the juxtaposition between the political and personal. By exploring the characters' most intimate dreams and illusions through the lens of a significant historic event, the audience could develop an emotional connection with these figures. Richard Nixon was no longer, at least for a few hours, a morally corrupted man, but a modern myth: a flawed human capable of great achievements who was also deeply insecure and full of self-doubt. Through music and poetry, Adams and Goodman went beyond a simple reproduction of the historic events. They provided a new interpretation that, as music historian Timothy Johnson has noted, 'was missing from, or merely latent in, the newsreel and other documentary evidence of Nixon's historic trip to China.'[20]

This could have been achieved only through opera. No other artistic form would have allowed for such dramatic representation of characters. As historian William Germano argues, opera is not interested in the fine details of war and treaties because it is a mytho-poetic form that puts personal conflict centre stage. In other words, 'it is the musical exploration of a character in crisis.' Who better than Richard Nixon to explore the concept of crisis? His entire political career had been underpinned by his ability to turn a crisis to his own advantage. His first autobiography alone, *Six Crises*, which Goodman refers to in the libretto, would make a perfect script for an opera. He was the greatest comeback artist of the twentieth century. His shrewd use of the media enabled him to reinvent himself after each crisis. Every time a 'new' Nixon entered the stage, a new aspect of his personality was revealed, thus making his image increasingly multi-faceted. In meeting the challenges presented by its main character, the Adams opera offers an insightful and credible portrayal of Nixon's complexity.[21]

The opera's first act belongs to the men. Scenes 1, 2 and 3 are an accurate re-telling of Nixon's arrival in Beijing, his meetings with Zhou En-lai and Mao Zedong and the lavish banquet at the end of the first day of the visit. Act 2 belongs to the women. In Scene 1, first lady Pat Nixon is taken on a sightseeing tour of Beijing. In Scene 2, Madame Mao hosts a revolutionary ballet performance for the guests. In Scene 1 of Act 3, all the characters come together to reflect on the events of the previous days and past experiences.[22]

The dialogue in the scenes re-enacting historical events comes almost verbatim from Nixon's memoirs and the documentation available at the time. Goodman drew heavily on these authoritative historical sources, but she skilfully altered the language to suit its poetic presentation. For the fictional scenes that explore the characters' thoughts and emotions, Goodman declared that they revealed her own understanding of these people, but more than that, they also reflected a part of herself: 'Nixon, Pat, Mme. Mao, Kissinger and the chorus were all "me." And the inner lives of Mao and Chou En-Lai, who I couldn't find in myself at all, were drawn from a couple of close acquaintances.'[23]

As with other postmodern operas, *Nixon in China* has elements of minimalism. Originated in the United States in the 1960s, the style is characterized by repetitions and steady pulses. One of its most famous exponents, Philip Glass, heavily influenced Adams during his formative years in San Francisco. But as *New York Times* critic Allan Kozzin observed, the score is more than just a minimalist piece, it is actually quite 'eclectic … in the orchestral interludes one hears references, both passing and lingering, to everything from Wagner to Gershwin and Philip Glass.' The opera is scored for an orchestra without bassoons, French horns and tuba, but it is very heavy on brass and there are four saxophones and a synthesizer. The percussion section incorporates numerous special effects, including a wood block and sandpaper blocks. At times, when focusing on Nixon and the first lady for example, it is white, big band music from the 1930s and early 1940s, which is, as Adams pointed out, 'when Dick and Pat fell in love.' When wanting to evoke the enormity of the landscape and the mystery of China's past, however, Adams relies on the chorus. The overall effect is a distinctive form of music that is capable of expressing the sudden changes in the mood of the characters.[24]

The Operatic Nixon

The stage for Nixon as a modern myth is set right from the beginning of the opera. Act 1, Scene 1 begins as dawn breaks over China, symbolizing not just a new day, but a new era of discovery. Contingents of army, navy and air force personnel gather at the airfield outside Beijing and sing 'The Three Main Rules of Discipline and Eight Points of Attention,' based on Mao's military doctrine issued in 1928 when the Communists were fighting against the Nationalists. The chorus gives a first glimpse into unknown China and reminds the audience that Nixon is about to embark on a historic mission. The image is sealed when Nixon and Pat disembark the 'Spirit of '76' plane to meet this crowd. The scene has almost a romantic feel: a man alone, supported by the partner of a life-time, is brave enough to venture into enemy territory for the sake of world peace.[25]

As the rest of the American party disembarks, the band strikes up. Zhou En-lai introduces Nixon to the official Chinese entourage, and together they review the massed ranks of the honoured guard. As hands are shaken, the audience becomes privy to Nixon's thoughts. To add drama and melancholy, he is cast as a baritone. His aria captures well the contrast between his public persona and his private fears, as the joy of anticipated triumph becomes the terrible expectation of failure. Nixon sings 'news' at least twelve times to reflect his obsessive need to control his public image, but also as a tragic forewarning that it will be the press that eventually will bring him down.

By 1972, Nixon's relationship with the media, in particular newspapers, was very strained. Fully aware that he needed journalists and correspondents to report that he 'had made history,' he micromanaged every aspect of his trip. Television dominated the coverage of his visit to China. A charter plane with sixty-eight staff from the three big networks (ABC, NBC and CBS) and only twenty-eight print reporters arrived ahead of the presidential party in order to hit 'prime time in the USA. Yesterday night. They watch us now; the three main networks' color glow,' Nixon sings. The 'Spirit of '76' landed in Beijing at 11.30 am which was 10.30, Sunday evening, on the East Coast, a time when families are together after dinner and 'dishes are washed and homework done, the dog and grandma fall asleep.'[26]

Goodman then introduces a reference to the landing-on-the-moon mission. 'We came in peace for all mankind,' Nixon sings. The president had actually uttered the famous sentence before departing by helicopter from the White House lawn on 17 February. But including it in the libretto heightened the significance of the historical moment and created a positive association with the heroic image of Apollo 11 astronauts Neil Armstrong and Buzz Aldrin. The triumphant moment is immediately followed by self-doubt and paranoia, however: 'We live in an unsettled time. Who are our enemies? Who are our friends?' The audience is unclear whether Nixon is singing about the international situation? Or his life? Or both? As the lighting and the music change to reflect his pensive mood, the scene shifts from Beijing airport to Nixon's hotel bedroom where he has retired to take a nap. While dreaming, he starts singing about his anxiety and concerns over the trip. He imagines 'rats chewing the sheets' and he can hear 'murmuring.' He shifts between melody and a rambling, conversational style. 'Nobody is a friend of ours. Let's face it. If we don't succeed at this summit, our name is in the mud.' Kissinger, then, suddenly wakes him up and informs him that Chairman Mao wants to see him.[27]

In Scene 2, the opera switches back to the historical event. In Mao's faithfully reproduced study, full of books and papers, the audience once again meets Nixon the statesman. The scene further highlights Nixon's complexity by bringing on stage 'new' versions of the man. The contrast between the Communist leader and the president is striking. Mao is portrayed as a frail man who can only walk with the support of three secretaries/nurses. At times, he is confused and falls asleep while talking. His declining health seems a metaphor for Communist power. He is disappointed with history and revolution, as he sings: 'the revolution does not last.' Adams casts him as a tenor, the male role in opera with a high range, which gives Mao vocal power. According to Kissinger, Mao still exuded an immense power, despite his frailty. Nixon, on the other hand, is calm, focused and ready to talk about important issues: Taiwan, Vietnam, bringing the boys home. Ever so conscious of the importance of history, he sings 'let us join hands, make peace at once. History is our mother, we best do her honor in this way.' But Mao replies, 'history is a dirty sow,' and reminds the audience that there are always multiple purposes behind Nixon's actions. He might be on a peace mission, but this is very conveniently taking place in an election year. Mao has read Nixon's first autobiography, *Six Crises*. He knows that behind 'a man of the people' exterior, there is a shrewd politician.[28]

In the final scene of the first act, the Americans are being feted in the Great Hall of the People. The stage directions tell us that outside the roof is outlined by strings of lights while inside there are tables set for nine. Against the far wall, a small platform supports several microphones. The American and the Chinese flags are in the background. The president and the first lady sit on either side of Premier Zhou, their backs to the flags, and gaze across the tables where the newsmen and the important Chinese sit. In a most accurate reproduction of the venue, we meet yet another Nixon. The atmosphere is cheerful and he feels strangely joyful and lightheaded, emotions to which he is unaccustomed. He sings, 'it is like a dream.' In his toast, he says 'never have I so enjoyed a dinner, nor have I heard played a better music that I love outside America.' But in a clear reference to his inability ever to relax and let his guard down, he suddenly remembers the cameras: 'no one is out of touch ... telecommunication has broadcast your message into space.' With history and his place in it always at the forefront of his mind, he sings, 'we must seize the hour and seize the day, this is the hour.' Meanwhile, Pat reinforces the significance of her husband's mission by making a reference to one of the most beloved US presidents, George Washington.[29]

Nixon does not feature prominently in the second act, which belongs to Pat and Madame Mao. We meet him again in the final act. Here the opera abandons the historical facts and delves into a deep exploration of the main characters' minds and emotions. The scenery is devoid of all props and the bright lights that characterize the state visit scenes. There are only six beds, one for each character: Dick, Pat, Henry (Kissinger), Zhou, Madame Mao and Mao. This is a true operatic moment when the characters reveal themselves earnestly. As they shift their focus from the intense political talks that had dominated through the week, they reflect on their lives and past challenges and how they overcame them. The stage directions tell us that Nixon is tired and the first lady looks fragile and overwhelmed. Through their melancholy, the audience gets a glimpse into their marriage.[30]

Much speculation has surrounded the Nixon marriage. To historian Will Swift, their union was a true love story, albeit one with its ups and downs. In his estimate, Nixon heavily relied on his strong wife, the only human being he ever fully trusted. By contrast, Herbert Parmet believed that the Nixons had a very unhappy relationship, one in which the first lady 'did all the right things' to support her husband at the expense of her own happiness. The creators of *Nixon in China* endorsed this latter version. At the beginning of the act, Nixon reproaches Pat that her lipstick is crooked, something he often enjoyed doing in public too.[31]

Pat is homesick, not for the White House, but for the simpler life she had in California as a young wife. In sweeping melodic lines, she sings, 'Oh! California! Hold me close.' She recalls their first home as a newly married couple and even though she 'squeezed [the] paycheck until it screamed,' she has fond memories of it: 'that place was heaven next to this.' It is not clear whether she is referring to China or life as a first lady. Her American dream was clearly much more modest than her husband's. She tells him, 'the trouble was, we moved too much. We should have stayed put Dick.'[32]

For Nixon, youth is synonymous of the Second World War. As he sings about his experience in the Pacific, new aspects of his character come through. 'There was so much I couldn't tell,' he sings, referring to war operations, but also to his difficulties in opening up and sharing his deepest feelings, even with his wife. As he recalls the details of his participation in the war effort, he first sings of the fear and trauma of a nightly bombardment, thus projecting an image as a war hero. Then, he remembers enthusiastically his make-shift hamburger stand, 'Nick's Snack Shack,' for pilots and crew on refuelling stops. The passage evokes feelings of friendship and camaraderie, but the audience does not have the time to warm to this idea of a young, caring Nixon. Pat suddenly reminds us that her husband was also a very able poker player. She sings, 'you won at poker.' And he replies:

I sure did. I had a system.
Five card stud taught me a lot about mankind.
Speak softly and don't show your hand
Became my motto.

Thus, the image of a friendly Nixon is crushed by the image of a manipulative Nixon and the duplicity that is associated with the game of poker.[33]
Nixon's last words in the opera appear to refer back to Nick's Snack Shack:

rare, medium, well-done, anything
you say. The customer is King.
Sorry we are out of relish. Drinks?
This is my way of saying thanks.

According to historian Fawn Brodie, Nixon had feelings of shame at not having taken part in actual combat despite being an officer in uniform.[34] This might be the case, but the passage can also be interpreted as referring to one of Nixon's major shortcomings as a human being: his inability to express his feelings, indeed his fear of doing so. Regret is the dominant emotion here – regret for failing to live a full life by refusing to trust those around him. As Pat and Dick share this intimate exchange on stage, conversations between other characters begin to overlap. Madame Mao and Mao playfully discuss their early days too.

The Rest of the Cast

While Nixon is undoubtedly the protagonist of the opera, the rest of the cast performs an important role in expanding our understanding of the former president. Through lyrics and music, we learn about aspects of their personalities too, and these, in turn, shed new light on Nixon's image.

The first lady is the character with whom an American audience can most empathize. She is introduced as the ideal Republican housewife, quiet, supportive of her husband and ready to sacrifice her own needs, even though she found public life difficult. Adams thought she had a genuine smile that disguised her unhappiness: 'you know there is a lot of pain behind it.'[35] While the men are busy discussing the important issues, in Act 2, Scene 1, Pat Nixon is taken on a tour of

Beijing, first to a market and then a school. This scene provides the most extensive development of her character, as she is free, away from her husband, to express her thoughts and personality.

As she interacts with her Chinese hosts, Pat reveals many details of her background. She comes from a poor family too and once raised pigs. She used to be a teacher before marrying Nixon. She sings of everyday values and her music reflects the simplicity of her story. Adams casts her as a soprano. Her arias are much softer and more lyrical than her husband's. Most of all, they are free from doubts, uncertainties and paranoia. Instead, the Pat Nixon created by Adams and Goodman is a stoic woman who understands her place in society and believes in fate and the power of optimism. She is the true embodiment of the American Dream. Her strength of character is in stark contrast to Nixon's but this does not detract from him. On the contrary, her practical approach to life and her understanding of the realities of American society make her the perfect companion/advisor for the president. She sings, 'Never have I cared for trivialities.' She is a positive influence who can give good advice and steer his attention towards less glamorous but more important everyday concerns for the American people. Ultimately, if such a charming and vital woman can love Nixon, then the audience can, at least, give him the benefit of the doubt.[36]

The portrayal of Jiang Qing (Chiang Ching) or Madame Mao reinforces the positive aspects of the first lady's character, and by extension of Nixon's. If Pat is the gentle and supportive wife, Jiang is the leader of the Cultural Revolution. Rather than being her husband's source of comfort, she derives her own power from him. As she dramatically sings in her aria, 'I am the Wife of Chairman Mao.' Musically, too, she distinguishes herself from Pat and the rest of the cast. She has a distinct harmonic structure, loud and uncontainable, that retraces her journey from a shady Shanghai actress to the second most important person in the history of Communist China. Adams stated that he did not want her to be just a 'shrieking coloratura' in the opera. Instead, he wanted to show the audience the extent of her involvement in 'the catastrophic Cultural Revolution,' the dark chapter in recent Chinese history. She is depicted as both a serious politician and a highly erotic woman who through her sexuality climbed her way up the political ladder.[37]

This image is reinforced in Act 2, Scene 2, by the re-enactment of *The Red Detachment of Women,* a play within the play. Jiang had created this three-hour ballet as a denunciation of the feudal system and to highlight the oppression of women in 1964. It was Peter Sellars's idea to include it in the opera, not only because this had actually been performed during Nixon's 1972 visit, but also because it gave a chance to explore further the comparison between Pat and Nixon on the one hand, and the rest of the cast on the other. The plot revolves around Wu Qinghua, the daughter of a poor peasant who is whipped to death by the sadistic factotum of her evil landlord, Lao Si, for trying to run away. The first lady's reaction to the ballet is very emotional. She is distressed by the physical abuse of the young girl. She eventually intervenes and tries to revive Wu. The president, on the other hand, seems undisturbed by the beating. He tells Pat not to get involved. The whole episode further highlights the moral bankruptcy of the

Cultural Revolution and of one of its main instigators, Jiang Qing, thus making the first lady look even more humane and caring.[38]

Jiang Qing also represents one of Mao's many flaws. Adams and Goodman cast the Communist leader as a shrewd and dangerous character. His meeting with Nixon in Act 1 highlights his physical frailty but his mind is still very sharp. He sings, 'after the founders come the profiteers,' to signal that he is not entirely impressed by Nixon and Kissinger. He knows the meeting will be used to increase their power and prestige both at home and abroad, but he is equally ready to exploit the occasion to his own advantage. He has met 'capitalists' before and he has skilfully manipulated them to keep the revolution going. Compared to this Mao, Nixon almost looks like a good man.[39]

In the final act, the Mao of the Great Leap Forward is transformed into a young and more humane man dreaming of a revolution to free his people. As Pat and Dick sing about their early years in California and the Pacific, Mao and Jiang dance and flirt remembering the days when they met and fell in love. In an interview in 2006, Sellars said that this had been done in order to create a sense of shared humanity. The Nixons and the Maos, an American marriage, a Communist marriage, signify that beneath whatever differences exist, we are all human beings who share the same fears and insecurities. The comparison not only evokes a sense of shared humanity but also makes the Nixons look more like a traditional and respectable middle-class American family. While Mao and Jiang indulge in sex fantasies and revolutionary plans, Pat and Dick talk about their sacrifices as a young couple and their vocation to live a life of service, as a teacher and a Second World War soldier, respectively.[40]

Henry Kissinger is the only historical figure portrayed as a caricature in the opera. Although he appears in almost every scene, he does not say much, but he plays a very important role in making Nixon look like a better man. At the time of the trip in 1972, he was national security advisor to the president. His knowledge of diplomacy and international affairs and his influence on US foreign policy were extensive. It was Kissinger, after all, who had secretly and successfully brokered the historic visit. The opera does not reflect this. There is a brief mention of the secret negotiations in Act 1, Scene 2, when Nixon sings 'my right-hand man. You'd never think to look at him. That he's James Bond.' But the president uses the reference mainly to indicate that Kissinger is a womanizer, rather than a 'consummate diplomat.'[41] This unflattering image is reinforced by Kissinger's participation in *The Red Detachment of Women* where he plays beater and rapist Lao Si. This dual role makes him at the same time the buffo of the opera and the sinister advisor who is happy to manipulate behind the scenes and take care of Nixon's dirty business. The more ridiculous and shady Kissinger looks, the better Nixon appears.[42]

By contrast, as music historian Timothy Johnson argues, Zhou is 'the conscience of the opera.' Of all the characters, he is perhaps the one that Adams and Goodman admired most and this is reflected both in his lyrics and music. He is cast as a medium baritone, helping to give him an aura of wisdom and calm. His lines are more melodic and much softer compared to the other men on stage. His composed and stable attitude makes Nixon look even more insecure and paranoid. He is presented initially as the world-renowned diplomat who escorts the American guests throughout the trip, but his key moment comes in the third act when he sings the final aria of the opera. He reflects on the historical events, not just the recent ones. He is nostalgic for a simpler life and he craves peace. His closing line invites the audience to consider the events they have just watched and their historical significance: 'How much of what we did was good?'[43]

It is with this profound question that the opera reaches its apex. What the characters/historical figures did might or might not have been done in good faith, but after all they were just human beings, with faults and weaknesses like everyone in the audience. The pomposity of the official occasion might have given a different impression, but as they reach the end of their lives (at the time of Nixon's visit Zhou had been diagnosed with bladder cancer and passed away in 1976), they too had to come to terms with their failures and shortcomings.[44]

Reception and Audience

Nixon in China premiered on 22 October 1987 at the Houston Grand Opera. Nixon was invited and was sent the libretto but he declined on the basis of poor health and pressing work deadlines. The *Los Angeles Times* reported that when the curtains came down, the audience's reaction was a 'polite applause'. Reviews were split. John Von Rhein of the *Chicago Tribune* wrote that it was a 'triumph' and 'a thought-provoking beauty'. Mark Swed of the *Los Angeles Herald Examiner* thought that the opera's relevance went beyond the political event it portrayed. It was a magnifying glass on the constant tension between private and public life that each human being has to face. As such, it should be appreciated 'for as long as mankind cherished humanity'. Martin Bernheimer from the *Los Angeles Times* praised Alice Goodman's ability to turn diplomatic conversations into a 'couplet-dominated libretto'. The most generous review came from the British newspaper *The Guardian*, whose critic Nicholas Kenjon was struck by the in-depth exploration of the characters' emotions. This was quite surprising 'because the Nixons are the last people one would think of as having a deep interior life'.[45]

Overall, however, the critics failed to appreciate Sellars and Adams's attempt at going beyond Watergate and understanding these characters beyond their public roles. The vast majority of reviews focused on the production and the music score, but only a few commented specifically on how the opera addressed Nixon's image and reputation. Donal Henahan of the *New York Times* characterized the production as Sellars's 'variety show'. Both in life and in the opera, the Nixons appeared to be 'a confused Rotarian couple swept up by incomprehensible events'. In particular, he questioned Pat's portrayal that made her look like 'a pathetic loyal wife'. Similarly, Peter G. Davis of the *New York* magazine doubted that the opera would ever become a classic of the American repertory. While he praised James Maddalena's portrayal of Nixon as 'positively eerie. The tilt of his head, the jerky walk, the nervous hand movements, even the way he sits and crosses his legs are Nixon to the life', he predicted that the work would soon land into oblivion once initial public curiosity subsided. In similar vein, *St Louis Post-Dispatch* reviewer James Wierzbicki labelled the opera a 'novelty ... not much more.'[46]

Over the years, the opera opened in several theatres in the United States and Europe. For the 1990 Los Angeles production, Sellars made revisions that included a reference to the tragic events of Tiananmen Square. The opera took nearly a quarter-century to receive a warmer reception. With the Nixons' daughter, Tricia Cox Nixon, in the audience, the New York Metropolitan Opera's 2011 production received an enthusiastic reception from the first-night audience and later ones. It also received a considerably more favourable critical approval, if not a universal approbation. In reviewing it for a second time, Mark Swed noted that a work once belittled as a 'CNN opera of no lasting merit, ... has clearly remained relevant,' and had finally been hailed as a classic. Anthony Tommasini of the *New York Times* observed that all historical players, with the exception of Kissinger, had been treated seriously and 'given dignity.' In particular, he praised the authors' efforts at restoring Nixon's reputation as a Cold Warrior who was 'piloting towards an unknown shore' to bring peace to the world.[47]

In 1987, critics had found it difficult to imagine Nixon and the rest of the cast as historical characters. Many of them were still alive. The Watergate scandal was still fresh in the memory of the vast majority of the American people. The process of rehabilitating Nixon's reputation, initiated by the former president himself, was still ongoing. But by 2011, Nixon revisionism had reached its peak. Scholarly and popular works now fully acknowledged the significance of his many foreign policy achievements, including his trip to China. This, combined with his passing in 1994, had allowed for a new appreciation of the opera to emerge.

Often compared to Verdi's *Aida* because of its skilful mixture of personal passions and social and political conflict, *Nixon in China* is now one of the most produced US operas. New generations are, however, drawn to broader political themes, such as the rise of China or the ongoing repercussions of the Cold War, rather than Nixon's portrayal. Indeed, Sellars himself declared that the opera should now be seen in the context of 'our interdisciplinary, intercultural, interdependent generation.' Nixon, he remarked, could easily feature in Sellars's production of Handel's *Giulio Cesare*, staged as *The American President Visits the Middle East*.[48]

Despite the opera's belated popularity, one question remains: How much influence did *Nixon in China* have in reshaping the former president's image? The operatic Nixon is inevitably less accessible that the television drama or cinematic one. Opera has traditionally been considered an elite product. In 2018, the *Seattle Times* reported that the largest segment of the Houston Grand Opera's audience was between sixty-five and seventy-two years old. Even the New York Metropolitan's average audience age is fifty-eight years. Opera-goers also tend to be more affluent and better educated than the societal average. That said, the number of people going to the opera has increased and grown more diverse in recent years. The National Endowment of the Arts reported that between 2008 and 2012, the percentage of African Americans attending increased by 59 per cent, Hispanic attendance grew by 8.3 per cent and other non-white groups grew by 19.4 per cent. Young audience segments have also increased. Attendance in the 18–24 age bracket grew by 43.2 per cent and in the 25–34 bracket 33.8 per cent. This is mainly due to a wider distribution through recordings and cinematic live-casts. The Houston production of *Nixon in China* had its PBS Great Performances television premiere in April 1988 and won an Emmy for Outstanding Classical Program in the Performing Arts. The 2011 Met premiere was simultaneously broadcast live in movie theatres on 2 February as part of the groundbreaking series *The Met, Live in HD*, which transmits live performances to more than 1,500 movie theatres and performing arts centres in forty-six countries around the world. It was also recorded for DVD and later Blue Ray distribution. Accordingly, it is safe to say that over the years, *Nixon in China* has reached quite a broad audience.[49]

Conclusion

Although the public's appreciation of *Nixon in China* has changed over the last thirty years, there is no doubt that the opera has made a positive contribution to the vast scholarly literature and cultural productions on the former president. It was one of the first art works to offer a new interpretation of the president's ambiguous personality. It is not a psychological work but it is an exercise in empathy and compassion through a musical and lyrical rollercoaster. While the initial focus is on the diplomatic achievement, the audience is soon invited to explore behind the scenes and discover the man without his political mask. In just a few hours, we meet Nixon the statesman, the paranoid, the insecure, the cheerful, the introvert, the explorer, the Second World War hero, the friend, the poker player, the co-dependent husband, the rude husband, the lonely. Ultimately this complicated mosaic leads to the opera's key message: there was more to Nixon than just the Watergate scandal.

Seven years after *Nixon in China* premiered, Oliver Stone's Oscar-nominated movie, *Nixon*, brought a similar image to the big screen. Actor Anthony Hopkins portrayed the president as a man whose ambitions and intelligence were often curbed by insecurities and paranoia. From the mid-1990s onwards, too, with the benefit of newly available archival sources, historians have increasingly presented a convincing image of a multi-layered Nixon. For example, Joan Hoff's seminal work, *Nixon Reconsidered*, argued that the president's legacy had been largely misunderstood. While many remembered him because of Watergate and Nixon himself had tried to rebuild his reputation using his foreign policy expertise, she chided scholars for failing to acknowledge the impact of his domestic agenda, notably his environmental policy, social reforms and expansion of civil rights. This analysis of Nixon's domestic policy brought to light a new image: Nixon the liberal.[50]

The debate over Nixon's complicated character is far from over and much more will be written about his achievements and shortcomings in the future. There is no doubt, however, that his image has been a major feature of American political life since he joined the House Committee on Un-American Activities in 1947. In the evolution of that image, John Adams's opera *Nixon in China* continues to play a notable role for its positive portrayal of him in contrast to the many negative ones. It can never help to put to rest the debate about who the 'real' Nixon was, however. As scholar Daniel Frick has remarked, 'When we fight about Nixon, we are fighting about the meaning of America, and that is a struggle that never ends.'[51]

Notes

1   MacMillan, Margaret, *Nixon and Mao: The Week That Changed the World* (New York: Random House, 2007), p. 21; Oliva, Mara, *Eisenhower and American Public Opinion on China* (New York: Palgrave Macmillan, 2018), p. 213; Nixon, Richard, *RN: The Memoirs* (New York: Grosset & Dunlap, 1978), p. 559.

2   Frankel, Max, 'Historic Handshake,' *New York Times* [*NYT*], 21 February 1972, https://www.nytimes.com/1972/02/21/archives/a-quiet-greeting-no-airport-speeches-plane-stops-in-shanghai-an.html; Silk, Leonard, 'A New Marco Polo?,' *NYT*, 16 February 1972, https://www.nytimes.com/1972/02/16/archives.html; Reston, James, 'Mr. Nixon's Finest Hour,' *NYT*, 1 March 1972, https://www.nytmes.com/1972/03/01/archives.html; Gallup, Inc., 'Presidential Approval Ratings'; Gallup.com, Gallup, 10 January 2017, http://news.gallup.com/poll/116677/presidential-approval-ratings-gallup-historical-statistics-trends.aspx; Saad, Lydia, 'Nixon's China Visit Was a Game Changer,' *Gallup Vault*, 17 February 2017, https://news.gallup.com/vault/204065/gallup-vault-nixon-china-visit-game-changer.aspx.

3   Greenberg, David, *Nixon's Shadow: The History of an Image* (New York: W. W. Norton, 2003), p. 297; Kohut, Andrew, 'How the Watergate Crisis Eroded Public Support for Nixon,' 8 August 2014, http://www.pewresearch.org/fact-tank/2014/08/08/how-the-watergate-crisis-eroded-public-support-for-richard-nixon/.

4   Frick, Daniel, *Reinventing Richard Nixon: A Cultural History of an American Obsession* (Lawrence: University of Kansas, 2008); Keener, John, 'Writing the Vacuum: Richard Nixon as Literary Figure,' *Critique*, 41:2 (2000): 129–51.

5   Quoted in Brodie, Fawn, *Richard Nixon: The Shaping of His Character* (New York: Norton, 1981), p. 414.

6   Minett, Mark, '*Millhouse*: The Problems and Opportunities of Political Cinema,' *Film History*, 26:1 (2014): 108–35; Vidal, Gore, *The Best Man* (New York: Dramatists Play Service Inc., 1960); Roth, Philip, *Our Gang* (New York: Random House, 1971).

7   Greenberg, *Nixon's Shadow*, pp. 232–69; Morgan, Iwan, 'Nixon Biographies,' in Melvin Small, ed., *A Companion to Richard M. Nixon* (Chichester, UK: Wiley-Blackwell, 2011), pp. 11–13.

8   Wise, David, 'Are You Worried about Your Image, Mr President?' *Esquire*, May 1973, p. 119; Nixon, *RN*, p. 354; Haldeman, H.R., with Joseph diMona, *The Ends of Power* (New York: Times Books, 1978), p. 70.

9   Greenberg, David, *Republic of Spin: An Inside History of the American Presidency* (New York: Norton, 2016), pp. 397–400.

10 Morgan, Iwan, 'Richard Nixon, Reputation and Watergate,' in Michael Genovese and Iwan Morgan, eds., *Watergate Remembered* (New York: Palgrave Macmillan, 2012), p. 108.

11　Aitken, Jonathan, *Nixon: A Life* (Washington, DC: Regnery Publishing, 1996), p. 535; Ambrose, Stephen, *Nixon: Ruin and Recovery 1973–1990* (New York: Simon & Schuster, 1991), p. 512.

12　Frick, *Reinventing Richard Nixon*, p. 23; Greenberg, *Nixon's Shadow*, p. 271.

13　Greenberg, *Nixon's Shadow*; Gaddis, John Lewis, *Strategies of Containment: A Critical Appraisal of Postwar American National Security Policy* (New York: Oxford University Press, 1982); 'He's Back: The Rehabilitation of Richard Nixon,' *Newsweek*, 19 May 1986, https://www.newsweek.com/nixon-hes-back-again-204460; 'Nixon Meets with Gorbachev,' *Washington Post*, 19 July 1986.

14　Bokina, John, *Opera and Politics, from Monteverdi to Henze* (New Haven, CT: Yale University Press, 1997), p. 2; 'The Myth of History,' *The Metropolitan Opera Playbill*, 9 February 2011, pp. 6–9.

15　Bokina, *Opera and Politics*, pp. 200–1.

16　*Playbill*, 2011; Pauly, Louis, 'The Political Resonance of Nixon in China,' *University of Toronto Quarterly*, 81:4 (2012): 824.

17　Oliva, *Eisenhower and American Public Opinion on China*, pp. 157, 214.

18　Steinberg, Michael, 'Nixon in China,' in *Nixon in China: An Opera in Three Acts by John Adams*, compact disc liner notes (New York: Elektra/Nonesuch, 1987) pp. 14–25.

19　*Playbill*, 2011.

20　Johnson, Timothy, *John Adams' Nixon in China* (New York: Routledge, 2011), p. 3.

21　Germano, William, 'Opera as News: Nixon in China and the Contemporary Operatic Subject,' *University of Toronto Quarterly*, 81:4 (2012): 797–804; Nixon, Richard, *Six Crises* (New York: Doubleday & Co, 1962).

22　Goodman, Alice, *History Is Our Mother: Three Libretti* (New York: New York Review of Books, 1987).

23　Gurewitsch, Matthew, 'Still Resonating from the Great Wall,' *NYT*, 26 January 2011, https://nytimes.com/2011/01/26/archive.html.

24　Kozinn, Allan, 'Nixon in China,' *Oxford Music Online*, 2007; *Playbill*, 2011.

25　Goodman, *History Is Our Mother*.

26　Ibid.

27　Ibid.

28　Ibid.; Daines, Matthew, 'Nixon's Women: Gender Politics and Cultural Representation in Act 2 of Nixon in China,' *Musical Quarterly*, 79:1 (1995): 16–17.

29　Ibid.

30　Ibid.

31　Swift, Will, *Pat and Dick, the Nixons: An Intimate Portrait of a Marriage* (New York: Simon & Schuster, 2014): Parmet, Herbert, *Richard Nixon and His America* (Boston, MA: Little Brown, 1990), p. 286.

32　Goodman, *History Is Our Mother*.

33　Ibid.

34　Brodie, *Richard Nixon*.

35　*Playbill*, 2011.

36　Goodman, *History Is Our Mother*.

37　Ibid.; *Playbill*, 2011.

38　Goodman, *History Is Our Mother*.

39　Ibid.

40　Ibid.

41　Ibid.

42　Ibid.

43 Ibid.

44 Ibid.

45 Gurewitsch, 'Still Resonating from the Great Wall'; Bernheimer, Martin, 'Gala Opera Premiere: John Adams' Nixon in China in Houston,' *Los Angeles Times* [*LAT*], 24 October 1987, https://www.bl.uk/collection-guides/newspapers.

46 Bernheimer, 'Gala Opera Premiere'; Davis, Peter G., 'Nixon – The Opera,' *New York Magazine*, 9 November 1987, pp. 102–4, https://www.bl.uk/collection-guides/newspapers.

47 Swed, Mark, 'Nixon in China at the Metropolitan Opera,' *LAT*, 13 February 2011, https://www.bl.uk/collection-guides/newspapers; Tommasini, Anthony, 'President and Opera on Unexpected Stages,' *NYT*, 3 February, 2011, https://www.bl.uk/collection-guides/newspapers.

48 Gurewitsch, 'Still Resonating from the Great Wall'; Reveles, Nic, 'Only Nixon Could Go to China,' *San Diego Opera Talk*, 9 February 2015, https://www.youtube.com/watch?v=x5e9ni-WCfQ.

49 Grey, Tobias, 'Is Opera Audience Aging? Not in Paris,' *Seattle Times*, 23 February 2018, https://www.seattletimes.com/entertainment/is-opera-audience-aging-not-in-paris/; 'How Technology Influences Arts Participation,' National Endowment for the Arts Report, 2010, https://www.arts.gov/sites/default/files/New-Media-Report.pdf.

50 Stone, Oliver, *Nixon*, 1995, https://www.imdb.com/title/tt0113987/; Hoff, Joan, *Nixon Reconsidered* (New York: Basic Books, 1994).

51 Frick, *Reinventing Richard Nixon*, p. 17.

Chapter 8

JIMMY CARTER: THE UNRAVELLING OF AN IMAGE

Bob Green

When Jimmy Carter announced he was running for president in 1976, even his local paper, the *Atlanta Constitution*, dubbed him 'Jimmy Who?'[1] Carter won office by promoting himself as a leader whom the American people could trust. Lacking public recognition, he had to build an image from scratch, but this was an advantage in the context of the 1976 election. The optimism of the 1960s had given way, in the words of cultural critic Joe Queenan, to a 'widespread feeling America had taken a wrong turn in the 1970s.'[2] The Vietnam War and the Watergate scandal undermined public confidence in politicians, political institutions and the presidency. A poll in 1975 indicated that 69 per cent of respondents felt that 'over the last ten years this country's leaders have consistently lied to the people.'[3] The nature of news had changed to become more immediate with a focus on investigation by journalists more sceptical of government information. Disillusioned voters wanted a candidate who was competent, untainted by Washington politics and trustworthy. Carter projected an image that met these expectations but his success as president would depend on how well he lived up to it in the eyes of the media and the public. His failure to build a record of legislative success, curb inflation and resolve the Iranian hostage crisis undermined his ability to control the presidential narrative. This opened the way for the media to reshape his image in negative terms that were damaging to his re-election prospects.

When Carter decided to run for president, he was largely unknown outside Georgia, where he had served as state senator and governor. He represented a breed of 'New South' governors who came to power in the 1970s on an agenda that combined acceptance of the civil rights revolution with emphasis on economy and efficiency in government. He was also part of a growing southern upper-middle class whose focus was on business development, balanced budgets and governmental reform.[4] Lacking a political image on the national stage, he had to fashion one for the 1976 campaign which he did in part by seeking to influence key journalists and opinion formers. These were national figures, but many such as Tom Wicker of the *Washington Post* were southerners who disdained the segregationist George Wallace and wanted someone to present the new political face of their region to the rest of America.[5]

Carter's low public profile enabled him to create an image that not only suited the campaign but him personally. Although he had a strong team of advisors, it was he who decided, sometimes against their recommendations, what emphasis would be placed on his character. He had debuted on the national stage with a speech at the National Press Club on 12 December 1974. In this he defined himself by the roles that he played: 'I am a farmer, an engineer, a businessman, a planner, a scientist, a governor and a Christian.'[6] All of these roles were a true reflection of who he was and proved a potent weapon for his campaign. At no point did he compromise on the fundamentals of his identity, certainly not his faith nor his Southern background.

Although somewhat at odds with his actual status as an agri-businessman, his self-claimed identity as a farmer struck a chord with rural America. In combination with his New South background, it also differentiated him from the discredited Washington elite. One of his most effective lines on the campaign trail was: 'I have been accused of being an outsider and I plead guilty.'[7] By contrast, Carter's ten-year military service as a US Navy officer was not an advantage in the first post-Vietnam presidential election. Instead, emphasizing his background as scientist and engineer, skills acquired in the navy, Carter projected himself as a problem-solving politician, an image reinforced in the language he used when talking about his policies. Words such as 'rational', 'efficient', 'logic', 'study' and 'comprehensive solutions' were a regular feature of his election rhetoric. This chimed with the assertion in his campaign biography, 'Government at all levels can be competent, economic and efficient.'[8] The final characteristic that Carter brought up in virtually all his speeches was his devout Christianity. A regular church-goer, he experienced a profound spiritual re-awakening that lifted him out of depression brought on by failure to win the Democratic gubernatorial nomination in 1966. Being 'born again' put him on a par with millions of Americans who had undergone the same experience, many of them resident in the South, a key battleground for the election. All of this enabled him to project a multi-faceted image of moral leader, outsider and tough problem-solver who could be trusted to clean up Washington.

Attuned to the national mood in 1976, the image that Carter created in his presidential campaign appealed to voters' deeper needs for honesty and efficiency in government. He presented himself as a man of faith who could be trusted to make government work for all. His simple style, candour about religion, and 'I will never lie to you' promise all helped to project a calm persona that harked backed to a simpler time of a stable America, an image with considerable appeal for the more conservative public mood of the 1970s. Vietnam, inner-city unrest and the white South's reaction to the civil rights revolution had accelerated the fragmentation of the voter coalition that had underwritten Democratic national ascendancy since the New Deal era. Carter seemed well suited to lead America in a post-liberal era when old orthodoxies were breaking down. As one analyst noted, if he was an 'outsider,' it had become 'increasingly hard to locate the mainstream to which he does not belong.'[9]

Although calculated to appeal to the electorate, Carter's image was a fair reflection of Carter the man. However, the public's perception of him in three areas presented his campaign team with major challenges. These were: confusion over his ideology; concerns about his religion; and the sense that he was something of an oddball. These impressions, which troubled Carter throughout his presidency, reflected public confusion over his identity and what he stood for. 'Carter is a complex man.' Chief of Staff Hamilton Jordan later acknowledged, 'And we began to realize, much to our dismay, that even by 1980 ... the American people still did not have a clear picture of who he was.'[10]

Carter refused to categorize himself by ideology. His National Press Club speech was notable for making no mention of the Democratic Party. When cornered on this issue, he said, 'I never characterise myself as a conservative, liberal or moderate and this is what distinguishes me from them (the other candidates).'[11] To many presidential candidates, this stance would have been a tactic to avoid losing support from sections of the electorate, but it truly reflected Carter's view. Explaining his approach to policy issues, he avowed, 'I have tried to analyse each question individually. I've taken positions that to me are fair and rational and sometimes my answers are complicated.'[12] This left him open to accusations of 'fuzziness' and did not stop speculation by politicians and the press regarding his ideological credentials. Whilst the Democratic Party mainstream retained its liberal philosophy, in Congress there remained a significant conservative minority and a group of newly elected moderates who straddled the ideological divide. The difficulty for Carter was that none of these groups were natural supporters of his broad legislative programme. Liberal Democrats considered him too conservative and conservative ones thought him too liberal.[13]

Carter faced similar misunderstanding over his religious faith that he considered an integral element of his character. Far from being an electoral disadvantage, he considered his 'born again' evangelicalism a positive draw in the South and helpful to his image of trustworthiness elsewhere if he could allay suspicions that he was a zealot. His infamous *Playboy* magazine interview attempted to provide reassurance that he was not intent on turning America into a theocracy if elected president. It would forever be remembered, however, for some unfortunate concluding comments made in a likely effort to play to a younger audience. Carter's use of phrases like 'lusting in his heart' over women and 'screwing around' grabbed the headlines.[14] This language and the choice of medium to publicize his views shocked pietistic supporters and reinforced an image of strangeness with the rest of the electorate. Carter found it difficult to deal with how his faith was perceived by the public. He felt, correctly in the 1976 campaign, that the American people would take his beliefs as an indicator that he could be trusted to do the right thing in office. In trying to reassure those who found his 'born again' credentials strange or even threatening, however, he failed to understand that to the religious right his faith signalled support for a political agenda of socio-moral conservatism. This would eventually prove extremely damaging to his image in the eyes of white evangelicals, who ranked among his major supporters in 1976.

The third issue that Carter and his team found themselves addressing was his 'Southerness' and how it added to the feeling that he represented something unusual. Communications director Gerald Rafshoon described this phenomenon as 'the weirdo factor'.[15] As the first president from the Deep South since the Civil War, Carter represented something quintessentially different from his modern predecessors. His accent and mode of speech were very different. His rhetoric was laced with biblical references and his style was more akin to a preacher than a politician. His 'born again' credentials, deemed 'normal' in the Bible Belt, were often viewed as strange in the rest of the country. This reinforced his image as an outsider that was an electoral advantage in 1976 but was less of an asset in the presidency. His efforts to appear hip to youth only added to uncertainty about him, as when he claimed in a Georgia Law Day address in May 1974 that Bob Dylan was 'a friend of his'.[16] Carter's unusual family also provided journalists with plenty of copy to reinforce his image of strangeness. As younger brother Billy remarked of their eccentricities, 'My mother went into the Peace Corps when she was sixty-eight. My one sister is a motor cycle freak. My other sister is a Holy Roller evangelist and my brother is running for president. I'm the only sane one in the family'.[17]

These issues obscured the image of Carter that the 1976 campaign aimed to foster and often contradicted the persona he was trying to promote to a public that did not know him. The close-run Carter–Ford race of 1976 also compelled some blurring of his outsider status. His presidential nomination acceptance address at the Democratic National Convention highlighted his anti-Washington credentials through its negative references to economic and political elites, bloated bureaucracy and secrecy in government.[18] His outsider persona became less clear-cut as he was forced during the campaign to endorse core Democratic programmes in order to ensure grass-roots party support. Carter's victory was a remarkable achievement: a virtually unknown candidate (his national recognition when he started was 1 per cent[19]) became president by creating an image that won the trust of the electorate in 1976. Although criticized for vagueness on policy issues, by the end of the campaign he had taken fifty-one positions and made 186 pledges, many of which were traditional liberal commitments.[20] This not only created expectations by which his presidency would be measured but also raised doubts about his capacity to deliver on his promises. In post-election polls, the public recognized Carter's strong moral character (83 per cent) but less than a third thought that he had the programme to move the country forward or that he was a strong leader.[21] If he was to succeed in the White House, it was those leadership qualities that he needed to demonstrate.

Given his narrow victory by 50.1 to 48 per cent in popular vote terms and 297 to 240 votes in the Electoral College, Carter required a broader image to sustain his public support. Political scientist Bruce Miroff has argued that to be successful, 'the qualities of the presidential character must not only be appealing, they must be magnified by spectacle'.[22] Spectacle can be described as a symbolic event designed to reinforce an image. Carter was no stranger to symbolism and had used it widely as governor, notably when dedicating Martin Luther King's portrait in the Georgia State Capitol to symbolize acceptance of the civil rights revolution. In the White House, Carter displayed an aversion to pomp and ceremony that not only reflected his Baptist background but was part of a wider strategy to promote an image of him representing all the people.[23] He sought to restore the republican frugality of his office by rejecting the trappings of the 'imperial presidency': Carter and his wife Rosalynn walked down Pennsylvania Avenue to the White House following his inauguration, he carried his own bag onto Air Force One, he sold the presidential yacht, he stopped serving alcohol at White House dinners, and he reduced the use of 'Hail to the Chief.' To maintain contact with the electorate, the White House devised 'people program' events where Carter could talk directly to ordinary members of the public. During the first eighteen months in office, he communicated through television addresses, a radio phone-in and a series of town hall meetings (thirteen by October 1979). In addition, he encouraged his 'constituents' to write to him, thereby generating a volume of mail that swamped the White House staff charged with providing weekly reports of public concerns.[24]

For this strategy to be effective, Carter needed the press to act as a channel for his message. The administration committed to fortnightly presidential news conferences, which Carter handled with confidence and answered questions freely. In addition, his aides organized meetings with reporters and editors from outside Washington and ensured that nationally eminent correspondents received invitations to White House dinners. However, Carter and his staff remained suspicious of reporters, particularly those based in Washington. The president often called the editors of journalists whose coverage displeased him and reportedly denied White House access to *New York Times* correspondent and fellow Southerner James Wooten because of his critical articles.[25] Carter expressed shock in an interview with Bill Moyers on 13 November 1978 about the 'irresponsibility of the press.'[26] For the journalists following the president, the suspicion was mutual. In addition, Carter's mastery of detail was taken as a challenge by reporters who wanted to trip him up and, in the post-Watergate climate, catch him in a lie.

This did not mean that his communication strategy was ineffective, at least not initially. The announcement of the administration's approach to the energy crisis was supported by a series of coordinated events that included town hall meetings, inviting reporters to a Cabinet meeting and a helicopter visit to Pittsburgh when the city suffered fuel shortages during a spell of extreme cold. These activities were the lead-up to the president's televised address to the nation on energy problems on 18 April 1977. Rejecting his wife's advice to don a jacket to look presidential, Carter delivered it wearing a cardigan and sitting before an open fire to reinforce his man-of-the-people image.[27]

Early assessment of Carter's public presidency was generally positive. Impressed by the Clinton, Massachusetts, Town Hall meeting on 17 March 1977, David Broder of the *Washington Post* commented, 'In his first two months as President Jimmy Carter has achieved a triumph of communication in the arena of public opinion. He has transformed himself from a shaky winner of a campaign into a popular President whose mastery of the mass media has given him real leverage with which to govern.'[28] To Carter's dismay, his honeymoon with the media was of short duration. Hoping to put things right once more, he appointed Gerald Rafshoon, a fellow Georgia who had worked on the 1976 campaign as communications director in charge of media liaison. The new man attempted to control the style and form of White House communications but fell afoul of the press's post-Watergate determination not to be manipulated by presidential spin. To make matters worse, Carter's folksy style was wearing thin with many

Figure 8.1 Just plain folks: Jimmy Carter addresses the nation on energy problems in his cardigan, 18 April 1977. Source: US National Archives and Records Administration.

journalists, notably *Time* White House correspondent Hugh Sidey, who adjudged him simply not presidential.[29] Compounding this negative imagery, he came under press criticism for surrounding himself with home-state aides, the so-called 'Georgia Mafia', whom many reporters deemed not up to the job because of their inexperience in the ways of Washington.[30]

Ultimately the administration's success was dependent upon Carter's ability to persuade the public of the wisdom of his policies. The best channel to achieve that was television. Early in the 1976 campaign, Carter's friend Charles Kirbo had arranged for him to have a test in front of the cameras. The feedback from the consultants was that the maximum time for him to be on TV would be five minutes.[31] Disliking set-piece speeches, Carter felt much more comfortable interacting spontaneously with smaller groups of people. Nevertheless, he gave three televised addresses during the first three months of his presidency to explain complex subjects like energy and inflation. As would be the case with much of his later rhetoric, he adopted a preachy style that set a pessimistic tone, exemplified by his energy address to Congress in April 1977: 'This cannot be an inspirational speech tonight. I don't expect much applause. It's a sober and a difficult presentation.'[32] Many pundits questioned whether such sombre messaging could gain popular support. The public did appreciate, at least initially, Carter's objective style that one historian ascribed to him being 'a trained engineer who prided himself on making technical judgements unburdened by ideology'.[33] To be seen as effective, however, he had to be able to work with Congress to pass legislation and there were early questions about his ability or even willingness to do this.

In 1976 Carter had presented himself to the public as someone who would make government work for the people. The outsider image had helped him win office but as president he needed to display competence by delivering on his substantive promises. Carter's commitment to provide comprehensive solutions to complex problems, like energy, tax fairness, healthcare and welfare, raised expectations that were politically impossible to fulfil. Unwilling to make compromises to broaden support for his core proposals in Congress, he never fully delivered on his ambitious agenda. When briefing staff before a key vote on energy policy, Carter acknowledged the political risks of failure: 'If we get whipped on this then incompetence and weakness will be perceived. This may be unfair, but this will be our image and it will become a reality.'[34] Without a legislative record to match his promises, the image of competency that was key to his success as president began to unravel.

Early legislative failure over his energy and tax reform bills contributed to a drop from 55 per cent to 34 per cent in Carter's approval ratings in the first six months of his presidency.[35] However, it was the failure of his economic policy, specifically his inability to control runaway inflation, that inflicted greatest damage on his reputation for competence. Inflation that brought about double-digit rises in the consumer price index during his last two years as president had both an economic and a psychological impact. Unlike unemployment, price instability affected everyone and created uncertainty that influenced investment decisions by business, wage demands by labour and consumer purchasing. Carter introduced five anti-inflation initiatives and made three televised addresses on inflation, but price instability got worse over the course of his presidency. This record earned Carter unwanted comparison with another engineer-president, Herbert Hoover. Dubbed 'Jimmy Hoover' by some commentators, he was accused of making 'his name a synonym for economic mismanagement' to rival Hoover's 'dawdling at the onset of the Great Depression.'[36]

Carter's various policy failures led to growing criticism of his leadership by politicians, interest groups and the press. A narrative initially developed that his inexperienced Georgian staff were to blame for things going wrong. Aides such as Hamilton Jordan and Frank Moore stood accused of failure to consult Congress, ignorance of correct protocol and general ineffectiveness. Budget Director Bert Lance's resignation over his financial dealings in Georgia in August 1977 further damaged the White House. Carter's handling of the issue damaged his reputation for moral probity because he had clearly underestimated the gravity of the charges against a close friend. Staffing reforms in April 1978 and in July 1979 improved the White House's efficiency, but this did little to make Congress more willing to cooperate with it. With their eyes on the 1980 elections, Republicans had nothing to gain from making Carter look good and Democrats had no incentive to associate themselves with a president sinking in the polls. Accordingly, the perception of presidential incompetence persisted but with the added dimension of Carter personally rather than his staff being increasingly blamed for the administration's problems.

It was not unreasonable for journalists to question Carter's political acumen as he had made several mistakes in trying to pass legislation. His failure to establish priorities resulted in a legislative logjam in Congress that facilitated opposition efforts to delay or even defeat his major bills. Congressional Democrats also resented his unwillingness to make the necessary deals to enact legislation. When there were successes, Carter let his Cabinet claim the credit but when there were failures he was the one who accepted the blame.[37] As Carter's signature legislative initiatives on energy, tax reform and hospital cost-containment underwent defeat or delay in Congress, he became personally associated with an image of failure. Journalists now focussed not on his intellectual strengths and his mastery of detail but his perceived inability to prioritize and delegate. They used stories of Carter controlling who used the White House tennis court and reading hundreds of pages of documents as signs of his mania for micromanagement that lost sight of the big picture.[38]

The president's reluctance to cut deals with key members of Congress did display a lack of political acumen, but much of the criticism was unfair. Despite a Democratic majority in both House and Senate, Congress was both ideologically and regionally divided on important matters of policy. An unholy alliance of conservatives from southern and western oil states allied and northern liberals concerned to protect automobile manufacturing consigned the president's oil conservation bill to defeat. There is no evidence of Carter being overwhelmed or indecisive in the face of his myriad problems. He clearly retained his capacity to absorb detailed information quickly as the basis for his decision-making, but the dominant political narrative of his inability to deliver change had become widely entrenched among political elites and the public by the midway point of his term.

Confusion over Carter's ideology continued to present problems. He always avoided being labelled as either liberal or conservative, preferring to define himself by issues rather than ideology. He stuck by his campaign self-description of being 'a fiscal conservative but quite liberal on such issues as civil rights, environmental quality, and helping people lead fruitful lives.'[39] Liberal Democrats wanted a more full-blooded ideological commitment to the reforms promised in the 1976 campaign, particularly on healthcare, welfare and taxation. They ended up bitterly resentful of Carter's failure to deliver substantively on these pledges and of his insistence on controlling inflation as his economic priority – even at cost of a recession in 1980 that violated the party's historic commitment to jobs. Their dissatisfaction helped feed negative stories in the press. According to Gerald Rafshoon, disgruntled Democrats were the chief source for the negative media coverage of the president.[40] Carter also had to contend with the hostility of his former Christian right supporters for not delivering on their socio-moral agenda of criminalizing abortion, legalizing school prayer and removing tax restrictions on faith schools for not meeting racial diversity requirements in their student body. Following a private prayer meeting between the president and a group of evangelical leaders, pastor Tim LaHaye issued a public prayer: 'God, we have to get this man out of the White House and get someone in here who will be aggressive about bringing back traditional moral values.'[41]

By the summer of 1979, with inflation rising and a second energy crisis underway, Carter's image as a competent president who would make government work for the American people had largely disappeared. His pollster, Pat Caddell, had carried out a survey in late 1978 which confirmed that Americans were pessimistic about the future and had lost faith in Carter, or any other politician, being able to fix the nation's problems. The only positive element for the president from this survey was the continued belief that he was a good, moral man.[42] In July 1979, his advisors called for a national address to 'reverse the image of drift, confusion and vacillation'[43] Carter's postponement of the speech and the consequent invitation to public officials from all levels of government to consult with him at Camp David were designed to create a sense of drama.[44] Hoping to relaunch his presidency, the eventual speech sought to project him as the healer of the 'crisis of spirit' that ailed the nation amid the energy crisis. However, the president's ill-advised decision to remove five cabinet members in the wake of the address and the continued failure of his legislative programme in Congress soon extinguished whatever good it had done for his public image.

To sustain public support and promote his message, a president needs the cooperation or, at the very least, the acquiescence of the media. Not only was Carter denied this for most of his time in office, but he also faced arguably more sustained criticism of his leadership capability than any modern occupant of the Oval Office. James Reston of the *New York Times* subsequently contended, 'The press is primarily responsible for destroying Carter's political reputation.'[45] Initial criticism triggered by failure of his key legislative initiatives developed into more fundamental questioning of whether he had what it took to be president. Bert Lance believed that the Carter White House was the victim of the Washington elite's regional prejudice.[46] The Georgians on the staff were openly mocked for their lack of Washington experience, but it often went well beyond that. Journalist Patrick Anderson, a one-time Carter speechwriter, later described Hamilton Jordan and Jody Powell as 'a couple of raw boned, narrow eyed South Georgia thugs.'[47] Negative stories about Jordan, largely unfounded, appeared throughout Carter's term of office. The most serious was that he snorted cocaine at a New York disco, but an official investigation found no evidence to substantiate this and his accusers were charged with perjury. Highly respected CBS anchor Walter Cronkite later adjudged the network's coverage of the cocaine allegations as the 'worst story he had ever broadcast.' Nevertheless, Carter and his aides continued to be held in low esteem by the press. When Ronald Reagan won the 1980 presidential election, Hugh Sidey would remark, 'Now maybe we'll have a little class.'[48]

Some of the press attitude had its roots in a dissonance between Carter's simple 'never lie to you' image and his sophisticated media operation that journalists felt was manipulative. A Watergate-jaundiced press questioned the sincerity of his message and image as managed by Rafshoon.[49] Such scepticism found its most damaging expression in media stories, widely believed by the public, that Carter would stage-manage the release of the US Embassy hostages held by Iran to win the 1980 election. In an effort to allay these suspicions, Rafshoon's department was closed in the run-up to the election, but the harm done to Carter's image as a moral man was serious.

In common with his aides, Carter felt mistreated by the press, commenting in a 1997 interview that he had only one month of positive coverage out of forty-eight.[50] His sense of hurt was still evident nearly forty years after leaving office in his public criticism of the mainstream media's negative coverage of President Donald Trump.[51] Eminent journalist Haynes Johnson acknowledged that Carter 'received credit for almost nothing.'[52] Whilst members of the press respected his intelligence, they did not warm to him personally. Carter prided himself on being able to answer any question at press conferences, but his attempts at wit would often descend into sarcasm.[53] The frequency of press conferences declined along with his standing in the polls. Jordan believed that the Washington press felt duped by Carter as he was not what they expected.[54] His non-ideological stance made it difficult for journalists to describe him coherently and they questioned his underlying motives. Carter's image as a moral man who would 'never lie' to the American public was sometimes regarded as a challenge by reporters determined to prick hypocrisy and call politicians to account. Stories about policy conflicts within the Cabinet, the White House failure to deal with Congress and the scandal over Lance's financial dealings all conspired to keep Carter's message off the front pages.

Despite these problems, Carter still had opportunities to reinforce his image by talking directly to the American people. While his performance on a radio phone-in and town hall meetings showed him at his best as a public communicator, he really struggled to get his message across in set-piece speeches. On taking up his media liaison role, Rafshoon counselled the president not to go on television so often, but the real problems lay with Carter himself, the message he was putting across and the way he delivered it. As a scientist and engineer, he understood complex issues but the moralist in him refused to simplify and sugar-coat the problems he was seeking to solve. His exhortations that the nation should live within its energy and economic limits could work only if Americans were prepared to listen, but not enough did. One analyst commented, 'Carter has been rather at odds with the temper of his time – the bearer of bad news and belt-tightening programs to a nation unprepared to believe than an energy crisis existed.'[55]

As his support waned, Carter would not adjust his message, nor would he articulate a positive theme that the sacrifices would be worthwhile. The overall tone of his speeches was pessimistic, containing such dark phrases as: 'Tonight I want to have an unpleasant talk with you.'[56] Although Carter's public speaking style had been integral to his outsider image in the successful 1976 campaign, more was expected of him as president. He continued to write most of his own speeches and declined any coaching, perhaps because he feared it might modify his voice. He also refused to use any rhetorical devices suggested by his speechwriters, such as articulating an overall theme to his policies. The idea of the 'New Foundations' received an airing in his State of the Union Address in 1979, only to be talked down in a later press conference.[57] With some justice, columnists Rowland Evans and Robert Novak described Carter's speeches as 'allergic to all efforts at eloquence.'[58]

Carter's last national address on energy, delivered after much deliberation on 23 July 1979, offered the ultimate proof of his failure to get his message across to the public, even though it was initially well received as an attempt 'To lift a nation's spirit.'[59] This went down in history as the 'malaise' speech, a term Carter never used but the press fixed upon it to suggest that the president was blaming the American people for their attitude to self-sacrifice. In the opinion of Bill Clinton, then Arkansas governor, salvationless jeremiads of such ilk made Carter sound more like 'a 17th Century New England Puritan than a 20th Century Southern Baptist.'[60] The air of pessimism pervading the speech coupled with the mistimed decision to remove five cabinet members could not halt his continued decline in the polls. More damaging for Carter's image was the fact that liberal and conservative opponents would reference the 'malaise' address' to claim that the country's long-term problems were down to its president. Pessimism – or put another way, a lack of faith in America – was to be part of Carter's image, and that became a major political problem for him in the 1980 election.

In common with a negative press, satirical comedy was instrumental in saddling Carter with an unwanted image. The mockery of presidents has a long tradition in American popular culture. Satire receded somewhat with the dawning of the nuclear age in the 1950s but revived in the 1960s. The genre hit new heights in the 1970s thanks to Herblock's anti-Nixon cartoons in the *Washington Post* as the Watergate scandal unfolded. Presidential impersonation then became a staple of the popular *Saturday Night Live Show* on television later in the decade. Ominously for Carter, persistent comedic attacks on presidents have caused political damage. Pictures of Gerald Ford falling over created a perception of clumsiness that was the antithesis of the dignified image that all presidents seek to cultivate.

Satire that focussed on Carter's perceived weaknesses and apparent eccentricities had a corrosive effect on his image. Jokes about his southern oddness persisted throughout his term in office. Initial focus was on his accent, the slow-paced southern drawl that prompted such publications as William Maloney's *How to Understand Your President and Speak Southern* and Jake Moon's *The Dixie-Doodle Dictionary*. Jokes about Carter family members were legion, with brother Billy mercilessly lampooned as a redneck: one jibe asked what his favourite seven-course meal was, with the answer being 'a six pack and a racoon.' Carter's evangelicalism was also a source of humour, its image of strangeness outside the South not helped by a popular song of the day entitled 'Drop Kick Me Jesus through the Goalposts of Life.'[61]

Although the satirical narrative was a product of general ignorance and snobbishness, Carter's own behaviour contributed to it, notably regarding the 'Killer Rabbit' incident. In August 1979, Press Secretary Jody Powell let slip that whilst fishing on holiday in Georgia, the president had beaten off a wild rabbit that had been in the water and tried to get into his boat. In a quiet news month, the media reported the story in a humorous way. Instead of killing it by saying nothing further, Carter issued repeated 'clarifications' in a vain attempt to be believed, but this only encouraged press ridicule of him. The story prompted a cartoon entitled 'Paws,' which spoofed the poster from the film *Jaws* by showing Carter in a boat with the 'killer rabbit' below the surface coming up fast to attack. The face of Senator Edward Kennedy, expected to challenge Carter in the Democratic primaries, was superimposed onto the rabbit's.[62] Adding to Carter's discomfort, folk-singer Tom Paxton satirized the episode in a self-penned ditty 'I don't want a bunny wunny.'[63] The overall effect was to make Carter appear to be not only a weirdo but also a wimp, thereby feeding the already rich seam of comedy about his leadership style.

Early representations of Carter's intellect and his range of knowledge were the subject of gentle parody on the *Saturday Night Live* television programme. In May 1977, it spoofed the president's successful radio phone-in with actor Dan Ackroyd, as Carter, answering questions in detail from a frustrated postal worker complaining about a new automatic postal sorter and a young man who had taken some 'bad' drugs. More seriously, in September 1978 the same show lampooned Carter's anti-inflation policy by having a presidential impersonator remarking that inflation might be uncontrollable but it would at least enable everyone to become millionaires as wages rose to compensate for the declining purchasing power of the dollar.[64] Although this sort of humour was damaging to Carter, more worrying for the White House was coverage on more established television shows. Rafshoon was concerned that jokes about his leadership style featured on the Johnny Carson Show would gain much wider credence with the American people.[65] The most famous was where Carson in his alter-ego 'Carnac the Magnificent' pretended to divine the answer to a question in a sealed envelope. On this occasion, he predicted 'Yes or No, Pros and Cons, For and Against' as the answer to the question 'Describe Jimmy Carter's position on three major issues.' This reference to alleged indecisiveness became so famous that after his presidency Carter himself played Carnac in a charity event.[66] Satirists did not always need to create material as the White House provided it for them. Carter's trip to Europe in late 1977 featured mistranslations by his interpreter in Poland who had the president saying that he had abandoned America to come live there and that he wanted to have sex with its women.

The thirty-ninth president also came in for some particularly rough treatment from cartoonists, and not just in the case of 'Paws.' In March 1977, Gary Trudeau's Doonesbury strip began to satirize the administration's media tactics by introducing the Duane Delacourt character in his role as Carter's Secretary of Symbolism. In one of his first moves, he announces that 'a major symbolic event will take place tonight at 9 pm Eastern Standard Time.' A newscaster then announces, 'NBC News will of course be providing live coverage of the gesture.'[67] Lampooning of this ilk raised questions about administration efforts to manipulate the media that undercut Carter's image of straightforward honesty. His portrayal in cartoons became more negative as his presidency unfolded. Whilst his distinctive smile remained, his body shrunk, his collar became too big and his ears became prominent, all of which made him look 'wimp-like.'

The comedic and cartoon Carter was weird, incompetent and a political featherweight, but this caricature was closer than White House image-making was to how many Americans saw him. In 1976, Carter had created an appealing persona from a blank canvass, but his record in office had tarnished this. Pat

Caddell's survey data confirmed that voters no longer regarded him as competent but, fortunately for the president, they did not believe that any politician could solve America's problems. The one feature on which Carter's poll results remained positive was his image as a moral man. Unable to run on his record, he would campaign for re-election on his personal qualities and on the dangers a Ronald Reagan presidency posed to the economy and relations with the Soviet Union, but this strategy carried with it the risk of a damaging contradiction.

By the time of the Democratic National Convention in mid-August, Reagan had a substantial lead in the polls, despite the efforts of Carter surrogates, notably Vice President Walter Mondale, to portray him as a threat to peace and prosperity. As there were three presidential contenders requiring media coverage (Congressman John B. Anderson of Illinois, a moderate Republican, was running as a third-party candidate), there was limited publicity for Mondale's speeches. Carter's frustration with his campaign's inability to get its message out induced him to lead the attack on Reagan in person. In three hard-hitting speeches, he came close to denouncing his opponent as a racial bigot, assailed him as a warmonger and condemned him as a polarizer rather than unifier by outlook.[68] These assaults prompted counter-accusations of meanness. The *Washington Post* accused him of running a 'mean and frantic campaign' that was consistent with his 'miserable record of personally savaging political opponents.' Despite toning down his attacks in response to this criticism, he could not undo the damage to his image as a moral man. The ABC/Harris Poll in mid-October 1980 found a doubling of those who doubted his integrity since its previous survey.[69]

Carter's political difficulties mounted as the campaign progressed. He had to deal with a second energy crisis, the Anderson campaign siphoning off liberal votes, the desertion of the evangelicals to Reagan and, above all, the ongoing crisis of the US hostages held in Tehran. Adding to his problems, Carter found himself distracted by a scandal involving allegations of his brother's influence-peddling as an agent of the Libyan government. The so-called Billygate episode took six weeks for Carter to resolve, killing off his hopes for a post-convention bounce in the polls.

As the election drew near, Carter's prospects appeared to depend on a successful performance in the single presidential debate with Reagan, held in Cleveland on 28 October, but the challenger's television prowess trumped his superior knowledge and intellect. Reagan's much more optimistic vision for America contrasted sharply with Carter's calls for sacrifice with little hope of progress to come. He also succeeded in framing the electorate's vote as a retrospective judgement on the incumbent's record rather than a prospective one on his putative presidency. Adding to his woes, Carter's image as a moral man continued to unravel. Some evangelicals questioned whether he was a true Christian and there was growing public belief that he would stage–manage the release of the Iranian hostages to 'steal' the election.[70] The increasingly predictable outcome saw Carter become the first elected incumbent since Herbert Hoover in 1932 to lose his bid for re-election. In what many pundits regarded as a rejection of his presidency rather than a positive approbation of Reagan, he won just 41 per cent of the popular vote and went down to heavy defeat in the Electoral College by 489 to 49 votes, winning just six states in the process.[71]

As the Democratic challenger in the 1976 presidential election, Carter had created a political image that both reflected the reality of his own persona and met the needs of post-Watergate America for a new style of leadership. As the Democratic incumbent in 1980, he needed an image based on a track record of success in office and awareness of the nation's changing aspirations amid economic and international crises. Instead voters were offered a choice between what they saw as Carter's pessimism and defeatism and Reagan's optimism and confident conservatism. Whereas Reagan, to quote the liberal editor of *The Nation*, 'radiated American values' in his certainty that the nation's best days lay ahead, Carter continued to see America's problems as deep-rooted and hard to solve.[72]

In July 1979, one of the public figures whom Carter invited to Camp David to advise him about his forthcoming energy speech was the young governor of Arkansas, Bill Clinton. He told Carter, 'Don't just preach sacrifice but liberation ... that it is an exciting time to be alive.'[73] Such an optimistic outlook was not in Carter's nature. To win in 1980, he needed to be a different Jimmy Carter from the one he presented in 1976 but fundamentally he had not changed. He was too moral a man and far too stubborn to substantially change his image to suit the political needs of the time. By November 1980, Carter's carefully crafted image had totally unravelled. His claim for competence based on his scientific/engineering training had been discredited by a series of policy failures particularly on the economy. His outsider status had been reinforced in negative fashion through media pejorative portrayal of the Georgia White House set, including himself, as backward and weird. In the 1980 campaign, perceptions of Carter's 'meanness' in his attacks on Reagan undermined his image as a moral man.

Whilst the building and sustaining of a positive image is important for all presidents, this can only be successful if it is supported by a credible track record of success, in terms of both domestic and foreign policy. For Jimmy Carter, the reality of his record, despite some significant achievement such as the Camp David Accords of 1978 that secured peace between Israel and Egypt and the major conservation initiative embodied in the so-called Alaska lands bill of 1980, simply did not match up to the competent image created in 1976. Since leaving office, Carter's simple lifestyle and his humanitarian work, for which he won the Nobel Peace Prize in 2002, have boosted his reputation. However, the contrast in his standing as the most venerated of America's post-presidents only underlines the image of failure that still clings to his actual presidency.

Notes

1   'Jimmy Who Is Running for What!?' *Atlanta Constitution*, 13 December 1974.
2   Quoted in Borstelmann, Thomas, *The 1970's: A New Global History from Civil Rights to Economic Inequality* (Princeton, NJ: Princeton University Press, 2012), p. 2.

3   Carroll, Peter, *It Seemed Like Nothing Happened. The Tragedy and the Promise of the 1970's* (New York: Holt, Rinehart, and Winston, 1982), p. 235.

4   Sabato, Larry, 'New South Governors and the Governorship,' in James Lea, ed., *Contemporary Southern Politics* (Baton Rouge: Louisiana State University Press, 1988), pp. 194–213; McMath, Robert, 'Jimmy Carter: A Southerner in the White House?' in Elizabeth Jacoway and Dan Carter, eds., *The Adaptable South: Essays in Honor of George Brown Tindall* (Baton Rouge: Louisiana State University Press, 1991), pp. 237–63.

5   Witcover, Jules, *Marathon: Pursuit of the Presidency 1972–1976* (New York: Viking, 1977), pp. 113–14.

6   Address Announcing Candidacy for the Democratic Presidential Nomination at the National Press Club, 12 December 1974, The American Presidency Project [APP], https://www.presidency.ucsb.edu/node/278527.

7   Borstelmann, *The 1970's*, p. 270.

8   Carter, Jimmy, *Why Not the Best?* (Nashville, TN: Broadman, 1975), p. 134.

9   Wrong, Dennis, 'Stumbling along with Carter,' *Dissent*, 25 (January 1978): 3–6 (quotation p. 6). See too Leuchtenburg, William E., 'Jimmy Carter and the Post-New Deal Presidency,' in Gary Fink and Hugh Davis Graham, eds., *The Carter Presidency: Policy Choices in the Post-New Deal Era* (Lawrence: University Press of Kansas, 1998), pp. 7–28.

10 Gaillard, Frye, *Prophet from Plains: Jimmy Carter and His Legacy* (Athens: University of Georgia Press, 2007), p. 15.

11 Shogan, Robert, *Promises to Keep, Carter's First One Hundred Days* (New York: Crowell, 1977), p. 30.

12 'Jimmy Carter: Candid Conversations with the Democratic Candidate for the Presidency' *Playboy Magazine*, November 1976.

13 Dumbrell, John, *The Carter Presidency: A Re-Evaluation* (Manchester: Manchester University Press, 1993), pp. 17–19.

14 'Jimmy Carter: Candid Conversations.'

15 Eizenstat, Stuart, *President Carter; The White House Years* (New York: St Martin's Press, 2018), p. 61.

16 Jimmy Carter, 'Georgia Law Day Address,' 4 May 1974, https://www.americanrhetoric.com/speeches/jimmycarterlawday1974.htm.

17 https://www.azquotes.com/author/2553-Billy_Carter%20.

18 'Our Nation's Past and Future': Address Accepting the Presidential Nomination at the Democratic National Convention in New York City, 15 July 1976, APP, https://www.presidency.ucsb.edu/node/244286.

19 Eizenstat, *White House Years*, p. 42.

20 Ribuffo, Leo, 'Jimmy Carter and the Selling of a President 1976–1980,' in Herbert Rosenbaum and Alexj Ugrinsky, eds., *The Presidency and Domestic Policies of Jimmy Carter* (Westport, CT: Greenwood, 1994), p. 141.

21 Morris, Kenneth J., *Jimmy Carter, American Moralist* (Athens: University of Georgia Press, 1996), p. 287.

22 Miroff, Bruce, 'The Presidency and Public Leadership as Spectacle,' in Michael Nelson, ed., *The Presidency and the Political System* (Washington, DC: CQ Press, 1988), pp. 271–89.

23 Kaufman, Burton I. and Scott Kaufman, *The Presidency of James Earl Carter* (Lawrence: University Press of Kansas, 2006), p. 36.

24 Johnson, Haynes, *In the Absence of Power. Governing America* (New York: Viking, 1980), p. 153.

25   Tebbel, John and Sarah Miles Watts, *The Press and the Presidency from Washington to Reagan* (New York, Oxford: Oxford University Press, 1985), p. 525.

26   Carter, Jimmy, *Keeping Faith: Memoirs of a President* (New York: Bantam, 1982), p. 125.

27   Eizenstat, *White House Years*, p. 161.

28   Quoted in Rozell, Mark, 'President Carter and the Press: Perspectives from White House Communications Advisers,' *Political Science Quarterly*, 105 (Autumn 1990): 19.

29   Wicker, Tom, 'Another PR Solution,' *New York Times*, 21 May 1978; Sidey, Hugh, 'But Is He Presidential?' *Washington Star*, 27 August 1978.

30   Fallows, James, 'The Passionless Presidency,' *Atlantic Monthly*, Part I, May 1979: 33–48, and Part II, June 1979: 75–81.

31   Thompson, Kenneth W., ed., *The Carter Presidency: Fourteen Intimate Perspectives of Jimmy Carter* (Lanham, MD: University Press of America, 1990), p. 68.

32   'Address Delivered before a Joint Session of the Congress on the National Energy Plan,' 20 April 1977, APP, https://www.presidency.ucsb.edu/node/243400.

33   Ribuffo, 'Jimmy Carter and the Selling of a President 1976–1980,' pp. 144–5.

34   Eizenstat, *White House Years*, p. 191.

35   NBC and AP Polls in Kaufman and Kaufman, *Presidency of James Earl Carter*, p. 97.

36   Melman, Sidney, 'Jimmy Hoover?' *New York Times*, 7 February 1979; Weintraub, Sidney, 'Carter's Hoover Syndrome,' *New Leader*, 24 March 1980: 5.

37   Peterson, Esther, Exit Interview, Jimmy Carter Presidential Library (JCPL) Atlanta GA, [30307–1498], pp. 8–9.

38   Fallows, 'The Passionless Presidency,' 75–81.

39   Carter, *Keeping Faith*, pp. 73–4.

40   Gerald Rafshoon Interview, Miller Center, https://millercenter.org/the-presidency/presidential-oral-histories/jimmy-carter, p. 13.

41   Quoted in Martin, William, *With God on Our Side: The Rise of the Religious Right in America* (New York: Broadway Books, 1996), p. 189.

42   Patrick Caddell, Memorandum to the President, 'Of Crisis and Opportunity,' 23 April 1979, Jody Powell Papers, Press Office Box 40, JCPL.

43   Bob Nesmith, Walter Schapiro and Gordon Stewart to Rafshoon and Rick Hertzberg, 29 June 1979, Speechwriters Subject Files, Box 8, JCPL.

44   Eizenstat, *White House Years*, p. 677.

45   Barger, Harold, *The Impossible Presidency. Illusions and Realities of Executive Power* (Glenview IL: Scott, Foreman, 1984), p. 127.

46   Lance, Bert with Bill Gilbert, *The Truth of the Matter. My Life In and Out of Politics* (New York: Summit Books, 1992), pp. 88–9.

47   Anderson, Patrick, *Electing Jimmy Carter. The Campaign of 1976* (Baton Rouge, London: Louisiana State University Press, 1994), p. 68.

48   Jordan, Hamilton, *No Such Thing as a Bad Day* (Atlanta, GA: Longstreet Press, 2000), p. 203; Anne Wexler Interview, Miller Center, 60, https://millercenter.org/the-presidency/presidential-oral-histories/jimmy-carter.

49   Rafshoon Exit Interview, JCPL.

50   Richardson, Don, ed., *Conversations with Carter* (Boulder, CO: Lynne Rienner, 1998), pp. 327–8.

51   Dowd, Maureen, 'Jimmy Carter Lusts for a Trump Posting,' *New York Times*, 21 October 2017.

52   Johnson, *Absence of Power*, pp. 228–30.

53   Ribuffo, 'Jimmy Carter and the Selling of a President 1976–1980,' p. 148.

54 Ibid., p. 164.

55 Goldman, Peter, 'The President Learning,' *Newsweek*, 26 December 1977, p. 26.

56 'Address to the Nation on Energy,' 18 April 1977, https://www.presidency.ucsb.edu/node/243395; 'Anti-inflation Program Address to the Nation,' 24 October 1978, https://www.presidency.ucsb.edu/node/243523.

57 'Interview with the President Remarks and a Question-and-Answer Session with Editors and News Directors,' 26 January 1979, https://www.presidency.ucsb.edu/node/247869.

58 Hahn, Dan F, 'The Rhetoric of Jimmy Carter,' *Presidential Studies Quarterly*, 14 (Spring 1984): 265–88.

59 'To Lift the Nation's Spirit,' *Newsweek*, 23 July 1979, p. 20.

60 Morgan, Iwan, *The Age of Deficits. Presidents and Unbalanced Budgets: From Jimmy Carter to George W Bush* (Lawrence: University Press of Kansas, 2009), p. 74.

61 Dudden, Arthur Power, 'The Record of Political Humor,' *American Quarterly*, 37 (Spring 1985): 50–70.

62 https://www.google.co.uk/search?q=jimmy+carter+paws+cartoon&tbm=isch&source.

63 https://www.azlyrics.com/lyrics/tompaxton/idontwantabunnywunny.html.

64 http://snltranscripts.jt.org/76/76ocarter.phtml. and http://snltranscripts.jt.org/78/78dcarter.phtml.

65 Rafshoon Interview, *Miller Center*, p. 14.

66 https://www.youtube.com/watch?v=RG1tpc5FjEQ.

67 Greenberg, David, *Republic of Spin: An Inside History of the American Presidency* (New York, London: W. W. Norton, 2016), p. 406.

68 Morgan, Iwan, *Reagan: American Icon* (London: I.B. Tauris, 2016), p. 139.

69 Ribuffo, 'Jimmy Carter and Selling of a President 1976–1980,' p. 157.

70 Bob Maddox, 8 December 1980, Exit Interview, JCPL; Germond, Jack and Jules Witcover, *Blue Smoke and Mirrors. How Reagan Won and Why Carter Lost the Election of 1980* (New York: Viking, 1981), p. 319.

71 For historical analysis of the contest and its outcome, see Busch, Andrew, *Reagan's Victory: The Election of 1980 and the Rise of the Right* (Lawrence: University Press of Kansas, 2005).

72 Troy, Gil, *Morning in America: How Ronald Reagan Invented the* 1980s (Princeton: Princeton University Press, 2005), p. 36.

73 Eizenstat, *White House Years*, p. 686.

Chapter 9

IN BLACK AND WHITE:
RONALD REAGAN'S IMAGE ON RACE

Iwan Morgan

As president, Ronald Reagan cultivated a self-image of colour-blind commitment to Martin Luther King's vision of an America 'rid of discrimination and prejudice, ... where people would be judged on the content of their character, not by the color of their skin.'[1] This was utterly at variance with the African American image of him. Most blacks regarded Reagan as the president of white America rather than of all Americans. As writer Alice Walker put it in a poem, 'We do not admire their president. We know why the White House is white.'[2] Giving voice to this sentiment, William Gibson, chair of the National Association for the Advancement of Colored People [NAACP], the nation's oldest civil rights organization, denounced Reagan as 'basically a reactionary and a racist.' An opinion poll taken in early 1986 found that 56 per cent of black respondents similarly thought of him as a racist.[3]

Skilled in symbolic leadership, Reagan created a trenchant presidential image that played well with white America. The fortieth president portrayed himself as the champion of America's exceptionalism as a nation of limitless potential based on its dedication to the values of freedom, a vision encapsulated in his frequent references to it as a 'shining city on a hill.'[4] Optimism, patriotism and a sense of national mission all found a place in his vision of the United States as 'the land of tomorrow .... [that] remains on a voyage of discovery, a land that has never become, but is always in the act of becoming.'[5] Anxiety about national decline felt by many Americans amid the economic woes, international reverses and the Watergate shame of the 1970s was heresy to Reagan. 'We are first; we are best,' he avowed in 1984. 'How can we not believe in the greatness of America? ... We're Americans.' Such conviction made him ideally suited to lead the nation out of an era of pessimism to renewed belief in its promise. In 1979, the Gallup poll reported that only 53 per cent of respondents were 'optimistic/very optimistic' and 39 per cent were 'pessimistic/very pessimistic' about America's future; in 1991, the respective scores were 75 per cent and 19 per cent.[6]

Reagan's image as the booster of America's best values and its unending capacity for self-renewal did not cross the racial divide. No modern president has avowed his colour-blind egalitarianism with such conviction as he did in seeking to depict himself as freedom's tribune and none has been held in such low esteem by black America, at least prior to Donald Trump.[7] This contradiction requires exploration because it suggests that presidential image is for the most part highly racialized in construction, reception and remembrance. Championship of black America has rarely been instrumental in forging the image of White House occupants from Theodore Roosevelt to Donald Trump. The standout exceptions are Lyndon Johnson and Barack Obama. In a bleak but accurate assessment, historian Kenneth O'Reilly commented, 'An urge to confront race and racism head on has appeared in the Oval Office as often as [Haley's] comet cuts the earth's heavens.'[8]

Ronald Reagan's presidency underlined this reality. In 1983, when a cornucopia of rights groups ranging from the NAACP to the Nation of Islam held a twentieth-anniversary commemoration of the 1963 March on Washington in the nation's capital, what united them, historian George Lewis noted, was 'outright opposition to the Reagan administration in general, and a willingness to obstruct his mooted return to the White House in 1984 in particular.'[9] Observing the almost complete absence of African Americans from commemorations that followed Reagan's death in 2004, black columnist Joe Davidson remarked, 'The gushy tributes … might be understandable eulogies, but they also are a testament to the persistence of two Americas, one black and one white. The two don't see things the same and the reaction to Reagan is just one more example.'[10] In a starker expression of black disdain, Mike 'Killer Mike' Render rapped in his song 'Reagan' off the 2012 album *R.A.P. Music*, 'I leave you with four words: I'm glad Reagan dead.'[11]

Through speeches, memoirs and private letters written to African Americans, Reagan attempted to craft an image of being completely free from racial prejudice. In his telling, uppermost in ensuring his lack of bigotry were his father Jack, whose own experience of anti-Catholicism made him detest prejudice of any kind, and his mother Nelle, a devotee of the Disciples of Christ Church who took to heart its belief in the brotherhood of man. As proof of his parents' racial values, and his own absorption of them, Reagan often recounted how they had welcomed two black fellow members of the Eureka College football team whom he had brought home for the night after they had been denied accommodation at a whites-only hotel in his hometown of Dixon, Illinois, while on the way to play another college in the 1931 season. This was a tale he frequently told when meeting or corresponding with blacks as president. Another, dubbed the 'Jackie Robinson story' by White House aides, featured his opposition to the practice of barring black players from major league baseball when he was a sports broadcaster in Des Moines, Iowa, in the mid-1930s.[12]

Beyond that point in time, Reagan had few stories about what he had done for blacks as a Hollywood actor, California governor and US president because there was precious little to tell. The anti-racist speeches delivered as a spokesman for the leftist Hollywood chapter of the American Veterans Committee (AVC) in the immediate aftermath of the Second World War constituted the high-watermark of his racial progressivism. Still an adherent to the liberal values he had espoused during the New Deal era, Reagan was forthright in attacking not only the Ku Klux

Klan but also police brutality against returning African American veterans in the South as fascist stains on America.[13] During a long career as the champion of the right, Reagan never referred to this brief anti-racist crusade, which ended when the AVC became tarred as communist-dominated during the Hollywood Red Scare. He also drew a veil over his role in an anti-KKK Hollywood movie.

Reagan's father had once forbidden him from seeing D.W. Griffith's racist classic *Birth of a Nation* (1915) on one of its 1920s re-runs because it glorified the Ku Klux Klan. Some thirty years later, he wrote a friend about starring in *Storm Warning* (Warner Bros., 1951), in which '[I] lick the KKK....Wouldn't Jack have been pleased!'[14] Reagan garnered good reviews for his performance as a district attorney fighting Klan corruption and intimidation in a Southern town, but the movie did not revive his flagging Hollywood career. A weak script had the protagonists deliver over-preachy lines in confrontational scenes without adequately exploring their inner selves. Producer Jerry Wald had wanted the story to focus on the conflicting emotions of the two lead characters to allegorize the ambivalence of local communities that tolerated the Ku Klux Klan instead of standing up to it. Played somewhat one-dimensionally by Ginger Rogers, an out-of-town witness to the local Klan's murder of an investigative journalist initially places family loyalty above duty rather than testify against her brother-in-law, whom she saw fire the fatal shot. Reagan's lines failed to reveal the dilemma that Wald had wanted his character to experience between doing his civic duty in ensuring justice at the likely cost of his personal hopes for re-election and political advancement.[15] In the less-than-credible final scene, good triumphs over evil when the murderer is exposed and the Grand Wizard who ordered the hit is abandoned to the law by the other Klansmen.

Life did not imitate art in the case of Reagan's encounters with racial prejudice as a politician. When *Storm Warning* appeared, he was in the early stages of a political odyssey that would transform him from liberal Democrat into conservative Republican and from actor into office-holder. Recollections of his earlier confrontations with racists, whether real or celluloid ones, found no place during a career in government built in part on being the most successful white-backlash politician in American history.[16] This is not to suggest that Reagan was racially prejudiced, an accusation guaranteed to get him steamed up. His only premature departure from a political stage occurred early in his 1966 gubernatorial campaign when he faced allegations of racism for opposing the Civil Rights Act of 1964 from a Republican rival during their joint appearance before the California Negro Republican Assembly. 'I resent the implication that there is any bigotry in my nature,' he shouted before storming out of the auditorium.[17]

Ironically, it was not racial prejudice but his concept of freedom that shaped his image of insensitivity to African American concerns. As historian Eric Foner observed, 'No idea is more fundamental to Americans' sense of themselves as individuals and as a nation than freedom.' Nevertheless, its meaning has metamorphosed over time in step with changing beliefs about the benefits of strong national government. Mid-twentieth-century liberals regarded the state's role in promoting economic growth, social welfare and civil rights as the fundamental security for personal liberty. As Reagan moved rightward, he became a powerful advocate of a competing vision that restoration of the free market, termination of confiscatory taxation and roll-back of government regulation would allow Americans the freedom to achieve their full potential as individuals.[18] This put him on a collision course with African Americans, for whom a benevolent federal government was the necessary guarantor of their civil rights, educational and employment opportunities, and social welfare. Conversely, Reagan's ideas appealed to many working-class and lower-middle-class whites, core Democratic constituencies during the heyday of the New Deal order, who felt their jobs, homes and neighbourhoods under threat from government-sponsored black advancement.

From his very first campaign for office, Reagan established an image of being sympathetic to white discontent and its racial undertones. His Democratic opponent in 1966, Governor Pat Brown, complained that he was 'riding the [white] backlash ... and perhaps even subtly contributing to it.'[19] Reagan was highly adept at so-called 'dog-whistle politics', the use of coded language that appeared benign but had specific meaning for targeted constituencies.[20] In defending the freedom of private owners to sell their property to whomsoever they wished as an inalienable right, he effectively sided with white suburbanites worried that house values would collapse if blacks moved into their neighbourhood. In condemning public-assistance handouts for able-bodied layabouts, he exploited white conviction that state taxes were rising to fund black welfare abuse. Finally, Reagan played on white concerns about liberal mollycoddling of black criminality through regular use of the 'jungle' metaphor for the Brown administration's failure to uphold law and order. 'Every day the jungle draws a little closer', he avowed in declaring his candidacy for governor. 'Our city streets are jungle paths after dark.'[21] As journalist Hale Champion commented, 'The whites thought ... there would be a different kind of atmosphere if Reagan were governor.'[22]

Reagan's image on racial issues and the strategy that shaped it carried through into his presidential campaigns. In 1968, frontrunner Richard Nixon worried that the California governor might deny him the Republican presidential nomination by sweeping Southern primaries and state conventions, but his declaration of candidacy came too late to be a serious threat. 'Reagan's strength', a Nixon campaign memo remarked, 'derives from ... the ideological appeal of the Right and the emotional distress of those who fear or resent the Negro, and who expect Reagan somehow to keep him "in his place" or at least to echo their own anger and frustration.'[23] In 1976, Reagan's more serious challenge came close to denying incumbent Gerald Ford the GOP presidential nomination through a campaign that exploited the racial concerns of white taxpayers. To highlight welfare abuse, Reagan attacked the food-stamp programme for allowing recipients to buy 'T-bone steaks' while hard-working citizens had to make do with 'hamburger.' Many speeches told of a Chicago 'welfare queen', who had fabricated 'eighty names, thirty addresses, twelve Social Security cards, and is collecting veterans' benefits on four non-existent husbands' to make an annual tax-free income of $150,000 in government benefits. Though he never mentioned race in these anecdotes, the not-so-subliminal messaging played on white concerns about black welfare cheating. Undeterred that the woman in the 'welfare queen' story was convicted in 1977 of using just two identities to defraud $8,000 in public aid checks, Reagan would often tell its original version as gospel in meetings with congressmen and even some foreign leaders when president.[24]

Though ultimately unsuccessful, Reagan's 1976 campaign for president was critical in shaping his image on race at the national level. It was also instrumental in creating a Republican Party that was fundamentally lilywhite in voter perceptions. This was the last election in which African Americans had any significance in GOP politics. In an extraordinarily tight race, the dwindling numbers of black Republicans went overwhelmingly for Ford, helping to deny Reagan victory in the pivotal states of Kentucky and Tennessee, whose delegates would have given him the margin to win the nomination. Conversely, Reagan had strong appeal in states like Michigan and Texas to crossover supporters of former Alabama Governor George Wallace, a powerful articulator of white rage against racial progressivism, following his withdrawal from the contest for the Democratic presidential nomination after a string of primary losses to Jimmy Carter. Ford's private pollster found that Reagan supporters were almost indistinguishable from Wallace ones in their racial perspectives.[25] Over the next decade, white southerners and northern white ethnics would realign with the Reagan-led Republican Party to help it win three consecutive presidential elections. It was a case, one analyst noted, of George Wallace meeting Archie Bunker (the name of a bigoted character in the popular television sitcom, *All in the Family*, about a blue-collar family in Queens, New York) in their new GOP home.[26]

In many regards, the 1984 presidential election encapsulated Reagan's dichotomous racial image in the eyes of white America and black America. The incumbent president swept to landslide victory over Democrat Walter Mondale with a campaign that celebrated America's exuberant recovery from the disillusion of the 1970s, a theme encapsulated in the signature 'Morning in America' ad. The idea, White House aide Richard Darman asserted in a memo, was 'to paint RR as the personification of all that is right with, or heroized by, America. Leave Mondale in a position where an attack on Reagan is tantamount to an attack on America's idealized image of itself – where a vote against Reagan is, in some subliminal sense, a vote against a mythic "AMERICA."'[27] It was evident, however, that the message of national renewal under Reagan carried racial meaning for many blue-collar whites.

After Reagan swept Michigan counties that had been solidly Democratic for decades, the state Democratic party commissioned Stanley Greenberg to conduct a post-election survey to ascertain why he had run so strongly in these places. The pollster concentrated his investigations on Macomb county on the outskirts of Detroit where many habitually Democratic whites had voted Republican. 'These white defectors,' he concluded after conducting focus-group sessions with them,

> express a profound distaste for blacks, a sentiment that pervades almost everything they think about government and politics....The special status of blacks is perceived by almost all these individuals as a serious obstacle to

their personal advancement. Indeed, discrimination against whites has become a well-assimilated and ready explanation for their status, vulnerability and failures.... Ronald Reagan's image formed against this backdrop – disorder and weakness, passivity, and humiliation and a [Democratic] party that failed to speak for the average person. By contrast, Reagan represented a determined consistency and an aspiration to unity and pride.[28]

A broader national survey, commissioned by the Democratic National Committee, reached similar conclusions about Reagan's appeal to blue-collar whites, many of whom now saw the Democrats as 'the giveaway party [and] "giveaway" means too much middle-class money going to blacks and the poor.'[29]

White defections contrasted with steadfast black loyalty to the Democratic Party that had endured since the 1930s. In 1984, African Americans cast judgement on Reagan's disregard for their interests by giving him just 9 per cent of their ballots, by far the lowest share of any demographic group in the electorate, whether based on race, class or age. For some blacks, such as controversial Chicago Democratic congressman Gus Savage, the racial polarization of the electorate signified that 'white Americans had voted en masse to accept the Reagan philosophy of narrow individualism, me-tooism and greed.' Others, like NAACP organizer Joseph Madison, viewed it somewhat differently as a white backlash based on fears of blacks 'getting too big for their political breeches.'[30]

African Americans' perceptions of Reagan in 1984 confirmed their gloomy foreboding about what his election as president four years earlier would mean for them. Though he had not given dog-whistle politics as much prominence in 1980 as in 1976, one incident had crystallized black concerns about his stand on racial issues. Shortly after accepting the Republican presidential nomination, Reagan visited Philadelphia, Mississippi, to speak at the Neshoba County Fair on 3 August. 'I believe in states' rights,' he told the predominantly white audience. 'I believe we have distorted the balance of our government today by giving powers that were never intended to be given in the Constitution to that federal establishment.' He promised to 'restore to states and local governments the power that properly belongs to them.'[31] Had Reagan uttered these words outside the South, they may have seemed a benign declaration of support for revitalizing state government, a cause that claimed bipartisan support in the National Governors Association. In Dixie, however, 'states' rights' had the coded meaning of opposition to federal efforts to promote civil rights. Even worse, Reagan was speaking close to where three civil rights workers had been murdered by racists during the Mississippi Freedom Summer of 1964. His remarks may well have helped him carry Mississippi by a narrow margin of 12,000 votes in the presidential election, but they confirmed his racist image in the eyes of many African Americans.[32]

Linking Reagan's comments with the revival of Ku Klux Klan activism in the late 1970s, Patricia Harris, Secretary of Health and Human Services in Jimmy Carter's administration, charged that many blacks would see 'the specter of the white sheet behind him.' Former Martin Luther King aide Andrew Young went even further in asserting that Reagan's remarks were 'like a code word to me that it's going to be all right to kill niggers when he's president.' King's widow, Coretta Scott King, voiced her fears that if Reagan won the White House, 'we are going to see more of the Ku Klux Klan and a resurgence of the Nazi Party.'[33]

Having started badly, Reagan's relations with black leaders deteriorated over the course of his presidency. His address to the NAACP's annual convention in June 1981 showed utter insensitivity in asserting that government programmes had subjected the African American poor to a new form of enslavement to departmental empire-building federal bureaucrats. Decrying government's ability to move people up the economic ladder, he declared, 'I believe many in Washington, over the years, have been more dedicated to making needy people government dependent rather than independent. They've created a new kind of bondage, because regardless of how honest their intention in the beginning, those they set out to help soon became clients essential to the well-being of those who administered the programs.'[34] Displeased with his chilly reception, Reagan never appeared before this august body again. He also stopped meeting with the Congressional Black Caucus early in his presidency for the same reason.

Occasionally Reagan reached out to individual black critics but usually just to tell them stories about his upbringing in a household that was free of bigotry. A telephone call of this ilk cut no ice with former LBJ Justice Department official Roger Wilkins, the author of a highly critical newspaper column about the racial effects of Reagan's economic and civil rights policies. 'Any fair reading of that column would reveal that I had called him an ignorant bigot,' Wilkins later observed, 'and any fair reading of my mind would reveal that this was exactly what I think.'[35] Legendary civil-rights champion Thurgood Marshall, appointed the first black Supreme Court justice by Lyndon B. Johnson in 1968, was another to receive the Reagan treatment after declaring his civil rights record the worst of any modern president. 'I think he's down with [Herbert] Hoover and that group. [Woodrow] Wilson. When we really didn't have a chance,' he asserted in a 1987 television interview. Such public criticism of an incumbent president by a sitting justice was almost unprecedented. A worried Reagan invited Marshall to the White House to 'tell him my life story & how there was not prejudice in me.' He reported in his diary that night, 'I think I made a friend,' but this was wishful thinking.[36]

More habitually Reagan dismissed the criticism of African American leaders as a deliberate misrepresentation of what he had done for black America. In 1983, he wrote to an unemployed black Vietnam veteran complaining about the 'constant drumbeat of propaganda' depicting him as a racist. 'Some leaders of black organizations have joined in this,' he remarked, 'whether to enhance their own stature by arousing their membership to anger or not I don't know.'[37] In 1988, at the annual dinner of the Gridiron Club, Washington's most exclusive journalistic organization, he buttonholed its first black president, Carl Rowan, the author of a number of critical columns about him, to say: 'You never really understood me on this business of racism .... I tried hard to win friendship among blacks, but I couldn't do it. I talked to black leaders after my election in 1980, and they went out and criticized me in horrible ways .... They attacked me at the outset, so I said to hell with 'em.'[38]

As far as Reagan was concerned, black America was doing better than ever before on his watch.[39] In material terms, there was some basis for this belief as many blacks experienced improvement in their economic and social status. In 1983, 30 per cent of African Americans considered themselves middle class, double the level in the late 1960s, a trend reflected in increasing university enrolments, entry into the professions and suburban residency. There was also a growing black presence in the mainstream cultural media, exemplified by Michael Jackson's pop music mega-stardom, Oprah Winfrey's debut on a Chicago television station in 1984, and the launch of *The Cosby Show* – the most watched television series of the decade that focused on a black upper-middle-class family – in the same year. Meanwhile black unemployment fell from its Reagan-era high of 19.5 per cent in recession-hit 1983 to 11.5 per cent in 1988, when the economy was in a prolonged cycle of growth. For Reagan, all this was vindication of his vision that 'the well-being of blacks – like the well-being of every other American – is linked directly to the health of the economy.'[40]

African Americans did not share the president's rosy image of 1980s America. Their attention focused on his administration's welfare spending cuts that hit the black poor hard, its diminished enforcement of civil rights regulations in housing, school and college enrolment, and its efforts to roll back affirmative action. Prior to his meeting with black clergy in early 1982, a White House staffer warned Reagan that he would likely face strong criticism because of administration failures to communicate all the good it had done for civil rights. 'While no single category of acusation [*sic*] might in and of itself present a cause for alarm,' the aide remarked, 'the cumulative effect of all of them together has created distrust and bitterness within the minority community…there is a widespread sentiment that the Administration is "anti-black" or engaged in a systematic effort to roll back civil rights achievements of the past.'[41] This showed scant understanding of African American discontent and its consequences. Seeing themselves under attack, blacks experienced a growing sense of racial solidarity regardless of their socio-economic class. In the 1980s, more than two-thirds of African American respondents replied 'yes' to opinion survey questions like: 'Do you think your fate is linked to that of black people?' The higher the education status of those polled, the more likely they were to answer in the affirmative.[42]

Black consciousness of race was directly at odds with the efforts of the Reagan administration and the broader conservative movement to depict a 'color-blind America.' The concept derived from Justice John Marshall Harlan's solitary dissent in the Supreme Court's *Plessy v. Ferguson* 'separate but equal' ruling of 1896 that legitimized segregation of public facilities provided the separate ones for blacks and whites were equal in quality. Despite his unqualified belief in white racial superiority, Harlan insisted that the Constitution had to be 'color-blind.' This became the watchword of the NAACP's judicial campaign against segregation in the quarter-century after the Second World War until opposing lawyers began deploying the term to challenge desegregation plans that took account of race in the late 1960s. Just over a decade later, the Reagan administration incorporated colour-blindness as the cornerstone of its civil rights strategy to justify rollback of affirmative action, established in the 1970s to ensure equality of outcome for groups historically victimized by discrimination.[43]

Reagan had avowed in the 1980 election campaign, 'We must not allow the noble concept of equal opportunity to be distorted into federal guidelines or quotas ... to be the principal factor in hiring or education.'[44] The official selected to head the civil rights division of the new administration's Justice Department offered a symbolic image of its determination to champion individual opportunity over group entitlement at his Senate confirmation hearing. Waving a copy of the Constitution above his head, William Bradford Reynolds asserted that on every question relevant to civil rights, the nation's supreme law was 'color-blind.'[45] Regarding the phrase as nothing more than an attempt to deny that groups were relevant to justice, civil rights leader Jesse Jackson expostulated, 'Race. Don't run from that. That's just real in this culture .... When you reduce our entire struggle to one guy's manhood, it distorts the bigger picture.'[46]

Reagan's most significant appropriation of color-blind imagery was to recast himself as the legatee of Martin Luther King in his remarks signing into law a national holiday for the slain civil rights leader on 2 November 1983. His words that day belied his low opinion of King in the 1960s. Reagan had criticized the Civil Rights Act of 1964 and the Voting Rights Act of 1965, the great legislative achievements of the King-led civil rights movement, as unjustifiable expansions of federal authority at the expense of the states. As late as 1980, he told one journalist that the second of these measures had been 'humiliating to the [white] South.' The statement Reagan issued when King was murdered in Memphis, Tennessee, on 4 April 1968 had implicitly condemned his use of protest tactics to promote civil rights. It was 'a great tragedy that began when we began compromising with law and order and people started choosing which laws they'd break.'[47] As president, Reagan had dragged his heels about whether King should be honoured by having a national holiday named after him. At one juncture he appeared to imply agreement with Senator Jesse Helms of North Carolina, an ultra-conservative Republican who had labelled the civil rights leader a law-breaking Communist agitator. To his embarrassment, Meldrim Thomson, a former Governor of New Hampshire and current member of the far-right John Birch Society who shared Helms's concerns, released a letter from Reagan saying, 'I have the same reservations you have but ... the perception of too many people is based on an image not a reality.'[48] However, the overwhelming level of bipartisan support for the King holiday left him little option but to approve the bill that established it.

In signing the legislation, Reagan paid tribute to King's role in securing the landmark civil rights measures of 1964–5 but presented these as the guarantees of a color-blind America. 'There was not just a change of law; there was a change of heart,' he asserted. 'The conscience of America had been touched. Across the land, people had begun to treat each other not as blacks and whites, but as fellow Americans.'[49] At the time black leaders focused more on the passage of the legislation than the president's signing remarks. Jesse Jackson, for example, declared

Figure 9.1 Ronald Reagan signs the Martin Luther King Holiday legislation on 2 November 1983, flanked on his right by Coretta Scott King. White House Photo, PD, Source: Wikimedia. Public domain, unrestricted use.

that it had 'institutionalized' the black freedom struggle and its significance in American history. When analysts paid more heed to the signing statement words, they realized that Reagan had co-opted an image of King that turned him into what scholars Justin Gomer and Christopher Petrella called 'the de facto patron saint of color-blind ideology.'[50]

The Martin Luther King that Reagan honoured was the one who had delivered the 'I Have a Dream' speech promoting a utopian vision of a colour-blind America during the March on Washington for Jobs and Freedom in August 1963. 'Finding material for the remarks was easy,' speechwriter Peter Robinson later commented, 'I kept finding passage after passage in King's work that Reagan might almost have written himself.'[51] This imagery obliterated King's radical criticisms of US capitalism, imperialism and racism and his call for an economic restructuring of American society during the last three years of his life from 1965 to 1968. Reagan's signing remarks effectively portrayed King's fundamental legacy as an America where racial injustice no longer existed: 'He symbolized what was right about America.... His nonviolent campaigns brought about redemption, reconciliation, and justice.' It therefore followed that any past injustices were not at issue, so there was no longer any need for remedial affirmative action programmes. Nor did white America need to feel guilty about the past because the future was colour-blind. Following the celebrations of the first Martin Luther King holiday, Reagan reiterated his racial vision that precluded acceptance of affirmative-action quotas for hiring: 'We want what I think Martin Luther King asked for. We want a colorblind society.'[52]

In the three decades since the fortieth president left office, his image on race has remained highly contested. During the Obama era, many conservatives appropriated it to attack what they regarded as the forty-fourth president's quasi-socialist resurrection of big government. Reeling off statistics to show how much better off blacks had been in 1989 in terms of employment, business starts-ups and middle-class growth, Heritage Foundation scholar Lee Edwards claimed that the color-blind Reagan had done far more for African Americans than the first black president by freeing them from the dead-hand of government to share in market-maximized prosperity.[53] Assertions of this kind ignored how the excesses of the free market had produced the financial crash of 2007–8 and the resultant Great Recession that impacted disproportionately on African Americans in the lower half of the income distribution. Showing the same disregard for historical context, Ronald Reagan's adopted son, conservative commentator Michael Reagan, marked the twenty–fifth anniversary of the Martin Luther King Holiday and the hundredth anniversary of his father's birth by effectively depicting him as America's 'first black president.' African American writer Toni Morrison had famously used this phrase to describe Bill Clinton, but she was allegorizing his treatment by political enemies during the 1998 impeachment crisis as typifying the experience of black men as 'the always and already guilty "perp."' Michael Reagan was using it to claim that in terms of promoting their material improvement, 'Ronald Reagan was a far better friend to black Americans than Barack Obama has been.' To give the anti-Obama message a color-blind coating, he concluded, 'History does not judge presidents by the color of their skin, but by the content of their policies.'[54]

In 2013, conservatives rushed to defend Reagan against a Hollywood movie that depicted him as racially insensitive. Directed by Lee Daniels, *The Butler* (Laura Ziskin Productions) tells the story of Cecil Gates (played by Forest Whitaker) who experiences extreme racism during his rural Georgia upbringing and goes on to serve as a White House butler for thirty-four years, during which he witnessed eight presidents grappling with civil rights issues. Though based on the true story of Eugene Allen, chronicled in a *Washington Post* article of 2008 by Will Haygood, it is a largely fictional production. Ronald and Nancy Reagan, well played against their progressive political grains by British Labour Party activist Alan Rickman and political activist Jane Fonda, strike up a friendly relationship with Gates. The president encourages him to ask for a pay rise and then invites him to attend rather than wait on a state dinner. On the other hand, Reagan is shown refusing to budge in his opposition to imposing economic sanctions on South Africa's apartheid regime, even though a Republican lawmaker urges him to support this action as morally right. In the movie, the hitherto apolitical Gates joins his son in a Free South Africa Movement demonstration in support of sanctions legislation, which results in both being arrested for public disorder.

The real Eugene Allen was never arrested for demonstrating in support of sanctions against South Africa and remained especially fond of the Reagans, but the film captures very well the two sides of Reagan on race.[55] There are plenty of instances of him doing kindnesses for individual African Americans as president but he showed little capacity for outreach on issues of broader concern to the black community.[56] Reagan did everything in his power to frustrate the enactment of sanctions legislation, even casting a futile veto of the Comprehensive Anti-Apartheid Act of 1986 in the face of overwhelming bipartisan support for it in Congress. Despite this, conservative historians complained that *The Butler* failed to explain his stand of constructive engagement on South Africa that struck a balance between pressing the Pretoria regime to undertake gradual reform of apartheid and not undermining a key ally in the regional Cold War in Africa.[57] Their criticisms glossed over the reality that black South Africans were strong supporters of sanctions in the justified belief that they would hasten the downfall of apartheid, which duly followed in 1990. When Nelson Mandela, the first leader of post-apartheid South Africa, died in 2013, one-time Reagan aide James Baker tried to soften his old boss's image as a supporter of the apartheid regime by claiming that he came to regret his veto of the sanctions bill, but there is no evidence to support this assertion. Ten months after casting it, Reagan told one correspondent, 'I wish my veto of the sanctions bill had been upheld.'[58]

Rather than his stand on South Africa, it was Reagan's efforts to support the Contra rebels' campaign to overthrow the Sandinista government of Nicaragua that led a younger generation of African American musicians to demonize him in rap and hip hop as the villainous architect of the crack epidemic of the 1980s and the resulting chaos in ghetto communities. The first ever hip hop hit, 'Rapper's Delight' by the Sugarhill Gang, entered Billboard's R&B chart in November 1979 just as Reagan announced his candidacy for president in 1980. Thereafter, Rap and Reagan had an indelible connection that went through three discernible stages, each one progressively more antagonistic to him. The conservative celebration of his 2011 centenary produced a determined counter-movement by rappers. 'There is an active marketing campaign to lionize Reagan,' Killer Mike declared, 'and I'm here to say it is a lie.'[59]

In the 1980s rap music presented an image of low-income ghetto life, hard hit by the Reagan budget cuts to public assistance and related programmes, as a desperate struggle for survival that bore no resemblance to 'Morning in America.' In their 1982 classic, 'The Message,' Grandmaster Flash and the Famous Five captured the stress of poverty with the lines 'Rats in the front room, roaches in the back/Junkies in the alley with the baseball bat' and the chorus refrain 'It's like a jungle sometimes/It makes me wonder how I keep from going under.' In the 1990s, hip hop entered a new phase with the emergence of 'gangsta rap,' featuring groups like N.W.A. whose music focused on the drugs and violence of the Compton area of Los Angeles. This genre required its artists to have had the shared experience of hustling out of poverty in the Reagan era. It was the music of those who had escaped ghetto entrapment by themselves running with gangs and drug-dealing. The early twenty-first century then saw the emergence of new performers who were the children of the ghetto generation caught up in the 1980s drug chaos.[60]

The latter hold Reagan responsible for government-sponsored flooding of cheap drugs from Central America into black neighbourhoods to fund Contra military operations in violation of congressional prohibitions on the United States helping either side in the Nicaraguan civil war. As the price of a kilo of cocaine tumbled from $60,000 to $9,000 in the 1980s, a cheap derivative known as crack gained popularity in inner cities, giving rise to the so-called crack epidemic and increasing gang violence to control territorial distribution. This in turn precipitated an intensified War on Drugs on the part of federal and local law enforcement bodies against drug use as well as supply. The outcome was a disproportionate rate of incarceration of young black males that continues down to the present day.[61]

To African American critics, like civil-rights advocate and litigator Michelle Alexander, black incarceration represented a deliberate government policy to establish racial control over non-whites. It was certainly a cruel parody of Reagan's vision of America in his farewell address as 'a tall, proud city built on rocks stronger than oceans, windswept, God-blessed, and teeming with people of all kinds living in harmony and peace.'[62] In a powerful volume of poetry, *Bastards of the Reagan Era*, Reginald Betts recounts how he slipped from honours student to teenage drug dealer, received an eight-year prison sentence for armed car-jacking at age sixteen, and found salvation behind bars through completing his high school education (on release, he gained an undergraduate degree and went on to study at Yale Law School). His poems draw analogies between the chains used to shackle prisoners and the chains of slavery. Born in 1980, Betts considers himself one of the bastards of the Reagan era in the dual sense that the abundance of drugs in the ghetto led him into bad ways and condemned him to become one of many young blacks living a parentless life in prison.[63]

The second generation of rappers was the first to identify Reagan as the culprit for the destructive lifestyle, violence and repression of the inner cities. In 2007, one-time drug dealer Jay-Z's 'Blue Magic' contained the lines, 'Blame Reagan for making me into a monster. Blame Oliver North and Iran-Contra. I ran contraband that they sponsored.' The next generation saw themselves, in Compton rap star Kendrick Lamar's words, as the 'children of Ronald Reagan.' On his 2011 album, *Section 80*, he referenced gangsta rappers as: 'The dysfunctional bastards of the Ronald Reagan era. Young Men that learned to do everything spiteful.' By contrast, Lamar saw his own ghetto cohort as innocent children born in the 1980s and trapped in the 'hood' by the awful conditions created by Reagan. His 2012 album *Good Kid, M.A.A.D. City* portrayed their traumatic experience of being raised by adults whose own opportunities were crushed by presidential policies.[64]

Kendrick Lamar received something of an official imprimatur of approval when Barack Obama invited him to the White House in November 2015 to talk over the problems of the inner cities and their solutions.[65] Nevertheless, the president did not share his guest's low opinion of Reagan. Coming of age in the 1980s, Obama had decided to become a community organizer out of discontent with Reagan's neglect of inner-city neighbourhoods. By the time he became president, his image of Reagan had become more positive. 'I think Ronald Reagan changed the trajectory of America,' he declared in 2008. 'He put us on a fundamentally different path because the country was ready for it.' Obama hoped to emulate his predecessor as a transformative president by putting America on a new track to becoming a post-racial, less unequal society.[66] The durability of the racial contours evident in Reagan's America ensured that he fell well short of this goal.

'For all my powers of communication,' Reagan had lamented in 1987, 'I was never able to convince many black citizens of my commitment to their needs. They often mistook my belief in keeping government [out] of the average American's life as a cover for doing nothing about racial injustice.'[67] If anything, his reputation has become even more tarnished in the eyes of black America with the passage of time. As the principal symbol of distrust for rap, now the most influential cultural genre of the twenty-first century, it remains to be seen how long Reagan's image as the embodiment of national pride in the eyes of many aging whites can endure in an America undergoing major demographic and generational changes. The transformation of America into a 'minority white' nation, due to occur in the mid-2040s according to recent census projections, could well be accompanied by a parallel shift from positive to negative remembrance of the fortieth president.[68] In an election-eve national broadcast in November 1984, Reagan had declared his re-election necessary for his country's continued revival from its 1970s low. 'We can say to the world and pledge to our children,' he avowed, 'America's best days lie ahead, and you ain't seen nothin' yet.'[69] Insofar as his image is concerned, however, its best days very probably lie in the past rather than the future.

Notes

1   'Radio Address to the Nation on Civil Rights,' 15 June 1985, Online by Gerhard Peters and John T. Woolley, The American Presidency Project [APP], https://www.presidency.ucsb.edu/node/260375.

2   Walker, Alice, 'Each One, Pull One,' in *Horses Make a Landscape Look More Beautiful* (San Diego: Harcourt Brace Jovanovich, 1984), p. 51 (also available at http://www.ctadams.com/alicewalker1.html).

3   'Rights Group Leader Calls Reagan a Racist,' *New York Times* [*NYT*], 19 May 1985; 'Reagan Rating Falls in Poll of Blacks,' *Washington Post* [*WP*], 18 January 1986, https://www.washingtonpost.com/archive/politics/1986/01/18/reagan-rating-falls-in-poll-of-blacks/b452138c-46ba-4353-b6d7-eb895d650bdc/?noredirect=on&utm_term=.52fcf214573f.

4   Foner, Eric, *The Story of American Freedom* (London: Papermac, 2000), pp. 320–1; Cannon, Lou, 'Why Reagan Was the "Great Communicator",' *USA Today*, 6 June 2004; Morgan, Iwan, *Reagan: American Icon* (London: I.B. Tauris, 2016), pp. 326–7.

5   'Republican National Convention address,' 17 August 1992, https://www.youtube.com/watch?v=WxL3OU1dwml.

6   'Address before a Joint Session of the Congress on the State of the Union,' 25 January 1984, APP, https://www.presidency.ucsb.edu/node/261634; Jones, Jeffrey M., 'Majority of Americans Optimistic about US in the Future,' Gallup, 4 January 2010, https://news.gallup.com/poll/124910/majority-americans-optimistic-future.aspx. See too Rogers, Daniel, *Age of Fracture* (Cambridge, MA: Belknap Press, 2011), pp. 17–40.

7   Bump, Philip, 'Nearly 9 in 10 Black Americans Believe President Trump Respects People of Colour Less than Whites, Finds Poll,' *Independent*, 10 December 2017, https://www.independent.co.uk/news/world/americas/black-americans-president-trump-respect-coloured-people-less-than-whites-mississippi-civil-rights-a8101936.html.

8   O'Reilly, Kenneth, *Nixon's Piano: Presidents and Racial Politics from Washington to Clinton* (New York: Free Press, 1995), p. 2.

9   Lewis, George, 'Memories of the Movement: Civil Rights, the Liberal Consensus, and the March on Washington Twenty Years Later,' in Robert Mason, and Iwan Morgan, eds., *The Liberal Consensus Reconsidered: American Politics and Society in the Postwar Era* (Gainesville: University Press of Florida, 2017), p. 268.

10 Davidson, Joe, 'Reagan: A Contrary View,' *NBC News Commentary*, 7 June 2004, http://www.nbcnews.com/id/5158315/ns/us_news-life/t/reagan-contrary-view/#.WzUDuNVKiM8

11 Duggan, Bob, 'Why Rap Artists Still Hate Ronald Reagan,' *Big Think* (no date), https://bigthink.com/Picture-This/why-rap-artists-still-hate-ronald-reagan.

12 Reagan, Ronald, *My Early Life: or Where's the Rest of Me?* (1965; London: Sidgwick & Jackson, 1981), pp. 63–4; Reagan Ronald, *An American Life* (London: Hutchison, 1990), p. 52; Cannon, Lou, *President Reagan: The Role of a Lifetime* (New York: Simon & Schuster, 1991), pp. 519–20.

13 Reagan, Ronald, 'Fascist Ideas Are Still Alive in US,' *AVC Bulletin*, 15 February 1946.

14 Edwards, Anne, *Early Reagan: The Rise to Power* (New York: Dutton, 1987), pp. 53, 397–400.

15 Jerry Wald to Daniel Fuchs, 31 October 1949, 3 November 1949, 21 November 1949, 13 December 1949, '*Storm Warning* – Stories, Memos, Correspondence Folder,' Warner Bros. Archives, University of Southern California, Los Angeles.

16 Rossinow, Doug, *The Reagan Era: A History of the 1980s* (New York: Columbia University Press, 2015), p. 8; Morgan, *Reagan*, p. 241.

17 DeGroot, Gerard, *Selling Ronald Reagan: The Emergence of a President* (London: I.B. Tauris, 2015), pp. 167–70.

18 Foner, *American Freedom*, p. xiii; Medhurst, Martin, 'LBJ, Reagan, and the American Dream: Competing Visions of Liberty,' *Presidential Studies Quarterly*, 46 (March 2016): 98–124.

19 DeGroot, *Selling Ronald Reagan*, p. 252.

20 Lopez, Ian Haney, *Dog Whistle Politics: How Coded Racial Appeals Have Reinvented Racism and Destroyed the Middle Class* (New York: Oxford University Press, 2015), esp. pp. 55–76.

21 'Reagan Shuns Image of Goldwater in Coast Race,' *NYT*, 1 June 1966; Evans, Robert, and William Novak, 'Inside Report: The Anti-Welfare State,' *WP*, 22 September 1966; Reagan, Ronald, 'A Plan for Action,' 4 January 1966, Ronald Reagan Gubernatorial Papers, Box C30, Ronald Reagan Presidential Library [RRPL].

22 DeGroot, *Selling Ronald Reagan*, p. 161.

23 Quoted in McGinnis, Joe, *The Selling of the President 1968* (New York: Trident Press, 1969), p. 170.

24 Edsall, Thomas Byrne, with Mary Edsall, *Chain Reaction: The Impact of Race, Rights and Taxes on American Politics* (New York: Norton, 1992), p. 148.

25 Mayer, Jeremy, *Running on Race: Racial Politics in Presidential Campaigns, 1960–2000* (New York: Random House, 2002), pp. 134–6.

26 Schneider, William, 'An Insider's View of the Election,' *Atlantic* (July 1988): 38.

27 Quoted in Goldman, Peter, 'Making of a Landslide,' *Newsweek* (December 1984), Election Extra: 88.

28 Greenberg, Stanley, *Report on Democratic Defection* (Washington, DC: Greenberg Research, 1985), pp. 13–18, 28.

29 Kotler, Milton, and Nelson Rosenbaum, *Strengthening the Democratic Party through Strategic Marketing: Voters and Donors* (Washington, DC: CRG Research Institute, 1985), p. 1.

30 Quoted in Marable, Manning, 'Race and Realignment in American Politics.' https://www.versobooks.com/blogs/2496-race-and-realignment-in-american-politics-part-iii.

31 'Ronald Reagan's Neshoba County Fair Campaign Speech,' https://www.youtube.com/watch?v=450DA4AZG6U; Greenberg, David, 'Dog-Whistling Dixie: When Reagan Said "States' Rights," He Was Talking about Race,' *Slate*, 20 November 2007, http://www.slate.com/articles/news_and_politics/history_lesson/2007/11/dogwhistling_dixie.html?via=gdpr-consent.

32 'Chilling Words in Neshoba County: Is Reagan Saying That He Intends to Turn the Clock Back to Mississippi Justice of 1964?' *WP*, 11 August 1980.

33 Quotations drawn from Hayward, Steven, *The Age of Reagan: The Fall of the Old Liberal Order, 1964–1980* (Roseville CA: Prima, 2001), pp. 696–7.

34 'Remarks in Denver, Colorado, at the Annual Convention of the National Association for the Advancement of Colored People,' 29 June 1981, APP, https://www.presidency.ucsb.edu/node/247463.

35 Wilkins, Roger, *A Man's Life* (New York: Simon & Schuster, 1982), pp. 369–70.

36 'Justice Marshall Rips Reagan,' *NYT*, 9 September 1987; Reagan, Ronald, *The Reagan Diaries*, ed. Douglas Brinkley (New York: HarperCollins, 2007) [17 November 1987], p. 549.

37 Reagan to Leonard Kirk, 23 March 1983, in Skinner, Kiron, Annelise Anderson, and Martin Anderson, eds., *Reagan: A Life in Letters* (New York: Free Press, 2003), p. 13.

38 Rowan, Carl, *Breaking Barriers: A Memoir* (Boston: Little, Brown, 1991), pp. 322–3.

39 Reagan to NAACP Executive Director Benjamin Hooks, 12 January 1983, Presidential Handwriting File [PHF], Box 5, RRPL.

40 Troy, Gil, *Morning in America: How Ronald Reagan Invented the 1980s* (Princeton: Princeton University Press, 2005), pp. 91, 175–6; 'Remarks in Denver, Colorado, at the Annual Convention of the National Association for the Advancement of Colored People,' 29 June 1981. See too 'Radio Address to the Nation on Martin Luther King, Jr., and Black Americans,' 18 January 1986, APP, https://www.presidency.ucsb.edu/node/259262.

41 Edwin Harper to Ronald Reagan, 5 March 1982, Office of the President, Presidential Briefing Papers, Box 20, RRPL.

42 Rogers, *Age of Fracture*, p. 118.

43 For the racially progressive origins of colour-blindness, see Kull, Andrew, *The Color-Blind Constitution* (Cambridge, MA: Harvard University Press, 1992). Its conservative usage is critiqued in Bonilla-Silva, Eduardo, *Racism without Racists: Color-Blind Racism and the Persistence of Racial Inequality in America* (Lanham, MD: Rowman & Littlefield, 2006).

44 Quoted in Rossinow, *The Reagan Era*, p. 43.

45 Rogers, *Age of Fracture*, pp. 129–30. See too Reynolds, William Bradford, 'Our Nation's Goal: A Color-Blind Society,' *Lincoln Review*, 4 (Winter 1984): 31–40.

46   Jackson, Jesse, *A Conversation with the Reverend Jesse Jackson* (Washington, DC: AEI, 1978), p. 14.

47   Barrett, Lawrence, *Gambling with History: Reagan in the White House* (New York: Doubleday, 1983), p. 426; Mayer, *Running on Race*, p. 153.

48   Reagan to Meldrim Thomson, 3 October 1983, PHF, box 7, RRPL.

49   'Remarks on Signing the Bill Making the Birthday of Martin Luther King, Jr., a National Holiday,' 2 November 1983, APP, https://www.presidency.ucsb.edu/node/262014.

50   Gomer, Justin, and Christopher Petrella, 'Reagan Used MLK Day to Undermine Racial Justice,' *Boston Review*, 15 January 2017, http://bostonreview.net/race-politics/justin-gomer-christopher-petrella-reagan-used-mlk-day-undermine-racial-justice. See too West, James, 'A Hero to Be Remembered: *Ebony* Magazine, Critical Memory and the "Real Meaning" of the King Holiday,' *Journal of American Studies*, 52 (May 2018): 503–27.

51   Skinner, Kiron, 'The Odd Couple,' *NYT*, 19 January 2004, https://www.nytimes.com/2004/01/19/opinion/the-odd-couple.html.

52   'The President's News Conference,' 11 February 1986, APP, https://www.presidency.ucsb.edu/node/257723.

53   Edwards, Lee, 'Dismantling Liberal Myths: A Refresher Course on Ronald Reagan,' *National Review*, 3 June 2015, https://www.nationalreview.com/2015/06/ronald-reagan-liberal-myths-debunked/.

54   Reagan, Michael. 'Ronald Reagan – Our First Black President? Asks Adopted Son,' *Hudson County People*, 20 January 2011, https://www.nj.com/hudson/voices/index.ssf/2011/01/ronald_reagan_–_our_first_bla.html; Morrison, Toni, 'Comment,' *New Yorker*, 5 October 1998, https://www.newyorker.com/magazine/1998/10/05/comment-6543.

55   Dockterman, Eliana, 'The True Story of "The Butler",' *Time*, 16 August 2013, http://time.com/2219/what-the-butler-really-saw/.

56   Morgan, *Reagan*, pp. 242–3.

57   Hayward, Steven, Paul Kengor, Craig Shirley, and Kiron Skinner, 'What "The Butler" Gets Wrong about Ronald Reagan and Race,' *WP*, 29 August 2018, https://www.washingtonpost.com/opinions/what-the-butler-gets-wrong-about-ronald-reagan-and-race/2013/08/29/5f6aa21e-0e87-11e3-8cdd-bcdc09410972_st.

58   Morgan, *Reagan*, pp. 244–6; Reagan to John Kehoe, 10 August 1987, PHF, box 18, RRPL.

59   Duggan, 'Why Rap Artists Still Hate Ronald Reagan.'

60   'Rap vs. Reagan,' *Carolina Political Review*, 4 November 2017, https://www.carolinapoliticalreview.org/editorial-content/2017/11/4/rap-v-reagan.

61   Alexander, Michelle, *The New Jim Crow: Mass Incarceration in the Age of Colorblindness* (New York: New Press, 2012), pp. 5–6, 50–6.

62   Ibid.; 'Farewell address to the nation,' 11 January 1989, APP, https://www.presidency.ucsb.edu/node/251303.

63   Betts, Reginald Dwayne, *Bastards of the Reagan Era* (New York: Four Way Books, 2015).

64   'Rap vs, Reagan,' *Carolina Political Review*; Crunkite, Walter, 'Rap vs. Ronald Reagan,' 16 January 2012, https://genius.com/posts/775-Rap-vs-ronald-reagan.

65   Kreps, Daniel, 'Kendrick Lamar Talks Oval Office Meeting with Barack Obama,' *Rolling Stone*, 12 January 2016, https://www.rollingstone.com/music/music-news/kendrick-lamar-talks-oval-office-meeting-with-barack-obama-68115/.

66 Cillizza, Chris, 'Barack Obama 2012 = Ronald Reagan 1984?' *The Fix*, 5 October 2012, https://www.washingtonpost.com/news/the-fix/wp/2012/10/05/barack-obama-2012-ronald-reagan-1984/?utm_term=.86760bf5e07a. See too Duffy, Michael, and Michael Scherer, 'The Role Model: What Obama Sees in Reagan,' *Time*, 27 January 2011, http://content.time.com/time/magazine/article/0,9171,2044712,00.html.

67 Reagan, Ronald, *Speaking My Mind: Selected Speeches* (New York: Simon & Schuster, 1989), p. 163.

68 Frey, William H., 'The US Will Become "Minority White" in 2045, Census Projects: Youthful Minorities Are the Engine of Future Growth,' *The Avenue*, 14 March 2018, https://www.brookings.edu/blog/the-avenue/2018/03/14/the-us-will-become-minority-white-in-2045-census-projects/.

69 'Address to the Nation on the Eve of the Presidential Election,' 5 November 1984, APP, https://www.presidency.ucsb.edu/node/260734.

Chapter 10

BILL CLINTON'S PRIMARY COLOURS: MAKING THE IMAGE OF THE FORTY-SECOND PRESIDENT

John Dumbrell

Introduction: Clinton, Kennedy and Slippery Images

Four months before President John F. Kennedy was assassinated, the young Bill Clinton, on a visit to the White House, was treated to a presidential handshake. As the Hot Springs High School delegate to the American Legion Boys' Nation programme, Clinton was photographed with JFK. His intense emotional reaction was evident in a second photograph, taken with him still in frame but when the president had moved on to the next delegate. To those who now view the photographs through a haze of memories of the two presidencies, the resemblance – the 'spark' between the schoolboy and JFK – seems remarkable.[1]

A very different pictorial image of a much older Bill Clinton was produced in 2006 by Nelson Shanks, painter of Clinton's official portrait (and best known in the UK for his portrait of Princess Diana). The Clinton portrait is of a standing ex-president, with a shadow to his right. Shanks subsequently revealed that the shadow was cast by a mannequin in a blue dress. Shanks had put the mannequin in place when Bill Clinton was not actually posing. Shanks later described Clinton as 'probably the most famous liar of all time' and acknowledged the 'secret reference' to the 'primary' Monica Lewinski scandal and the 'shadow' it cast over the Clinton presidency.[2]

The 1963 and 2006 Clinton pictorial images illustrate the sheer slipperiness and contingent nature of presidential image-making. The 1963 photo with JFK was in no sense manufactured. The young Clinton was delighted to be given a copy of the JFK photographs. Clinton was pleased and flattered to be associated with Kennedy and later was happy for his photographed handshake with JFK to stand as a symbol of his own youthful purpose and ambition. The positive charge of the image was only slightly lessened by the ease with which later critics were able to draw parallels between Kennedy's sexual misconduct in the White House and the Lewinsky affair during the Clinton presidential years. The Shanks portrait, ostensibly a celebration of Clinton's place in history, was much more negative in its impact. Bill and Hillary Clinton made no secret of their unhappiness with

Shanks's secret reference.[3] There was, too, yet another Kennedy connection. Shanks's ambivalence towards his sitter brought to mind Pietro Annigoni's 1962 portrait of JFK for *Time* magazine. Annigoni's painting showed a self-doubting, slightly dishevelled president, rather than the confident and glamorous Man of the Year. The Shanks painting of Clinton is, in effect, a portrait of a dishevelled presidency. Its primary colour is not the red of Clinton's tie but the blue irradiated from the mannequin/Lewinsky dress.

The complexity and uncontrollability of 'image', now defined more broadly than simple pictorial image, dominate this chapter's discussion of image-making and President William J. Clinton. On the one hand, Bill Clinton's image has been defined and promoted in terms of his role as a product and exemplar of the socially liberal values of the 1960s, sometimes filtered through his parallel status as a relatively cautious and fiscally conservative New Democrat. On the other, various texts and memories have defined Clinton's image in terms of sexual indiscretion, political deviousness and compromised values. The chapter begins with a brief survey of Clinton's changing public reputation, constantly buffeted by political shifts and especially by the changing political and electoral fortunes of his wife. Subsequent attention focuses on *Primary Colors*, the novel published anonymously in January 1996 and revealed in July 1996 as the work of journalist Joe Klein. The chapter ends with consideration of a highly unusual and unexpected effort at post-White House image-making: Bill Clinton's 2018 co-written political thriller, *The President Is Missing*.[4]

Clinton's Reputation and the 'Character Issue'

It is argued below that Joe Klein's novel, *Primary Colors*, played a key role in the fixing – if only as far as such a slippery concept as 'image' can be fixed – of Bill Clinton's presidential image. The image which emerged from Klein's novel was not entirely negative. Klein's president-in-waiting was a socially liberal and intellectually robust politician, a leader who was able to respond both to the upheavals of the 1960s and to the crisis of post–Great Society liberalism. On balance, however, Klein presented a political character who was profoundly flawed, not only in terms of sexist behaviour which belied a professed adherence to progressive feminist values, but also in more general terms relating to a lack of personal and political integrity.

It should be noted that many of the tensions within Clinton's character – tensions reflected in his presidential record – were widely debated before 1996. The chief tension lay between Clinton's charm, sharp intellect and ability to reflect, even to embody, changing facets of American liberalism, on the one hand, and his apparent cynicism, sense of entitlement and excessive desire to please all sides, on the other. On the positive side, Clinton was widely perceived early on as a candidate and a leader who combined an extraordinary knowledge of political minutiae, an avalanche of charm, instinctive electoral skills, *and* a genuine enthusiasm for policy detail. This was an unusual combination. Political scientist Fred Greenstein wrote in 1995: 'It is as if the more cerebral side of John F. Kennedy's approach to leadership were writ large and amalgamated with Lyndon Johnson's proclivity to press the flesh, find ways to split the difference and otherwise practise the art of the possible.'[5] The reverse side of the coin of Clinton's supposed incarnation of a synthesis of JFK and LBJ was, of course, the familiar charge of deviousness, linked to obsessive 'triangulation' and lack of clear direction. Arthur Schlesinger Jr. wrote in 1997: 'Middle-roading may be fine for campaigning, but it is a sure road to mediocrity in governing.' Clinton, argued Schlesinger, 'must liberate himself from polls and focus groups.'[6] Describing the early Clinton White House, journalist Elizabeth Drew commented: 'It wasn't policy-making. It was group therapy.'[7]

Clinton's style of leadership – balancing, listening, constantly adjusting – has always had its defenders. In her memoir, *Living History*, Hillary Clinton wrote: 'One of Bill's great strengths is his willingness to invite disparate opinions and then sort them out to reach his own conclusion.'[8] Former Treasury Secretary Robert Rubin commented: 'Clinton listened so sympathetically that people who were unaccustomed to him often took it as duplicitous when he later came out against their positions.'[9] Political consultant and scholar Benjamin Barber, essentially an admirer of Clinton, wrote in 2001 that the forty-second president 'didn't like hard choices.' When more or less forced to choose between competing positions, he continued to believe 'he could always do "some of both."'[10]

However one interprets the synthetic, accumulative, often sinuous style of Clinton's leadership, the image of him as malleable and lacking core beliefs had been established well before the publication of *Primary Colors*. This image was reinforced in rather brutal ways in various published interviews with associates from pre-presidential days in Arkansas. Many of these interviewees, it should be remembered, had a host of personal scores to settle. For Arkansas journalist Max Brantley: 'He crawls into your soul for a minute or two, and then he looks over your shoulder for the next guy in the room he's going to do the same thing to.'[11] Political opponents were quick to exploit Clinton's developing reputation. *Slick Willie*, a book written by Floyd Brown, who had played a controversial role in President George H. W. Bush's 1992 campaign, appeared in 1993.[12]

Bill Clinton's 'character issue' extended beyond the stereotype of 'Slick Willie'. It included Clinton's sexual adventurism, involving (as with Kennedy) an apparent attraction to risk. Almost as enduring as Clinton's reputation as a reckless philanderer is, despite his humble origins, his perceived sense of entitlement, developing sometimes into self-pity. Towards the end of the first term, *Time* magazine attributed Clinton's problems, including the mid-term electoral reversals, to his overconfidence. Clinton had interpreted the 43 per cent of the vote he received in the 1992 presidential election as 'an imperial mandate to rearrange the planet.'[13] George Stephanopoulos, in his 1999 memoir *All Too Human*, recalled Clinton complaining to his staff in December 1993 (i.e. well before Kenneth's Starr's investigation): '*No* president has ever been treated the way I've been treated.'[14] For David Broder in 2000, Bill Clinton's underpinning flaw was an excessive faith in his status as 'fortune's favoured child.'[15] Barack Obama, in *The*

Audacity of Hope (2006), attributed many of the problems of the Clinton era to a kind of 'psychodrama' between different factions of the baby-boomer generation. The United States, wrote Obama, should be 'led, not by polls, but by principle; not by calculation, but by conviction.'[16]

Bill Clinton became a very popular president as his tenure progressed. His overall average Gallup approval rating was 55 per cent but the first-term figure of 50 per cent was significantly lower than the second term's 61 per cent. Impeachment only seemed to boost public approval. There is no evidence that Americans actually approved of his apparent perjury in connection with the Lewinsky affair – or, for that matter, of the affair itself – but they soon appeared to tire of the intricate and far-from-compelling details of his Whitewater real estate transactions. Rather, Clinton in his second term benefitted from a buoyant national economy, public support for anti-terrorism initiatives and a kind of resigned affection for the good 'bad boy' in the White House. Arthur Schlesinger concluded that the American people came to see Clinton as an 'endearing rogue.'[17] Clinton's Gallup approval score on leaving office was 66 per cent (compared to Reagan's 51 per cent, George W. Bush's 25 and Barack Obama's 59 per cent). Interestingly, a Gallup survey of February 2018 of public approval of the last ten US presidents (not including Donald Trump) put Clinton in fifth place, behind Kennedy, Reagan, George H. W. Bush and Obama.[18]

Clinton's reputation has seesawed during his post-presidency. His departure from presidential office in January 2001 was accompanied by intense criticism, not least from former president Jimmy Carter, relating to the pardon extended to Marc Rich, American tax fugitive and Friend-of-Bill. Despite the bursting of the dot.com bubble in 2000, a *New York Times* survey of the presidency, published in December 2000, stressed Clinton's role as a president in prosperous times. Richard Stevenson saw Clinton as the president of globalization and economics-first, who 'let the good times roll,' linking himself to the 'widespread sense that times, for most people, have never been better.'[19] Subsequent economic travails were to stimulate the kind of nationalist reaction to globalization that led eventually in 2016 to the election of Donald Trump. Clinton, the president of globalization, saw his reputation fade accordingly.

The terror attacks of 9/11 drew attention to putative mistakes made by the Clinton administration in handling the threat of radical Islamist terror. The 9/11 Commission made the following assessment its record on this score: 'The US government took the threat seriously, but not in the sense of mustering anything like the kind of effort that would be gathered to confront an enemy of the first, second, or even third rank.'[20] The agonies of the George W. Bush administration arguably led to something of a revival for Bill Clinton, despite his wife's Senate vote in favour of the 2003 US invasion of Iraq.

The repeal in 1999 of the 1933 Glass-Steagall Act, which had separated commercial and investment banking activities, was criticized for facilitating the financial crash which began in 2007. The further rise of extreme partisan divisions and 'culture wars' after 2000 also had an impact on Bill Clinton's reputation. For many conservatives, he was the amoral 'counter-culturalist in chief.'[21] On the liberal side, Clinton was regularly seen as having overreacted to the Republican mid-term electoral victory of 1994 by moving sharply rightwards.[22]

Various specialist studies of the Clinton presidency combined praise for particular policies, and sometimes even for Clinton's leadership, with important reservations about Clinton's sense of direction and about the 'character issue'. For *Washington Post* political reporter John Harris, author of *The Survivor* (2006), Clinton practised a defensible kind of opportunism. He 'understood the transformational character of his times,' but suffered too many 'self-inflicted wounds' and too often allowed policy to drift. For Harris, Clinton could not be admitted to the 'elite gallery' of great presidents.[23] In tune with this judgement, American historians, polled by C-Span in 2009, ranked Clinton the fifteenth best-ever US president, the same position he would occupy in its 2017 survey; a parallel 2011 poll, organized by British academics, ranked Clinton at nineteenth.[24]

By the middle and latter part of the first decade of the new century, the default view was that Clinton was a lucky president who managed to scrape through his two terms. His image still partook of being a leader in good times. In Joseph O'Neill's novel *Netherland* (2008), Clinton is referred to as having done 'little more than oversee the advent of a national fortunateness.'[25] He was the quite attractive and engaging leader of a nation which had been taking its collective eye off the ball. A broadly sympathetic portrayal of President Josiah Bartlet, a character who embodied some of Clinton's more positive characteristics, appeared in the TV series *The West Wing*, which ran from 1999 to 2006.[26] Against this background, Clinton made his first major effort to further refashion his image – by publishing his presidential memoir, *My Life*, in 2004.[27]

Clinton's autobiography, apparently written in longhand by the ex-president himself, ran to around half a million words. The book contained a vivid account of his childhood and especially of the violent conduct of his stepfather. Bill Clinton recorded himself as living 'parallel lives': an inner life of fear and uncertainty and an outer, public life of confident gregariousness. Novelist Larry McMurtry, reviewing the book for the *New York Times*, considered it 'the richest presidential autobiography.' He thus rated it more highly than the two frequently most admired volumes of presidential memoir, those of Ulysses S. Grant and Richard Nixon. For McMurtry, Clinton's autobiography brought to mind the work of North Carolinian Thomas Wolfe, author of *Look Homeward, Angel* (1929), 'the big ghost from the other side of the South.'[28] Most reviewers were less kind. Another piece in the *New York Times* saw *My Life* as a reflection of the Clinton presidency itself: 'lack of discipline leading to self-indulgence and scattered concentration.' The book was like the man: sentimental, superficial and tending to self-pity.[29] The publication of *My Life* in 2004 very nearly coincided with the death of Ronald Reagan, with several commentators finding unlikely parallels between the two leaders. Joe Klein himself identified links between two outgoing and optimistic small-town sons from troubled family backgrounds.[30] Robert McCrum in the London *Observer* commented: 'Clinton's tragedy is Sisyphean: he will always be rolling the horrendous boulder of his flawed presidency uphill.'[31] William Berman remarked on what he saw as the shallowness and disingenuousness of

Figure 10.1 Bill Clinton signs copies of his memoir, *My Life*, in Dublin, Ireland, August 2004. Source: https://commons.wikimedia.org/wiki/File:Bill_Clinton_signs_My_Life_in_Dublin_(303067).jpg

Clinton's outward good nature: the former president seemed to like 'virtually everybody whose name he mentions in his memoirs save Saddam Hussein and Kenneth Starr.'[32]

My Life was far too long. The accounts of childhood troubles and of his early political career are riveting and (despite a degree of self-serving self-analysis) genuinely revealing. The pages on the presidency, however, degenerate into a rather tedious recitation of meetings and events, presumably constructed from the presidential diary. Clinton admits an 'inappropriate encounter' with Monica Lewinsky.[33] The impeachment is attributed entirely to malicious political partisanship. The structure of the presidential sections reinforced the view of presidential policy as reactive and lacking clear direction. The meeting-by-meeting, event-by-event discussion of foreign policy caused one British reviewer to recall Theodore Roosevelt's dismissal of President William McKinley as a leader with 'the backbone of a chocolate éclair.' Clinton's foreign policy, according to Tim Hames, had 'the backbone of a raspberry pavlova.'[34]

The post–George W. Bush presidential years saw Clinton's reputation fluctuating in line with the political and electoral fortunes of his wife. The leading account of the 2008 presidential campaign depicts Bill Clinton as a heavyweight loose cannon, not least because of continuing extra-marital involvements, during the primary contest between Barack Obama and Hillary Clinton.[35] The ex-president's relationship with Obama, who had opposed the welfare reform programme signed by President Clinton in 1996, was fraught, but in office the forty-fourth president did reach out to him after 2010. Bill Clinton gave a vigorous and well-received address in strong support of Obama to the 2012 Democratic National Convention. Clinton's agenda in these years featured his own putative establishment as a Democratic Party elder statesman for a globalized age.[36]

During the 2016 Democratic primary contest between Bernie Sanders and Hillary Clinton, Sanders and other leftist Democrats attacked Bill Clinton for excessive softness as president on the issue of Wall Street regulation. The general election contest, however, involved extraordinary attacks on Bill Clinton by Republican candidate Donald Trump. As Amy Chozick later put it, Trump 'effectively turned Bill Clinton into a human shield.' When the *Access Hollywood* tape was released with Trump's obscene boasting about his own sexual misconduct, Trump remarked that 'Bill Clinton has said far worse to me on the golf course.'[37] Trump attacked Hillary Clinton as an 'enabler' for Bill, who was 'the single greatest abuser of women in the history of politics.'[38] Trump invited three women who had accused Bill Clinton of sexual harassment to the presidential debates, appearing with them in public to denounce the behaviour of his opponent's husband. Newspaper photographs of Bill Clinton and Donald Trump apparently behaving as close golfing friends seemed to harm Bill (and possibly Hillary) Clinton more than Trump.[39] Written against the background of the #MeToo movement, a 2018 piece in the *Washington Post* referred to Bill Clinton's portrayal of himself as somehow a victim of 'imagined facts' and partisan investigations as – the ultimate in bitter invective – 'Trumpian.'[40] By this time, many American commentators were simply fatigued by discussion of Bill Clinton's libido. P. J. O'Rourke, describing the 2016 presidential election in tones of incredulity, wrote: 'We know more about Bill Clinton's sexual peccadilloes than we can, if we're of a certain age, remember about our own.'[41]

Primary Colors

Primary Colors: A Novel of Politics was a phenomenon. Its sales, for a political novel, were exceptional.[42] An indication of the book's impact was provided in the 2015 film about the writer David Foster Wallace, *The End of the Tour*. Set in 1996, the film featured a succession of characters holding and/or reading hardback copies of *Primary Colors*.[43] The novel, *Primary Colors*, formed the template for a 1998 film, starring John Travolta. For Bill Clinton, *Primary Colors* was 'that damned book.'[44] The breathless hunt for the author of the anonymous publication itself generated massive interest and debate.

Primary Colors is actually a very good novel. Klein consciously set it in the tradition of Robert Penn Warren's *All the King's Men*, a book about Governor (later Senator) Huey P. Long of Louisiana (Willie Stark in the novel), which is narrated by Jack Burden, reporter and aide to Stark. In Klein's book, Jack Burden becomes the African American politico-narrator Henry Burton. Burden's view of the deeply flawed Long is echoed in Burton's developing judgements about the character of Jack Stanton.[45] Klein's characters have direct real-life counterparts: Stanton is Clinton; Burton is an African American version of George Stephanopoulos; Luther Charles is Jesse Jackson; Richard Jemmons is a grotesque version of James Carville; Orlando Ozio is Mario Cuomo; Cashmere McLeod is Gennifer Flowers; Richmond Rucker is New York City Mayor David Dinkins. The tone of the book is a kind of ironic exaggeration, suffused with the manic energy of a campaign. Some of the real-life correspondences are more exact than others, and the plot heads off in its own directions. As with Robert Penn Warren's novel about Huey Long, *Primary Colors* is a work of fiction, more properly a *roman à clef*. A factually accurate (and also gripping) account of Clinton's 1992 campaign – and of the roles played particularly by George Stephanopoulos and James Carville – is provided, not by Joe Klein, but by the 1993 documentary film *The War Room*.[46]

Roughly the first half of the book is concerned with the New Hampshire primary, which Stanton loses narrowly to the cerebral Lawrence Harris. In 1992, Clinton narrowly trailed Paul Tsongas in New Hampshire, enabling James Carville, following the various scandals which had erupted in the campaign, to dub Clinton 'the comeback kid.' In Klein's book, Stanton's difficulties include the emergence of information concerning his relationship with his wife's hairdresser (Cashmere McLeod), his involvement in anti–Vietnam War protest and misuse of influence to extricate himself from trouble, and baseless allegations of racial insult towards Luther Charles. Klein's handling of these events frequently veers away from what actually happened in the 1992 campaign. He invents a plot twist whereby Stanton is accused of impregnating the daughter of Fat Willie, an African American barbecue restaurateur. Stanton's self-identification as a politician who is able to identify with the aspirations and concerns of African Americans is thus undermined in Klein's narrative. The various problems raised by Stanton's behaviour are negotiated by campaign staff, sometimes operating under the direction of Stanton's wife, Susan. Henry Burton himself sets on a course of morally questionable behaviour in pursuit of a cause – Stanton's presidential campaign – in which he still genuinely believes.

Following the story of the New Hampshire primary, the plot veers further into the realms of fiction. The Stanton team launches a negative campaign against Harris, who is accused of seeking to cut benefits to the elderly and of being unfriendly to Israel. Harris suffers two heart attacks and is replaced as a candidate by Florida Governor Fred Picker, a Harris backer. Picker has no obvious real-life counterpart, though his 'New South' politics cause Burton to recall the appeal of Jimmy Carter. Picker's rhetoric also echoes some themes of Ross Perot's 1992 presidential campaign. Henry and Susan Stanton have sexual relations following the latter's discovery of details of the former's efforts to resolve the problems posed by Fat Willie. Stanton's campaign flounders amid sexual allegations. Picker wins decisively in New York. For Burton, 'Fred Picker seemed to be campaigning from Mount Olympus,' while 'we were neck-deep in the Augean Stables.'[47] Burton and campaign 'dustbuster' Libby Holden (probably a version of Bill Clinton's long-time aide Betsey Wright) duly seek out evidence of skeletons in the Picker cupboard. Burton describes himself and Holden acting 'almost ironically, standing at a distance from ourselves, curious about where we were going, how far we'd be willing to go.'[48] They uncover evidence of past cocaine use and of homosexuality. Libby commits suicide, while Burton resolves to break his association with Stanton. The book ends with Stanton's presidential inauguration and with continuing uncertainty about Burton's future.

The novel is not without its weaknesses. The New Hampshire section is by far the strongest. The distance between fiction and reality, particularly in the book's later pages, is not consistently well handled. Some reviewers accused Klein/'anonymous' of distorting the role of the press corps (the 'scorps' in the terminology of Stanton's staff). Journalist Alexander Cockburn, who believed that the press actually gave Clinton a relatively easy ride in 1992, criticized the book for focusing too little on issues of fund-raising for the campaign.[49] For some, the impact of the book was blunted by the familiarity of some of its themes. Tales of compromised political conscience do run the risk of eliciting yawns from a public saturated by such fare. *Primary Colors* sounds familiar notes of lost innocence, idealism betrayed and the corruption of ambition. These themes are scarcely original. They surface across the history of world literature, as well as in imaginative portrayals of American politics. The 1979 film *The Seduction of Joe Tynan*, starring Alan Alda and dealing with the moral dilemmas of a progressive Democratic senator with presidential ambitions, is a case in point.[50] Despite all this, the central theme of *Primary Colors* – the tension between the characters of Stanton and Burton – is handled with considerable subtlety and originality. Klein achieves a kind of focused and realized ambiguity. The skill of his presentation of Stanton's character, as filtered through the conscience and consciousness of Henry Burton, accounts for the potency of Klein's fixing of Clinton's character in political memory.

As portrayed by Klein, Stanton is considerably less driven and commanding than his wife Susan, who resembles Lady Macbeth as much as Hillary Clinton. Stanton's appeal is largely a product of political skill. He practises 'aggressive listening'; 'he would never leave a room … without knowing everyone's name, and he would *remember* them.'[51] Stanton's understanding of, and sympathy for, social deprivation is profound. Burton recognizes Stanton's genuine empathy with the problems of African Americans, though also discovers that such empathy does not prevent Stanton from maltreating Fat Willie. Stanton's emotions constantly bubble up – sometimes cynically controlled, sometimes not. His intellect is also sharp and well honed. He is a serial philanderer and, at times at least, an amoral political operator. Stanton's disquisition on political leadership, delivered to Burton before the inauguration, is the nearest the (now) president-elect comes to self-awareness: 'We smile, we listen…. We do our pathetic little favors. We fudge when we can't. We tell them what they want to hear – and when we tell them something they *don't* want to hear, it's usually because we've calculated that's what they really want. We live an eternity of false smiles – and why? Because it's the price you pay to lead.'[52]

Primary Colors played a major role in honing and setting Bill Clinton's already less-than-stainless public image. Klein had written a piece in *Newsweek* (May 1994) entitled 'The Politics of Promiscuity.' Obliquely referenced in *Primary Colors*, the 1994 article, which followed on the heels of Klein's previously positive coverage of Clinton's 1992 campaign and early presidency, constituted something of a dry run for the later novel. Klein's disillusion would seem to have tracked Burton's. Another possible personal correspondence relates to the criticism that Klein received for dissembling over several months about the true authorship of *Primary Colors*. Not only did the early 'anonymous' status of the book cause difficulty for other possible authors, notably George Stephanopoulos, but Klein's dissembling might also be seen as 'Stantonian'. *The Running Mate*, a Klein-authored sequel to *Primary Colors*, appeared in 2000. *The Running Mate* focused on the 'Charlie Martin' character (a version of Bob Kerrey, Vietnam veteran and primary candidate in 1992) from *Primary Colors*. In *The Running Mate,* President Stanton is a somewhat remote figure, though rarely referred to in anything other than a negative light. The book was also implicitly critical of intrusive media coverage of candidates' sexual behaviour.[53]

In *The Natural* (2002), Joe Klein provided a fairly straightforward journalistic/ contemporary historical account of the Clinton presidency. Klein denied any malice towards Clinton. *Primary Colors*, wrote Klein in *The Natural*, had been 'incorrectly' construed as an attack on Clinton. Klein described his novel as a defence of 'larger-than-life politicians – who, inevitably, have mythic weaknesses entangled with their obvious strengths.' *The Natural* certainly drew attention to several of these weaknesses: not only sexual scandal, but also bouts of temper and childishness. There was some sympathy for Clinton's political pragmatism, even if it did pull him in unsustainable directions: 'A pattern appeared in the 1992 campaign and continued through his presidency: Clinton would initially succeed as a moderate, then he would try to move left and plummet, then he would shuffle back to the center again.' Joe Klein suggested in *The Natural*, however, that Clinton's loss of moral authority was not entirely due to sexual scandals. Rather, it derived from 'snuggling too close to us ... by trying so hard to please.'[54] In other words, Clinton's presidential leadership became compromised by the kind of indiscriminate people-pleasing that Stanton described to Henry Burton before the inauguration. Yet Klein's Clinton is not unprincipled. Rather, principles – relating to fairness, the ability of government to alleviate hardship and indeed to centre-left politics generally – are too often sacrificed on the altar of short-term advantage and the desire to please. It was precisely Klein's (and Burton's) genuine admiration for Stanton/Clinton, however qualified, which made the image construction in *Primary Colors* so powerful.

The most important spin-off from the 1996 novel was the 1998 film starring John Travolta and Emma Thompson. The film dropped the sexual encounter between Burton and Susan Stanton but otherwise remained more or less faithful to the novel. If John Travolta was not entirely convincing as Stanton, the film contained strong performances from Thompson as Susan and especially from Kathy Bates as the profoundly troubled Libby Holden. Somewhat ironically, the film's impact was lessened to some extent by the onset of the Lewinsky scandal – something which made the (real-life) upsets of the 1992 campaign seem like small beer. Bill Clinton was probably more discomfited by the political backlash from the 1997 film *Wag the Dog*, starring Dustin Hoffman and Robert De Niro, which featured the artificial manufacturing of a foreign policy crisis by a scandal-hit president.[55] *Wag the Dog* briefly preceded not only the Lewinsky affair but also Clinton's military response in Sudan and Afghanistan to terror attacks on US targets. Commentators such as Christopher Hitchens were not slow to see dogs being wagged by the impeachment-threatened Clinton.[56]

In the late Clinton and George W. Bush presidential years, several novels seemed to draw on themes from the Clinton presidency. Erik Tarloff, sometime member of the wider Clinton circle, wrote a 1998 novel about a presidential love affair.[57] Ethan Canin, in his novel *America, America* (2008), presented, in the person of Henry Bonwiller, a flawed liberal Democratic senator and aspiring president, an apparent amalgam of Edward Kennedy and Bill Clinton. Canin's narrator argued that 'power comes first through character – that combination of station and forcefulness that produces not just intimidation, which is power's crudest form, but flattery too.' Bonwiller is depicted as someone genuinely seeking to move from a purely character-driven form of power towards a more mature, more outward-oriented understanding of political leadership: 'He must change his personal ambition into ambition for his country.' Canin's point seems to be that Bonwiller, like Edward Kennedy and Bill Clinton, was unable to effect the change.[58]

Primary Colors had some important antecedents and some interesting repercussions. It stands in a tradition of fictionalized political writing which stretches back to Anthony Trollope. Klein's novel has obvious links not only to *All the King's Men*, but also to Norman Mailer's account of the 1968 presidential race. In addition, *Primary Colors* arguably displays the more recent influence of the New (later, 'Gonzo') Journalism, associated particularly with Hunter S. Thompson.[59] The novel and film versions of *Primary Colors* were not quickly forgotten. The book may well have provided part of the inspiration for *The West Wing*. The novel's themes and reputation also fed into the scurrilous and libellous treatment of the Clintons doled out by rightist and conspiracist outlets such as the *American Spectator* and the Drudge Report. The influence of *Primary Colors* on John Heilemann and Mark Halperin's vivid account – factual but written in a lively and sometimes semi-speculative style – of the 2008 presidential election is also evident.[60]

William J. Palmer identified the film of *Primary Colors* as an example of 1990s 'new historicism': the melding of fact and fiction which developed partly from the New Journalism but mainly from postmodernist ideas about history.[61] It is not difficult to read *Primary Colors* as a self-consciously postmodernist novel. In 2011, it was the model for another anonymously published book, *O: A Presidential Novel*, concerning the forthcoming 2012 electoral defence of his presidency by Barack Obama.[62] Lastly, crudely and unfairly, *Primary Colors* was recruited into the abuse-laden discourses of the 2016 presidential election. Rudy Guiliani, former mayor of New York City, stated at the 2016 Republican Party National Convention: 'Bill Clinton was a predator president with a wife who enabled him ... you've seen the movie with John Travolta.'[63] By this time, Joe Klein had completely lost control of the image he himself had done so much to construct.

Imaginative Literature and the Presidency: *The President Is Missing*

Presidential association with musical (especially jazz) and literary culture formed an important part of Clinton's agenda. John Kennedy's Camelot provided the obvious model. In 2014, Clinton, the saxophone-playing former president, received a special award from the Thelonious Monk Institute for a lifetime of jazz advocacy. For his first presidential inauguration, Clinton echoed JFK's decision to invite the poet Robert Frost to read at the 1961 inaugural. At the 1993 inauguration, Maya Angelou read her poem, 'On the Pulse of Morning.' Clinton developed an enthusiasm for the poetry of Seamus Heaney, making a private visit to the Irish poet's hospital bedside in Letterkenny, County Donegal, in 2006. Clinton's quotation from Heaney – his invocation of a time when 'hope and history rhyme' – in the course of a speech in Derry in 1995 represented a highly effective and emotionally charged moment on the road to a peace agreement in Northern Ireland.[64]

Bill Clinton was not the first president with serious literary interests. John Quincy Adams translated Horatian odes, while the young Abraham Lincoln and the young Barack Obama wrote poetry. Jimmy Carter published a book of poems in 1995, following this in 2001 (approaching eighty years old) with a novel, *The Hornet's Nest*, set during the American Revolutionary War in the South.[65] In 2018, Bill Clinton entered the fray with a co-written thriller entitled *The President Is Missing*. The book is a breezy page-turner, lacking the seriousness and research depth of Carter's novel, but not without merit. As with the reaction to the Clinton autobiography, the critical response to Clinton's novel was mixed at best. Writing in the *Washington Post*, Ron Charles saw the book as a simple and crude effort to redeem the Clinton presidency in fiction: 'As a fabulous revision of Clinton's own life and impeachment scandal, this is dazzling.'[66] A review in the London *Times* noted that the book's hero and prime narrator, President Jonathan Lincoln Duncan, is 'far too busy to splash DNA on interns,' while a *New York Times* review allowed that the book was 'ambitious and wildly readable.'[67] Most reviewers attributed the plot development (in 513 pages and 127 chapters) to James Patterson, Clinton's co-author, while detecting the ex-president's hand in the more reflective passages, notably the final presidential address to a joint session of Congress. In the final speech, President Duncan sounds some characteristic Clinton themes updated to the era of Trump. In an 'environment so covered in a blizzard of information and disinformation,' the country needs to return to 'what's brought us so far: widening the circle of opportunity, deepening the meaning of freedom, and strengthening the bonds of community.' The way forward includes commitments to social inclusion, protection of voting rights, gun control, action on climate change and immigration reform.[68]

At one level, *The President Is Missing* is an enjoyable, if formulaic, adventure. Yet it is also a direct and fairly unapologetic effort at presidential image manipulation, and as such it deserves some serious analysis. *The President Is Missing* is a *roman à clef*, albeit one of inferior quality in comparison with *Primary Colors*. President

Duncan is a former Southern governor. His father died before Duncan could get to know him. He is under unfair threat of impeachment for apparently 'coddling' terrorists during an incident in Algeria. Duncan has one daughter. Yet, President Duncan is also an Iraq war hero and a widower. His chief political adversary is House Speaker Lester Rhodes, a character whose portrayal evokes more than a hint of Newt Gingrich (Republican Speaker of the House of Representatives from 1995 to 1999). Duncan comes close to losing his temper with the bumptious Rhodes: 'He's only been Speaker for five months. He doesn't realize his limitations yet. . . . The only thing he cares about is returning to his caucus and telling them he stood up to me.'[69] Journalist Robbie Millen, reviewing the book, found Jonathan Lincoln Duncan 'a mix of Jack Ryan' (Tom Clancy hero and sometime fictional US president), Senator 'John McCain, Jed Bartlet and, yes, William Jefferson Clinton.'[70] Like Bartlet, Duncan has a serious illness. There are echoes of Hillary Clinton's problems, as secretary of state under President Obama, in relation to the 2012 terror attack on Benghazi. During the course of the plot, Duncan does not actually go missing. He does, however, rather like King Henry V in Shakespeare's play, mix incognito with some unknowing 'ordinary' people. Rather than soldiers prior to battle, Duncan meets a deserving and destitute armed services veteran. He witnesses police misbehaviour towards African Americans. He is consistently compassionate, sensitive, optimistic and supremely intelligent. There are references to Russian meddling in US elections. The nearest the book comes to acknowledging some doubt about the Clinton presidency comes in relation to the expansion of NATO in the 1990s: 'The expansion of NATO to the Russian borders . . . has been the cause of great consternation in the Kremlin.'[71] (Although Poland, Hungary and the Czech Republic joined NATO in 1999, NATO expansion to Russia's borders did not occur until Clinton had left office.) Interspersed with the rapid-fire action are reflections on matters such as the 'false equivalency' of media reporting of presidential behaviour: 'when you find a mountain to expose in one person or party, you have to pick a molehill on the other side and make it into a mountain to avoid being accused of bias.'[72]

There are holes and inconsistencies in Clinton and Patterson's thriller. How does 'false equivalency' fit with a world of polarized media? The impeachment threat is far less credible than that which faced Clinton. The presidential image burnished by Clinton and Patterson is nonetheless clear. As filtered through the hybrid figure of Duncan, Clinton emerges as a figure much more sinned against than sinning: a mixture of philosopher-king and loyal servant of the people. Authoring such a book exposed Bill Clinton to the kind of ridicule he received in some of the reviews quoted above. The book arguably contributed to the strand of liberal opinion which saw both Trump and Clinton as narcissistic figures. For journalist Frank Bruni, Clinton and Trump were 'sultans of self-pity' – 'self-righteous, self-pitying and suffused with anger that anyone would peddle a version of events less heroic than the one that he proffers.'[73] Whatever its faults, *The President Is Missing* clearly does represent Clinton's own image of himself. Despite a degree of ridicule, it swept to the top of best-seller lists.

Bill Clinton's image, as it developed in the post-presidential years, was a complex product of competing texts, memories and memorializations. Clinton, notably in *My Life* and (to a lesser extent) in *The President Is Missing*, sought to shape his own image as a Southerner who embraced the social liberalism of the 1960s, along with more cautious and conservative attitudes, especially in financial matters, characteristic of a New Democrat.[74] Joe Klein himself was not entirely unsympathetic to this view of Clinton as a political leader who sought a fruitful fusion of sixties 'newness' with the self-consciously 'sensible' attitudes of a post-Great Society, post-tax-and-spend liberal. However, *Primary Colors* also emphasized the degree to which compromised values spread across Stanton/ Clinton's entire campaign, calling into question the value and integrity of the political commitments which underpinned his bid for the White House. The image of Clinton which emerged from the novel *Primary Colors* still dominates our understanding of what was in so many ways a very successful presidency.

Notes

1   See Marannis, David, *First in His Class: The Biography of Bill Clinton* (New York: Touchstone, 1996), p. 11; White, Mark, 'Son of the Sixties: The Controversial Image of Bill Clinton,' *History*, 103 (January 2018): 100–23.

2   Kaplan, Rebecca, 'The Hidden Image in Bill Clinton's Official Portrait,' *CBS News*, 2 March 2015, https://www.cbsnews.com/news/hidden-image-bill-clintons-official-portrait/.

3   Ibid.

4   Anonymous, *Primary Colors: A Novel of Politics* (London: Vintage, 1996); Clinton, Bill, and James Patterson, *The President Is Missing: A Novel* (London: Century, 2018). See also White, 'Son of the Sixties.'

5   Greenstein, Fred, 'Political Style and Political Leadership: The Case of Bill Clinton,' in Stanley A. Renshon, ed., *The Clinton Presidency: Campaigning, Governing and the Psychology of Leadership* (Boulder, CO: Westview, 1995), pp. 134–50, 140.

6   Schlesinger Jr, Arthur M., 'Rating the Presidents: Washington to Clinton,' *Political Science Quarterly*, 112 (Summer 1997): 179–91 (quotations p. 187).

7   Drew, Elizabeth, *On the Edge: The Clinton Presidency* (New York: Simon & Schuster, 1996), p. 150.

8   Hillary R. Clinton, *Living History* (London: Headline, 2003), p. 289.

9   Rubin, Robert E., and Jacob Weisberg, *In an Uncertain World: Tough Choices from Wall Street to Washington* (New York: Texere, 2003), p. 133.

10 Barber, Benjamin R., *The Truth of Power: Intellectual Affairs in the Clinton White House* (New York: Norton, 2001), p. 495.

11 Gallen, David, *Bill Clinton as They Knew Him: An Oral Biography* (New York: Gallen Publishing, 1994), pp. 152–3; see also Rubenzer, Steven J. and Thomas R. Faschingbauer, *Personality, Character and Leadership in the White House* (Washington, DC: Brassey's, 2004), p. 193.

12 Brown, Floyd G., *Slick Willie: Why America Cannot Trust Bill Clinton* (Annapolis, MD: Annapolis Publishing, 1993).

13 *Time*, 18 November 1996, p. 31.

14 Stephanopoulos, George, *All Too Human: A Political Education* (London: Hutchinson, 1999), p. 143.

15 Cited in Smith, Sally Bedell, *For Love of Politics: The Clintons in the White House* (London: Aurum Press, 2007), p. 444.

16 Obama, Barack, *The Audacity of Hope: Thoughts on Reclaiming the American Dream* (New York: Crown, 2006), p. 171.

17 Schlesinger Jr, Arthur M., *Journals, 1952–2000* (London: Atlantic Books, 2007), p. 853.

18 Jones, Jeffrey M., 'Obama's First Retrospective Job Approval Rating Is 63%,' Gallup, 15 February 2018, https://news.gallup.com/poll/226994/obama-first-retrospective-job-approval-rating.aspx. See also Brian Newman, 'Bill Clinton's Approval Ratings: The More They Change, the More They Stay the Same,' *Political Science Quarterly*, 117 (2002): 789–804.

19 Stevenson, Richard, W. 'The Wisdom to Let the Good Times Roll,' *New York Times* [*NYT*], 25 December 2000, p. A1.

20 *The 9/11 Commission Report: Final Report of the National Commission on the Terrorist Attacks on the United States* (New York: Norton, 2004), p. 340.

21 See Robert E. Denton, *Moral Leadership and the American Presidency* (Lanham, MD: Rowman and Littlefield, 2005).

22 See Dionne, E. J., and Robert Kuttner, 'Did Clinton Succeed or Fail?,' *American Prospect*, 11 (August 2000): 24–33.

23 Harris, John F., *The Survivor: Bill Clinton in the White House* (New York: Random House, 2006), p. 434. For historians' evaluations that reach similar conclusions, see White, Mark, ed., *The Presidency of Bill Clinton: The Legacy of a New Domestic and Foreign Policy* (London: I.B. Tauris, 2012); and Maney, Patrick J., *Bill Clinton: New Gilded Age President* (Lawrence: University Press of Kansas, 2016).

24 C-Span, *Presidential Historians Survey 2017*, https://www.c-span.org/presidentsurvey2017/?personid=1651; Morgan, Iwan, 'The Top US Presidents; First Poll of UK Experts,' *BBC News: US & Canada*, 17 January 2011, https://www.bbc.co.uk/news/world-us-canada-12195111. See also Michael Nelson, 'Evaluating the Presidency,' in Michael Nelson, ed., *The Presidency and the Political System* (Washington, DC: CQ Press, 2003), pp. 87–102.

25 O'Neill, Joseph, *Netherland* (London: Fourth Estate, 2008), p. 88.

26 Created and developed by Aaron Sorkin, *The West Wing* (which originally ran on NBC) contained characters with apparent real-life counterparts from the Clinton White House. The clearest such example was C.J. Cregg, who was plausibly derived from Dee Dee Myers, White House press secretary from 1993 to 1995, who advised on the development of the series.

27 Clinton, Bill, *My Life* (New York: Knopf, 2004).

28 McMurtry, Larry, 'My Life: His True Love Is Politics,' *New York Times*, 23 June 2004, https://www.nytimes.com/2004/06/23/books/review/my-life-his-true-love-is-politics.html.

29 Kakutani, Michiko, 'Books of the Times: A Pastiche of a Presidency, Imitating a Life, in 957 Pages,' *NYT*, 20 June 2004, https://www.nytimes.com/2004/06/20/us/books-of-the-times-a-pastiche-of-a-presidency-imitating-a-life-in-957-pages.html.

30 Klein, Joe, 'Citizen Clinton,' *Time*, 28 June 2004.

31 Robert McCrum, 'Still Pressing the Flesh,' *The Observer*, 27 June 2004, https://www.theguardian.com/books/2004/jun/27/biography.politicalbooks1.

32 Berman William, '*My Life*,' *Reviews in American History*, 33 (2005): 126–33 [quotation p. 127].

33　Clinton, *My Life*, p. 362.

34　Tim Hames, 'Clinton: Egotist and Wrecker', *The Times*, 21 June 2004, p. 27.

35　John Heilemann and Mark Halperin, *Race of a Lifetime: How Obama Won the White House* (London: Penguin, 2010), pp. 207–15.

36　See Clinton, Bill, *Giving: How Each of Us Can Change the World* (New York: Knopf, 2007); Clinton, Bill, *Back to Work: Why We Need Smart Government for a Strong Economy* (New York: Knopf, 2011). See also Lizza, Ryan, 'Let's Be Friends', *The New Yorker*, 10 September 2012, pp. 34–42.

37　Chozick, Amy, *Chasing Hillary: Two Years, Two Presidential Campaigns, and One Intact Glass Ceiling* (New York: HarperCollins, 2018), p. 323.

38　Healy, Patrick, and Maggie Haberman, 'Donald Trump Opens New Line of Attack on Hillary Clinton: Her Marriage', *New York Times*, 30 September 2016, https://www.nytimes.com/2016/10/01/us/politics/donald-trump-interview-bill-hillary-clinton.html.

39　Michele Gorman, 'A Brief History of Donald Trump and Bill Clinton's Friendship', *Newsweek*, 27 May 2016, https://www.newsweek.com/history-donald-trump-bill-clinton-friendship–464360.

40　Milbank, Dana, 'How Bill Clinton Cleared a Way for Donald Trump', *Washington Post*, 4 June 2018, https://www.washingtonpost.com/opinions/how-bill-clinton-cleared-a-path-for-donald-trump/2018/06/04/e024c388-6834-11e8-9e38-24e693b38637_story.html?utm_term=.0355e584fe2f.

41　O'Rourke, P. J., *How the Hell Did This Happen? A Cautionary Tale of American Democracy* (London: Grove Press, 2018), p. 187.

42　Wood, Gaby, 'Interview with Joe Klein', *The Guardian*, 6 August 2006, https://www.theguardian.com/books/2006/aug/06/usa.shopping.

43　*End of the Tour*, directed by James Ponsoldt, 1996. See too Scordelis, Alex, 'A Look Back at "Primary Colors," Which Changed the Way We Talk (and Joke) about Politics', *Esquire*, 30 August 2016, https://www.esquire.com/author/16704/alex-scordelis/.

44　*Primary Colors* (film), directed by Mike Nicols, 1998; Tarloff, Erik, 'Loyalty, Decency, Campaigning, Love', *NYT*, 23 April 2000, http://movies2.nytimes.com/books/00/04/23/reviews/000423.23tarloft.html.

45　Lewis, Michael, 'Review of *Primary Colors*', *NYT*, 28 January 1996, http://movies2.nytimes.com/books/98/03/29/bsp/klein-primary.html; Warren, Robert Penn, *All the King's Men* (New York: Harcourt, Brace, 1946).

46　*The War Room*, directed by Chris Hegedus and D.A. Pennebaker, 1993.

47　Anonymous, *Primary Colors*, p. 291.

48　Ibid., p. 310.

49　Cockburn, Alexander, 'White House Farce', *The Observer*, 3 March 1996, https://www.theguardian.com/theobserver/1996/mar/03/featuresreview.review.

50　*The Seduction of Joe Tynan*, directed by Jerry Schatzberg and written by Alan Alda, 1979.

51　Anonymous, *Primary Colors*, pp. 4, 33.

52　Ibid., p. 364.

53　Klein, Joe, *The Running Mate* (New York: Dial Press, 2000).

54　Klein, Joe, *The Natural: The Misunderstood Presidency of Bill Clinton* (London: Coronet Books, 2002), pp. 27, 33, 165, 208.

55　*Wag the Dog*, directed by Barry Levinson, 1997.

56　Hitchens, Christopher, *No One Left to Lie To: The Triangulations of William Jefferson Clinton* (London: Verso, 1999), p. 89.

57   Tarloff, Erik, *Face-Time* (New York: Random House, 1998).

58   Canin, Ethan, *America, America* (London: Bloomsbury, 2008), pp. 297–8.

59   Mailer, Norman, *Miami and the Siege of Chicago: An Informal History of the Republican and Democratic Conventions of 1968* (New York: Random House, 1968); Thompson, Hunter S., *Fear and Loathing in Las Vegas: A Savage Journey to the Heart of the American Dream* (New York: Random House, 1971).

60   Heilemann and Halperin, *Race of a Lifetime.*

61   Palmer, William J., *The Films of the Nineties: The Decade of Spin* (New York: Palgrave Macmillan, 2009), pp. 19, 79–128; White, Hayden, *Metahistory: The Historical Imagination in Nineteenth-Century Europe* (Baltimore, MD: Johns Hopkins University Press, 1973). See also Parry-Giles, Shawn J., and Trevor Parry-Giles, *Constructing Clinton: Hyperreality and Presidential Image-making in Postmodern Politics* (New York: Peter Lang, 2002).

62   Anonymous, *O: A Presidential Novel* (New York: Simon and Schuster, 2011).

63   Quoted in Scordelis, 'A Look Back at "Primary Colors."'

64   See McDonald, Henry, 'Heaney Tells of Stroke Ordeal,' *The Observer*, 19 July 2009, https://www.theguardian.com/books/2009/jul/19/seamusheaney-ireland; Wilson, R., 'Days Like These,' *New Statesman*, 15 December 1995; Dumbrell, John, *Clinton's Foreign Policy: Between the Bushes, 1992–2000* (New York: Routledge, 2009), pp. 88–92.

65   Elliott, Clare Frances, 'A Poetic Presidency: Abraham Lincoln, Walt Whitman, and the Second American Revolution,' in Michael Patrick Cullinane and Clare Frances Elliott, eds., *Perspectives on Presidential Leadership: An International View of the White House* (New York: Routledge, 2014), pp. 41–56; Carter, Jimmy, *Always a Reckoning and Other Poems* (New York: Times Books, 1995); Carter, Jimmy, *The Hornet's Nest: A Novel of the Revolutionary War* (New York: Simon and Schuster, 2001).

66   Charles, Ron, 'Bill Clinton and James Patterson's *The President Is Missing* Is an Awkward Duet,' *Washington Post*, 4 June 2018, https://www.washingtonpost.com/entertainment/books/bill-clinton-and-james-pattersons-the-president-is-missing-is-an-awkward-duet/2018/06/01/adca8530-64dd-11e8-a768-ed043e33f1dc_story.html?utm_term=.47d0c045ff6e.

67   Millen, Robbie, 'Welcome to Clintonland,' *The Times*, 9 June 2018; Wallace, Nicole, 'Bill Clinton and James Patterson Have Written a Thriller: It's Good,' *NYT*, 5 June 2018, https://www.nytimes.com/2018/06/05/books/review/president-is-missing-clinton-patterson.html.

68   Clinton and Patterson, *The President Is Missing*, pp. 500–08, 505.

69   Ibid., pp. 50, 58.

70   Millen, 'Welcome to Clintonland.'

71   Clinton and Patterson, *The President Is Missing*, p. 293.

72   Ibid., p. 60.

73   Bruni, Frank, 'Bill Clinton and Donald Trump, the Sultans of Self Pity,' *NYT*, 5 June 2018, https://www.nytimes.com/2018/06/05/opinion/bill-clinton-trump-sexual-harassment.html.

74   See Parry-Giles and Parry-Giles, *Constructing Clinton*; and White, 'Son of the Sixties.'

Chapter 11

HIP HOP AND HOPE: MANAGING THE OUTLIER STATUS OF BARACK OBAMA

Clodagh Harrington

Hip hop is more than a musical genre: it's a philosophy, a political statement, a way of approaching and remaking culture.[1]

In the 2008 presidential election, Barack Obama presented himself as an outsider, a candidate like no other. Not everyone embraced this 'otherness' but for those who did, the promise of change seemed real. As a candidate, Obama broke boundaries via his ability to transform the Democratic Party's voter base. The liberal youth of America were inspired by the Hope and Change agenda on offer, with 66 per cent of voters aged 18–30 supporting him on election day.[2] Many unconventional cultural threads highlighted the distinctive appeal of this self-described 'skinny kid with a funny name,' starting with the use of graffiti artist Shepard Fairey's iconic imagery on the campaign trail. Further cementing his outlier status, Barack Obama was lauded as America's 'first hip hop president,' and his wife, Michelle Obama, became revered as 'the Beyoncé of First Ladies.'[3] More than a nod to ethnicity, this perception reflected belief that the Obamas appreciated the cultural significance of rap music. Young people were intrigued, some electrified, to hear the new president declare that he saw a place for hip hop in the nation's dialogue. During his time in office, rappers and poets were invited to perform at the White House and praised for their artistic contribution.

As the first African American president, Barack Obama's musical tastes and preferences were more consequential owing to the significance of the youth vote, and therefore more scrutinized than those of his predecessors. His electoral appeal reached beyond that of the usual presidential candidate. Overall, young Americans identified music as a significant life influence. As the musical preference of the harder-to-reach African American youth tended towards R&B and hip hop, rather than traditional white rock-and-roll, it was clear that a candidate who not only looked like them, but also appeared to relate to them on a musical and cultural level held unprecedented appeal. The more overtly Obama was associated with hip hop and with specific rappers, however, the easier it became for some political opponents to draw negative conclusions about his plans for America.

Whatever musical strategy Obama embraced, first as a candidate and later in the Oval Office, there were inevitable challenges in presenting himself as sufficiently authentic and aware of the *zeitgeist* whilst not scaring more traditional Democrat voters. Born in 1961, Obama positioned himself as coming from the generation prior to hip hop, publicly stating that he was present for its early inception in the 1970s but casting himself more as an uncle in relation to the movement. In doing so, he could appreciate its merits, offer criticism where appropriate and maintain sufficient distance. Therefore, his own reputation as a serious presidential contender and later incumbent was not threatened by a genre that, despite its twenty-first-century global reach, many Americans over a certain age were ignorant of, intimidated by or simply did not comprehend.

The relationship between Obama and hip hop cannot be considered a one-way or even a two-way street, being more of a multi-lane highway, laden with junctions, about-turns and cul-de-sacs. Obama utilized hip hop as he shaped his pre-presidential image, and this was sufficiently authentic for the genre to reciprocate, despite its 'historically indignant attitude toward the state.'[4] There is no single category or neat conclusion to be drawn from how hip hop interpreted the first black president and contributed to shaping his image. This chapter offers some observations on overlapping and often conflicting sets of interactions, along with the challenges a president faces when engaging with a movement known for offering unfiltered criticism of the establishment.

Hip Hop and the Shaping of Obama's Image

When considering how Obama utilized hip hop to craft his image, the content of relevant speeches and interviews provides clues to his thinking about those artists he referenced and invited to the White House. In addition, continuous media attention focused on performers who he had on speed-dial and on his iPod, who he (usually mildly) criticized, and who he distanced himself from. It was notable, however, that the relationships and outreach were not necessarily continuous or linear. There were ebb and flow, with campaign and first-term peaks followed by evident troughs over time.

A preliminary research question concerns the style-to-substance ratio, namely the extent to which Obama's engagement with hip hop was genuine and consequential. An examination of style *as* substance can be a challenging task. The Obama-Jay-Z bromance, for example, provided liberal media optics from heaven but beyond the powerful imagery, it is worth considering how far there their relationship had real meaning beyond the exchange of cool and kudos. In the words of Bakari Kitwana, co-founder of the first US National Political Hip-Hop Convention, listening to Jay-Z and watching *The Wire* were not sufficient to make Obama the 'hip hop president.' What really mattered, Kitwana averred, was 'the organizing and the issues.'[5] Thanks to a graffiti artist, social media and music, the first African American president connected with sections of the youth vote in a way his political opponents and presidential predecessors simply could not. How successful and reciprocal this outreach really was is a matter for debate, as Obama elicited a complex range of responses from the sprawling cultural form that is twenty-first-century American hip hop.

Crafting a Visual Image of 'Hope'

Prior to the Obama years, hip hop with its four components of rapping, dj-ing, graffiti and break-dancing had little formal interaction with national politics, although as a sub-culture it had a lot to say on the topic.[6] In an early indication of candidate Obama's unconventional appeal, street artist Shepard Fairey requested approval to create a piece of visual art in support of his 2008 campaign. The iconic 'Hope' image that he produced became a cultural phenomenon that gave the Democratic Party nominee unparalleled kudos. The 'Hope' artwork, a stylized stencil piece that was recreated extensively, became *the* image of the 2008 'Hope and Change' campaign. That a black man was the presidential nominee for a major political party was groundbreaking, but in addition he was youthful and intellectual, and considered handsome and charismatic in a manner reminiscent to many of Jack Kennedy.

For those with an eye on the nation's civil rights chronicle, this was arguably the most significant development since the heady days of JFK's election as president in 1960. Nearly half a century before Obama's triumph, another glass ceiling had been broken, albeit a less dramatic one, as a young Catholic made it to the Oval Office and offered more than a nod to the burning issue of minority rights. As the first television president, who came to power at a time of growing social change and ensuing civil unrest, the visual imagery surrounding Kennedy was laden with significance. Inevitable comparisons were drawn with Obama, as once again liberals swooned with optimism and conservatives wondered what would become of their country. One CNN poll from the euphoric post-election week in 2008 showed that 80 per cent of African Americans agreed with the statement that 'Obama's election was a dream come true.'[7] Foreshadowing the intense conservative resistance that the forty-fourth president would encounter, an earlier CNN survey found that 70 per cent of white respondents disagreed with the statement that the Obama nomination 'was a dream come true.'[8] Not all Americans were ready for a black man in the White House.

There was no precedent for a presidential candidate using a street artist's visual image of him as the symbol of his campaign. It was testament to the outlier status of both that the skinny kid with the funny name utilized the work of a thirteen-times arrested graffiti artist, whose creative *raison d'etre* was to challenge convention and mainstream political views. The power of employing Fairey's work, as opposed to, for example, that of even a hip graphic design company, was significant. It demonstrated Obama's capacity to engage beyond the mainstream. Fairey's art attempted to speak truth to power, or at least question it, with reference to oppression, exploitation, prejudice and discrimination.[9] Already facing sustained criticism for being too liberal and inexperienced, candidate Obama would have to tread lightly around the artist's challenging and provocative agenda.

Fairey's inspiration derived in part from an earlier iconic image, Robert Rauschenberg's silk-screen print of John F. Kennedy looking upwards in embodiment of hope.[10] The mainstream appeal of Obama and his populist image was cemented as *Time* magazine asked Fairey to design its 'Person of the Year' cover in December 2008. In offering such a plaudit to the president-elect, *Time* merged the Hope portrayed by the man and image on the covers of all editions. Fairey later created a Hope poster for the *Occupy Wall Street* [OWS] movement, with similar imagery, but instead using the darker visage of a Guy Fawkes mask. Initially, the text read 'Mr President, we HOPE you are on our side,' but after discussion with *OWS* this was changed to 'We are the Hope,' which was more in keeping with the movement's non-partisan ethos.[11] Writing in 2011, Fairey outlined his motivation for supporting both OWS and President Obama, arguing that voters simply turning up on election day was not enough. In keeping with hip hop's broader philosophy, Fairey reinforced the importance of individual activism in the push for social progress. In common with many hip hop performers, Fairey later expressed disappointment with Obama's record in office, voicing particular concern about drone attacks and surveillance abroad and the lack of social progress at home.[12] To put its ultimate dissatisfaction with Obama in context, it is useful to consider the genesis and evolution of political hip hop in terms of its expectations and experience.

The 1970s Hip Hop Generation

There is some dispute about the genesis of the connection between graffiti and hip hop, with some commentators insisting that it was merely a 1980s media construct.[13] They are more commonly seen as two strands of creativity coming out of poorer urban areas, most notably in the Brooklyn and Bronx boroughs of New York City, where the creators led lives light years removed from the wealth of lower Manhattan, despite their geographical proximity. Coming into being in the 1970s, the first hip hop generation made its presence felt in outdoor block parties where young blacks could congregate to rap, breakdance and socialize for free. Tagging graffiti on the subway as it headed for the other-world of Manhattan was also a fun and free pastime. None of these activities required the conventional trappings of a venue, equipment, instruments or staff, hence they were fully and authentically grassroots and real. Crucially, they brought young African Americans together in creativity and unity. Hence, the components of hip hop were far removed from engagement with government or the establishment in any form. One notable exception, albeit a negative one, was the relationship with the police, particularly in the aftermath of President Richard Nixon's declaration of a 'War on Drugs' in 1971. Perpetuated by succeeding administrations, both Republican and Democrat, this resulted in a disproportionate rate of imprisonment for young black males and appeared to make incarceration a new form of racial control.[14]

As a relatively homogenous entity in its earlier days, hip hop often referenced politics, policy and individual presidents in largely negative terms. It focused mainly on domestic issues pertaining to institutional racism and social policy, but foreign policy criticism was also an important strand in the genre. Hip hop opinion on US military actions and illegal covert operations abroad chimed with that of the American left. Political rappers offered insightful musings on the how the leader of the free world often failed to practise what he preached both at home and abroad. Years later, when hip hop had become a far broader, more globally established and fragmented entity, it did not guarantee Barack Obama a free pass when responding to his presidency. He was lauded, without doubt, but also criticized in two main regards. As a black man, or at least as bi-racial man who chose to identify as black, he was inevitably held to a higher standard by many of those who viewed him as one of their own. He was also taken to task, at times with vitriol, by those who took exception to, for example, his drone usage abroad and immigration restrictions at home.[15]

1980s Anti-GOP Rapping

From 1980 onwards, following changes in the criminal justice system, the rate of black male incarceration increased dramatically. This predominantly related to drug use and sales, rather than violent crime.[16] Some black political musicians of the 1970s sent an angry message to their government through their song lyrics. As president, Obama's inclusion of Gil Scott Heron on his iPod playlist made interested observers take note.[17] Earlier in his career, the soul and jazz poet, often considered the godfather of political rap, had continuously compared his country to South Africa. He gave clear instruction to the next generation of political rappers to engage politically and offer a positive message of change.[18] Taking their cue from him, newer acts such as Public Enemy offered biting criticism of the 1980s establishment in their condemnation of the prison-industrial complex, the war on drugs, foreign policy hypocrisy, the mainstream media and, of course, individual presidents. By now a robust genre, hip hop was facing up to twelve years of Republican rule in the White House, and rappers found plenty to criticize during the Reagan–Bush Sr. years.

As the hip hop genre matured in the 1980s and beyond, the splintering of styles and priorities demonstrated that it categorically was not an ideological monolith. The division lines of age, class, gender, colour and sexuality ensured that not everyone sang from the same rap sheet. Hip hop had long become a vibrant form of expression for Latinos, Filipino Americans and other ethnicities – not least Arab-Americans, all of whom had their own, sometimes overlapping, story to tell. For the casual observer, it may be a reasonable assumption that contemporary hip hop leans more towards the material plane than the political. To a large extent, this is correct, and there are certain high-profile strands of the genre – what could be termed 'unconscious' rap – that seemingly focus only on conspicuous consumption, notably regarding money, drugs, cars, guns, glorification of violence and objectification of women. With 'mainstreaming', many components of the genre became the seeming antithesis of early hip hop through their focus on the material over the political. This is a far cry from the powerfully eloquent diatribes of Public Enemy and their contemporaries. However, there has been some value to the mainstreaming of hip hop in that it has become a culture consumed and appreciated by those far beyond the ghettos of its genesis. In addition, movements such as Black Lives Matter have reignited the decades-old call for African Americans to 'get woke' and effectively broadcast this message using social media as well as more traditional hip hop channels.[19]

'America's First Black President'

As the American presidency moved towards the twenty-first century, the 1992 election of 'the first black president' brought with it interactions and images that would have been unthinkable even one administration earlier.[20] Despite his 'Sister Souljah moment' (which happens 'when a candidate publicly rejects an easily recognisable extremist in his or her own political party'), Bill Clinton was embraced by much of black America in an unprecedented manner.[21] At a 1992 pre-inauguration event, a stellar line-up of African American musical royalty performed in support of the president-elect. It was unthinkable that his opponent George H. W. Bush could have gathered Diana Ross, Stevie Wonder and Michael Jackson alongside the Queen of Soul, Aretha Franklin, to appear on stage.[22] A decade and a half later, Barack Obama appeared to have his own 'Sister Souljah' moment on 29 April 2008 when, in his much-lauded campaign speech on race, he distanced himself from long-time mentor Reverend Jeremiah Wright.[23] This time, the stakes were far higher in that the Democratic Party candidate actually *was* black, and, unlike Clinton, his public repudiation was directed at an individual with whom he had a deeply meaningful relationship.

Bill Clinton had successfully ventured where his predecessors could not go, notably when appearing on the Arsenio Hall Show during the 1992 campaign. Geared towards a young urban audience, the show's tone and content could not be described as hard-hitting, but it engaged the MTV Generation, the notoriously difficult-to-reach voting demographic of 18- to 29-year-olds. Clinton's saxophone rendition of *Heartbreak Hotel* was a defining moment for his presidential candidacy because he successfully presented his brand, first to late-night television viewers and then to the nation, as cool.

One measure of Clinton's success came in the form of a national poll showing that if he ran for re-election in 1996 against Colin Powell, over two-thirds of black voters would have supported the southern white man over the African American Four-Star Army General and Chairman of the Joint Chiefs of Staff from New York.[24] It is worth bearing in mind that this poll was done after the introduction of the infamous 'Three Strikes' law (formally the Violent Crime Control and Law Enforcement Act of 1994), which brought in mandatory life prison sentences for those who had committed a severe or violent felony after two previous convictions. Addressing the National Association for the Advancement of Colored People in 2015, Clinton expressed regret for approving the measure because of its disproportionate impact on African Americans.[25]

Clinton's relationship with black America was inevitably complex, and over time a generational shift appeared as older voters maintained some loyalty to the family brand and their off-spring gravitated first towards Barack Obama and later Bernie Sanders. Commenting in 1998 on how Bill Clinton displayed 'almost every trope of blackness,' Toni Morrison argued that this was reflected in both his upbringing and later his treatment by the establishment, rather than his policy initiatives or his capacity to sound soulful.[26]

Clinton's case had some pertinence for Barack Obama, whom many black commentators criticized for not being sufficiently black and for not having direct empathy with the African American experience. In his essay 'Fear of a Black President,' Ta Nehisi Coates reminded readers that the only way an African American could win election to the highest office was to be 'twice as good' and 'half as black.'[27] Hence the role of Michelle Obama was significant, as she provided full authenticity with her blackness and her modest beginnings. For those eager to criticize the first half-white president, his choice of spouse inevitably gave them pause. She was Chicago South Side born-and-bred and was open about the slave aspects of her ancestry.[28]

It is worth considering the balancing skills Obama required to manage brand and persona to win bi-racial voter support. His appeal to progressive whites did not always sit well with some African Americans. Harvard law professor Randall Kennedy cites his position on gay rights, especially same-sex marriage, as a prime example of the tightrope he had to walk on this score.[29] Back in 1996, Obama was clear in his support for same-sex marriage, but the need to mobilize African American support likely influenced a later reversal of position. In 2008, a mere 24 per cent of black Christians approved of gay marriage compared with 41 per cent of white ones.[30] There are no figures readily available regarding how those involved with or culturally invested in hip hop perceived Obama in relation to his stance on gay marriage, but the genre had long manifested homophobia. One only needs listen to a sample of lyrics to get a sense of how certain influential rappers perceived gayness, until very recently at least. Some, including Ice-T, matured with age and publicly rejected the homophobic lyrics of their youth, whereas others clung to old prejudices. The Goon Sqwad's Trick-Trick, for example, advocated violence against lesbians as recently as 2008. In a fitting microcosm of the genre's partial evolution, Snoop-Dogg's 'Moment I Feared' video openly mocked sexually ambiguous rapper Young Thug.[31]

Clearly, Obama had no intention of pandering to the ignorance of a few rappers, but Randall Kennedy condemned him for fitting his 'retrograde religiosity' into his electoral strategy 'with uniform snugness.'[32] An alternative assessment of Obama's position might be that no politician ever made it to the pinnacle of power without a finely tuned political ear and a capacity for compromise. The evidence suggests that he was attempting to accommodate the (very slow) evolution of socially conservative black Christians who may have been ready for an African American man in the White House but were not at a point, yet at least, of embracing the rights of gay Americans to marry.

Judicial developments would demonstrate how far the nation travelled on this issue over the course of Obama's presidency. His nomination of two Associate Justices who were supportive of gay marriage opened the way for the Supreme Court's landmark 2015 ruling, *Obergefell v Hodges*, that the right to marry is guaranteed to same-sex couples by the 'Due Process' clause and the 'Equal Protection' clause of the US Constitution. If Barack Obama was playing the long civil rights game back in 2008, then it was a resounding success for gay America. Whilst hip hop may not have unconditionally embraced this development, it was having some great leaps forward of its own. When Jay-Z's 4:44 was released in 2017 to huge acclaim, one of the album tracks shared the story of how his mother came out as a lesbian to her son. He wrote the song *Smile* the following day, featuring a poignant monologue delivered by Gloria Carter.[33] It is difficult to measure the soft power of an internationally successful rap artist accepting his mother's sexuality so publicly, but it was likely very considerable. The tandem progress of government and culture helped to reinforce the new normal of marital equality.

One Hip Hop Voice against Bush 43

Political hip hop had remained vocal throughout the George W. Bush years, starting with responses to the chaotic Florida 2000 election process, in which black voters made up 11 per cent of the electorate but 44 per cent of those citizens barred from voting because of previous conviction for a felony. On top of this, there were apparently numerous bureaucratic errors on the purge list that resulted in some eligible African American voters being denied their legitimate suffrage rights.[34] Unsurprisingly, the playlist on George W. Bush's 'iPod One' consisted mainly of country music and classic rock with 'a little bit of hard core and honky-tonk.'[35] The forty-third president did reach out to African Americans, albeit cautiously and within the confines of his party's limited record on black engagement. (In 2000 less than one in twenty black Americans was a registered Republican voter.) Candidate Bush discussed race on the campaign trail via safe topics such as education and the economy, but he had little chance of generating a sea change of black voting in his favour.[36]

Post-9/11 developments diminished the already slim prospects of enhanced socio-economic progress and opportunity for low-income African Americans. In addition, the inept federal government response to Hurricane Katrina in 2005 did nothing for relations between the Bush administration and the world of hip hop. At a Hurricane Relief concert, co-host Kanye West went off script to declare that 'George Bush doesn't care about black people.'[37] Long before the New Orleans disaster, however, it was clear that African Americans did not care for Bush, who received just 10 per cent and 11 per cent of their votes in 2000 and 2004, respectively.[38]

Black disdain for the forty-third president was also on display in other ways. If the urban poetry of hip hop offered a channel for the anger and dissatisfaction felt by much of young America, other creative communities shared their displeasure in a range of ways. One less beat-driven form of verbal protest, conventional poetry, had much to say about the foreign policy direction of the Bush administration. Clearly, this had not come to the attention of the first lady's staff when Laura Bush arranged a 'Poetry and the American Voice' event at the White House in February 2003. Some invitees, including Wanda Coleman, Yusef Komunyakaa and former US poet laureate Rita Dove, refused to attend. In the heated moment before the US invasion of Iraq, poets around the world joined together in verse to repudiate the government's decision. Poet Sam Hamill refused his invitation and put out a call for contributions to an anti-war poetry compilation that received over 8,200 responses.[39] Unsurprisingly, therefore, the first lady's event never took place.[40]

Michelle Obama experienced her own White House poetry challenge, albeit for different reasons. In contrast to her predecessor, she was not unaware of the public relations challenge that would come with inviting those who had so vocally disparaged other presidents. Her 2011 'Evening of Poetry' guests included the rapper 'Common,' whose critical musings on George W. Bush's war in Iraq made it a challenge for Press Secretary Jay Carney to manage the news cycle that followed. The invitation to this controversial figure brought a plethora of responses, with *Fox News* and Sarah Palin voicing outrage at a 'thug' being invited to the White House and the *Atlantic* magazine reminding readers that he was a Grammy-winning cerebral artist with a positive message.[41] In a nation divided on the topic of the first black president, the presence of rappers in the White House was as thrilling to some as it was offensive to others.

America's First Hip Hop President

If Bill Clinton was perceived as 'America's first black president' on account of his life experience rather than his skin colour, then the actual first black president embraced a more specific role, that of the nation's first hip hop chief executive. Reflecting on the responses from this subcultural genre to Obama as White House candidate and subsequently president, suffice it to say that there was a wealth of unconditional positive regard in the early days. Obama ran, initially at least, on a post-racial ticket in 2008. There was a brief period when colour was not at the forefront of the national dialogue, or at least a pretence that it was not. However, President Obama found himself dealing with problems that disproportionally impacted Americans of colour, including the economic collapse and ensuing housing crisis.[42]

Four Hip Hop Interpretations of Obama

Once the Obama presidency was underway, several categories of hip hop response to it became apparent. These were inevitably overlapping, but each had its own characteristics, some more positive than others. They can be termed 'effusive,' 'instructive,' 'adversarial' and 'unconscious.' This classification is not intended to categorize all the hip hop interpretations of the Obama presidency. The aim instead is to offer some snapshots on how hip hop, in its various forms ranging from politically oblivious to 'woke,' responded to the unprecedented accession of a young black progressive man as the leader of the free world.

The 'Effusive' Category

This involved the highest profile hip hop artists, most notably Jay-Z, coming out loudly in support of candidate and later President Obama. The Carter-Knowles billionaire power couple, namely Jay-Z and Beyoncé, embodied individualistic mainstream corporate success, and if Obama had a best friend in hip hop, it was Shawn Carter. Others in this category, including megastars Sean Combs and Kanye West, had influence and appeal that reached far beyond a black youth audience, and all campaigned loudly and effectively for their candidate in 2008. On Inauguration Day 2009, as an estimated crowd of 2 million gathered in Washington DC to witness the presidential swearing in, soul legend Aretha Franklin sang 'My Country, Tis of Thee.' Later, Beyoncé performed at the Neighbourhood Ball and nearby, at the Hip Hop Youth Ball, Kanye West delivered a bespoke version of 'Heartless' in which he adjusted the lyrics to fit the occasion.

> From miles around they came to see him speak
> The story that he told
> To save a country that's so blue
> That they thought had lost its soul
> The American Dream come true tonight. [43]

In many ways, West personified the strand of hip hop that demonstrated clear and expected enthusiasm for the first black president. When candidate Obama appeared on the Black Entertainment Television show 'What's in It for Us?' in 2008, he informed his host that as part of his voter outreach efforts, he had met with Kanye and Jay-Z.[44] Clearly this was a canny move in terms of joining the dots of the enthusiasm he was igniting with the practicalities of getting the hard-to-reach youth vote to the polling booth on election day. It was evident that Kanye was impressed with Obama, and the connection could only be of benefit to a rapper who liked to share stories of his own mother's role in the civil rights movement. Like Jay-Z, Kanye demonstrated his support, but the quality and sustainability of their relationships with the First Couple differed significantly. The Carters and the Obamas held unparalleled positions in their respective spheres and each could reinforce the kudos of the other. Kayne West was more of a loose cannon and Obama was mindful of this. Suddenly the nation's highest role model, Obama had to watch his footing amidst relentless media scrutiny, the rise of the Tea Party movement and accompanying heightened racial aversion.

The 'Instructive' Category

Perhaps the most meaningful, if not the most high-profile, hip hop response was the 'Instructive' category, which could be described as engaged and expectant in relation to their president. There was also the potential for anger if he did not live up to expectations. Some of this group were peers of Obama, with direct experience of living through earlier administrations and their civil rights developments and setbacks. The most notable was Chuck D, who coined the phrase that rap was 'CNN for black people.'[45] Considered by many to be the most credible voice in American hip hop, the highly cerebral Public Enemy frontman maintained a reputation for consistently speaking truth to power since the Reagan era. The furious energy of their 'Fear of a Black Planet' album remained central to the established rap cannon long after its 1990 release.[46] In later years, Chuck D was as likely to be found lecturing from a university podium as rapping on stage, and his tone towards Barack Obama tended towards the constructive, albeit at times critical, something akin to a fond but stern older brother. More recently, Killer Mike, one half of Run the Jewels, stepped up in a similar manner, albeit more overtly voicing his condemnation.[47]

The 'Adversarial' Category

It is worth noting that not all black Americans were overjoyed with the rise of Obama. High-profile Republican conservatives such as Tim Scott, whose election as South Carolina senator in 2012 made him the first black member of the upper house from the South since Reconstruction, and self-described 'right-wing extremist' Congressman Allen West of Florida did not hesitate to criticize the relatively inexperienced senator from Illinois.[48] Unsurprisingly, there is no evidence of hip hop criticizing Obama for not being progressive enough, but he was taken to task by some on the left of its political spectrum. A relatively niche sub-genre, this third category of hip hop responses to Barack Obama may not have lost him many votes, but it did cause him to lose credibility among the thinking person's rappers, such as Killer Mike. Run the Jewel's frontman compared the first black president to Ronald Reagan, especially on foreign policy issues as 'just another talking head telling lies on teleprompters.'[49] Others, such as Lupa Fiasco, went further, in both lyrics and interviews, in accusing the forty-fourth president of being 'a terrorist.'[50]

From this perspective, Obama faced harsh criticism in print and verse from commentators who censured not only his foreign policy priorities but also his preference for the 'universal' as opposed to race-specific responses to social inequalities. In 2010, Michael Eric Dyson complained that Obama 'runs from race like a black man runs from the cops.'[51] In his book *The Black Presidency*, Dyson expanded his criticism, accusing Obama of 'racial procrastination.' Clearly, he was frustrated that whilst the presidency was of 'great symbolic value' to black America, it 'has hardly put a dent in the forces that pulverise black life: high infant mortality rates, high unemployment, atrocious educational inequality, racial profiling and deadly police brutality.'[52] The harsh critique offered by this Georgetown sociology professor chimed with the views of political rappers frustrated with Obama. On the more acerbic end of the spectrum, academic Cornel West echoed the sentiments of rapper Killer Mike about the shortcomings of Obama's presidency. The Princeton professor disparaged him as a 'Rockefeller Republican in blackface,' a president 'more interested in Wall Street and drone strikes than the needs of black America.'[53]

West's criticisms continued into Obama's post-presidency. In a 2017 opinion piece for *The Guardian*, he referred to Obama 'cheerleader' Ta Nehisi Coates as 'the neoliberal face of the black freedom struggle.'[54] In accusing Coates of ignoring Obama's failure to tackle poverty at home and curb American imperialism abroad, his grievances mirrored hip hop's disappointment that the forty-fourth president had failed to deliver the Hope and Change promised in 2008. As the writer of the *Black Panther* comic, and contributor to the subsequent movie which was a mainstream box-office smash, as well as acclaimed literary works, Coates could claim credentials relating to high and low culture in a way that few can. Though not unconditionally supportive of Barack Obama, he cut the president slack, not least in making the valid point that one president, however visionary and capable, faced inevitable constraints.[55] The theme of saviour, and its associated myths, is a recurrent feature in much of the left-leaning academic and rap commentary on President Obama, but even his critics acknowledge the fallacy of expecting a single individual to bring about fundamental societal change.[56]

The 'Unconscious' (or 'Unintentionally Injurious') Category

The final category of unconscious rapper is one where artists not renowned for their self-awareness or emotional maturity were supportive of America's first black president. Receiving public support from those whose lyrics were, for example, laden with misogyny, homophobia or profanities brought challenges for Obama. Whilst the enthusiasm of these rappers was clearly authentic, it also had the potential to be unintentionally injurious to the first black president.

Kanye West offered one high-profile example as a global hip hop superstar who commanded immense influence with his fans but did not necessarily engage in a meaningful way with Obama. Having campaigned not only for Obama but also the Democratic Party, he met with the president several times, but their relationship was less than harmonious. There were times when West's controversial public behaviour ensured considerable international media attention. It was not in the president's interest to be too closely associated with such a volatile artist. Obama famously referred to Kanye as a 'jackass' and Kanye publicly stated that the president had done nothing for his adopted home town of Chicago during his tenure.[57] Much to the bemusement of at least some of his fan-base, Kanye voted for Donald Trump in 2016. He also announced his own intention to run for president in the future. Further reinforcing the theme of individual choice, fellow-Chicagoan Chance-the-Rapper reminded his millions of Twitter followers that 'Black people don't have to be Democrats.'[58]

There is clearly no obligation for any hip hopper to be the voice of his/her generation or race or to adhere to an expected narrative or political position. Nonetheless, when an artist possesses the powerful platform that fame brings, he or she arguably has some responsibility to demonstrate at least a basic level of self-knowledge and political sensitivity. Supporting a presidential candidate by rapping about attacking his opponent is a textbook example of providing unintentionally injurious support. For every teenager who may have gasped in delight at Lil Wayne's Sarah Palin references, there were older voters horrified at the prospect of their president being associated with gangsta rap and its offensive themes. Unsurprisingly, Obama demonstrated high awareness of potential image tarnishing when referencing hugely successful and controversial artists such as Lil Wayne and Ludacris.[59]

Hip Hop Strands of the Obama Legacy

During his presidency, Obama often justified his policy priorities via the adage that 'a rising tide lifts all boats.' If some of the boats were so battered and damaged, critics observed that the rising tide would just fill them with water. Hence, such policy developments as the Affordable Care Act, the increase in the federal minimum wage and prison reform did not always receive an unconditionally positive response from those with an eye on the disproportionate socio-economic challenges faced by African Americans.[60] Rappers, pundits and academics often chimed in their frustration. Criticism also followed Obama's key post-presidential initiative, *My Brother's Keeper*, a 'mentoring legacy' focusing on the attainment gap of young African American men and their need for positive role models in the absence of (some) fathers.[61] Coates, among others, argued that the challenges were structural and were about far more than absent fathers.

During his White House years, Obama was often disparaged for his paternalistic approach, and his apparent willingness to blame young black men for contributing to their own problems. His invitation to Compton-born Kendrick Lamar, a devout Christian, to become a custodian of *My Brother's Keeper* was an astute move. The Pulitzer Prize-winning hip hop superstar and creator of the *Black Panther* musical score personified socially conscious or 'woke' rap, in the context of the Black Lives Matter era. Here was a strand of the Obama legacy reminiscent of his Chicago activist days when community engagement was key. In November 2015, the pair met in the Oval Office to talk over inner-city problems as they pertained to black youth. Obama also pronounced Lamar's 'How Much a Dollar Cost' his favourite song of 2015.[62]

With hindsight, Obama and some of his hip hop critics took too much for granted in assuming that the progressive style and substance of his two terms in office would be continued under the next president. In the run-up to the

Figure 11.1 Barack Obama with rappers Kendrick Lamar and Janelle Monae at the 2016 White House Independence Day celebrations. (Photo by Aude Guerrucci-Pool/Getty Images.)

Clinton–Trump election in 2016, almost no one, including Team Trump, believed that the former reality television star could become the leader of the free world. As the political environment around the forty-fifth president grew rapidly toxic, more overt expressions of racism were given airings in a manner that many hoped had been consigned to history. As a consequence, the earlier fissures between Obama and hip hop rapidly came to look irrelevant.

'Make America Woke Again'

Rapper Ice-Cube referred to Obama as 'an anomaly' because of his unique engagement as president with hip hop.[63] It is fair to say that whoever won in 2016 could not connect with the genre in the way that he did. Had Hillary Clinton triumphed, she could not have attempted anything similar. In the post-Obama political environment, with many suffering from what Kimberlé Crenshaw termed 'post-traumatic Trump syndrome,'[64] it is more necessary than ever for hip hop to embrace and act upon its original and fundamental philosophical message – that of self-sufficiency. From this perspective, anyone hoping that President Obama could have acted as a saviour, or in the words of Killer Mike, a 'wizard,' was deluded.

One core element of hip hop is a focus on what happens outside of formal political structures. The significance and legacy of a progressive black man in the White House for two terms can and are being continued via grassroots energy and an ongoing push for social change and racial justice. In addition, there are new and vibrant strands including the expansion of feminist rap and the impact of the #Me Too movement. The Obama years provided political hip hop with a platform that was previously unthinkable. Now that the black man has left the White House, he has been succeeded by, in the words of Ta Nehisi Coates, the 'first white president.' Coates talks of the passive power and implicit whiteness of those presidents who preceded Obama, which has now been replaced by the explicit whiteness of Donald Trump. He reminds readers that Trump has facilitated the comfort of white supremacists, exemplified not least by the president's response to the Charlottesville, Virginia, neo-Nazi and counter-protests of August 2017, when he talked of 'very fine people on both sides.'[65]

While Trump's presidential agenda lacks any notable ideological underpinning, it is evidently focused on the de-Obamafication of the office and recent policy legacy. From efforts to repeal Obamacare to a tightening of immigration policy, along with staffing diversity within the highest echelons of government, it is increasingly clear to 'woke' America (black or white) that the Republican Party of Donald Trump lacks an inclusive agenda. With the formal unravelling of so much of what was achieved during the Obama years, a hip hop–infused grass-roots pushback has gathered pace.

Regardless of its imperfections, Obama's presidential tenure made real what was previously unthinkable, namely a black man in the White House. Long before coming to office, he had warned reporters, '[I]t's important that stories like mine aren't used to say everything is OK for blacks.'[66] Offering its own set of checks and balances, hip hop made sure that such a false narrative would never find acceptance. Thinking rappers did not hesitate to call out the shortcomings, as they saw it, of Obama's agenda and rhetoric. Generally, they did so from a supportive perspective and out of at least qualified loyalty for the first black president. At the other end of the political spectrum, Obama's racially anxious opponents were determined to ensure that stories like his would not become the norm.

Despite the severe and ongoing challenges to racial equality in the United States, there is no doubt that hip hop played an important role in the forty-fourth president's breakthrough. Its reward was unprecedented participation in the nation's political discourse. At no point did Obama have real agency over how hip hop interpreted and reacted to him. He would have been foolish to try and manipulate how such a sprawling and diverse genre projected his image. Instead, he engaged with it and, whilst establishing some parameters, let it settle on him in its own manner. The strategy worked. The words of rapper Nas (Nasir bin Olu Dara Jones) encapsulated how much of the genre, with all its criticisms, perceived the cultural significance of Obama: 'He is hip hop. It makes him real.'[67]

Notes

1   Hsu, Hua, 'The End of White America?' *The Atlantic*, January/February 2009, https://www.theatlantic.com/magazine/archive/2009/01/the-end-of-white-america/307208/.

2   Keeter, Scott et al., 'Young Voters in the 2008 Election,' Pew Research Center, 13 November 2008, http://www.pewresearch.org/2008/11/13/young-voters-in-the-2008-election/.

3   Gosa, Travis L., 'Not Another Remix: How Obama Became the First Hip-Hop President,' *Journal of Popular Music Studies*, 22:4 (2010); (Rapper) Lizzo interview with Deena Zaru, 16 August 2017, CNN, https://edition.cnn.com/2016/11/03/politics/lizzo-hillary-clinton-michelle-obama/index.html.

4   Ossei-Owusa, Shaun, 'Barack Obama's Anomalous Relationship with the Hip-Hop Community,' in Charles P. Henry, Robert Allen, and Robert Chrisman, eds., *The Obama Phenomenon: Towards a Multi-Racial Democracy* (Urbana: University Press of Illinois, 2011), p. 224.

5   Kitwana, Bakari interviewed by Berry, Elizabeth Mendez, 'It's Bigger than Barack,' in Travis L. Gosa, and Erik Nielson, eds., *The Hip-Hop and Obama Reader* (New York: Oxford University Press, 2015), p. 69.

6   For a detailed analysis of political hip hop, see Chang, Jeff, *Can't Stop Won't Stop: A History of the Hip-Hop Generation* (New York: St Martin's Press, 2005).

7   Steinhauser, Paul, 'In Poll, African-Americans Say Election a "Dream Come True",' CNN.com, 11 November 2008, http://edition.cnn.com/2008/POLITICS/11/11/obama.poll/.

8   Gerstle, Gary, 'Civic Ideals, Race and Nation,' in Julian E. Zelizer, ed., *The Presidency of Barack Obama: A First Historical Assessment* (Princeton, NJ: Princeton University Press, 2018), p. 261.

9   Young Caruso, Hwa, 'The Art of Shepard Fairey: Questioning Everything,' *International Journal of Multicultural Education*, 10:2 (2008), http://ijme-journal.org/index.php/ijme/article/viewFile/180/220.com.

10 Fisher, William W. et al., 'Reflections on the Hope Poster Case,' *Harvard Journal of Law and Technology*, 25 (Spring 2012), http://jolt.law.harvard.edu/articles/pdf/v25/25HarvJLTech243.pdf.

11 Judkis, Maura, 'Shepard Fairey Changes Occupy Wall Street Sign after Complaints,' *Washington Post*, 23 November 2011, https://www.washingtonpost.com/gdpr-consent/?destination=%2fblogs%2farts-post%2fpost%2fshepard-fairey-changes-occupy-wall-street-sign-aftercomplaints%2f2011%2f11%2f23%2fgIQADCDgoN_blog.html%3f&utm_term=.4a3120228b7f.

12 Fairey, Shepard, 'Occupy Hope,' 18 November 2011, https://obeygiant.com/occupy-hope/.

13 Ehrlich, Dimitri and Gregor Ehrlich, 'Graffiti in Its Own Words,' *New York Magazine*, 25 June 2006, http://nymag.com/guides/summer/17406/.

14 (No author cited) 'Nixon Adviser Admits War on Drugs Was Designed to Criminalize Black People.' Equal Justice Initiative, 25 March 2016, https://eji.org/news/nixon-war-on-drugs-designed-to-criminalize-black-people.

15 For context, see Chang, *Can't Stop, Won't Stop*; and Gosa, Travis L. and Erik Nielson, eds., *The HipHop and Obama Reader* (New York: Oxford University Press, 2015).

16 (No author cited) 'Criminal Justice Facts,' The Sentencing Project (ongoing project, no date), http://www.sentencingproject.org/criminal-justice-facts/.

17 Forman, Murray, 'Obama/Time: The President in the Hip-Hop Nation,' in Gosa and Nielson, *The Hip Hop and Obama Reader*, pp. 155–75.

18 Scott-Heron, Gil, 'The Revolution Will Not Be Televised,' in *Pieces of a Man* (New York: RCA Studios, 1971), offers one example.

19   Kitwana, Bakari, *Why White Kids Love Hip Hop: Wankstas, Wiggers, Wannabes, and the New Reality of Race in America* (New York: Basic Books, 2006), offers an informative look at the mainstreaming of hip hop.

20   Morrison, Toni, 'The Talk of the Town: Comment,' *New Yorker*, 5 October 1998, https://www.newyorker.com/magazine/1998/10/05/comment–6543.

21   Bill Clinton speaking on C-Span, 13 June 1992, https://www.youtube.com/watch?v=xtSifopiL1g; *Political Dictionary*, https://politicaldictionary.com/words/sister-souljah-moment/; Roper Center, 'How Groups Voted in 1992,' https://ropercenter.cornell.edu/polls/us-elections/how-groups-voted/how-groups-voted–1992/.

22   (No author cited) 'Inaugural Events Sing a Song of Diversity,' *Los Angeles Times*, 12 January 1993, http://articles.latimes.com/1993-01-13/entertainment/ca-1347_1_inaugural-events.

23   Barack Obama public address, 29 April 2008, https://www.c-span.org/video/?205102-1/obama-reaction-reverend-wright; Dowd, Maureen, 'Praying and Preying,' *New York Times*, 30 April 2008, https://www.nytimes.com/2008/04/30/opinion/30dowd.html?_r=1&hp&oref=slogin.

24   Germond, Jack and Jules Witcover, 'Poll Numbers Light Up for Colin Powell,' *Baltimore Sun*, 16 August 1995, http://articles.baltimoresun.com/1995-08-16/news/1995228157_1_colin-powell-powell-retired-republican-presidents.

25   'Bill Clinton Address to NAACP Convention, Philadelphia,' 15 July 2015, https://www.nbcphiladelphia.com/news/politics/Bill-Clinton-NAACP-Convention-Philadelphia-315320831.html.

26   Morrison, 'The Talk of the Town.'

27   Coates, Ta-Nehisi, 'Fear of a Black President,' in Coates, *We Were Eight Years in Power* (London: Hamish Hamilton, 2017), pp. 119–50.

28   'Michelle Obama's Slave Ancestry, Ann Romney's Atheist Immigrant Father and Presidential Identity Politics,' *National First Ladies Library* (undated), http://www.firstladies.org/ancestral-obama.aspx.

29   Kennedy, Randall, *The Persistence of the Color Line: Racial Politics and the Obama Presidency* (New York: Vintage, 2012), p. 22.

30   Pew Fact Sheet, 'Changing Attitudes on Gay Marriage: Public Opinion on Same Sex Marriage,' *Religion and Public Life*, 26 June 2017, http://www.pewforum.org/fact-sheet/changing-attitudes-on-gay-marriage/.

31   Lewis, Brittany, 'Hip Hop's History of Homophobia,' 18 September 2012, https://globalgrind.cassiuslife.com/1889805/hip-hops-history-homophobia-list-videos/; Blistein, Joe, 'Watch Snoop-Dogg's 'Moment I Feared' Video, *Rolling Stone*, 21 June 2017, https://www.rollingstone.com/music/music-news/watch-snoop-doggs-tongue-in-cheek-moment-i-feared-video–194559/.

32   Kennedy, *Persistence of the Color Line*, p. 24.

33   Jay-Z (featuring Gloria Carter), 'Smile,' *4:44* (Hollywood: Roc Nation, 2017), https://www.youtube.com/watch?v=SSumXG5_rs8.

34   Berman, Ari, 'A Botched Voter Purge Prevented Thousands from Voting - And Empowered a New Generation of Voting-Rights Critics,' *The Nation*, 28 July 2015, https://www.thenation.com/article/how-the-2000-election-in-florida-led-to-a-new-wave-of-voter-disenfranchisement/.

35   Gorzelany-Mostak, Dana, 'Keepin' It Real (Respectable) in 2008: Barack Obama's Music Strategy and the Formation of Presidential Identity,' *Journal of the Society for American Music*, 10:2 (May 2016), https://www.cambridge.org/core/journals/journal-

of-the-society-for-american-music/article/keepin-it-real-respectable-in-2008-barack-obamas-music-strategy-and-the-formation-of-presidential-identity/4F9A98491F2BC4736B33E0E4B419B33A.

36 Kettle, Martin, 'Bush Woos Black Vote for 2000 Election,' *The Guardian*, 27 November 1999, https://www.theguardian.com/world/1999/nov/27/uselections2000.usa.

37 Billboard News, 'Kanye West Rips Bush during NBC Telethon,' *Billboard*, 3 September 2005, https://www.billboard.com/articles/news/61564/kanye-west-rips-bush-during-nbc-telethon.

38 Roper Center, 'How Groups Voted' [2000 and 2004 surveys], https://ropercenter.cornell.edu/polls/us-elections/how-groups-voted/).

39 Hamill, Sam, ed., *Poets against the War* (New York: Thunder's Mouth Press, 2003).

40 Hamill, Sam et al., 'Poets Against the War,' *The Nation*, 19 February 2003, https://www.thenation.com/article/poets-against-war/.

41 Eichler, Alex, 'So What Actually Happened at the White House Poetry Night?' *The Atlantic*, 12 May 2011, https://www.theatlantic.com/politics/archive/2011/05/so-what-actually-happened-white-house-poetry-night/350583/.

42 Ferro, Shane, 'The Great Recession Was Much, Much Worse for African Americans,' *Business Insider*, 25 June 2013, http://uk.businessinsider.com/great-recession-exacerbated-a-big-racial-disparity-in-the-housing-market-2015-6?r=US&IR=T.

43 Pareles, Jon, 'Music for Many Firsts at Inauguration Event,' *New York Times*, 21 January 2009, https://www.nytimes.com/2009/01/22/arts/music/22conc.html.

44 Barack Obama interview with Jeff Johnson, 'What's in It for Us?' *Black Entertainment Television*, 3 February 2008, https://www.youtube.com/watch?v=pFSVG7jRp_g.

45 Williams, Stereo, 'Is Hip-Hop Still "CNN for Black People?"' *The Daily Beast*, 24 March 2015, https://www.thedailybeast.com/is-hip-hop-still-cnn-for-black-people.

46 See Chuck, D. and Yusef Jah, *Fight the Power: Rap, Race and Reality* (New York: Payback Press, 1999).

47 Arnold, Paul, 'Killer Mike Explains His Comparison of Barack Obama to Ronald Reagan,' HipHopdx.com, 21 May 2012, https://hiphopdx.com/interviews/id.1896/title.killer-mike-explains-his-comparison-of-barack-obama-to-ronald-reagan-his-brotherly-bond-with-el-p#.

48 Kennedy, *Persistence of the Color Line*, p. 242.

49 Madden, Michael, 'Killer Mike – RAP Music,' *Consequences of Sound*, 17 May 2012, https://consequenceofsound.net/2012/05/album-review-killer-mike-r-a-p-music/; Nielsen, Erik, 'How Hip-Hop Fell Out of Love with Obama,' *The Guardian*, 23 August 2012, https://www.theguardian.com/music/2012/aug/23/why-hip-hop-deserting-obama.

50 Coplan, Chris, 'Lupe Fiasco – Laser,' *Consequences of Sound*, 9 March 2011, https://consequenceofsound.net/2011/03/album-review-lupe-fiasco-lasers/; Perpetua, Matthew, 'Lupe Fiasco Declares Obama a Terrorist,' *Rolling Stone*, 9 June 2011, https://www.rollingstone.com/music/music-news/lupe-fiasco-declares-obama-a-terrorist-98109/.

51 Dyson, Michael Eric on MSNBC, quoted in cganemccalla [*sic*] 'Dyson Says Obama "Runs from Race Like a Black Man Runs from a Cop",' *Newsone.com*, 12 January 2010, https://newsone.com/410402/michael-dyson-says-obama-runs-from-race-like-a-black-man-runs-from-a-cop/.

52 Dyson, Michael Eric, *The Black Presidency: Barack Obama and the Politics of Race in America* (Boston: Houghton Mifflin Harcourt, 2016), pp. 156, 68.

53 'Smiley, Tavis and Cornell West on the 2012 Election and Why Calling Obama
    "Progressive" Ignores His Record,' *Democracy Now!* 9 November 2012, https://www.
    democracynow.org/2012/11/9/tavis_smiley_cornel_west_on_the.

54 West, Cornel, 'Pity the Sad Legacy of Barack Obama,' *The Guardian*, 9 January 2017,
    https://www.theguardian.com/commentisfree/2017/jan/09/barack-obama-legacy-
    presidency.

55 Coates, *We Were Eight Years in Power*.

56 Powell, Kevin interview, 'There Are No Saviours,' Gosa and Nelson, *The Hip Hop and
    Obama Reader*, p. 70.

57 Barack Obama interview on CNBC, 15 September 2009, https://www.youtube.com/
    watch?v=078BGtKNL1o; @kanyewest, 'Obama Was in Office for Eight Years and
    Nothing in Chicago Changed,' 25 April 2018, www.twitter.com

58 Chance the Rapper, 'Black People Don't Have to Be Democrats,' 25 April 2018,
    Twitter, https://twitter.com/chancetherapper/status/989260195598688257?lang=en.

59 Larson, Jeremy D., 'Lil Wayne Offers Non-Apology Apology for Controversial Lyrics
    about Emmet Till,' *Consequences of Sound*, 1 May 2013, https://consequenceofsound.
    net/2013/05/lil-wayne-offers-non-apology-apology-for-controversial-lyrics-about-
    emmett-till/; Smith, Ben, 'Obama Camp Condemns Song: Ludacris "Should Be
    Ashamed,"' *Politico*, 30 July 2008, https://www.politico.com/blogs/ben-smith/2008/07/
    obama-camp-condemns-song-ludacris-should-be-ashamed–010659.

60 Coates, Ta-Nehisi, 'A Rising Tide Lifts All Yachts,' *The Atlantic*, 3 October 2013,
    https://www.theatlantic.com/politics/archive/2013/10/a-rising-tide-lifts-all-
    yachts/280224/.

61 My Brother's Keeper Mentoring Legacy, 27 February 2014, https://obamawhitehouse.
    archives.gov/my-brothers-keeper.

62 Kreps, Daniel, 'Kendrick Lamar Talks Oval Office Meeting with Barack Obama,'
    Rolling Stone, 12 January 2016, https://www.rollingstone.com/music/music-news/
    kendrick-lamar-talks-oval-office-meeting-with-barack-obama–68115/.

63 (No author cited) 'Rappers Salute Barack Obama, the President Who Bridged the Gap
    between Hip Hop and Politics,' *Billboard*, 19 January 2017, https://www.billboard.
    com/articles/columns/hip-hop/7661746/barack-obama-hip-hop.

64 Crenshaw, Kimberlé, 'The Post-Racial Condition of Trump's Possibility,' Douglas W.
    Bryant Lecture, Eccles Centre, British Library, 16 May 2017.

65 Coates, Ta Nehisi, 'The First White President,' *The Atlantic*, October 2017, https://
    www.theatlantic.com/magazine/archive/2017/10/the-first-white-president-ta-nehisi-
    coates/537909/.

66 Butterfield, Fox, 'First Black Elected to Head *Harvard Law Review*,' *New York
    Times*, 6 February 1990, https://www.nytimes.com/1990/02/06/us/first-black-elected-
    to-head-harvard-s-law-review.html.

67 Quote from Nas in 'Rappers Salute Barack Obama.'

Chapter 12

'ALL PUBLICITY IS GOOD PUBLICITY': DONALD TRUMP, TWITTER AND THE SELLING OF AN OUTSIDER IN THE 2016 PRESIDENTIAL ELECTION

Tim Stanley

The 2016 presidential election victory of Donald J. Trump came as a shock to the world. In retrospect, however, it was predictable. Explanations range from the Democratic campaign's strategic errors to the Republican candidate's exploitation of fears related to immigration, industrial decline, crime and terrorism.[1] This chapter focuses on Trump's use of social media, specifically Twitter, to define and project his image. When he declared his candidacy in 2015 for the Republican nomination, we might have assumed that Trump's Twitter account would be a problem.[2] The businessman tweeted on the go, without filter and sometimes after limited sleep – and this meant the candidate was voluntarily exposing himself to risk and scrutiny.[3]

Here was easily accessible evidence of Trump changing his mind on important issues. He retweeted white nationalists; he insulted war veterans. On 22 October 2015, ahead of the Iowa Republican caucus, he retweeted a suggestion that the voters of Iowa might have 'issues in the brain.' Trump blamed the retweet on a 'young intern' in control of his account but returned to the theme himself in November when the surgeon Ben Carson pulled ahead of him in local polls.[4] 'How stupid are the people of Iowa?' Trump asked a rally of Iowans. 'How stupid are the people of the country to believe this crap?'[5]

Trump narrowly lost Iowa to Senator Ted Cruz but went on to win the GOP nomination comfortably and the general election with a majority of the electoral college votes. He did all of this despite being considerably outspent by his rivals and, in a sense, victory on the cheap was the best endorsement of Trump's social media strategy one can think of.[6] The evidence suggests he led Hillary Clinton on Twitter, Instagram and Facebook in terms of posts, free advertising and shares – at a time when 75 per cent of Americans owned a smartphone and 65 per cent said they took their news from a digital source.[7] It was Twitter, however, that arguably won him the most coverage and was the best example of medium and message finding synthesis. It helped Trump communicate directly with voters in a written style closely approximating his own voice, to dominate the debate and to burnish his image as a plain-spoken businessman taking on the established order. Crucially, this was an image already well embedded in American life.

Trump's victory can be traced back to long-term changes in popular culture, a culture he had always kept in step with, and while he was undoubtedly the champion of social media politics in 2016, one of his greatest achievements was using Twitter to manipulate old-fashioned television coverage. Trump professes to hate what conservatives call the 'mainstream media', and many journalists in TV and the written press probably dislike him in turn. But their relationship has always been and remains symbiotic.[8]

The Creation of an Image

Born in 1946, Trump entered his father's real estate business and rose to become one of the most recognizable business celebrities of the Reagan era. His approach towards media relations can be summed up with two maxims. First: 'go to Hell.' Roy Cohn, the New York lawyer who had served as chief counsel to Senator Joe McCarthy of Wisconsin during the anti-communist scare in the early 1950s, schooled Trump in this approach. Cohn and Trump met in 1973 when Trump was facing a federal suit for discrimination against black tenants. Should he settle, Trump asked Cohn? Cohn said not: in fact, he told Trump to counter sue for $100 million and accuse the government of discriminating against *him*. Trump did so in a blaze of publicity, and although the strategy still resulted in a settlement, the fight created a narrative that Trump believed he was innocent and was prepared to stand up for himself. Never back down: if hit, hit back harder.[9]

Trump's second maxim could be paraphrased as 'all publicity is good publicity', and in his early years of business most of the publicity was flattering.[10] Journalists covered him because he told them he was immensely rich and so, consciously or subconsciously, they played his game of over-valuing his financial worth.[11] This in turn made creditors more likely to lend to Trump, creating almost a 'virtuous circle' of wealth distortion: public speculation about the size of Trump's fortune helped him to accumulate more of it. In a 1976 interview with the *New York Times*, Trump estimated his worth at north of $200 million. This was contradicted by a casino commission report which put his taxable income that year at just $24,594.[12]

Trump's architectural projects – notably the completion of Trump Tower in 1983 – his colourful marriages and ostentatious style made him a figurehead of the hyper-capitalism of the eighties and encouraged talk in 1987 of a presidential run. Between then and 2000, Trump was often a guest on talk shows, and was invited to articulate not just his business philosophy but his views on politics. Trump may have changed his party registration several times but his outlook has remained largely consistent. America's allies, he wrote in a *New York Times* ad in 1987, should pay for their own defence. The United States should protect its manufacturing from foreign competition, he told *Playboy* in 1990, and act ruthlessly: 'People need ego; whole nations need ego.' As summarized by historians Charlie Laderman and Brendan Simms, Trump has talked to the public for decades about 'the power of human agency to bring about fundamental change, particularly when that agency is himself.'[13] There was an actual presidential run on an independent ticket in 1999 which, while brief, demonstrated Trump's ability to court headlines and TV interviews in a cultural context that thrived on the kind of contrived drama normally associated with pro-wrestling.[14] It is no coincidence, say some observers, that the businessman has been a promoter of wrestling panto, or that his political personality is eerily similar to the 'heel character' in the ring – a deliberately obnoxious fighter who riles up the crowd.[15]

At the turn of the millennium, television's coverage of politics was changing character, becoming a fusion of fact and entertainment, a confusion that was also reflected in the rise of reality TV. This new strand of broadcasting promised to make the viewer the star, offering sensational drama with real-life consequences.

In fact, reality TV could be almost as choreographed as pro-wrestling, as demonstrated by NBC's rating hit *The Apprentice*, which launched in 2004. It starred Donald Trump as one version of himself, a successful capitalist who hires and fires desperate job applicants. 'The Apprentice,' wrote Emily Nussenbaum of the *New Yorker*, 'is set in a patriotic world of capitalist potential, where the boss takes you in a helicopter to view the Empire State Building (he boasts, deceptively, about his stake in it), and to gaze at the sunset-lit Statue of Liberty.' When he signed up to host, Trump predicted it would be 'good for the brand' – and it was.[16]

Jim Dowd, the head of public relations for NBC on the East Coast, claimed in an interview that *The Apprentice* transformed Trump's public image. By 2004, he had been written off by many as a throwback to the eighties, with two broken marriages and a handful of bankruptcies under his belt. Immediately after *The Apprentice* premiered, Dowd witnessed viewers embracing Trump on the streets in a new way. 'All of a sudden, there was none of the old mocking.... He was a hero and he had not been one before .... That was the bridge to the [2016] campaign.' Dowd believed that it was *The Apprentice* that reignited Trump's interest in the presidency, noting that he began appearing more frequently on right-wing talk radio and Fox News: 'Foreign policy, jobs, immigration, all the topics that he's speaking about now, he was talking about in 2004 with [Don] Imus and [Bill] O'Reilly and others.'[17]

The date is important because it shows just how long and hard Trump thought about running for the presidency, but also highlights the entertainment industry's part in his reinvention. For over a decade, 2004–15, the media knew exactly what kind of politics Trump embraced and it continued to lend him a platform.

In 2011, he flirted with a run in the Republican presidential contest and horrified many by pushing the Birther conspiracy theory, which claimed that Barack Obama was a constitutionally illegitimate president because he was born outside the United States.[18] For all the controversy, however, he remained host of *The Apprentice* franchise until NBC dropped him in 2015.[19] Trump was not made of Teflon, as was said of Ronald Reagan, the conservative to whom mud never stuck. Many accusations stuck messily to Trump, but they did not slow him down. On the contrary, voters may have inferred that his willingness to be outrageous was a facet of his enormous wealth: he was so rich, he could afford to say anything. The media helped sustain this appearance.

A telling example was when on 15 March 2011, at the height of the Birther controversy, Comedy Central broadcast a roast of Donald Trump. It might have been an attempt to deflate Trump by employing comedians to mock him, but it backfired and became rather emblematic of his ability to wind up and manipulate media liberals, some of whom do not appreciate Trump's own line in self-deprecating humour. Trump frequently invites others to laugh at him. From appearing in *The Fresh Prince of Bel-Air* sitcom to singing the theme tune to 'Greenacres' at the 2006 Emmys (dressed in dungarees), Trump has encouraged the impression that his persona is a joke that he is in on. He asked on the Roast: 'What's the difference between a wet racoon and Donald Trump's hair? A wet racoon doesn't have seven billion fucking dollars in the bank.' The audience laughed. Behind the scenes, however, certain aspects of his image were not up for discussion or satire: Trump told Comedy Central there could be no gags about the rumoured size of his wealth, and they apparently complied. The racoon joke originally stated that Trump's hair has '$2 billion in the bank.' Comedian Jimmy Fallon recalls that Trump demanded the figure be $10 billion and finally settled on seven. The punchline was treated like a business negotiation.[20]

Trump ended the 2012 speculation in an air of ambiguity: had he been serious or just enhancing the brand? The answer was provided in November, when he quietly applied to trademark the phrase 'Make America Great Again,' which would be his 2016 campaign slogan.[21] Astute observers might have noted that by this point he had collected an astonishing 2 million followers on Twitter.

Trump Uses Twitter to Test the Waters

Twitter was launched in 2006 and its name, according to cofounder Jack Dorsey, was meant to evoke 'a short burst of inconsequential information' – a single online message of 140 characters in which users would have to be as concise as possible. Readers could either like or retweet what they saw.

The new platform gave Americans a chance to interact with the rich and the powerful, and the powerful found themselves under an avalanche of initially uncensored criticism. Populists prospered. Some analysts argue that Twitter reduced the electorate's patience; others insist it raised sophistication by spreading information and increasing participation. Twitter became first a way of relaying the news and commenting on it and then an alternative news source in itself, possibly even of 'fake news' generated by political activists and foreign regimes.[22] And its punchy style, which encouraged debate through slogans, seemed perfectly suited to someone whose syntax almost matched the limits and potential of 140 characters.[23]

The history of Trump on Twitter charts the evolution of the platform's political role. At first, he used it for free and succinct promotion: Trump's premier tweet, on 4 May 2009, flagged up an appearance on the David Letterman show.[24] For two years his output was largely factual and said what he was up to: 'The [Scottish] Dunes are amazing,' he reported from a scouting trip to find a site for a new golf course, 'and they're how I learned about geomorphology, which is the study of movement landforms.'[25] Even when he teased America with a presidential run in early 2011, his tweets remained banal ('Watch my speech', 'Check out my [website]' etc.). Notable by its absence was any comment – none at all – on Trump's attendance at the 2011 White House Correspondents Dinner, at which Obama ridiculed the businessman for his obsession with his birth certificate. It is often speculated that this event was critical in encouraging Trump to run in 2016, out of revenge, yet the most he could drum up on Twitter was to announce the results of a Fox News poll and a sale of mattresses.[26]

We can infer that Trump realized the political potency of the platform only in the summer of 2011 as that season's Republican presidential auditions got underway. His output accelerated from no more than about 150 tweets a year to more than 100 tweets per month (by 2016, he would average 375 per month). His first-ever online comment about policy was on 7 July 2011. 'Republicans should not negotiate against themselves again with @BarackObama in today's debt talks – First and foremost CUT, CAP and BALANCE.'[27]

Short, direct and capitalized words drew the eye of even casual readers; the content allied Trump with fiscal conservatives. After that tweet, there was no holding back. Trump used Twitter to pursue vendettas against the president ('Let's take a closer look at that birth certificate') and his political allies (Joe Biden 'never wastes an opportunity to say something stupid').[28] Trump quickly realized that Twitter could be used to 'troll' his critics and start fights that would generate publicity. When the singer Cher tweeted that the Republican nominee, Mitt Romney, and his supporters were bigots, Trump replied: '@Cher should stop with the bad plastic surgery and nasty statements about good people running for office.'[29]

Trump's tweets put him on the side of every conservative cause going – everything from the 'war on Christmas' to the supposed link between vaccines and autism – and with such success that counting his likes and retweets became a method of discerning what was really on the mind of conservatives. The following resulted in over 100,000 retweets for Trump: 'The concept of global warming was created by and for the Chinese in order to make US manufacturing non-competitive.'[30] Trump's doubts about global warming tapped into his long-running concern that America was being exploited by its clever competitors, and putting the idea out there on Twitter offered the opportunity, in effect, to conduct a free poll of public sentiment (campaigns normally paid thousands for such things).

By the end of the 2012 presidential contest, Trump had found a new metric of success akin to his bank balance: his number of followers. 'I picked up 70,000 twitter followers yesterday alone,' he boasted in a tweet.[31] Trump's newfound reach offered an answer to what many in the conservative movement regarded as the central impediment to taking back the White House: the alleged bias of the 'mainstream media.'[32] The libertarian muckraker Andrew Breitbart famously complained that 'politics is downstream from culture,' meaning that the Left's alleged stranglehold over the media not only squeezed out Right-wing voices but also fostered a popular culture in which conservatism was increasingly unviable – politically incorrect, anachronistic, unfashionable among the young.[33]

The theory of a media conspiracy against the Right has a long pedigree: the Nixon administration routinely complained that the press distorted its record.[34] In the eighties and early nineties, conservatives tried to get around the TV networks with direct mail campaigns and talk radio. In 1996, Roger Ailes, a former image consultant for Richard Nixon, launched Fox News as a conservative news organization. And beneath the radar, younger conservatives were tapping into the potential of the internet, pursuing a vendetta against a media culture in which many of them – like Trump – operated but never felt entirely accepted. One of the key players in the war against President Bill Clinton was the online news aggregator, the Drudge Report, which began life as an email briefing about celebrity and political gossip; founder Matt Drudge had once sold T-shirts at the CBS Studios gift shop. He partnered with Andrew Breitbart, another Angelino, who later founded his own news agency with Steve Bannon, a Nixon fan and businessman who had tried with mixed success to make it in movies. Bannon later emerged as Trump's campaign strategist, providing philosophy, greater message discipline and, argues Bannon's biographer, a connection to online conservatives otherwise hidden in message boards – 'millions of intense young men … who disappeared for days or even weeks at a time into alternate realities.'[35]

Breitbart died of a heart attack in 2011. His creation, Breitbart.com, would become the most consistent supporter of Donald Trump and the source of a great deal of what critics called 'fake news.' By the middle of the 2016 election campaign, Breitbart was the single most shared publisher of political content on Facebook and Twitter: 8,112,163 interactions in a month on the former, 985,850 on the latter.[36] In short, conservatives had both the will to take on the mainstream media and, finally, the platforms from which to do it. All they needed was the candidate whose methods and image best suited their agenda: Donald Trump.

That said, while Trump was building an online presence, much of his attention was still firmly fixed on the TV. As he explained to Fox News: 'Tweeting is like a typewriter. When I put it out, you put it immediately on your show.' For Trump, the beauty of Twitter was not just that he could trot out instant reactions read by millions but that each reaction generated enough buzz to cut straight through the traditional gatekeepers of the media – such as producers and editors – and appear largely unfiltered in print or on TV. This would then be followed up by a request for him to come on a show and defend his views.[37] Trump had no intention of bypassing the old media. He wanted to conquer it.

Trump Takes Control of the GOP

Trump declared his presidential candidacy on 16 June 2015 with a speech at Trump Tower. Its most controversial line was his assertion that illegal immigrants from Mexico were rapists and murderers. ('And some of them, I assume, are good people.') This led some to conclude that Trump's candidacy was doomed to failure, either in the primaries against more disciplined candidates, or in the general election against a presumed opponent, Hillary Clinton, who was already using sophisticated tools of voter identification to target moderate swing voters.[38] Trump's campaign was aimed at the conservative base he had discovered during his 2011 Birther period but never actually tested in an election. Surely his image would alienate large swathes of the electorate in 2016, such as independents and moderate Republicans. Yet Trump went on in the primaries not only to beat representatives of traditional, big money elite politics (Jeb Bush) but also candidates with narratives of change, including rising ethnic minority stars Senator Marco Rubio of Florida and Senator Ted Cruz of Texas, the latter also a favourite of the Christian Right.

Trump was not running to be a traditional, consensus-orientated presidential candidate, so it would have made no sense for him to behave like one. He styled himself as a disruptor, someone conservatives voted for precisely because he was unpolished, a businessman outsider who would get the best deal for America. The proof? His wealth. He would not need any special interest lobby money, he said, because 'I'm really rich ... I'm not saying that bragging, that's the kind of mind set you need for this country.'[39]

'There you go!' he quoted a supporter on Twitter. 'Everyone loves Donald Trump bcuz he's the real thing, not a politician.'[40] Another: 'If I had a dollar for every time a politician lied, I'd be as rich as @realDonaldTrump.'[41] And in the context of a hunger for change – for an alternative to the politics of establishment insiders embodied by Jeb Bush and Hillary Clinton – his image was enhanced by controversy, not undermined by it. Twitter operated like a live-feed running straight from Trump's brain, allowing readers to follow his thinking in real time and see that he thought largely like them. Trump's radicalism could actually be reassuring to supporters because it proved that he was not holding anything back: as one of these tweeted, 'Awesome interview. You are always honest with the American people Thank you Mr. Trump!!'[42]

At the first GOP debate in Ohio on 6 August 2015, Trump refused to say he would vote for the eventual nominee, demonstrating that he was not just another boilerplate Republican loyalist. At the South Carolina debate on 13 February 2016, he attacked former President George W. Bush – and, despite handwringing from his opponents, still won the primary a week later. Trump was the second most discussed item on TV news in late 2015 (after winter weather) and by March 2016 had earned more coverage than all the Democrats combined. This was paydirt for the networks (CNN charged forty times its normal rate to advertisers during one debate) and Trump dominated the conversation even when he was not there.[43]

When Trump skipped a debate in January in Iowa, the first question put to those present was what they thought about his absence: 'the elephant not in the room.' A Twitter analysis found that 37 per cent of the online debate mentions that night were about Trump, far ahead of his nearest rival, Ted Cruz, on 18 per cent – and, to repeat, Trump was not present. The other Republicans found that their candidacies were judged largely in terms of how they related to Trump, a phenomenon undoubtedly helped by social media.[44]

Trump used Twitter not only to promote his outsider reputation but to define the images of his opponents. He proved adept at identifying a weakness, preferably one they were conscious of and embarrassed by, and turning it into a nickname, which Twitter, the ultimate soundbite medium, was ideal for spreading. Marco Rubio, a smallish man, was 'Little Marco:' Jeb Bush, a floundering moderate, was 'Low energy'; Ted Cruz, who had a reputation for being hard to work with, was 'Lyin' Ted.'[45] An analysis conducted for *Politico* found that Trump tweeted adjectives more than any other candidate except Democrat Bernie Sanders. His favourite was 'great,' which related to himself thirty-two times. 'Light-weight' was next (used to describe Rubio forty-seven times), followed by 'weak' (Jeb Bush six times), 'failed' (Mitt Romney nine times), 'crazy' (Fox anchor Megyn Kelly eight times) and 'nasty' (Ted Cruz four times).[46]

Twitter could sometimes save Trump's bacon. At a debate in Texas in February, Cruz and Rubio ganged up on him and Trump looked momentarily weak. Afterwards, he tweeted: 'Lightweight Marco Rubio was working hard last night. The problem is, he is a choker, and once a choker, always a chocker [*sic*]! Mr. Meltdown.'[47] This so-called Twitter storm was picked up by the media as a story in and of itself, giving it almost equal weight to a debate that, by some judgements, Trump had lost. On the TV shows next morning, Rubio found himself talking not just about his own performance but also about Trump's tweets. He conceded that in this toxic environment, he too would have to go personal, and walked straight into a trap.[48]

Rubio mocked Trump's tan ('he should sue whoever did that to his face') and implied that his 'small hands' might mean he had small genitalia. At a rally in Texas, Rubio read out Trump's tweets from his phone and corrected their spelling mistakes. Playing nasty did not work: out of the eleven Super Tuesday contests on 1 March, Rubio won just Minnesota. Trump had forced Rubio to vacate the higher ground; political scientist Sheri Berman argues that the growing 'incivility' of Trump's critics galvanized his supporters by 'reminding them how "bad" and "threatening" the other side is.'[49] Trump laughed off Rubio's attacks: at a debate in Detroit on 3 March, he reassured viewers that his penis was of satisfactory size. On 9 March, Rubio expressed regret at the direction of his own campaign: 'My kids were embarrassed by it. My wife didn't like it. I don't think it reflects good. That's not who I am. That's not what my campaign is going to be about or will ever be about again.' Six days later, Rubio lost Florida, his own state, to Trump.[50]

The primaries showed that Trump had learned how to use social media not only to reinforce his own image but to destroy the reputations of his opponents. By May, Trump had sewn up the nomination and in July he was officially nominated by the Republican Party. Rubio and Jeb Bush did not attend the convention.

Taking on Hillary Clinton

Trump essentially repeated his primaries strategy in the general election. He continued to tweet, apparently without discipline, and handed control of his account over to his campaign team only during the debates with Hillary Clinton. (At 3.14 am after the first debate, he was already back online, claiming victory.)

Trump also continued that old tactic of nicknaming and denigrating his opponent. In the space of just seven minutes on 28 July 2016, Trump said that 'Hillary will never reform Wall Street. She is owned by Wall Street'; Clinton wanted 'a borderless world'; 'her wars in the Middle East' had unleashed the Islamic State terrorist group; and 'No one has worse judgement than Hillary Clinton.'[51] Clinton, meanwhile, told audiences that she was following Michelle Obama's famous advice: 'When they go low, we go high.' It sounded laudable but in fact she had no choice. To acknowledge Trump's insults or fight fire with fire risked hurting Clinton, as the candidate learned on 9 September when she said that half of Trump's supporters could be put in a 'basket of deplorables.... They're racist, sexist, homophobic, xenophobic, Islamophobic, you name it.'

Trump accused her of slandering 'patriotic Americans.' Others concurred that she sounded elitist and that no matter how deplorable their opinions might be, Trump's working-class supporters were arguably victims of free-trade policies that the Clintons had promoted in office. Within twenty-four hours, Clinton had backtracked.[52] An attempt at positivity, motherliness and statesmanship followed, on the presumption that the more Trump spoke, the less presidential he sounded – and the more likely that a coalition of minority voters and disgusted moderates would coalesce around the Democratic ticket. Trump's base was loud but assumed to be part of a dwindling angry white vote, so why not just write it off? Bill Clinton argued behind the scenes that blue-collar whites were in fact still important and the campaign had both a tactical and moral responsibility to establish a dialogue with them. His argument was dismissed. 'Go high' was the strategy Hillary Clinton more or less stuck with through to Election Day.[53]

The problem was that Trump's age-old maxims of 'go to Hell' and 'any publicity is good publicity' – amplified entirely for free via social media and reported ad infinitum by press and TV – kept dragging the campaign back down to his level, helping him survive even the most devastating revelations. On 7 October the *Washington Post* released video of Trump bragging about sexual assault. The moment occurred during the filming of a 2005 episode of NBC's *Access Hollywood*, in which Trump, unaware that his audio was being recorded, described how easy it was for celebrities to get women: 'When you're a star, they let you do it. You can do anything. Grab them by the pussy.' Even Trump's running mate, Mike Pence, said he was 'offended.' Congressman Paul Ryan of Wisconsin, the Republican Speaker of the House of Representatives, announced that he could no longer campaign for the presidential ticket.[54]

Trump, unusually, said sorry: 'it was wrong, and I apologize.' The way the statement was made was significant. Rather than a press conference or a one-on-one televised interview, it was recorded in-house by the campaign, posted on Facebook and advertised on Twitter, which meant that Trump was totally in control of both the message and its visuals – demonstrating how social media makes it easier to dictate not just the production of an image but its dissemination. Moreover, Trump's *mea culpa* came with rather lawyerly caveats. First, he reminded voters: 'I've never said I'm a perfect person, nor pretended to be someone that I'm not.' This was not only a fair comment but part of his appeal – the paradoxical integrity of being openly flawed – and a reminder that he was running not as a career politician but as a political neophyte. The voters, he seemed to be saying, never expected him to be an angel, so what did the *Access Hollywood* audio really matter?

As a second part of this strategy, Trump went on the attack. 'Bill Clinton has actually abused women,' he claimed, 'and Hillary has bullied, attacked, shamed and intimidated his victims. We will discuss this more in the coming days.'[55] Trump had made this threat before. He tweeted on 24 September that he was tempted to invite Gennifer Flowers, a woman who had an extra-marital affair with Bill Clinton, to attend the first presidential debate – a tweet that, in the view of the *Washington Post*, had dominated pre-debate discussion.[56] After the release of the *Access Hollywood* tape, Trump threw a photo-op with four women who had been sharply critical of Hillary Clinton, three of whom had accused her husband of sexual harassment. Then, to the astonishment of the press corps, he brought the four along to the second presidential debate on 9 October.

The presence of these women in the audience presumably sent the message that although Trump was guilty of misbehaviour, so were the Clintons – and, given the equal moral quality (or depths) of both candidates, the choice was between a sleaze who would at least fight for America (Trump) versus a sleaze who was the preferred candidate of Washington (Clinton).[57] Trump successfully moved the debate on from allegations against him and towards a scandal involving the wiping of Clinton's email server, which – conservatives insisted – was deliberate and potentially criminal. Clinton told the debate audience that America was lucky a man of Trump's temperament was not in charge of enforcing the law. Trump replied: 'because you'd be in jail.'[58]

This was a major theme of the last few days of the campaign. Online, Trump referred constantly to Clinton as 'Crooked Hillary.' A final, misleading FBI announcement that it was reopening an old investigation into her confirmed for many voters that, once again, Trump's characterization of an opponent, no matter how nasty, was essentially accurate.[59] By early November, one poll found that Trump led Clinton on the issue of trust.[60]

In the context of Trump's many recorded lies and distortions, some may find that finding hard to believe. But to understand why Trump found a sympathetic audience, we have to go back to that decades-long battle between the Right and the liberal part of the media, which had popularized the idea that the Democrats were shielded by pliant journalists. 'I am not only fighting Crooked Hillary,' Trump tweeted on 14 August, 'I am fighting the dishonest and corrupt media.'[61]

'The failing @nytimes has become a newspaper of fiction,' Trump tweeted.[62] The *Washington Post* published 'inaccurate stories.'[63] '@CNN is unwatchable. Their news on me is fiction.'[64] Trump's media war extended to conservative critics. Although Fox eventually became friendly towards Trump, its journey was uneven: Trump boycotted one of its debates during the primaries, citing bias. In early 2016, there was a concerted effort by pro-Trump outlets such as Breitbart to delegitimize Fox and force it to accept the candidate or lose its status as the most trusted news source for the American Right. Among Breitbart's top twenty most shared stories on social media was 'The Anti-Trump Network: Fox News Money Flows into Open Borders Group.' This campaign worked on Twitter at least. The attention paid to Fox among conservative social media users fell in the early part of the election season, when it was regarded as anti-Trump. It later rose when the network reconciled itself to his candidacy.[65]

It was only after the general election that Trump finally tweeted the words 'FAKE NEWS!', but the epithet had broadly come to reflect how both sides saw coverage of the campaign.[66] Trump supporters believed that a media cabal backed Clinton and had destroyed whatever pretence of objectivity it might have had by throwing its journalism behind her. Trump's critics, on the other hand, believed that his candidacy could only have flourished in a media environment in which conservatives manipulated data gathering and flooded the market with cheap propaganda (possibly even financed by Russia).[67] David Frum, a prominent Never Trump conservative, noted after the election that the most well-circulated fake story of the cycle was not about Hillary Clinton's emails or Bill Clinton's sexual history, it was something aimed at Catholic voters. In June 2016, a website designed to look like a local TV station (WTOE 5 News) announced that Pope Francis had endorsed Trump. This generated about 100,000 engagements online. In late September, another website called Ending the Fed reposted the story. This time it won over a million Facebook engagements.[68]

Trump's electoral triumph on 8 November thus seemed to be a victory over not only Clinton but also the media, which Trump accused of deliberately talking down his chances.[69] Widespread predictions that Trump would lose were in fact half correct: he lost the popular vote. He won the Electoral College thanks to rustbelt states defecting from the Democrats to the Republicans. Trump did particularly well in areas that had shipped significant job numbers overseas and which previously had gone for Obama. It is often pointed out that Trump's coalition included many traditional Republican elements – social conservatives, the rich, rural voters – and that it could be described as an across-the-board white backlash rather than a class vote. Certainly, there is always a risk when focusing on the rustbelt swing states of missing other narratives taking place elsewhere.[70]

Trump, though, did do better than previous GOP candidates among the working class and in such a way as to make a difference between winning or losing. According to CNN, he won white men without a college degree by 71 to 23 per cent, a group that backed Romney by 64 per cent and John McCain by only 59 per cent. In 660 counties that are at least 85 per cent white and with incomes below the national median, Clinton won just two. Two decades earlier, her husband had won half of them.[71]

Trump's issues, notably immigration and trade, and his image were critical to his success, in both a negative and a positive sense. Negatively because those looking for, say, an uncouth, Islamophobic candidate with an antediluvian attitude towards women clearly had their man. Of his Republican opponent, Carly Fiorina, Trump said: 'Look at that face. Would anyone vote for that?' Positively because anyone searching for a clear break with the past could be certain on the basis of Trump's media profile that the candidate offered precisely that. Exit polling revealed anger towards political elites and frustration at the direction of America. Clinton was perceived as the very model of an identikit politician even if, as a woman, she actually represented change.[72] Trump, by contrast, scored highly throughout the race on the basis of his outsider status and business credentials – and whatever one thought of his personal morals, said some voters, his ruthlessness was probably the norm in business and might even prove useful in government.[73]

It must have helped that Trump not only got 150 per cent more coverage on Twitter than Hillary Clinton but also about 50 per cent more coverage on TV, which all added up to an estimated $800 million in free earned broadcast media, compared to $666 million for Clinton.[74] As columnist Ross Douthat argued in the *New York Times*, the notion that Trump's victory was solely down to the internet was hard to prove given that Trump's voters tended to be older and less likely to go online, and he had in fact done less well among regular internet users than Romney did. So, it was not just social media but a synthesis of internet and TV coverage that made the difference.[75] 'You could argue, all those tweets mattered mainly because they kept being quoted on TV,' concluded academic Richard Perloff. 'He not only tweets, but the media then writes about those tweets. And the mainstream media – despite his criticism of it – gives him a degree of legitimacy.'[76] This pattern came to be dubbed a 'feedback loop,' a cycle of news reporting and response that became even more pronounced when Trump entered the White House.

The new president liked to watch hours of cable TV every day, keeping it on mute during meetings. He was accused of live-tweeting shows on Fox News. For example, on 3 January 2018, Fox reported that North Korean dictator Kim Jong-un had warned the United States that he had a nuclear button on his desk. This was at 7.37 pm. At 7.49 pm Trump tweeted that his own nuclear button was 'bigger and more powerful.' Veteran journalist Bob Woodward wrote: 'The president of the United States was practicing a scene out of Dr Strangelove.'[77] Some pundits have argued that Trump does not set the news agenda so much as follow and contribute to it, that America under Trump has become a runaway reality TV train separated from material reality.[78]

Conclusion: President Trump

Trump's election immediately posed a challenge to his communications strategy: would he continue to tweet? Giving up Twitter or handing it over to a White House team would suggest some evolution from candidate to president, and Trump hinted at first that he might tweet less. Then he decided against it. 'It's working,' he told British MP Michael Gove. 'I thought I'd do less of it, but I'm covered so dishonestly by the press – so dishonestly – that I can put out Twitter ... I can go bing bing bing and I just keep going and they put it on and as soon as I tweet it out – this morning on television, Fox – "Donald Trump, we have breaking news."'[79] Over the course of his first year in office, Trump continued deploying all the tactics he had used in the primaries and general election: nicknames (Kim Jong-un was 'rocket man'), attacking the media ('failing @nytimes') and hammering home his key issues such as tax cuts (mentioned ninety-seven times) and jobs (ninety-two

Figure 12.1 As president Donald Trump has continued to use Twitter to dominate the news agenda and mobilize his base, a strategy complemented by public appearances before his supporters, such as this one at the Conservative Political Action Conference, 2 March 2019. White House official photograph, no restrictions on use, public domain.

times). In total, there were 2,417 posts (including deleted ones) in twelve months, amounting, by the estimate of the *Boston Globe,* to about forty hours of manpower. A third of his activity took place between 5 am and 8 am, in time for the morning TV shows. Most tweets got between 20,000 and 200,000 likes.[80]

Trump's election sparked soul-searching in Silicon Valley. One of the most politically liberal parts of America had created the technology that helped elect the most conservative president since Ronald Reagan, a man who tried to ban migrants from some Muslim-majority countries, exclude transgendered personnel from the military, dismantle aspects of Obamacare, appoint conservative judges and tear up environmental regulations. Could Twitter not simply ban Trump? Users do access the platform at the discretion of the company, and by 2017 it was cracking down on abusive and extremist content.[81] But Twitter had become institutionalized as part of the political process: it was now recognized as so essential to American democracy that to pick and choose who could use it would validate Trump's accusation that the elites want nothing less than to silence the conservative movement. After the president said that an MSNBC journalist was 'dumb as a rock' and 'bleeding from a face-lift,' he came under pressure yet again to moderate his language. Trump tweeted: 'The FAKE & FRAUDULENT NEWS MEDIA is working hard to convince Republicans and others I should not use social media – but remember, I won the 2016 election with interviews, speeches and social media.'[82] He added: 'My use of social media is not Presidential – it's MODERN DAY PRESIDENTIAL.'[83] (This logic, that the president has a right to be heard, works both ways. Seven of Trump's followers brought a legal action when he blocked them, insisting they had a constitutional right to read the words of their president. The court found in the plaintiffs' favour.[84])

President Trump was never going to change his social media strategy because it helped put him in office. Unfiltered use of Twitter was as important and beneficial to his image as radio was to Franklin D. Roosevelt or television to John F. Kennedy, communication tools that allowed them to speak directly to the people. Twitter fulfilled a long-held conservative dream of bypassing the so-called mainstream media. Trump could disseminate his own version of events, set the day-to-day agenda, divert attention and define his opponents. Attempts to fight back, including via Twitter, have often forced his critics to join Trump in the wrestling ring and thus legitimize his brand of reality TV politics.

In the past, presidents have tried to craft an image only to see it undermined or turned against them: Jimmy Carter's anti-establishment message won him the White House in 1976, but in office his outsider status was reinterpreted by critics as naiveté and incompetence. Trump, by contrast, has remained in control of his image throughout his career (even when accused of not having as much money as he claims). The Trump of *The Apprentice* is more or less the same character as the Trump in the Oval Office, and this consistency of personality and opinion – interpreted by fans as honesty and incorruptibility – has helped cement loyalty among the conservative base. The downside is that because Trump has never softened or compromised his image, he has failed to reach beyond his natural demographic to the wider population, and never enjoyed an approval rating higher than about 45 per cent despite peace and prosperity. His image, though expertly defined and projected, repels as much as it attracts, suggesting he is no Ronald Reagan, who was able to use rhetoric and television to transcend partisan politics. Trump is a populist but not necessarily popular.

Notes

1   Dovere, Edward-Isaac, 'How Clinton lost Michigan – and Blew the Election,' *Politico*, 14 December 2016, https://www.politico.com/story/2016/12/michigan-hillary-clinton-trump–232547; Hooghe, Marc, and Ruth Dassonneville, 'Explaining the Trump Vote: The Effect of Racist Resentment and Anti-Immigrant Sentiments,' *Political Science and Politics*, 51:3 (2018): 528–34.

2   It was even suggested that he didn't know how the platform worked. Cillizza, Chris, 'RESOLVED: Donald Trump Isn't Very Good at Twitter,' *Washington Post*, 25 August 2015, https://www.washingtonpost.com/news/the-fix/wp/2015/08/25/resolved-donald-trump-isnt-very-good-at-twitter/?noredirect=on&utm_term=.e5520a7dbb05.

3   Whitten, Sarah, 'Can 140 Characters Affect the 2016 Presidential Election?,' *CNBC*, 5 November 2015, https://www.cnbc.com/2015/11/05/can-140-characters-affect-the-2016-presidential-election.html.

4   Collins, Eliza, 'Trump Blames Intern for Tweet Mocking Iowans,' *Politico*, 22 October 2015, https://www.politico.com/story/2015/10/trump-retweet-blunder–215072.

5   Habberman, Maggie, 'Donald Trump Asks Iowans: "How Stupid" Are They to Believe Ben Carson?,' *New York Times*, 13 November 2015, https://www.nytimes.com/politics/first-draft/2015/11/13/trump-asks-iowans-how-stupid-are-they-to-believe-carson/.

6   Associated Press, 'Here's How Much Less than Hillary Clinton Donald Trump Spent on the Election,' *Fortune*, 9 December 2016, http://fortune.com/2016/12/09/hillary-clinton-donald-trump-campaign-spending/.

7   Denton Jr., Robert E., Robert V. Friedenberg, and Judith S. Trent, *Political Campaign Communication: Principles and Practices* (Lanham, MD: Rowman & Littlefield, 2018), pp. 10–12.

8   Rutenberg, Jim, 'The Mutual Dependence of Donald Trump and the News Media,' *New York Times*, 20 March 2016, https://www.nytimes.com/2016/03/21/business/media/the-mutual-dependence-of-trump-and-the-news-media.html.

9   Johnston, David Cay, *The Making of Donald Trump* (New York: Random House, 2017), pp. 33–9; Brenner, Marie, 'How Donald Trump and Roy Cohn's Ruthless Symbiosis Changed America,' *Vanity Fair*, August 2017, https://www.vanityfair.com/news/2017/06/donald-trump-roy-cohn-relationship.

10 Trump, Donald, *The Art of the Deal* (New York: Random House, 1987), pp. 56–8.

11 Bump, Philip, 'The Rise of Donald J. Trump — as Told in the Pages of the New York Times,' *Washington Post*, 30 July 2015, https://www.washingtonpost.com/news/the-fix/wp/2015/07/30/the-rise-of-donald-j-trump-as-told-in-the-pages-of-the-new-york-times/?utm_term=.94b6e39c5fac.

12 Fisher, Marc, and Michael Kranish, *Trump Revealed: The Definitive Biography of the 45th President* (New York: Simon & Schuster, 2018), p. 294.

13 Laderman, Charlie, and Brendan Simms, *Donald Trump: The Making of a World View* (London: I.B. Tauris, 2017), p. 5.

14 Timothy Stanley, *The Crusader: The Life and Tumultuous Times of Pat Buchanan* (New York: Thomas Dunne, 2012), pp. 331–4.

15 Newkirk III, Van R., 'Donald Trump, Wrestling Heel,' *The Atlantic*, 15 March 2016, https://www.theatlantic.com/politics/archive/2016/03/trump-politics-and-professional-wrestling/473652/.

16 Nussbaum, Emily, 'The TV That Created Donald Trump,' *New Yorker*, 31 July 2017, https://www.newyorker.com/magazine/2017/07/31/the-tv-that-created-donald-trump.

17 Fisher and Kranish, *Trump Revealed*, p. 217.

18 Habberman, Maggie, 'Donald Ducks,' *Politico*, 16 May 2011, https://www.politico.com/story/2011/05/the-donald-ducks–055052.

19 Nguyen, Tina, 'NBC Drops Donald Trump over Racist Comments,' *Vanity Fair*, 29 June 2015, https://www.vanityfair.com/news/2015/06/nbc-drops-donald-trump-racist-comments.

20 Jung, Alex, 'Donald Trump Edited Jokes at His 2011 Comedy Central Roast to Make Himself Seem Richer,' *Vulture*, 11 October 2016, http://www.vulture.com/2016/10/donald-trump-edited-jokes-at-his-roast-to-seem-richer.html.

21 Long, Heath, 'Donald Trump Trademarks "Make America Great Again",' *CNN*, 8 October 2015, https://money.cnn.com/2015/10/08/investing/donald-trump-make-america-great-again-trademark/index.html.

22 For overviews of the impact of social media, see Denton, Friedenberg and Trent, *Political Campaign Communication*, pp. 14–15; Lewis, Helen, 'How Britain's Political Conversation Turned Toxic,' *New Statesman*, 29 August 2018, https://www.

newstatesman.com/politics/uk/2018/08/how-britain-political-conversation-turned-toxic; Bartlett, Jamie, *The People vs Tech: How the Internet Is Killing Democracy (and How We Save It)* (London: Ebury Press, 2018).

23 The best study of this subject is Oborne, Peter, and Tom Roberts, *How Trump Thinks: His Tweets and the Birth of a New Political Language* (London: Head of Zeus, 2017).

24 @realDonaldTrump, 4 May 2009, https://twitter.com/realdonaldtrump/status/1698308935?lang=en.

25 @realDonaldTrump, 27 May 2009, https://twitter.com/realdonaldtrump/status/14848387814?lang=en.

26 @realDonaldTrump, 13 May 2011, https://twitter.com/realdonaldtrump/status/69120590535081987.

27 @realDonaldTrump, 7 July 2011, https://twitter.com/realdonaldtrump/status/89005019432620032.

28 @realDonaldTrump, 18 May 2011, https://twitter.com/realDonaldTrump/status/203568571148800001; @realDonaldTrump, 9 May 2011, https://twitter.com/realdonaldtrump/status/200300700658442240.

29 @realDonaldTrump, 11 May 2012, https://twitter.com/realdonaldtrump/status/201044011954348032?lang=en.

30 @realDonaldTrump, 6 November 2012, https://twitter.com/realdonaldtrump/status/265895292191248385?lang=en.

31 @realDonaldTrump, 7 November 2013, https://twitter.com/realdonaldtrump/status/266227159528534017.

32 Mahaskey, Scott, 'The Deep Roots of Trump's War on the Press,' *Politico*, 26 April 2018, https://www.politico.com/magazine/story/2018/04/26/the-deep-roots-trumps-war-on-the-press–218105.

33 York, Byron, 'In Politics Fight, Breitbart Knew Culture Is Key,' *Washington Examiner*, 1 March 2012, https://www.washingtonexaminer.com/in-politics-fight-breitbart-knew-culture-is-key.

34 Rosen, Jay, 'Why Trump Is Winning and the Press Is Losing,' *New York Review of Books*, 25 April 2018, https://www.nybooks.com/daily/2018/04/25/why-trump-is-winning-and-the-press-is-losing/.

35 Joshua Green, *Devil's Bargain: Steve Bannon, Donald Trump, and the Storming of the Presidency* (London: Scribe, 2018), pp. 79–88.

36 Benkler, Yochai, Robert Faris, Hal Roberts and Ethan Zuckerman, 'Study: Breitbart-Led Right-Wing Media Ecosystem Altered Broader Media Agenda,' *Columbia Journalism Review*, 3 (March 2017), https://www.cjr.org/analysis/breitbart-media-trump-harvard-study.php.

37 Shepherdson, David, 'Trump Defends Tweets as Key to White House Victory,' *Reuters*, 22 October 2017, https://www.reuters.com/article/us-usa-trump-tweets/trump-defends-tweets-as-key-to-white-house-victory-idUSKBN1CR00B.

38 Manjoo, Farhad, 'The Trouble with Twitter,' *New York Times* [*NYT*], 19 May 2016, p. B1.

39 Strauss, Daniel, 'Donald Trump's New Pitch: I'm So Rich I Can't Be Bought,' *Politico*, 28 July 2015, https://www.politico.com/story/2015/07/donald-trumps-so-rich-i-cant-be-bought–120743.

40 @realDonaldTrump, 21 October 2015, https://twitter.com/realdonaldtrump/status/656672410025009152.

41 @realDonaldTrump, 7 July 2015, https://twitter.com/realdonaldtrump/status/618270248811266048.

42 @realDonaldTrump, 6 December 2015, https://twitter.com/realdonaldtrump/
    status/673562693983412224.

43 Huddleston Jr., Tom, 'How Media Giants Are Profiting from Donald Trump's Ascent,'
    Fortune, 21 March 2016, http://fortune.com/2016/03/21/tv-debates-trump-media/.

44 Bruenig, Elizabeth, 'Minutes: Notes and News,' *New Republic*, 29 January 2016,
    https://newrepublic.com/minutes/128674/donald-trump-won-debate-didnt-
    attend.

45 Flegenheimer, Matt, 'Band of the Insulted: The Nicknames of Trump's Adversaries,'
    NYT, 5 January 2018, https://www.nytimes.com/2018/01/05/us/politics/trump-
    nicknames.html.

46 Lazer, David and Oren Tsur, 'I. You. Great. Trump. A Graphic Analysis of Trump's
    Twitter History, in Five Slides,' *Politico*, May/June 2016, https://www.politico.com/
    magazine/story/2016/04/donald-trump-2016-twitter-takeover–213861.

47 McCaskill, Nolan D., 'Angry Trump Lashes Out in Typo-Ridden Twitter Tirade,'
    Politico, 26 February 2016, https://www.politico.com/blogs/2016-gop-primary-live-
    updates-and-results/2016/02/donald-trump-twitter-rant-debate–219846.

48 Wright, David, 'Marco Rubio: Not Going to Turn over GOP to "Con Artist" Donald
    Trump,' *CNN*, 26 February 2018, https://edition.cnn.com/2016/02/26/politics/marco-
    rubio-donald-trump-morning-show-attacks/index.html.

49 Berman, Sheri, 'Why Identity Politics Benefits the Right More Than the Left,' *The
    Guardian*, 14 July 2018, https://www.theguardian.com/commentisfree/2018/jul/14/
    identity-politics-right-left-trump-racism.

50 Holland, Steve, 'Rubio Says He Regrets Getting Personal with Donald Trump,'
    Reuters, 10 March 2016, https://www.reuters.com/article/us-usa-election-
    republicans/rubio-says-he-regrets-getting-personal-with-donald-trump-
    idUSMTZSAPEC3AT263LZ.

51 Bakkila, B.C., 'Donald Trump Fires Back at Hillary Clinton after DNC Speech: "No
    One Has Worse Judgement",' *People Magazine*, 29 July 2016, https://people.com/
    politics/donald-trump-fired-back-at-hillary-clinton-after-dnc-speech/.

52 Wallace-Wells, Benjamin, 'Clinton's Coming Struggle with Trump Supporters,' *New
    Yorker*, 10 October 2016, https://www.newyorker.com/news/benjamin-wallace-wells/
    clintons-coming-struggle-with-trump-supporters.

53 Chozick, Amy, 'Hillary Clinton's Expectations, and Her Ultimate Campaign Missteps,'
    NYT, 9 November 2016, https://www.nytimes.com/2016/11/10/us/politics/hillary-
    clinton-campaign.html.

54 Sarlin, Benjy and Ari Vitali, 'Donald Trump Defiant as Top Republicans Flee
    Candidacy,' *NBC*, 6 October 2018, https://www.nbcnews.com/politics/2016-election/
    gop-piles-donald-trump-over-remarks-women-n662276.

55 Nelson, Colleen McCain and Peter Nicholson, 'Trump Signals Attack on Bill Clinton
    in Coming Days,' *Wall Street Journal*, 9 October 2018, https://www.wsj.com/articles/
    trump-signals-attack-on-bill-clinton-in-coming-days–1476028692.

56 Blake, Aaron, 'Gennifer Flowers Said She Would Attend Debate for Trump,
    but Trump Camp Says No,' *Washington Post*, 25 September 2016, https://www.
    washingtonpost.com/news/the-fix/wp/2016/09/24/bill-clinton-accuser-gennifer-
    flowers-accepts-donald-trumps-invitation-to-attend-debate/?noredirect=on&utm_
    term=.bd48098faf5b.

57 Baker, Peter, '"What about Bill?" Sexual Misconduct Debate Revives Questions about
    Clinton,' *NYT*, 15 November 2016, https://www.nytimes.com/2017/11/15/us/politics/
    bill-clinton-sexual-misconduct-debate.html.

58 Roberts, Dan, Ben Jacobs and Sabrina Siddiqui, 'Donald Trump Threatens to Jail Hillary Clinton in Second Presidential Debate', *Guardian*, 10 October 2018, https://www.theguardian.com/us-news/2016/oct/10/debate-donald-trump-threatens-to-jail-hillary-clinton.

59 @realDonaldTrump, 12 October 2016, https://twitter.com/realdonaldtrump/status/786189446274248704.

60 Chan, Melissa, 'Donald Trump More Trustworthy than Hillary Clinton, Poll Finds', *Time Magazine*, 2 November 2016, http://time.com/4554576/donald-trump-trustworthy-hillary-clinton/.

61 @realDonaldTrump, 14 August 2016, https://twitter.com/realdonaldtrump/status/764867963845484545.

62 @realDonaldTrump, 13 August 2016, https://twitter.com/realdonaldtrump/status/764529295901528064.

63 @realDonaldTrump, 22 January 2016, https://twitter.com/realdonaldtrump/status/690682449387397120.

64 @realDonaldTrump, 9 September 2016, https://twitter.com/realdonaldtrump/status/774255510191239170.

65 Benkler, Faris, Roberts, Zuckerman, 'Right-Wing Media Ecosystem.'

66 @realDonaldTrump, 10 December 2016, https://twitter.com/realdonaldtrump/status/807588632877998081.

67 Fisher, Max, 'Russia and the U.S. Election: What We Know and Don't Know', *NYT*, 12 December 2016, https://www.nytimes.com/2016/12/12/world/europe/russia-trump-election-cia-fbi.html.

68 Frum, David, *Trumpocracy: The Corruption of the American Republic* (New York: HarperCollins, 2018), p. 25.

69 @realDonaldTrump, 22 August 2016, https://twitter.com/realdonaldtrump/status/767505383430782976.

70 Matthew Goodwin and Roger Eatwell, *National Populism: The Revolt against Liberal Democracy* (London: Pelican, 2018), pp. 17–20.

71 Francis, Robert D., 'Him, Not Her: Why Working-Class White Men Reluctant about Trump Still Made Him President of the United States', *Socius: Sociological Research for a Dynamic World*, 4 (2018), http://journals.sagepub.com/doi/pdf/10.1177/2378023117736486.

72 For the importance of gender to the election, see Valentino, Nicholas A., 'Mobilizing Sexism: The Interaction of Emotion and Gender Attitudes in the 2016 US Presidential Election', *Public Opinion Quarterly*, 82 (April 2018): 213–35.

73 Ayoola, Teniola, Taylor Kate Brown and Max Matza, 'Election 2016: Trump Voters on Why They Backed Him', *BBC*, 9 November 2016, https://www.bbc.co.uk/news/election-us-2016-36253275.

74 Stewart, Emily, 'Donald Trump Rode $5 Billion in Free Media to the White House', *The Street*, 20 November 2016, https://www.thestreet.com/story/13896916/1/donald-trump-rode-5-billion-in-free-media-to-the-white-house.html.

75 Douthat, Ross, 'Trump Hacked the Media Right before Our Eyes', *NYT*, 21 March 2018, https://www.nytimes.com/2018/03/21/opinion/trump-facebook-cambridge-analytica-media.html.

76 Buncombe, Andrew, 'Donald Trump One Year on: How the Twitter President Changed Social Media and the Country's Top Office', *The Independent*, 17 January 2018, https://www.independent.co.uk/news/world/americas/us-politics/the-twitter-president-how-potus-changed-social-media-and-the-presidency-a8164161.html.

77 Woodward, Bob, *Fear: Trump in the White House* (New York: Simon & Schuster, 2018), p. 301.

78 Matthew, Gertz, 'I've Studied the Trump-Fox Feedback Loop for Months. It's Crazier than You Think,' *Politico*, 5 January 2018, https://www.politico.com/magazine/ story/2018/01/05/trump-media-feedback-loop–216248.

79 Diekmann, Kai and Michael Gove, 'Full Transcript of Interview with Donald Trump,' *The Times*, 16 January 2017, https://www.thetimes.co.uk/article/full-transcript-of-interview-with-donald-trump-5d39sr09d.

80 Viser, Matt and Yan Wu, '11 Months, 1 President, 2,417 Tweets,' *Boston Globe*, 25 December 2017, https://apps.bostonglobe.com/opinion/graphics/2017/12/ president-twitter/.

81 Ortutay, Barbara, 'No, Twitter Will Not Ban Trump, Here's Why,' *National Post*, 23 July 2018, https://nationalpost.com/pmn/life-pmn/no-twitter-will-not-ban-trump-heres-why.

82 @realDonaldTrump, 1 July 2018, https://twitter.com/realdonaldtrump/status/8812717 48280365056?lang=en.

83 @realDonaldTrump, 1 July 2018, https://twitter.com/realdonaldtrump/status/8812817 55017355264?lang=en.

84 Herrmann, John and Charlie Savage, 'Trump's Blocking of Twitter Users Is Unconstitutional, Judge Says,' *NYT*, 23 May 2018, https://www.nytimes.com/2018/05/23/business/media/trump-twitter-block.html.

INDEX

Note: Page locators in "italics" indicate images